Violence in Schools

Violence in schools is a pervasive, highly emotive and, above all, global problem. Bullying and its negative social consequences are of perennial concern, while the media regularly highlights incidences of violent assault – and even murder – occurring within schools. This unique and fascinating text offers a comprehensive overview and analysis of how European nations are tackling this serious issue.

Violence in Schools: The response in Europe brings together contributions from all EU member states and two associated states. Each chapter begins by clearly outlining the nature of the school violence situation in that country. It then goes on to describe those social policy initiatives and methods of intervention being used to address violence in schools and evaluates the effectiveness of these different strategies. Commentaries from Australia, Israel and the USA and an overview of the book's main themes by eminent psychologist Peter K. Smith complete a truly international and authoritative look at this important – and frequently controversial – subject.

This book constitutes an invaluable resource for educational administrators, policymakers and researchers concerned with investigating, and ultimately addressing, the social and psychological causes, manifestations and effects of school violence.

Peter K. Smith is Professor and Head of the Unit for School and Family Studies at Goldsmiths College, University of London.

Violence in Schools

The response in Europe

Edited by Peter K. Smith

RoutledgeFalmer
Taylor & Francis Group

LONDON AND NEW YORK

First published 2003 by RoutledgeFalmer
11 New Fetter Lane, London EC4P 4EE

Simultaneously published in the USA and Canada
by RoutledgeFalmer
29 West 35th Street, New York, NY 10001

RoutledgeFalmer is an imprint of the Taylor & Francis Group

Typeset in 10/12pt Palatino by Graphicraft Limited, Hong Kong
Printed and bound in Great Britain by TJ International Ltd,
Padstow, Cornwall

British Library Cataloguing in Publication Data
A catalogue record for this book is available from the British
Library

Library of Congress Cataloging in Publication Data
A catalog record for this book has been requested

ISBN 0-415-27822-8 (hbk)
ISBN 0-415-27823-6 (pbk)

Contents

Figures

Tables

Contributors

Ana Tomás de Almeida is Assistant Professor of Psychology at the Instituto de Estudos da Criança, Avenida Central n° 100, Braga 4710, Portugal. aalmeida@iec.uminho.pt

Ron Avi Astor is Professor at the School of Social Work and School of Education, University of Michigan, Ann Arbor, Michigan, USA. rastor@umich.edu

Moira Atria is Member of the Scientific Staff in the Center for Educational Psychology and Evaluation, Department of Psychology, University of Vienna, Universitätsstraße 7, 1010 Austria. moira.atria@univie.ac.at http://www.evaluation.ac.at/

Rami Benbenishty is Professor at the School of Social Work, Hebrew University of Jerusalem, Jerusalem, Israel. msrami@mscc.huji.ac.il

Kaj Björkqvist is Professor of Developmental Psychology at the Åbo Akademi, POB 311, FIN-65101 Vasa, Finland. kaj.bjorkqvist@abo.fi

Gaute Bjørnsen is a social worker and teacher, and a research and project collaborator at the Centre for Behavioural Research, Stavanger University College, P.Box 8002, 4068 Stavanger, Norway. gaute.bjornsen@saf.his.no

Catherine Blaya is Co-Director of the Observatoire Européen de la Violence Scolaire, Université Bordeaux 2, 3 ter place de la Victoire, 33800 Bordeaux, France. Cblaya@aol.com

Carolien Bongers is co-ordinator of the project office Conflict Management and Social Competence in Education, at Sardes Educational Services, P.O. Box 2357, 3500 GJ Utrecht, The Netherlands. c.bongers@sardes.nl

Joana Campos is a researcher at the Centro de Investigação e Estudos de Sociologia, Av. das Forças Armadas, Ed° ISCTE, 1649-062 Lisboa, Portugal. ficus@mail.telepac.pt or jcampos@eses.pt

Helen Cowie is Research Professor and Director of the Centre for Research in Peer and Organizational Relationships in the School of

Psychology and Counselling, Roehampton University of Surrey, West Hill, London SW15 3SN, United Kingdom. h.cowie@roehampton.ac.uk

Monique D'Aes is a teacher at the Teacher Training Centre of Jette, Brussels, Belgium. bs173934@skynet.be

Eric Debarbieux is Director of the Observatoire Européen de la Violence Scolaire, Université Bordeaux 2, 3 ter place de la Victoire, 33800 Bordeaux, France. Debarberic@aol.com

John Devine is Co-Chair of the Academic Advisory Council of the National Campaign against Youth Violence, 45 Christopher Street, New York, NY 10014, USA. jfdevine@mindspring.com

Maria Doanidou is a school psychologist at the Department of Psychology and Counselling, The Moraitis School, Papanastassiou and Ag. Dimitriou Street, 154 52 Psihiko, Athens, Greece. admin@moraitis.edu.gr

Ebbe Ebbesen is a teacher, until June 2002 on leave from teaching at Hårby Skole (Public School) and Odense Socialpædagogiske Seminarium, Nørregade 72, DK5620 Glamsbjerg, Denmark. ubbebsen@post11.tele.dk

Isabel Fernández is Directora I.E.S. Pradolongo, Catedrática De Educación Secundaria, C/Albardín 6, Madrid 28026, Spain. isabel055@hotmail.com

Anastasia Houndoumadi is Professor and Psychology Area Co-ordinator at Deree College, The American College of Greece, Gravias 6, GR-15342 Aghia Paraskevi, Greece. ahal@hol.gr

Inge Huybregts is a researcher on the Research Group on Juvenile Criminology, Department of Criminal Law and Criminology, K.U. Leuven, Hooverplein 10, B 3000 Leuven, Belgium. inge.huybregts@law.kuleuven. ac.be

Viktoria Jansson is a Research Assistant at the Åbo Akademi, POB 311, FIN-65101 Vasa, Finland.

Dawn Jennifer is Research Consultant in the Centre for Research in Peer and Organizational Relationships in the School of Psychology and Counselling, Roehampton University of Surrey, West Hill, London SW15 3SN, United Kingdom. d.jennifer@roehampton.ac.uk

Niels-Jørgen Jensen is Pedagogue and Senior Lecturer at Odense Socialpædagogiske Seminarium, Rømers Vej 3, DK5200 Odense V, Denmark. nj.jensen@mail.tele.dk

Stefan Korn is a doctoral student and researcher at the Institute of Empirical Paedagogics and Educational Psychology of the Ludwig-Maximilians-University of Munich, Leopoldstr. 13, 80802 München, Germany. Stefan.Korn@gmx.net.

Hal A. Lawson is Professor of Social Welfare; Professor of Educational Administration and Policy Studies; and Special Assistant to the Provost for School–Family–Community Partnerships at the University at Albany, The State University of New York; 135 Western Avenue, Albany, NY 12222, USA. Hlawson@albany.edu

Gunnar Mandt is Assistant Director General at the Norwegian Ministry of Education and Research, Department of Education and Training, P.Box 8119 Dep., 0032 Oslo, Norway. gunnar.mandt@ufd.dep.no

Ersilia Menesini is a senior researcher at the Department of Psychology, University of Florence, Via S. Niccolò, 93 50125 Firenze, Italy. menesini@psico.unfi.it

Stephen Minton is a researcher at the Anti-Bullying Research and Resource Centre, Trinity College, Dublin 2, Ireland. sjminton@hotmail.com

Rossella Modiano is a junior researcher at the Department of Psychology, University of Florence, Via S. Niccolò, 93 50125 Firenze, Italy. rossmod@hotmail.com

Sólveig Norðfjörð is part-time Research Assistant at the Educational Testing Institute, Suðurgata 39, 101 Reykjavik, Iceland. solveign@hi.is

Mona O'Moore is Head of Education Department and Co-ordinator of the Anti-Bullying Research and Resource Centre in the School of Education, University of Dublin, Trinity College, Dublin 2, Ireland. momoore@tcd.ie

Ragnar F. Ólafsson is Visiting Lecturer in Methodology at the University of Iceland and Researcher at the Educational Testing Institute, Suðurgata 39, 101 Reykjavik, Iceland. rfo@namsmat.is

Rosario Ortega is Professor of Educational Psychology at the Department of Developmental and Educational Psychology, University of Seville, C/Camilo Jose Cela, s/n. 41018, Seville, Spain. ortegaruiz@us.es or edlorrur@uco.es

Lena Pateraki is Adjunct Professor in the Psychology Area at Deree College, The American College of Greece, Gravias 6, GR- 153 42 Aghia Paraskevi, Greece. apate@tee.gr

Frits Prior is at the Transfercentre 'Youths, school, safety and security', Postbox 85475, 3598 AL Utrecht, The Netherlands. f.prior@aps.nl

Rosario Del Rey is a researcher at the Department of Developmental and Educational Psychology, University of Seville, C/Camilo Jose Cela, s/n. 41018, Seville, Spain. delrey@us.es

Erling Roland is Professor, and Head of the Centre for Behavioural Research, Stavanger University College, P.Box 8002, 4068 Stavanger, Norway. erling.roland@saf.his.no

Claire Russon is at the Centre de Psychologie et d'Orientation Scolaires, 280 route de Longwy, L-1940 Luxembourg. claire.friedel@cpos.educ.lu

Mechthild Schäfer is a senior researcher at the Institute of Empirical Paedagogics and Educational Psychology at Ludwig-Maximilians University of Munich, Leopoldstr. 13, D-80802 München, Germany and Associate Lecturer at the Open University (West Midlands), 66 High Street, Birmingham, B17 9NB, United Kingdom. mechthild.schaefer@gmx.de

João Sebastião is a senior researcher at the Centro de Investigação e Estudos de Sociologia, Av. das Forças Armadas, Ed° ISCTE, 1649-062 Lisboa, Portugal. joao.sebastiao@netc.pt or jsebastiao@eses.pt

Sonia Sharp is Assistant Director of Special Educational Needs, Birmingham Education Authority, Council House Extension, Margaret Street, Birmingham B3 3BU, United Kingdom. sonia.sharp@birmingham.gov.uk

Phillip T. Slee is Associate Professor in Human Development, School of Education, Flinders University of South Australia, Australia. edpts@ flinders.edu.au

Peter K. Smith is Professor, and Head of the Unit for School and Family Studies, at the Department of Psychology, Goldsmiths College, University of London, New Cross, London SE14 6NW, United Kingdom. p.smith@gold.ac.uk

Christiane Spiel is University Professor, and Head of the Center for Educational Psychology and Evaluation, Department of Psychology, University of Vienna, Universitätsstraße 7, 1010 Austria. Christiane.Spiel@univie.ac.at http://www.evaluation.ac.at/

Georges Steffgen is Assistant Professor in Social and Work Psychology at the Department of Psychology, Centre Universitaire de Luxembourg, 162A, avenue de la Faïencerie, L-1511 Luxembourg. steffgen@cu.lu

Robert Svensson is Research Officer at the Crime Studies Division, National Council for Crime Prevention, P.O. Box 1386, SE-111 93 Stockholm, Sweden. robert.svensson@bra.se

Nicole Vettenburg is a researcher and Practical Lector with the Research Group on Juvenile Criminology, Department of Criminal Law and Criminology, K.U. Leuven, Hooverplein 10, B 3000 Leuven, Belgium. nicole.vettenburg@law.kuleuven.ac.be

Daniel Vidal is Proviseur, Lycée Professionnel Marcel Dassault, 33700 Mérignac, France. vidal.ayter@caramail.com

Guido Walraven is Unit Manager for Learning and Innovation at Sardes Educational Services, P.O. Box 2357, 3500 GJ Utrecht, The Netherlands. g.walraven@sardes.nl

Chapter 1

Violence in schools

An overview

Peter K. Smith

'School violence, having been dubbed a crisis, permeates the national consciousness and media outlets' (Mulvey and Cauffman, 2001, p.797). This perspective is from the USA; in Europe, violence in school and the concern about violence may not be at similar levels, but it is undoubtedly a topic of major concern. This book seeks to document what is known about school violence, and what can be done about it. It does so on the basis of experiences of the countries within the European Union. The comments of colleagues in Australia, Israel and the USA are included.

Schooling is a vital part of modern society. Intellectually, schools aim to educate pupils, to develop knowledge and skills that will help them achieve employment, further their adult career, and contribute to their society. Schools are also an immensely important social forum for children and young people. Over a period of some ten to twelve years, they will spend many thousands of hours at school with same-age and similar-age peers, as well as with teachers and other school personnel.

Each child brings their own personality and individuality to their school, no doubt influenced by their family environment. The peer groups they find themselves in start to introduce them to a somewhat autonomous 'peer culture' (Harris, 1995). The adults in the school try to inculcate certain ways of behaving in school. Everyone in the school community and in the families of the children, is influenced by the wider environment – the community which the school is in, the society which the community is in, even the global environment of international co-operation, international conflict, scientific and technological progress, and environmental degradation.

It is in these multiple contexts that we need to place the issue of violence in schools. There is no doubt that school violence is a topic of concern; those who doubt this need only read further in this book. This is not necessarily to sensationalize the issue. Despite some recent horrific incidents – such as the killing of head teacher Philip Lawrence outside his school gates in London as he intervened to break up a fight between pupils (and see also commentary from the US) – violence has always been with us, and it is not at all clear that violence in schools is actually getting worse. But many people perceive it as getting worse; and certainly it happens, in all of the countries represented in this book.

There are multiple reasons for concern about violence in schools. Most obviously and directly, it is damaging to the recipients of violence (or to the school environment, in cases of vandalism). More profoundly, it can create a climate of insecurity and fear which damages the whole purpose of the school – the case study of the Gran school in Norway describes what was one such example, now fortunately changed for the better. A climate of violence in school has repercussions for what is meant by 'education for citizenship', and for the rights of any individual to live a life free from fear and intimidation. This broader perspective also reminds us that violence in school is not a 'walled-in' problem (Lawson, 2001). In the wider society, violence is sometimes approved of, by many people and often a majority of populations, in certain circumstances – for example retributional violence resulting in people being forcibly imprisoned, or when retaliatory action is taken against political opponents or groups perceived as engaging in terrorist activities. Our concern for violence in school needs to be tempered by such awareness.

The background for this book

The opportunity for this book arose from an initiative of the European Commission under its Fifth Framework programme of research activities. This and related programmes aim to assist the cause of European integration by funding co-ordinated research which links different European partner groups. The Connect initiative was one programme within the Fifth Framework, aiming to enhance the nature of education and cultural opportunities in states in the European Union (EU). Over the period 1998–2002 some 60 educational projects were chosen for funding; six of these were on the topic of school violence, and this book results in large part from one of these [UK-001]. (For details of the five other projects on school violence, and the Connect initiative generally, see the website http://europa.eu.int/comm/education/connect/selection.html; see also the Connect fi 006 Proposal for an Action Plan to Tackle Violence at School in Europe, www.health.fi/connect; and the European Observatory of School Violence, www.obsviolence.pratique.fr.)

The UK-001 project aimed to get a report on the situation regarding violence in schools, in all fifteen member states, and two associated states. These form the basis of the subsequent seventeen chapters. Inevitably there are omissions: Liechtenstein, although an associated state, was omitted due to its very small size (population 27,000); Switzerland is the main central European state that is not an EU member; Malta has carried out substantial work on school bullying (Ministeru ta' l-Edukazzjoni,

1999); the eastern European countries are at present candidate members and they too are not represented here. Nevertheless there is complete coverage of the EU member states (at the time of writing), and a clear panorama of activities across countries in the north, west, south and centre of Europe.

Each of the seventeen states had two partner teams in the project; usually one representing an academic department or research institute with ready access to research findings, and the other representing practitioner bodies such as teachers, parent–teacher organizations, government departments, with expertise in areas of practical action. The major aim of the project was to obtain a report on Violence in Schools from each state. Another aim of the UK-001 project was to select three existing intervention projects in different states for some modest enhanced support and independent evaluation; those selected were peer support schemes in Italy, the broad approach exemplified in the Gran school work in Norway, and the Checkpoints for Schools initiative in the UK. These were evaluated by partners from Finland, Ireland, and France, respectively; evaluation reports can be found at the project website (www.gold.ac.uk/connect).

The project held a symposium at Goldsmiths College in London, in April 2001. At this meeting, draft reports were circulated, and critiqued in small groups. This proved an invaluable way of both promoting and exchanging ideas, and also helping get the reports into reasonably similar and complete formats. These reports were finalized in summer 2001, and posted on the project website in largely unedited form, in English, with summaries (and a few full reports) in French, German and Spanish.

For the purposes of this book, we went further; some revised guidelines were used to streamline each report (for example, omitting very detailed accounts of school systems), to update accounts up to the end of 2001 or early 2002, and to go through a rigorous editing procedure to ensure similar coverage and to clarify any ambiguities. In addition, three sets of commentators – from Australia, Israel, and the USA – were invited to set down their responses to these European reports, in the light of the situation in their own countries.

The reports from each state

Vettenburg (1999) had previously compiled a report for the Council of Europe on the topic of school violence, and other documents were available; the country reports took account of such prior work, either at a European level or in that country. A standard format for these reports was agreed.

In a first, *background* section, the context is set with a brief description of the country (population, major regional areas, major languages, major ethnic groups and minorities); the school system (age of compulsory and optional schooling; organization of schooling by age and by type of school; length and organization of school day; special schools and ways of coping with children with behavioural disturbance at the school organizational level; relevant curricular information); any linguistic/definitional issues (the words used to describe, define or delimit 'violence' in schools, for example in statistics or in school regulations); and the relevant historical background (recent developments relevant to current understanding of, action about and policies concerning violence in schools).

The second section concerns *knowledge* about school violence. This aims to cover any recent statistics at a national or large regional level on the incidence of violence in schools; information on different types of violence, and involving different dyads (pupil to pupil, pupil to teacher, teacher to pupil etc); age trends; sex differences; effects of factors such as ethnic group, socio-economic status, disability, special needs; and information relating to variations by school type, and school ethos.

The third section details *action* taken. This is intended to cover any policies at national (or large regional) level regarding violence, and bullying, in school; and any specific initiatives, taken at a regional or local level, to tackle violence in schools. Details of the nature of the initiative or programme, and of any evaluation carried out of its effectiveness, were asked for. Also included in some reports are case studies of particular schools, or small-scale initiatives, which are of particular interest or have had particular success, and which therefore may be applicable on a wider scale.

Definitional issues

What is 'violence'? Even the English word is open to different interpretations – and in this project we were coping with at least twelve other languages, each with their own terms, sometimes apparently similar, as in Italian *violenza*, sometimes quite different linguistically at least, as Greek βία or Icelandic *ofbeldi*. It was obviously important to try to reach some level of agreement about what should be covered, in our reports and discussions.

Initially, I proposed a definition that may be seen as a 'narrow' one – that proposed by Olweus (e.g. 1999, p.12). This states that violence or violent behaviour is 'aggressive behaviour where the actor or perpetrator uses his or her own body or an object (including a weapon) to inflict (relatively serious) injury or discomfort upon another individual'. Thus, violence refers to the use of physical force or power. It does not include verbal aggression, or relational/indirect aggression (such as rumour telling, social exclusion: Underwood, 2002). It does include physical bullying (in which the aggression is repeated, against a less powerful individual);

and also for example fights between equals, which are not bullying. Some report authors (e.g. Denmark, Germany) were quite satisfied using this definition.

However, there are 'broader' definitions of violence. The World Health Organization defines it as 'The intentional use of physical and psychological force or power, threatened or actual, against oneself, another person, or against a group or community, that either results in or has a high likelihood of resulting in injury, death, psychological harm, mal-development, or deprivation' (see fi-006: www.health.fi/connect). The emphasis here on threatened as well as actual violence can justify the inclusion of measures such as *feelings* of insecurity (see report from France). Further, some definitions embrace institutional violence, and violence due to inequalities, in which case school violence might be justified as retaliation (see e.g. reports from France and Greece, and discussion of *disagio scolastico* in Italy). Also, although both the Olweus definition and the WHO definition implicate violence as leading to relatively serious harmful consequences, the reports from Belgium and France make a strong case for including incidents of 'micro-violence' or 'incivilities', relatively minor impolitenesses and infringements of rules that might not count as 'violent acts' by the prior definitions, but which may be vital in understanding the origins and nature of school violence.

These differences were discussed at the symposium in April 2001, but could not be resolved. No consensus could be achieved. It was recognized that there are disciplinary and country differences in how violence is defined. However, each team was asked to make clear in their report what definition was used, or what kinds of definitions and methods were used in gathering any data that is reported on violence. Interestingly, the report from Spain highlights a concept that is an opposite of violence – that of *convivencia*, or living together in harmony.

Knowledge about violence in schools

There is great variation in the extent of our knowledge base on school violence. Although a range of statistics is available, many country reports deplore the lack of systematic data gathered on a large scale over time. This is only partly an issue of definition, important though that aspect is. Some reports struggle to find data on violence, and have to resort to other data beyond any usual definition; for example, to physical kinds of bullying (when surveys of bullying provide a main data source, e.g. reports from Greece, Iceland, Ireland, Italy); to official statistics on accidents caused by violence (Denmark report), and criminal statistics based on 'legal' definitions such as antisocial behaviour, juvenile delinquency, vandalism (which will also include damage to property, drug taking, other activities not necessarily 'violent') (as in the Belgium,

Iceland, Italy and Norway reports); and even to school exclusion data (as in the UK report).

Statistics of school violence *per se* are based on a variety of instruments. A common type, perhaps most common, is pupil questionnaire self-reports. A prominent example is the Olweus bully/victim questionnaire, by now used in many European countries. However, other data sources include victim surveys, structured interviews, teacher reports (e.g. of pupil violence) and, much more rarely, observations of violent behaviour.

Most countries provide some data on pupil to pupil violence. Other dyads are more rarely reported. This probably reflects a reality of available data, and of perceptions of the problem in these societies, since the report guidelines explicitly mentioned teacher–pupil and pupil–teacher violence. There is some data on pupil to teacher violence (reports from Austria, Germany, Ireland, Norway, UK), little on teacher to pupil (Ireland; the Germany report points out difficulty in even trying to get such data); adult to adult violence is also seldom reported, though some available data may come from research into workplace violence (reports from Ireland, UK).

The sections on knowledge also discuss (to varying degrees) the influence on frequencies of violence of factors such as the region of the country, and socio-economic circumstances; the type of school; and pupil characteristics such as age, sex, ethnicity, social class, family background, and special educational needs. Many findings here reflect rather well-established findings. For example, being a victim of violence often decreases with age, perhaps as potential victims become relatively stronger and more skilled at avoiding it; whereas being a perpetrator of violence shows some increase into mid- or late adolescence, perhaps as norm-breaking and risk-taking behaviours generally become more common and more sanctioned by the peer group (Arnett, 1992). Sex differences are evident, of course; especially when statistics are restricted to physical forms of violence, boys are much more in evidence than girls. Some statistics are available on sexual harassment, though (as remarked on in the Australia and US commentaries) this does not get the coverage it might be thought to deserve.

Noticeable here – and picked up in the opening background sections of most reports – is the increase in young people in school from immigrant groups to the European Union countries, which has accelerated since the early 1990s. Racial tensions are prominent in many countries, and these can be reflected in schools. Ethnic minority and immigrant children can experience racial harassment; and the young people themselves may bring different expectations, and experiences of deprivation and frustration, into the school (see, for example, reports from France, Norway; commentaries from Israel, USA).

Is violence on the increase?

Several teams are able to report some evidence on whether there have been changes over time, and thus address the common perception that violence is increasing (e.g. report from Germany). Perceptions do not always match reality. Often, older people look back to a supposed 'golden age' when things were better, one or two generations previously – even though, looking at perceptions held one or two generations earlier, just the same mantra was being reported (Pearson, 1983)! Some countries report little change, or only a slight increase (Germany, Norway); others a curvilinear increase then decrease (Italy); others mixed findings depending on type of violence (Austria).

Actions to reduce violence in schools

As noted in the Australian commentary, many European countries do not provide much information on, or do not have, legal requirements on schools to prevent violence, or bullying, in the school premises. Most national education ministries do have some sort of requirement for schools to 'have an environment of respect for others', a general aim which can embrace many facets; but a limited number have specific and legal requirements on violence. Those that do, include Belgium, Finland, France, Germany, Ireland, Luxembourg, Sweden, and the UK. For a review of these legal requirements (including those in other European countries such as Switzerland and Malta) see Ananiadou and Smith (2002). Legal requirements may suggest that schools develop some kind of whole-school approach or policy to deal with violence or bullying (as required in England and Wales, for example); such policies certainly put the topic on the agenda for action, can provide a framework, assign responsibilities, and suggest sanctions for non-compliance. However, in themselves they may do little to prevent violence unless combined with other initiatives.

There is a large range of initiatives, described in these chapters, to attempt to reduce violence in schools. Some actions have been tried in every country. Some of these actions are national initiatives, some are regional or local, some are simply in individual schools but noteworthy in the context.

The larger scale actions are often well-developed programmes that may include curriculum work, individual work with pupils at risk, and other measures. For example the Olweus anti-bullying programme is used widely in Norway (together with other initiatives), has been used in Austria, Finland and Germany, and is being considered in Iceland; the Safe School Programme has been used widely in Portugal; the SAVE programme has been developed in the Andalusia/Seville region of Spain; and the Farsta programme (amongst others) is often used in Sweden.

Generally these programmes are well described, with booklets and materials for teachers and pupils, and have a somewhat standardized form. Other initiatives reported to reduce violence, however, are of a less standardized kind.

Types of intervention

Some of the initiatives described do not focus very directly on violence, but attempt to improve 'preventive factors' such as a good school climate, and sense of pupil responsibility. The report from Denmark describes a Parliament Day for children, in which they can voice (and vote on) concerns regarding school and what should be improved, and how. Besides the general sense of participation and citizenship this may engender, some practical proposals regarding school violence may be included. Similar Parliament Days have been tried in France and Sweden.

General work to improve the climate of schools and classes, through teacher education, peer support systems, and enhanced personal and social education, feature in some countries. The Life Skills programme in Iceland is an example of such a broad approach. Some trends in The Netherlands and Norway suggest that this is regarded as more promising than programmes such as those of Olweus, which focus rather specifically on bullying (see too commentary from Israel on the issue of focused versus holistic interventions). General work to improve the school environment, including the physical environment, also features, for example in the report from Luxembourg. Smaller class sizes, and smaller schools (see commentary from the USA), and more (non-competitive) sports facilities, are other suggestions.

Some preventive interventions are focused more on individual pupils. Austria reports on a Social Competency training programme; and Belgium on a Positive Report Card scheme. A number of countries are developing peer mediation and conflict resolution skills (Austria, Italy, Leap Confronting Conflict in the UK), and finding ways of raising pupils' self-esteem (Pathways programme in Ireland). The Nuutinen slide show (report from Finland) aims to 'shock' pupils into a change of attitude regarding the acceptability of violence.

Other initiatives focus much more directly on dealing with violence when it happens, or providing less opportunity for it to happen. In several countries (Austria, Spain, UK) there are telephone hotlines or helplines for pupils as a way of seeking help when this is apparently not provided within the school. A more 'security' oriented focus can include employing school guards (as in the Safe School Programme in Portugal); strengthening general security in the school regarding weapons and unauthorized entry, perhaps by video surveillance; having a rapid response system to deal with violent incidents when they occur; and issuing vulnerable pupils with an 'alarm bracelet' so that they can call for help if threatened or attacked (report from Finland). Such 'security' responses may be necessary in some situations, but run the risk of being counter-productive in efforts to improve school climate and *convivencia*. The report from Portugal suggests that in that country, an earlier reliance on a security-based, Safe School approach is now giving way to one based more on pedagogical principles and encouraging pupil self-esteem and responsibility.

Some reports (e.g. Austria, The Netherlands) mention the development of class rules to deal with violence and to foster helping behaviours; other reports (e.g. UK) place more emphasis on whole-school policies. Teachers have a vital role in developing class rules or school policies with pupils. Support for teachers emerges as an important theme in intervention work. Although all members of the school community share the problem of school violence, teachers are generally in the forefront of dealing with pupil to pupil violence, when they see it happening or it is reported to them. A good whole-school approach will make the role of the teacher (and other school personnel and parents) clear; but in addition, there are examples of, and arguments for, specific teacher training in dealing with violence (reports from Ireland, Spain), more information and materials (such as the anti-bullying pack, report from the UK), and the provision of education assistants or *aide-éducateurs* (report from France), or learning mentors (report from the UK) to assist teachers in general or specific ways. Much more can probably be achieved in matters of teacher education; and very little seems to be done to provide help for non-teaching staff such as playground supervisors, janitors, cooks, and school nurses who may witness violence but be ill-prepared to react in a co-ordinated way. The reports also document very little activity on issues concerning the involvement of parents in work to reduce school violence.

Evaluation of actions to reduce school violence

The report from Austria comments on 'a wealth of materials but not based on empirical research'. A recurring theme in many reports is a lack of evaluation of many initiatives reported – even though some initiatives are implemented on a large scale. The report from Sweden points out the lack of independent evaluation even of the Farsta method, and the report from Portugal points out that no independent evaluation of the effectiveness of the Safe School Programme was ever published. Even when evaluations are published, they are usually in simple terms of percentage reductions, and do not attempt a cost effectiveness analysis of the interventions (report from Austria).

Independent evaluations of actions to reduce school violence are essential – as essential as independent evaluations of the effectiveness of medical treatments, drugs and therapies (commentary from Australia).

Every method has its proponent(s), and these people are likely – even with the best of intentions – to see their 'own' method (or one they have been heavily involved in) as successful; they probably hope this is the case, and a belief that this is so can also enhance their own self-esteem, assist in publishing their work, and increase sales of their books or packs describing the method. There may be political interests too in surmising the success (or not) of certain approaches; 'security' versus 'pedagogical' based interventions are certainly likely to elicit different levels of support from politicians of different viewpoints (report from Portugal). Thus, there are plenty of temptations to incorrectly evaluate the success of certain methods.

Evaluations can vary along several dimensions, for example who does the evaluation. Evaluation by the person or team who designed the intervention in the first place is relatively commonplace (it includes my own work in evaluating anti-bullying interventions in England: Smith and Sharp, 1994). However, the most convincing evaluations would be carried out by third parties who could never be accused of any vested interest in the outcome.

A second dimension concerns the source of data. Some evaluations are based rather loosely on teacher reports – whether teachers 'feel' or 'think' that the intervention has helped, for example. Though it has some value, this is rather 'soft' data; it relies on impressions of those involved and – unless the data is on violence experienced by teachers themselves – it is only an indirect reflection of what pupils may be experiencing. Other evaluations are based on school discipline records, expulsions, incident reports; these are certainly more 'objective', but many factors may go into deciding what becomes an incident. Evaluations based on pupil reports (self-reports, victim reports, reports of peers) may have most validity; observational data could also have high validity, though it is obviously difficult and expensive to obtain on any large scale.

A third dimension concerns the scale of the evaluation. Some evaluations are large-scale, and embrace many schools and thousands of pupils. Such studies may provide an opportunity to examine school variables, and class variables – but very often they do not do this, and limit themselves to statistical tests on individual variables such as pupil involvement in bullying. These evaluations may give a broad idea of whether an intervention is likely to work in other, similar, schools, and to what extent. If documented sufficiently, the cost-effectiveness of the intervention may be estimated. However, unless further multi-level analyses are carried out or supplementary, more qualitative data is obtained, we may not get much evidence as to the processes involved in the success or failure of the intervention.

There is a case to be made for the large-scale, multi-level, pre- and post-test designs to be usefully supplemented by more qualitative approaches and by single-participant designs. Qualitative methods (detailed interviews, focus groups) may enable us to understand more of the 'reality' of violence as perceived by different actors in the situation. They may help us to understand different pathways in and out of violence; different types of violence, of victim, or of perpetrator; different ways in which actions by teachers and other adults to reduce school violence are perceived by pupils. Such insights are not intrinsically unavailable to quantitative researchers, but they are often neglected. A broad-sweep quantitative statistical analysis may lump together different types or pathways, and produce a misleading null result or even a misleading positive finding.

I and my colleagues have attempted to combine quantitative and qualitative methods in, for example, looking at the effects of co-operative group work curricula in middle school classrooms (Cowie et al., 1994). We combined formal pre- and post-test procedures, with more open-ended interviews with pupils and teachers. We found that co-operative group work got a mixed reception. Many pupils liked it, but some actively disliked it. Victims of bullying and aggression were sometimes helped in gaining confidence and making friends, by co-operative group work. But aggressive and bullying children disliked it for just these reasons, and because their actions might be challenged; they often tried to 'sabotage' group work procedures. The point here is that some overall trends (e.g. for liking co-operative group work, or reduction in aggression) might be concealed or appear misleadingly simple, if the differentiation of experience for different individuals was not recognized – an area where qualitative methods have a particular strength.

There is a related case for what is called 'single-participant research design' (Morgan and Morgan, 2001). This would look in detail at the experiences and process of change in individuals – the phrase 'single participant' implies that this will be done on a one-by-one basis, though a thorough study would build in replication with a number of participants. In effect, these could be case studies of, for example, highly aggressive pupils, their experiences of school, and how school-based interventions impact on them.

Ways forward in Europe

These issues and many others are discussed, directly or indirectly, in the chapters that follow. Where do we go from here? Many suggestions on this, too, are made in the following pages. My own view is that there may be issues worth reflecting on, for researchers in education, practitioners in education, and for education authorities and regional and national ministries and governments.

I believe that researchers in this area need to reach out across disciplinary boundaries and more widely than conventional methods of thinking. My own background as a psychologist leads me to think of individual factors, violent pupils, temperament, family factors, and other risk factors for violent behaviour. I do believe there is some utility in this approach. Even in a perfectly just and egalitarian society (whatever that might mean), I think it likely that human motives of selfishness and opportunism will lead some pupils to be abusive and violent. The opportunities and rewards for violent behaviour have long been present in our evolutionary past – they are still often present today – and are likely to be present in human nature, not as a simple 'violent instinct', but rather as an inclination to use violent means in certain situations when advantages of status, and resources, will accrue from this. For example, Pellegrini and Bartini (2001) have indicated how some adolescent boys in US high schools use aggressive and violent behaviour to increase their status in boys' peer groups, and appear attractive to girls at an age when heterosexual relations are beginning to become important. There are probably, if unfortunately, aspects of violence quite deeply within us, that we need to recognize rather than deny.

However, it is easy for psychologists to ignore the wider social factors, in their emphasis on individual factors (commentary from the USA). The radical critique of the psychologist 'dealing with' an aggressive child (perhaps using drug treatments) while ignoring the social and economic conditions which have led this child to find advantages in aggressive behaviour, can ring true. It is the more sociologically oriented contributions in this book that point out how violence may be seen as justified if society, the community, and then the school itself are also violent, or at least carry through inequities and inequalities rather than providing an environment of respect and opportunity. The considerable differences found in violence between different schools (even in similar areas) point to the general importance of school climate in this respect. The report from Italy points to the existence of Mafia phenomena as a possible explanation for some regional variations in school violence. Changes over time, and possible differences between countries in rates of violence (always difficult to interpret) may reflect not only changes or differences in school systems, but also in patterns of violence in society, and the attention and respect given to violence in media presentations.

Practitioners – teachers, head teachers, education advisers – may welcome help in tackling violence in schools, but they need to be open to the requirement for evaluation. As discussed, this may take a range of forms. Evaluation is almost inevitably an extra burden for teachers and pupils as well as researchers, but unless it is done we will not accrue knowledge for the future.

Naturally, regional and national authorities need to provide resources for schools to tackle violence, and for researchers to develop and evaluate such resources. Examples of good practice in this respect are evident in some countries, but in others the problem is largely ignored. It will not go away. More widely, while helping schools is important, helping the communities that schools are embedded in is likely to be part of the solution. The extent to which 'walled-in', solely school-based solutions can work, independently of wider community and society action, is itself a matter of debate and research; but there seems little doubt that these wider factors have an impact (see commentary from USA and discussion of child abuse and neglect).

At the European level, initiatives such as those of Connect play a valuable role in collating and disseminating knowledge. I believe there is scope for further work at this level. Even at the level of definition, more could be done to agree on the range of actions and behaviours which might be considered as violence; comparative statistics across countries (and times and regions) may best be constructed on the basis of definitions clearly rooted in behaviours – or in the behaviours themselves – rather than on words such as 'violence' or 'bullying', on which there is only partial agreement. A systematic collation of evaluated interventions in the European Union countries – which, despite differences, share some cultural heritage and are working towards economic and educational integration – will be an invaluable resource for the future.

In all this, it is important not to overstate the problem. School violence may not be increasing (in many countries), and rates of serious violence in schools are generally low. Often, rates of violence outside school are higher. To quote the same source as at the start of this chapter, 'school hours are probably the safest time of the day for adolescents' (Mulvey and Cauffman, 2001). Schools should be a safe place. Some schools are not as safe as they should be. This book aims, in its own small way, to help share knowledge and endeavours and thus move to remedy that situation.

References

Ananiadou, K. and Smith, P.K. (2002). Legal requirements and nationally circulated materials against school bullying in European countries. *Criminal Justice*, in press.

Arnett, J. (1992). Reckless behavior in adolescence: a developmental perspective. *Developmental Review*, 12, 339–373.

Cowie, H., Smith, P.K., Boulton, M.J. and Laver, R. (1994). *Co-operative Group Work in the Multi-ethnic Classroom*. London: David Fulton.

Harris, J.R. (1995). Where is the child's environment? A group socialization theory of development. *Psychological Review*, 102, 458–489.

Lawson, H. (2001). Reformulating the school violence problem: implications for research, policy, and practice. Paper presented at the International Conference on School Violence and Public Policies, UNESCO, Paris, France.

Ministeru ta' l-Edukazzjoni (1999). *L-Imgiba Tajba fl-Iskejjel. Politika Nazzjonali u Pjan ta' Azzjoni dwar l-Ibbuljar* [Good Behaviour in Schools. National Anti-Bullying Policy and Action Plan]. Malta: Ministeru ta' l-Edukazzjoni.

Morgan, D.L. and Morgan, R.K. (2001). Single-participant research design. *American Psychologist*, 56, 119–127.

Mulvey, E.P. and Cauffman, E. (2001). The inherent limits of predicting school violence. *American Psychologist*, 56, 797–802.

Olweus, D. (1999). Sweden. In P.K. Smith, Y. Morita, J. Junger-Tas, D. Olweus, R. Catalano and P. Slee (eds). *The Nature of School Bullying: A Cross-national Perspective*. London and New York: Routledge. pp. 2–27.

Pearson, G. (1983). *Hooligan: A History of Respectable Fears*. London: Macmillan Press.

Pellegrini, A.D. and Bartini, M. (2001). Dominance in early adolescent boys: affiliative and aggressive dimensions and possible functions. *Merrill-Palmer Quarterly*, 47, 142–163.

Smith, P.K. and Sharp, S. (eds) (1994). *School Bullying: Insights and Perspectives*. London: Routledge.

Underwood, M.K. (2002). Sticks and Stones and Social Exclusion: Aggression among Girls and Boys. In P.K. Smith and C.H. Hart (eds). *Blackwell Handbook of Childhood Social Development*. Oxford: Blackwell.

Vettenburg, N. (1999). Violence in Schools: Awareness-raising, Prevention, Penalties. General report. In Council of Europe, *Violence in Schools: Awareness-raising, Prevention, Penalties*. Strasbourg: Council of Europe Publishing.

Part I

Central Europe

Chapter 2

Tackling violence in schools
A report from France

Eric Debarbieux, Catherine Blaya and Daniel Vidal

Background

The country

France has a population of 57.8 million, increasing at the rate of just over 0.3 per cent each year. Around 9 per cent of the working age population are currently unemployed. Foreigners account for 3.6 million and a further 1.3 million have recently become French by naturalization. Major ethnic groups come from former colonies, mainly north and west Africa. There are 96 metropolitan and 5 overseas *départements*. The official language of the whole country and educational system is French.

The school system

State-led education, which caters for more than 80 per cent of pupils, is secular. Approximately 17 per cent of pupils from nursery to upper secondary level currently attend private schools. Education is the top national priority. Its objective is 'to educate an entire age group to at least the level of a vocational aptitude certificate and 80 per cent to *Baccalauréat* level.' State secondary schools have legal responsibility and financial autonomy; head teachers are recruited through a ranking examination with a limited number of places. They enjoy a life-long special legal status as representatives of the Ministry and have no teaching duties. School life is governed by internal regulations voted annually by the board of governors. In all types of schools the national curriculum is designed by the Ministry. All public sector teachers are life-long civil servants.

Pre-school education (*Enseignement préélémentaire*) is from age 2 to 5 years. Compulsory education, from age 6 to 16 years, is submitted to a catchment area policy. It starts with primary education (*Enseignement élémentaire*), lasting five years or up to the age of 11. Primary schools have an average size of 100 pupils. In lower secondary education studies normally last four years in a *collège* with an average size of 500 pupils. Each school must organize assistance for pupils experiencing learning difficulties. Special sections exist in some *collèges* for pupils with learning difficulties. Pupils with very disturbed behaviour can be admitted to referral units (*Classes relais*). Medical schools admit emotionally disturbed or handicapped children.

The compulsory curriculum includes education for citizenship. Each secondary school has at least one education counsellor (*Conseiller d'éducation*) governing ancillary staff, in charge of organizing pupils' life in school, discipline and relationships between teachers, parents and pupils. Since 1997, educating-assistants (*aide-éducateurs*) have been appointed to all types of schools for educational tasks: mediation, organization of extracurricula activities, assistance with studies or prevention of violence.

General or technological *lycées* (*Lycées d'enseignement général et technologique*) prepare pupils in upper secondary education for the general or the technological *Baccalauréat*, a nationwide examination, in three years. It is the main way for admission to higher education. The average size of *lycées* is 1,000 pupils, and they often have more. Vocational *lycées* (*Lycées professionnels*) prepare for different vocational degrees up to a vocational *Baccalauréat*.

Violence in schools: linguistic and definitional issues

In France, the issue of the definition of violence in schools contrasts those who uphold a restricted definition of the term, and wish to confine the notion to a strictly penal definition (that is, 'violent' offences or infringements, Bonnafé-Schmitt, 1997), with those who prefer a wider and less constrained definition. We shall see that this debate permeates French research on the subject. As far as this chapter is concerned, we shall use a wide definition, and consider 'micro-violence' (incivilities, harassment, permanent disorder) as important as any other stress on victims in creating feelings of insecurity and disorder. Thus, we shall see how the French research approach, mainly based on incivilities and frequent disorders, allows the construction of both a 'victim' and a 'delinquent career'.

Violence is not only an exceptional, brutal, unpredictable fact originating outside school, but also the result of frequent banal irritating small aggressions. 'It is as much a climate as a fact' (Debarbieux, 1996). Violence will be viewed through three groups of variables: crime and offences, micro-violence and the feeling of insecurity.

We shall accept the recent definition stated by Denise Gottfredson (2001, p.4), that 'Many acts are behaviourally analogous to crime in terms of their causation, and attempts to understand their causes are unnecessarily constrained when the dependent variable is restricted to illegal acts'.

Historical background

From the 1990s, the increasing sensitivity of the French to this issue was unquestionably strengthened by the press. The problem of violence became a major ideological stake: the feeling of an overall decadence in educational values was linked to a decay in family norms, to political weakness and to a supposed lack of authority from teachers. Public policies were strongly questioned, and there is now an attempt to respond to strengthened social expectations. The trend is to try and tackle the difficulties due to inequalities in a positive way, trying to have a preferential policy towards schools recorded as being 'sensitive' according to social criteria.

Some particular measures taken show the centralized, state managerial way of dealing with education in France: no position being given to inexperienced teachers in difficult schools, initial and in-service training schemes, specific wage bonuses, setting up of intervention teams, summer universities and so on. Some actions try to deal with the problem in a better way: the setting up of a national observatory, and better communication between the relevant departments (mostly police and justice).

More accurate records of violent offences and infringements were started in 1993, mainly because of the apparently increasing number of assaults against students and teaching staff members. This reflects an expectation of high rates of occurrence. In fact the figures recorded in 1993 were rather low: 771 reported aggravated assaults (more than eight days' illness for the victim) on students and 210 on teachers. The perpetrators identified were mainly students from the same school. Contrary to what the French steadily tend to believe, most of the violence in school is not perpetrated by intruders, even though this sometimes happens. People lodge complaints more often when the aggressor is an intruder (90 per cent of the staff complain when offenders are not from the school, and only 53 per cent when it is a school student; Horenstein, 1997).

These figures suggest that school remains a rather safe place, whatever indicators are used. If compared with the number of students, the ratio seems very low: only 1,999 reported cases – including minor acts – out of 14 million pupils; that is, 0.015 per cent. This ratio should be compared with that of the entire French population, where it is 6.5 per cent (about 3,700,000 offences and infringements for 57 million people). Of course, the figures in school should be higher because, as assessed by the principals, about 80 per cent of the incidents are internally resolved by the school. Even correcting for this would show much lower rates of offence in school than in society generally.

Since 1993 the problem of violence in school has been considered a public safety concern. An invitation to tender for research was launched in 1994; seventy-five teams applied, nine of them were appointed, five have

(handwritten margin note: "How they gain statistics")

merged, and seven of the ongoing researches are in the sociological field. The methods used are multifaceted: accounts of violent acts, question-naires, workshops, individual interviews, victimization surveys, second-ary analysis of statistical data and administrative documents, ethnographic observations, case studies, intervention research through mediation, a global approach by social action.

This methodological variety allows considerable distance from the phe-nomenon. Nevertheless, the recently published works complied with a social and institutional demand. There is an important issue about whether the recorded facts about school violence are exaggerated. Is there an insecurity fantasy about violence in school that increases demands for stricter repression and greater undue social control? Perhaps earlier re-searchers had even fed this fantasy with their research. The low figures in the more recent officially reported facts could lead to a moderation of views of the importance of crimes and offences in schools and help us to understand this 'social fantasy'.

However, this pattern can be questioned on several points: the import-ance of a 'black hole' of non-reported offences; the non-consideration of victims; and the inability to determine what the major delinquency problem is composed of (namely, minor delinquencies) and to imagine the disorder that disrupts daily life in some schools.

Victimization surveys conducted steadily since 1993 have proved effi-cient in describing the development of the phenomenon and in evaluating the impact of public policies. The Observatory of Violence in Schools – created in 1998 – allowed, through empirical enquiries, a better know-ledge of the importance of real victimization and of safety and risk factors in schools.

Knowledge

A permanent census of violent incidents in schools has been continuing since 1996. During 1999, a total of 240,000 incidents of all sorts were registered in secondary schools; only 6,240 of these incidents, or 2.6 per cent, are regarded as 'serious' (mainly physical aggressions), and 1,750 were damage to property or belongings. The aggressors were mostly pupils (86 per cent); intruders (12 per cent) are in no way the main offenders, staff (1.3 per cent), or parents (0.7 per cent) even less so. The victims were also mainly pupils (70 per cent, mainly boys), followed by staff (20 per cent), and seldom intruders (1.6 per cent) or parents (0.4 per cent).

Serious incidents remain relatively exceptional, with only 0.12 per cent of all pupils being involved. These data have been supplemented by victim surveys, such as those initiated by the European Observatory of Violence in Schools (Debarbieux and Montoya, 2000). The 'black hole' of victimization is linked to the production of direct official statistics (Facy and Henry, 1997) and the only way of reducing it, is a victimization survey.

The epidemiological surveys concerning extortion provide some interesting information. A large survey by Choquet and Ledoux (1994, pp.155–173) reported that one youngster out of six stated that he had been a victim of physical assault. A survey by Carra and Sicot (1996, 1997, p.70) found that 4.3 per cent of students have experienced extortion, whereas a national sample in a survey by Debarbieux (1996) registered a rate of 9 per cent (Debarbieux, Dupuch and Montoya, 1997, p.30). Moreover, a survey by Horenstein (1997), a psychiatrist at the MGEN (Teacher's Social and Medical Care), reminds us that even if reported pupil victims are rare in privileged schools, teachers suffer a statistically rather high level of stress.

Level of stress ?
from concern of violence ?

Not giving the quantitative results their real importance would shut the victims into a guilty feeling and silence. Surveys change the way of approaching the problem and its definition. Visible, symbolic violence, as theorized by Bourdieu and Passeron (1970), is still the underlying pattern exploited in most research. Another point of view should be considered: this states that violence 'is first what I consider as such' (Debarbieux, 1990; Debarbieux, 1999; Carra and Sicot, 1996). This is not a subjectivist nor a solipsist position, but an attempt to gather data on all the acts considered as violent by the actors themselves (see also Coslin, 1997). The definition of such acts differs between students and teachers as well as, for instance, between teaching staff and administrative staff (Ballion, 1996).

Debarbieux (1996, 1997) has attempted an epistemological shift in this area, following the work of Roché (1993, 1994, 1996) that applied the North American concept of incivility to schools. The translation of the founding texts such as the famous 'broken windows' of Wilson and Kelling (1982), and the works and synthesis of Roché (1993, 1994) and Lagrange (1995), have contributed widely to engender a change in paradigm in the French way of thinking about insecurity through the concept of incivility. We can think of it as an interim concept awaiting further refinement but still useful. It is accepted by most of the research teams in France (Ballion, 1996, 1997; Carra and Sicot, 1997), but questioned by some because of its lack of precision (Bonnafé-Schmitt, 1997). Even if violent crimes have been decreasing for two centuries, there is evidence that minor delinquencies, or incivilities, have been increasing in French society for the last 30 years. As such, they are penalized and can be recorded. Yet nearly 80 per cent of the offences counted as small delinquencies are not solved; not because of failures of the police, but because the nature of delinquency has changed.

Victims of these small offences or infringements experience a global feeling of disorder, of violence in a world of confusion. This leads us to question whether a psycho-sociological pattern of insecurity is a 'fantasy': far from being an unjustified worry in a period when crime becomes scarce, insecurity is linked to micro-victimization that cannot be sorted out by the state. Moreover, these acts should not necessarily be penalized, but even in the most insignificant forms they are difficult to bear, because of the feelings of lack of respect they engender in the victim. In school, they have a profound impact upon pupils as well as teachers in terms of identity feeling, and the term most often used in discourse about them is 'respect', without which there is no possible self-esteem or strong social identity (Dhoquois, 1996; Carra and Sicot, 1996).

Everything leads us to take incivility seriously into account; while not constituting actual infringements or offences, incivilities are at the border of offence and contribute to a strong deterioration of climate in some schools. Incivility is one of the main factors determining school climate. This realization allows us to understand Dubet's statement (1991, p.144) that 'The climate of indiscipline is, paradoxically, more precise than the incidents which create it. . . . Violence is more a threat than a real fact.' Even tiny forms of violence, when added up, make our world unbearable.

Focusing on the issue of incivility should not be used to minimize the issues of violence and delinquency; nor should it be used excessively, thereby leading to an over-emphasis on school disorders, and thus miss the real meaning and foster a xenophobic culture.

The incivility we have to cope with at school should not be seen as a 'fight between the barbarians and the civilized ones'. Incivility does not mean non-civilization, nor merely 'bad education'. It is a conflict of civilities, but not between foreign civilities that are forever relative and irreducible. It is rather a matter of exchange and opposition between values and feelings of belonging to different cultures. Incivility might only be the basic form of the class relationships that reflect a disappointed regard for a school that cannot hold its promises of equality in social integration. All sociological researches underline this link between school violence and social unfairness.

Incivility does not mean bad citizenship. Incivility in school is a clumsy, most ineffectual answer to the inegalitarian system of the urban 'school market' linked to the strategies of middle class parents avoiding ordinary schools to keep their social privileges. This game of choosing the 'right school' (Ballion, 1991) questions republican egalitarianism much more than does violence from the victims of exclusion (Dubet, 1996). Today, in a context of widespread unemployment, the comprehensive system can no longer be regarded as a democratic process. To many authors (Dubet, 1994; Payet, 1995; Ballion, 1997), it produces more diversified and complex attitudes towards school and school work, weakening the school republican concept based on meritocracy.

Prost (1992) showed how the former education system resulted in an openly unequal system: primary schools for the working class and further education for the heirs of the middle and upper classes. 'Reforming secondary schools not only strengthened social stratification but legitimated it, since it was based on some supposed school criteria and not openly social ones any more.' We can see the origin of the change in the shift in the composition of the school population (Testanière, 1967). To Peralva (1997), the main effect of being excluded from school is now perceived as being socially excluded; this implies a change in the meaning of school assessment so that it becomes the assessment of one's destiny, responsible for violent acts.

Payet (1995), Montoya (1994) and Debarbieux (1996) question the role of selection and ability grouping in schools. Pupil violence is motivated by and is part of a process of protest and confrontation; this is one of the reasons why it is impossible to tackle the problem by eliminating the so-called 'hard core'. The most vivid problems are assessment and selection. Pupils resist in several ways, more often violently, in order to reduce the grip of negative school verdicts on themselves.

Peralva supports Dubet's analysis (1994): some types of violence are part of an 'anti-school' behaviour pattern; it is a way of resisting the negative image that school gives to some pupils and expressing a kind of rage which is the only way to 'differentiate themselves from the defamatory categories of banishment' (Dubet, 1994, p.25). Ballion (1997) stresses that a covert social stratification and segregation results in a 'diffraction' or distortion and fragmentation of a social consensus that used to ground the acceptance of school.

The ideological erosion of the consensus that allowed the 'tacit sharing' of relationships and enabled implementation of soft discipline and negotiations has entailed the disappearance of a consensus of opinion about the meaning of school and law (Charlot, 1987, 1994; Debarbieux, 1994b; Peralva, 1997). Ballion demonstrates that cultural agreement survives within the middle class, allowing implementation of rules in a clear and legitimate way. On the other hand, deprived suburbs in large cities experience a cultural fragmentation. In these schools the rates of victimization and infringements of rules (apart from drugs and theft) are three times higher than in average secondary schools.

In a broad comparative study covering more than 14,000 pupils and 600 teachers and education officers, Debarbieux's team (1996) showed that violence depends mostly on the socio-demographic conditions of the school population. The more the schools welcomed socially deprived pupils, the more offences and rule infringements there were. When the school climate declines, feelings of insecurity grow. There is a direct link between the increase in feelings of insecurity and actual rates of victimization, or to be more accurate, in the awareness of the victims of a victimization process (Grémy, 1996). Feelings of insecurity and exposure to risk are socially unfair and closely related to social and school exclusion.

Most researchers find a close relationship between violence and the process of exclusion within schools, often created by hidden segregation in secondary schools (Payet, 1995, 1997). Such segregation might include 'mixophobia' between French female pupils and North African male pupils, choice of valuable courses for middle class children, etc. Debarbieux and Tichit (1997a, b) showed how relationships within groups were influenced by a process related to labelling and self-designating race, contributing to the building of a 'delinquent career' for a certain category of pupils. For these authors, much repressive behaviour is ethnically and sociologically influenced, and the ethnicization of violence is the most serious concern for the republican school. This is not because it is an 'ethnic violence' due to some cultural characteristics, but because the difference first imposed is now claimed as a very identity (Barrère and Martucelli, 1997; Lorcerie, 1996). The social experience of ethnic minorities is less based on a cultural difference than on a stigma or exclusion experience. Their attitude, far from expressing an attempt to go back to their roots, takes a reactive, even opposing, ethnic dimension because of their difficulties in getting into the social game.

For most researchers, the causes of violence cannot merely be rooted beyond school, as if it was besieged from outside. However, by stressing the links between violence and social background, research could feed the idea of a violent social handicap, and thus produce a fatalistic inertia, as well as the idea of a sanctuary school assaulted by barbarians. Schools often consider that violence can only come from outside (usually perpetrated by coloured people from deprived suburbs), ignoring the role of the school itself in the occurrences (Payet, 1997). As a result of such a view, the school bears no responsibility, and violence is considered to be due to the outside environment. Certainly, a portion of the reported violent acts come from outsiders. Nevertheless, trespassers are rather scarce and, most of the time, they are not real outsiders. Syr's survey (1996, 1997) studied the files of teachers in an extremely sensitive area who were reported as victims. There were only thirty-three reported cases. Eighty-eight per cent of offenders were adults, among which 55 per cent were parents of a schoolchild. Even when offenders were not parents, they were in some way linked to the victims in 85 per cent of the reported cases.

This scientific debate is also a fundamental strategic one: should we protect the school from its environment and external aggression, or should a genuine partnership with the inhabitants of the area be the solution? Should the school be deeply involved in the outside community life or just be a school in a neighbourhood (Debarbieux, 1994a)? Are the causes of violence in school totally external, or is school responsible too?

Most researchers are studying deeply the internal aspects of the school that help explain its vulnerability to attacks or even its direct responsibility for violence (Ballion, 1997; Payet, 1995; Debarbieux, 1996, 1997; Carra and Sicot, 1996, 1997; Pain, 1996). Walgrave (1992) argues that the school is obviously influencing the origins of delinquency and that the 'socio-cultural atmosphere of the school, composed of values, common behaviours and attitudes' that we could call school climate, is the main discriminating factor.

This is a new research orientation. Previously the 'school effect' had been studied in France through school achievement (Cousin, 1993; Grisay, 1993). Contrary to recent findings on academic achievement (Bressoux, 1995), it seems that as far as violence is concerned, the 'school' effect is bigger than the 'class' one, as global order is shared by everybody. The places outside the classroom are the most dangerous and the least controlled by adults. Nevertheless, the impacts of class and course are very powerful (Montoya, 1994; Payet, 1995).

Debarbieux (1997) does not oppose these views. In secondary schools, the class impact relates to the general policy of the school that copes with heterogeneity by forming groups of students according to their level and guiding some of them on to selective courses. The class impact results from gathering students with learning difficulties into classes, that can then become tense.

The roles of the principal, of staff cohesion and motivation, and of institutional partnerships, are important too. Conflicts among adults seem to affect the school atmosphere through a deregulation leading to all forms of violence (Pain, 1993a, 1993b; Debarbieux, 1994a, 1994b). In this case, the 'intermediary' places – corridors, stairs, toilets, etc. – become very risky. The macro-sociological determinants of violence in school are huge, but they should not prevent people from thinking about the way they are working in the school. This approach considers that there is a genuine freedom of the actors and that acting is possible. It deconstructs the evidence of violence resulting from poverty and immigration and contradicts the fatalistic belief of 'social handicaps leading to violence' (Debarbieux 2001).

This French model is strongly influenced by its history and a more conformist school system than the Anglo-Saxon one. According to a comparative survey by Pain and Barrier (1997), school could be considered as a 'democratic education place' in Germany and England and as a 'teaching place' in France. The policy of the school board hardly gets to mobilize the local inhabitants like in England or the USA (Body-Gendrot 1997), and in France schools rely on other state services and social workers rather than on parents' commitment. The permanent French temptation is to consider 'behaviour policy' as a matter for specialists such as *Conseillers Principaux d'Education* (Educating Counsellors), whose position is unique in Europe (Roché, 1996; Pain and Barrier, 1997).

The recent works of Blaya (Blaya and Debarbieux, 2000; Debarbieux and Blaya, 2001) show well how educative tasks are more often neglected, and even refused, by teachers in France, even though tutoring (guidance) and socio-cultural activities, when accepted by teachers, prove to be efficient. This situation is encouraged by the existence of ancillary staff in secondary schools, recently further supported by the recruiting of thousands of 'educating assistants' (see below) supposed to be in charge of socio-cultural activities, mediation, socializing and study supervising. As a consequence, even though the academic level of French students is good, the climate in schools is often worse and shows a stronger opposition to adults, especially to teachers.

Action

School safety and government regulations to ensure security in schools

Since the 1990s, governments and ministries of education have tried to tackle the problem of violence; and the first scheme was set up by the Ministers of Education, of the Interior and Justice. Since then, schemes have been designed without really solving problems. When Minister Claude Allègre launched a 'new' anti-violence scheme in 1998, it originated in his desire for action to be assessed by scientific research, which had never been done before. The scheme was set up in 291 *collèges*, 65 *lycées*, and 54 *Lycées professionnels* (vocational *lycées*), and involved 270,854 pupils. It aimed to reduce the level of incivilities and violence by injecting new means (staff and money) into 'at risk' secondary schools.

One of the new ideas was the creation of a new position in schools called *aide-éducateurs* (educating assistants). Aged 21 to 29, they are supposed to assist relationships between adults and pupils in the schools, to help with some educational tasks, and to act as mediators, at the same time as gaining some professional experience within the education system.

The assessment of these schemes showed that the *aide-éducateurs* and the addition of extra money were useful to stabilize or reduce violence or a tense school climate in some areas, but not in others (Debarbieux and Montoya, 1999). The scheme worked out well where the school culture was strong, and staff turnover was low (that is to say in areas such as Marseille where usually people wish to stay because of the nice environment and climate) or in the North of France where teams proved to be stable and where the *aide-éducateurs* were welcomed by the whole school and used for the tasks for which their position was first created and not as wardens. However, it was not so efficient in areas such as the Paris suburbs, where the environment and teaching conditions can be difficult and which have poor reputations because of being 'at risk'.

The importance of justice in the approach was reflected in the implementation of the scheme, in the sense that penalties for violence in schools were increased (Law of 17/06/97), and the courts were supposed to feed back to the principals about decisions and sanctions taken. This had some unexpected side-effects, such as some principals calling for penalties when this was not relevant. Moreover, because of some structural difficulties and lack of means, the interval between the complaint and judicial measures can be very long, even though it is sometimes a matter of emergency. Minister Claude Allègre left the Ministry of Education in March 2000, after a spate of strikes and unrest amongst the teaching staff he had criticized for 'their lack of dynamism'. They demanded extra staff, extra financial support and less violence in schools. However, a second 'plan' was announced by January 2000. It concerned the extension of the previous scheme to 60 extra secondary schools with some 7,000 extra staff, the division of overcrowded secondary schools, the inclusion of education for citizenship in the national curriculum, and the creation of *Classes Relais* (Pupil Referral Units) to host pupils under 16 with behavioural difficulties for temporary periods, to help maintain them in mainstream education.

The newly appointed Minister of Education, Jack Lang, set up new initiatives such as the creation of an Anti-violence National Committee (19.10.2000), composed of thirty-six members from National Education, Ministries of Justice, Interior, Cities, Defense, Youth and Sports, parents and pupils' representatives, and one university researcher. The objective of this committee is to analyse and identify violence in schools and design prevention schemes and actions to tackle the issue with other ministries, as well as mobilizing pupils themselves against violence in schools.

As concrete measures, the new Minister of Education is planning the creation of 185,000 teaching positions, of which 33,000 will be entirely new. This measure may satisfy teachers, but we can ask what educational measures will also be taken to improve the situation, since financial improvements or adding more staff proved insufficient in the previous 'plan'. The mobilization of the new Minister was emphasized concretely by the funding (jointly with the European Commission) of the first International Conference on Violence in Schools and Public Policies, that brought together more than twenty-seven countries and 129 paper presentations in early March 2001. This conference, organized by the European Observatory of Violence in Schools, gave the opportunity for the Minister to announce some new measures, such as an improved software programme to report violent acts in schools.

A new scheme is to try and attract new and motivated teachers in the Paris area, where staff turnover is the greatest (Debarbieux and Montoya,

1999). This would entail a reduction of the weekly teaching time from 18 to 16 sessions, the two extra hours being dedicated to in-service training. In order to keep these teachers, they will benefit from an extra bonus in their assessment; moreover, the head teachers of the 100 secondary schools involved in this scheme will have the opportunity to appoint teachers appropriate to school needs. Another aspect is the twinning of well performing inner city secondary schools with 'at risk' schools located in the outskirts of Paris (*Le Parisien*, 24 April 2001, pp.2–3). In 2001 the Ministry of Education initiated a nationwide TV campaign where media stars addressed young people and called for 'respect'.

Regional and local initiatives

A pilot initiative in the region of Paris, launched in July 2000, concerns violence prevention in upper secondary schools (*lycées*). Volunteer pupils dedicate themselves to inform about, and mobilize their peers against, violence in schools. The originality of this project lies in the unusual partnership and co-operation of the national railway company (SNCF), the Paris underground company (RATP), and the Ministry of Education. This scheme, involving 470 state *lycées* and 200 private ones, has not yet been assessed.

The 'green ribbon' initiative was designed by the juvenile magazine *Okapi* to tackle violence and break the rule of silence. All secondary school pupils who wished to participate wore a green ribbon and 30,000 signed up for a charter against violence. Some 600 secondary schools participated, organizing information and projects. The campaign is being conducted again this year and supported by the Ministry of Education. A website was set up (www.rubanvert.net) where adults from the school community and pupils can communicate. A helpline is to be set up for pupils, adults, victims or witnesses of violence. The extent of participation in this initiative was quite surprising, reflecting the mobilization of the school communities about violence and also the need of pupils to talk about the issue.

Evaluation of public policies

The action initiated by the government in 1998 was experimental. It was evaluated by a research team from the Observatory of Violence in Schools. A sample of schools that belonged to the 'experimental sites' chosen by the 1998 Ministry plan had been previously studied during a survey conducted in 1995 (Debarbieux, 1996). This allowed a comparison between the situation in 1995 and in 1998, before and after the implementation of the programme. The measures implemented by the Ministry, particularly the efficiency of the appointment of extra staff, could thus be evaluated (Debarbieux and Montoya, 2000).

The feeling of insecurity had increased between 1995 and 1998. The rates of reported victimization did not increase, but they did appear to be more serious, and mainly regarding adults. While in 1995 it was found that 24 per cent of the 3,134 students thought that violence existed within their school, this figure was 41 per cent in 1998. In 1995, 7 per cent of the 314 teachers complained about pupils' aggressiveness to adults; this figure was 49 per cent in 1998. This degradation mainly reflected a change in certain aspects of violence. The classroom had become a violent place with an anti-school collective form of violence along with an increasing severity of offences. The evaluation of the plan showed an encouraging stability in the actual number of violent acts, but with strong disparities.

The climate proved to be better when the staff had remained stable and when the managing team was efficient. On the other hand, in the outskirts of Paris, the extra staff granted to schools was not really helpful. In some schools the staff turnover was too high (as much as 80 per cent leaving schools after one year). The schools had no actual ethos, and pupils had the strong feeling of being neglected. Such schools thus more often experienced violence. Consequently, public policies are now re-oriented to keep teaching staff in difficult zones by means of a variety of measures: financial bonuses, promotions, new ways of appointment, improved accommodation for heads, new teacher training.

The evaluation of the Ministry plan showed that human and financial measures were not sufficient. It stressed the need for fairness in school discipline management, and social mixing. Particularly, classes composed of 'at risk' students according to ethnic criteria are likely to induce a feeling of injustice and promote the constitution of so-called delinquent 'hard cores' (Debarbieux and Blaya, 2001).

Conclusion

Violence in schools has been a major concern for the past ten years in France. The situation as a whole remains rather good and has not apparently changed much; nevertheless, a minority of schools in underprivileged areas have experienced a considerable increase in aggression and offences from pupils. In these schools especially, the rate of anti-school violence reveals a greater distrust of a large part of the working-class youth concerning the education system. However, research has found evidence that violence is not a social inevitability in relation to socio-economic factors, and that the organization of schools can in itself generate violence. The importance of better stability and efficiency of the teaching and managing staff is often stressed.

The French research approach is not, in the main, behaviourist or psychological, although it does not of course deny the importance of a psychological approach. Deeply influenced by a critical sociological tradition, the French approach lays stress upon sociological, school management and organization factors, refusing to regard 'violence' at the level of single individual 'risk factors'.

Public policies have turned particularly towards the so-called 'at risk zones' where a need for emergency action is felt, making up for social difficulties by extra teaching provision and supplies, and attempts to solve the problem through a closer partnership with the police, justice officials, and social workers. This partnership has already shown promise in preventive as well as remedial fields, in some areas. Beyond this, the most unexplored field is that of an improved co-operation with parents and the whole community (although several such preventive actions and partnerships have been locally implemented in some places). A necessary reorganization of public policies concerning the issue should be designed, to try and face the urgent, though limited, worsening of the problem.

References

Ballion, R. (1991). *La bonne école, évaluation et choix du collège et du lycée*. Paris: Hatier.

Ballion, R. (1996). *La gestion de la transgression à l'école*. Bordeaux: CADIS-EHESS-CNRS.

Ballion, R. (1997). Les difficultés des lycées vues à travers les transgressions. In B. Charlot and J.C. Emin (eds). *Violences à l'école. Etat des lieux*. Paris: Armand Colin.

Barrère, A. and Martucelli, D. (1997). L'école à l'épreuve de l'ethnicité. *Les Annales de la Recherche Urbaine*, 75.

Blaya, C. and Debarbieux, E. (2000). Violence à l'école et politiques publiques. In P. Baudry, C. Blaya, M. Choquet, E. Debarbieux and X. Pommereau. *Souffrances et violences à l'adolescence*. Paris: ESF.

Body-Gendrot, S. (1997). La violence dans l'école américaine: une invitation à la réflexion. In B. Charlot and J.C. Emin (eds). *Violences à l'école. Etat des lieux*. Paris: Armand Colin.

Bonnafé-Schmitt, J.P. (1997). La médiation scolaire: une technique de gestion de la violence ou un processus éducatif? In B. Charlot and J.C. Emin (eds). *Violences à l'école. Etat des lieux*. Paris: Armand Colin.

Bourdieu, P. and Passeron, J.-C. (1970). *La reproduction. Eléments pour une théorie du système d'enseignement*. Paris: Minuit.

Bressoux, P. (1995). Les effets du contexte scolaire sur les acquisitions des élèves. *Revue française de sociologie*, XXVI, 2.

Carra, C. and Sicot, F. (1996). *Pour un diagnostic local de la violence à l'école: enquête de victimation dans les collèges du département du Doubs*. Convention de recherche IHESI/DEP, LASA/UFC.

Carra, C. and Sicot, F. (1997). Une autre perspective sur les violences scolaires: l'expérience de victimation. In B. Charlot and J.C. Emin (eds). *Violences à l'école. Etat des lieux*. Paris: Armand Colin.

Charlot, B. (1987). *L'école en mutation*. Paris: Payot.

Charlot, B. (1994). L'école en banlieue: ouverture sociale et clôture symbolique. *Administration et éducation*, 3.

Choquet, M. and Ledoux, S. (1994). *Adolescents*. Paris: INSERM.

Coslin, P.G. (1997). A propos des comportements violents observés au sein des collèges. In B. Charlot and J.C. Emin (eds). *Violences à l'école. Etat des lieux*. Paris: Armand Colin.

Cousin, O. (1993). L'effet établissement. Construction d'une problématique. *Revue Française de Sociologie*, XXXIV, 3.

Debarbieux, E. (1990). *La violence dans la classe*. Paris: ESF.

Debarbieux, E. (1994a). Ecole du quartier ou école dans le quartier. Violence et limites de l'école. *Migrants-formation*, 97.

Debarbieux, E. (1994b). Violence, sens et formation des maîtres. In H. Hannoun and A.M. Drouin-Hans (eds). *Pour une philosophie de l'éducation*. Paris: Dijon CNDP.

Debarbieux, E. (1996). *La violence en milieu scolaire. 1: Etat des lieux*. Paris: ESF.

Debarbieux, E. (1997). Insécurité et clivages sociaux. L'exemple des violences scolaires. *Annales de la Recherche Urbaine*, 75.

Debarbieux, E. (1999). *La violence en milieu scolaire. 2: Le Désordre des choses*. Paris: ESF.

Debarbieux, E. (2001). 'Noyaux durs'? In *Les Cahiers de la Sécurité Intérieure*, 23. Paris: IHESI.

Debarbieux, E. and Blaya, C. (eds) (2001). *La violence en milieu scolaire. 3: Dix approches en Europe*. Issy-les-Moulineaux: ESF.

Debarbieux, E., Dupuch, A. and Montoya, Y. (1997). Pour en finir avec le handicap socio-violent. In B. Charlot and J.C. Emin (eds). *Violences à l'école. Etat des lieux*. Paris: Armand Colin.

Debarbieux, E. and Montoya, Y. (1999). Unpublished typed copies. Université de Bordeaux II.

Debarbieux, E. and Montoya, Y. (2000). Unpublished typed copies. Université de Bordeaux II.

Debarbieux, E. and Tichit, L. (1997a). Ethnicité, punitions et effet-classe: une étude de cas. *Migrants-formation*, 109.

Debarbieux, E. and Tichit, L. (1997b). Le construit 'ethnique' de la violence. In B. Charlot and J.C. Emin (eds). *Violences à l'école. Etat des lieux*. Paris: Armand Colin.

Dhoquois, R. (1996). Civilité et incivilités. In *Les Cahiers de la sécurité intérieure*, 23. Paris: IHESI.

Dubet, F. (1991). *Les lycéens*. Paris: Seuil.

Dubet, F. (1994). Les mutations du système scolaire et les violences à l'école. In *Les cahiers de la sécurité intérieure*, 15. Paris: IHESI.

Dubet, F. (1996). La laïcité dans les mutations de l'école. In M. Wieviorka (ed.). *Une société fragmentée? Le multiculturalisme en débat*. Paris: La Découverte.

Facy, F. and Henry, S. (1997). Systèmes d'information sur le phénomène des violences à l'école: du signalement direct aux statistiques indirectes. In B. Charlot and J.C. Emin (eds). *Violences à l'école. Etat des lieux*. Paris: Armand Colin.

Gottfredson, D.C. (2001). *Schools and delinquency*. Cambridge: Cambridge University Press.

Grémy, J.P. (1996). La délinquance permet-elle d'expliquer le sentiment d'insécurité? In *Les Cahiers de la sécurité intérieure*, 23. Paris: IHESI.

Grisay, A. (1993). Le fonctionnement des collèges et ses effets sur les élèves de sixième et cinquième. *Education et formations*, 32.

Horenstein, M. (1997). Les enseignants victimes de la violence. In B. Charlot and J.C. Emin (eds). *Violences à l'école. Etat des lieux*. Paris: Armand Colin.

Lagrange, H. (1995). *La civilité à l'épreuve. Crime et sentiment d'insécurité*. Paris: PUF.

Lorcerie, F. (1996). Laïcité 1996. La République à l'école de l'immigration. *Revue française de pédagogie*, 117.

Montoya, Y. (1994). La violence en milieu scolaire. In *Phénomènes de violence: essai de structuration méthodologique*. Paris: MEN DLC.

Pain, J. (1993a). *La pédagogie institutionnelle d'intervention*. Vigneux: Matrice.

Pain, J. (1993b). Violences en milieu scolaire et gestion pédagogique des conflits. *Migrants-formation*, 92.

Pain, J. (1996). Violences à l'école, étude comparative. Rapport de recherche. Université Paris X.

Pain, J. and Barrier, E. (1997). Violences à l'école: une étude comparative européenne. In B. Charlot and J.C. Emin (eds). *Violences à l'école. Etat des lieux*. Paris: Armand Colin.

Payet, J.P. (1995). *Collèges de banlieue. Ethnographie d'un monde scolaire*. Paris: Méridiens Klincksieck.

Payet, J.P. (1997). Le sale boulot. Division morale du travail dans un collège de banlieue. *Les Annales de la Recherche Urbaine*, 75.

Peralva, A. (1997). Des collégiens et de la violence. In B. Charlot and J.C. Emin (eds). *Violences à l'école. Etat des lieux*. Paris: Armand Colin.

Prost, A. (1992). Ecole et stratification sociale. In A. Prost, *Education, société et politiques, Une histoire de l'enseignement en France de 1945 à nos jours*. Paris: Le Seuil.

Roché, S. (1993). *Le sentiment d'insécurité*. Paris: PUF.

Roché, S. (1994). *Insécurités et libertés*. Paris: Le Seuil.

Roché, S. (1996). *La société incivile. Qu'est-ce que l'insécurité?* Paris: Le Seuil.

Syr, J.H. (1996). *Les violences à l'école: l'exemple de l'Académie d'Aix-Marseille*. ISPC-LRDD. Exemplaire dactylographié.

Syr, J.H. (1997). L'image administrative des violences concernant les personnels. In B. Charlot and J.C. Emin (eds). *Violences à l'école. Etat des lieux*. Paris: Armand Colin.

Testanière, J. (1967). Désordre et chahut dans l'enseignement du second degré en France. Thèse de troisième cycle. Paris: Centre de sociologie européenne. Exemplaire dactylographié.

Walgrave, L. (1992). *Délinquance systématisée des jeunes et vulnérabilité sociétale*. Genève: Méridiens Klincksieck (Médecine et Hygiène).

Wilson, J.-Q. and Kelling, G.-L. (1982). Broken windows. *The Atlantic Monthly*. March, 29–38.

Chapter 3

Tackling violence in schools
A report from Belgium

Inge Huybregts, Nicole Vettenburg and Monique D'Aes

Background

The country

Belgium has a population of 10.2 million inhabitants, 8.7 per cent of whom are foreign (5.5 per cent citizens of the European Union, 3.2 per cent others). It is a federal state with three policy levels, each having their own responsibilities: the Federal State, the communities and the regions. The communities (Flemish, French and German-speaking) are based on language and 'linked' to the people. They are responsible for the cultural and personal affairs within a certain linguistic area. Therefore, almost all educational responsibilities are vested in the hands of the communities. The regions (Flemish, Walloon and Brussels-Capital) are institutional entities that are linked more to economic interests, themselves determined by specific geographical areas. The Brussels-Capital Region corresponds to the bilingual area of the capital city of Brussels, where French and Dutch have equal status.

The Belgian school system

The Federal State is responsible only for the pensions of the staff members of educational institutions, for laying down compulsory school attendance and for determining the minimum requirements to obtain a diploma. The 1983 Compulsory Learning Act obliges parents to have their children study for twelve years: from the year of their sixth birthday until the year in which they turn 18. Compulsory learning is full-time up to the age of 15 or 16; from then on it is only compulsory part-time. However, full-time education is opted for by the large majority of pupils (Tielemans, 1996).

Traditionally three educational levels exist in Belgium: elementary, secondary and higher education. Elementary education includes nursery and primary education. Nursery education is a three-year cycle provided for children aged 2½ to 6. Though it is optional, nearly all children attend nursery school in Belgium. Primary education is a six-year cycle, meant for children aged 6 to 12. Pupils receive a certificate of elementary education when they pass year six. Primary schools typically have 100 to 400 pupils (mean size in Flanders is 273 pupils). Secondary education is meant for youngsters aged 12 to 18 and consists of six years, divided into three grades of two years each. The first grade offers a range of general subjects. For pupils who did not receive their elementary education certificate or who are considered to be not academically strong enough to pass the first year of secondary education, one transitional year is offered during which the subject matter of primary school is repeated. Secondary schools typically have 200 to 600 pupils (mean size in Flanders is 447 pupils).

Starting the second grade of secondary education, pupils have a choice between five main types. General secondary education offers academic subjects only and prepares pupils for higher education. Artistic secondary education includes a combination of general and artistic subjects. Technical secondary education involves a combination of general, technical-theoretical and practical subjects. Vocational secondary education is a practical education form in which pupils learn a specific occupation. It prepares youngsters for a job. Part-time vocational secondary education is a practical education form in which youngsters attend only 15 periods of classes a week. Once a pupil passes the last year of full-time secondary education, s/he receives the leaving certificate of secondary education, giving the right to enter any college for *higher education* or any university of his/her choice (Ministère de l'éducation, de la recherché et de la formation, 1996).

Next to the traditional mainstream education levels, special education exists on the level of primary and secondary education. It is meant for children and adolescents with a mental, physical and/or sensorial handicap, with grave behavioural and/or emotional problems or children with serious learning difficulties (Tielemans, 1996).

Violence in schools: linguistic and definitional issues

Flanders

In Flanders there has been an unmistakable influence of Scandinavian, Anglo-Saxon and Dutch publications (Vettenburg, 1988). This explains why aggressive behaviour in school, at first, got public and scientific attention almost exclusively in terms of bullying. The most frequently used definition of 'bullying' is the one developed by Olweus (1991): 'a person is being bullied or victimized when he or she is exposed, repeatedly and over time, to negative actions on the part of one or more other persons'. Though Olweus' concept of bullying implies 'behaviour intended to inflict injury or discomfort upon another individual', it does not refer to the same reality as his concept of violence. Both phenomena are subsets of aggressive behaviour, but they each have their own specific characteristics. Bullying is characterized by repetitiveness and an asymmetric relationship; violence by the use of physical force of power (Olweus, 1999).

Next to 'bullying' the notion 'violence in schools' has become very common in recent years, especially in Wallonia. Though this notion is seldom defined, it generally is used to refer not only to physical violence, but to the whole spectrum of aggressive behaviour, going from verbal/psychological, over material, to physical violence (Buidin et al., 2000; Vettenburg and Huybregts, 2001).

More recently the concept 'antisocial behaviour in schools' has been used more as an alternative to 'violence in schools'. This concept was introduced in Flanders by Vettenburg (Vettenburg and Huybregts, 2001) in a research project on 'Violence in schools: feelings of lack of safety'. 'Antisocial behaviour in schools' refers to 'the full spectrum of verbal or non verbal interactions between persons active in or around the school and involving malicious or allegedly malicious intentions causing mental, physical or material damage or injury to persons in or around the school and violating informal rules of behaviour'. Again, contrary to Olweus' definition of violence, this concept refers not only to physical violence, but includes verbal/psychological and material violence as well.

Wallonia

Unlike Dutch-speaking Flanders, Wallonia has been hardly influenced or inspired by the Anglo-Saxon or Scandinavian views. Also, there is no good French translation for the term 'bullying'. In recent years the English word has been used more and more. That is why preference is given in Wallonia to the terms 'school violence' (*'violence(s) scolaire(s)'*) or 'violence in schools' (*'violence(s) à l'école'*). These terms denote the same reality as the Dutch term *'geweld op school'* and so are used not only to refer to physical violence, but to the whole spectrum of verbal/psychological violence, through material, to physical violence.

Knowledge

Neither in Flanders nor in Wallonia has any specific research been carried out into physical school violence so far. It is therefore impossible to make an accurate assessment of the situation. Still, a number of studies have been conducted into bullying and violence in schools in general. Some of these studies also address the issue of physical violence. We review some of these partial data below.

Empirical research focusing on bullying

Concerning the theme of aggressive behaviour in Flemish education, bullying is by far the most studied form (Vettenburg, 1999a). Of particular interest are two studies. Stevens and Van Oost (1994, 1995) used the Dutch translation by van Lieshout of the Classmates Relation Questionnaire, developed by Olweus (1991), and slightly adapted to the Flemish context; 10,000 pupils between ages 10 and 16, drawn from 84 primary and secondary schools were questioned. The Central Board for Study and Career Guidance (CSBO) (Vandersmissen and Thys, 1993) involved an inquiry among 1,054 sixth form pupils in mainstream full-time secondary education.

The study by Stevens and Van Oost found that 15.9 per cent of pupils in primary education bully other pupils regularly or often; 5.6 per cent do so at least once a week. In secondary education, these figures are 12.3 and 3.9 per cent respectively. In terms of victimization, 23 per cent of pupils in primary education report that they are victims of bullying regularly or often; 9.1 per cent report being bullied at least once a week. In secondary education, the percentages are 15.2 and 6.4 per cent respectively.

The CSBO study found that 18 per cent of secondary school pupils are being bullied to a lesser extent; 2.6 per cent of them report being bullied badly. The most frequent form of bullying is ridiculing (60 per cent of those bullied). Name calling (22.4 per cent) and social exclusion (20.5 per cent) are quite frequent, followed by hitting and pushing around (11.7 per cent), threatening (9.8 per cent) and destruction of possessions (6.3 per cent). Verbal types of bullying are clearly predominant.

Bullying and being bullied decrease with age. In the study by Stevens and Van Oost, the frequencies decrease significantly between ages 10 and 16. This decrease with age is confirmed by the CSBO study, though the age trend is found to be less pronounced among girls, since bullying is less frequent at a lower age.

Bullying and being bullied in general occurs more frequently among boys than girls, as the Stevens and Van Oost study found. This is especially the case with regard to direct, physical bullying. With regard to indirect bullying however, more girls report bullying and being bullied than boys. The CSBO also found more boys to be bullied than girls. Within the group feeling badly bullied, however, no sex differences were found.

Other empirical research

Flanders

Vettenburg (1988) asked 1,689 pupils in the first, third and fourth years of vocational education to state whether and to what extent they had committed acts of problem behaviour at school in the past school year. The acts of problem behaviour concerned were: theft, vandalism, involvement in fights, deliberate disruptive classroom behaviour and truancy. Fourteen per cent of pupils admitted to having been involved at least once in a serious fight at school in the past school year (11.1 per cent once, 2.9 per cent several times). In contrast to other types of problem behaviour, serious fights had a significantly higher incidence with first year than with third year and fourth year pupils. The interviews with pupils and teachers and non-participative classroom observations showed that a general positive attitude of the teacher has a favourable effect on his or her pupils' behaviour. This positive link is based on mutual respect and recognition and appears to be crucial for curbing or preventing problem behaviour (see: theory of social vulnerability, Vettenburg, 1988, 1999b).

In a large-scale youth research a representative sample of 4,829 school-going youngsters (from 94 secondary schools in Flanders) were interviewed in class on a large number of topics, including delinquent behaviour and school-related incidents (De Witte, Hooge and Walgrave, 2000). For the school-related incidents: 14 to 15 per cent disrupted the classroom deliberately, directed abuse at the teacher or skipped school; 13 per cent prevented fellow students from paying attention; 10 per cent bullied their fellow students and 7 per cent deliberately destroyed school property (Mertens and Van Damme, 2000). Secondary analyses showed that substantially more boys than girls and more youngsters in vocational than in technical or general secondary education say they have committed such behaviour in the past year. Stepwise multiple regression showed that the quality of the pupil–teacher relationship is the best predictor for antisocial behaviour in school (Vettenburg and Huybregts, 2001).

In a study commissioned by the Flemish Ministry of Education, linked to the large-scale youth research, Vettenburg and Huybregts (2001) asked 1,432 Flemish teachers in regular secondary education whether they had been the victims of (physical and/or other types of) violence committed by pupils at school; and whether they knew of any colleagues in their school who had become the victims of such violence. The results suggest that teachers are mostly the victims of verbal violence and to a much smaller extent of material violence. Hardly any physical violence was reported, either with regard to the teacher's own victimization or to that of their colleagues. Of the investigated facts involving physical violence committed against the respondents personally, robbery ranked first, reported by 2.1 per cent, followed by battery and assault, 1.2 per cent, and armed threats, 0.6 per cent.

Wallonia

In Wallonia, Ganty (1993) conducted research into the incidence of physical and other types of school violence in French-speaking education in Belgium. The school boards in primary and secondary mainstream and special education were asked to what extent their schools were confronted with eleven types of school violence. Two of these related to physical violence: against teachers and among pupils. For the different types of education, the percentages of school boards reporting physical violence against teachers and among pupils were: mainstream primary education: 2.3 per cent and 56.6 per cent respectively; mainstream secondary education: 7.5 per cent and 64.6 per cent; special primary education: 37.3 per cent and 84.9 per cent; special secondary education 54.1 per cent and 97.3 per cent.

By order of the Education Ministry of the French Community, researchers of the Universities of Liège (ULG) and Louvain (UCL) asked about 5,000 pupils in the first, third and fifth years of secondary education, in Wallonia and Brussels, and 1,500 teachers, school board members, pupil counsellors, school administrative and maintenance staff, whether they had been the victim of acts of physical and other forms of violence at school in the past five months (Buidin et al., 2000). Three of the eleven items related to physical violence: violent wrestling, armed threats and battery and assault. For physical violence against pupils, 26.1 per cent of the pupils claimed to have been the victim of battery and assault at least once during the past five months. The figures for violent wrestling and armed threats were 4.8 per cent and 3.4 per cent respectively. For physical violence against adults, like the Flemish study, the results suggest that adults in schools are mostly the victims of verbal and to a much smaller extent of material violence.

Other indicators of the incidence of physical school violence in Belgium

Very rough indicators of acts of physical violence are provided by industrial accident statistics. If a case of aggression at school causes bodily injuries to a staff member, the victim may report the incident as an industrial accident. In Flanders, thirteen cases were reported in 1998 that qualified as violence by pupils against staff members. None of these cases involved the use of weapons. The reported acts of violence were fighting, punching and pushing. Note that industrial accidents are caused more often by aggression from persons external to the school than by pupil aggression (Scheys, Dupont and Huylebroeck, 1999–2000).

Other indicators of physical school violence are police data. School violence statistics are not systematically kept by the police or by the judicial services. However, the boards of Antwerp schools are increasingly calling on the municipal police Youth Squad and Youth Violence Cell to intervene in conflicts involving pupils, and as a result the Youth Violence Cell is now recording the relevant information. In the 1997–1998 school year, the Antwerp police had to intervene 865 times. Offences against property were the most frequent cause. Theft and vandalism together accounted for almost 85 per cent of cases. Only 6.5 per cent of interventions were for violent offences (De Wit, 1998).

Features related to violence in school

In their research on violence in schools Vettenburg and Huybregts (2001) reviewed the recent Western research literature on pupil, family, peer-group and school features connected with (physical and other forms of) violence in school. Their conclusions can be summarized as follows. Among the student features, gender has by far the best predictive value. Boys systematically appear to commit more acts of all types of violence than girls. In addition, the preponderance of boys is more pronounced as the acts of violence become more serious. School fatigue, problems during the early school career, problem behaviour outside the school context and a more tolerant attitude towards violence appear to be closely connected to school violence as well. Although the differences are not equally significant in each study and for each type of violence, a general finding is that juveniles belonging to vulnerable social families, ethnic minorities and juveniles in lower levels of education, commit more acts of violence than more privileged, indigenous juveniles and juveniles in higher levels of education.

As far as the correlation between violence and family features is concerned, the qualitative features of the family appear to be most relevant. Young people having a good bond with their (prosocial) parents commit fewer acts of violence. Conversely, a strong bond between children and their antisocial parents increases the risk of more, and more serious, violence. The same goes for bonds with prosocial or antisocial peers. Finally, the school itself plays an important part in the development of school violence. Antisocial behaviour decreases as the school succeeds in establishing a better bond with pupils. To the extent that young people set greater store by teachers' judgements and expectations, invest more time and energy in school tasks and grow convinced of the usefulness of school regulations, they will enact less antisocial behaviour at school. A positive school climate and teachers' attitude towards the pupils appear to be especially important.

Action

Current national (regional) policies regarding violence in school

As stated above, education in Belgium is almost the exclusive province of the Flemish and the Walloon Communities. Although Flanders and Wallonia pursue individual policies, the principles underlying their policies for the prevention of (physical and other types of) school violence are broadly similar.

The Flemish community

Action plan

Up until now, there were very few indications that violence, in terms of verbal, material or physical aggression, was a major concern in Flemish schools. However, because the concern about violence in society as a whole as well as in schools is growing, the Department of Education worked out an action plan. The action plan starts from the definition of violence in terms of antisocial behaviour and integrates already existing and stimulates further preventive, remedial and curative work. The action plan goes along with a research project, intended to describe the phenomenon of antisocial behaviour in quantitative and qualitative terms (see Vettenburg and Huybregts, 2001).

Based on empirical evidence that schools can make a difference, enhancing educational quality is a key goal of the action plan. First has been the introduction of broader learning objectives such as group work, as the pre-eminent instrument to impart values and social skills to pupils. Second has been a reorganization of the inspection system, with inspection teams visiting schools to examine the performance of the school as a whole, away from the subject-oriented inspection or the checking of individual teachers. Third, the action plan aims at enhancing a positive school climate and feelings of success and well-being in pupils. The matter of rules and regulations (as set and applied) and students' rights in schools are given special attention and initiatives are taken to empower parents and students to participate better in these matters. Fourth, the needs of the teaching profession will be given further attention. In-service training programmes, selected on their relevance for implanting new practices at class and school level, are offered to schools.

Next to the general ambition of enhancing quality, specific remedial measures of positive discrimination are taken to improve the quality of the education of pupils with special needs, especially youngsters from ethnic minorities and vulnerable social groups. To combat the retardation problem of migrant students an educational priority policy was worked out, focusing on the stimulation of the school environment, to adapt to the special needs of this pupil group and the activation of the educational environment at home. This policy is now extended to the empowerment of the group of poor and underprivileged families who are not from an ethnic minority background. To combat the increasing concentration of ethnic minorities in a small number of schools, a desegregation policy at local community level has been started. It tries to avoid a situation in which immigrants are channelled to only a few schools with an open admissions policy or a positive attitude towards multiculturalism, or in which immigrants demand schools of their own religion for their children.

Next to the general preventive and remedial measures, the action plan outlines new curative policies. Extreme antisocial behaviour (such as physical violence) must be tackled. Alternative sanctions (e.g. based on a restorative justice approach) are promoted. Further work will be done on developing co-operative and intersectional youth care, with the centres of pupil guidance as crucial partners and co-ordinators (Scheys, Dupont and Huylebroeck, 1999–2000).

Support for 'schools with special needs'

This project was launched on 1 September 2000. It gives targeted support to the Flemish secondary schools that are most in need of help. Schools qualifying for participation in this project were given extra staff for counselling and monitoring pupils.

Youngsters for schools, schools for youngsters

This project involves 115 school dropouts in the fight against school violence, from 1 January 2001 onwards. Based on the number of pupils with educational needs, 135 schools with special needs were pre-selected in five cities to apply for participation in the project. The project has dual objectives: first, to allow dropouts to experience what it is like to have a job in education and encourage them to pursue this direction through additional training; second, to assign an extra staff member to schools with problem pupils, who can help create a positive climate at school and enhance contacts between teachers and foreign or deprived families.

The French community

General approach

In 1999 the Ministry of Education set up a Unit for prevention of violence in school. The objectives are: to stimulate schools to develop democratic structures (pupil consulting, pupils' parliaments), to facilitate collaboration between various partners (school, police, youth assistance) and to set up a structure for dealing with crisis situations including attention to any urgent needs of victims in school (Blomart et al., 2000).

As far as the curative aspect is concerned, the French Community pursues a much more elaborated policy – witness the decree of 30 June 1998. On the matter of preventing violence, this decree sets out provisions on access to school buildings and the conditions for expulsion of pupils following serious incidents. In addition, the Education Minister recently recommended that school boards should respond firmly and severely to any type of violence. For this purpose, the Minister recommended a manual prescribing the sanctions and measures to be taken not only against the culprits of all kinds of violent behaviour, but also on behalf of the victims and the school.

School mediation

In the wake of severe incidents of violence in Brussels in 1991, the French Community introduced a project of school mediation in twenty-eight schools. In September 1993, twenty-eight mediators were recruited in twenty-two French-speaking schools in the Capital Region of Brussels in order to stem the problems of dropping out and school violence. The function of a school mediator primarily involves detecting and heading off truancy, dropping out and violence in school. The mediator intervenes at the request of the pupil, a teacher, the head teacher or any parents who contact him or her.

Local initiatives or programmes

Besides government initiatives, a lot of useful work is done by local level agencies, as can be seen in a review of the educational literature. Different practices are described and worked out in practical manuals or handbooks, video materials, and training programmes. Strategies and models envisage both work at classroom and at school level. Because it is impossible to discuss all initiatives, we only discuss a few.

School adoption (Antwerp)

As part of its preventive action, the police of the city of Antwerp launched the school adoption project *Act normally!* during the 1998–1999 school year. This project is based on a similar Rotterdam-based project. One of the main objectives of the school adoption project was the prevention of antisocial or violent behaviour within and around Antwerp schools. To tackle these problems, police officers adopted one or two schools in their district and instructed the pupils in 'peer education'. The aim of this training was fourfold:

1   to make pupils aware of the group pressure exercised by (some of) their peers;
2   to teach pupils the skills to withstand this pressure;
3   to offer positive alternatives to antisocial behaviour; and
4   to boost pupils' self-confidence, communicative skills and decisiveness.

The teacher's participation in the lesson was required, so that (s)he could refer to the content of the 'adoption lesson' in subsequent classes (De Meyer and Massel, 1998).

By training pupils at school, the police not only want to prevent or curb problem behaviour but also to improve their relations with the school in general and with the pupils in particular. Since the adoption project was not launched until very recently, an in-depth evaluation is not yet possible. The Dutch project on which the Belgian one is based has a very sound scientific foundation. Evaluations of the Dutch project have been invariably positive, and it has been awarded several prizes (De Meyer and Massel, 1998).

Mikpunt (Ghent)

Mikpunt (Target) is a project for the prevention of youth violence developed by the pluralistic youth service for peace education *'Jeugd en Vrede'* (Youth and Peace), in co-operation with the educational service of the Ghent police. The project aims to sensitize young people aged 12 to 16 to the problem of youth violence. For this purpose, *Mikpunt* elaborated a training package to encourage an open-minded and frank discussion of violence.

The educational package consists of a trainer's manual with information on violence and aggression in general, possible preventive approaches and ways of coping with violence; plus five booklets comprising a theoretical part with background information and a practical part presenting methodologies. The five themes covered are: violence within and around schools, violence at mass events, violence on the road and in public transport facilities, vandalism, and sexual violence. The package also includes a video offering a visual representation of the five themes. This is expected to make the youngsters reflect on these issues and should spark off discussions. The pupil package includes a workbook with cartoons, press cuttings and blank exercises.

Schools have shown an overwhelming interest in the training package. Both the Ghent police and *'Jeugd en Vrede'* are receiving frequent requests from schools to organize exhibitions. The response of participants is positive. Teachers in particular feel that the resources offered provide an excellent basis for approaching the topic from a different angle (Verduyckt, 2000).

To become one's own mediator (Devenir son propre médiateur)

This programme intends to promote the development of prosocial behaviour with pupils. It is based on self-mediation and aims for harmonious and autonomous management of relationships, by teaching young children to be in control of the way they communicate. Thus they will be able to prevent conflicts in numerous situations, now and in the future, whether they be in school, with the family, with friends or at work. It is hoped that in the long run this project will change the attitude of teachers and bring about a better climate in class and school.

The programme was made and adapted by a team of teachers. It contains eleven themes, each consisting of various activities including: knowing oneself and others, recognizing one's needs and feelings, verbal and non-verbal communication, solving conflicts, mediation, responsibility and co-operation (Blomart et al., 2000).

The programme is part of an action research conducted at the University of Brussels. Within this research the programme was evaluated both qualitatively and quantitatively on its short-term effects. The qualitative evaluation was based on observations during the sessions with all parties concerned. The quantitative evaluation consisted of an inventory of the social and emotional development of the pupils by means of a questionnaire to measure social competences (adapted from Gresham and Eliot) and a scale to measure attitudes towards social interaction (based on the frustration test of Rozenzweig). The answers of the pupils and class tutors show less aggressive and arrogant and more prosocial behaviour among the pupils. They score higher on co-operation, self-esteem and self-control. The observations confirm this, and show a constructive attitude and behaviour pattern on the part of the teachers. They suggest a positive effect of the project within the classroom and in the whole school (Blomart et al., 2000).

The Linkedness project (Louvain)

This project starts from the reflection that, according to its Latin origin, 'de-linquency' literally means the 'absence of a link'. The project envisages global change of the school culture and school structure towards a school climate of linkedness. In order to obtain an integral prevention, five dimensions are distinguished in the programme of relinking: the link with oneself, the other, the material, and the larger social and ecological environment. The most important thing on each of these levels is not to carry out major projects, but rather to promote, by means of minor, concrete initiatives, a process of awareness. Another important starting point in this prevention project is the integration of all these initiatives by linking them to daily life.

The central method developed and used in the project is the 'School team based Process oriented Working method' (SPW-method). Working with the whole school team is necessary (Depuydt and Deklerck, 2000). This means that during the course of a school year the project co-ordinators meet with the entire school team about five times. During this year the school team works out small initiatives, which they can integrate into the school culture or school structure.

The Linkedness project started on a voluntary basis in 1990 and has been continued as a postgraduation project with one part-time staff member since 1994. It was worked out in a partnership between the Departments of Criminology and Education at the K.U. Leuven. Experiences in the fourteen pilot primary schools over the last ten years are now being carried forward to six pilot secondary schools.

Time-out projects with school replacing programmes

These programmes are aimed at youngsters who run a severe risk of dropping out of school and for whom all efforts to retain them in school have been to no avail. The pupils are temporarily removed from school with the purpose of unravelling the problematic situation. After a number of weeks they should ideally return to their former school and continue their education. During this intermission – which results in a break for the pupil and the school – the youngsters are closely followed and guided. At the same time support is given to the school with a view to the future integration of the pupil and a course of action aimed at the prevention of disruptive behaviour. During the 'time-out' period several partners work together: the school, the school psychologist and social worker, the parents and local welfare organizations.

Four time-out projects with school replacing programmes are co-financed by King Boudewijn Foundation and the Departments of Education and Welfare. These projects have been developed by a number of welfare services. In 2001 and 2002 the projects will be closely monitored and supported by 'inter-supervisory meetings'. Simultaneously a working group will prepare the further structural embedding. The evaluation of the projects will be done on the basis of data that register the development of and impact on the pupil and the school. Apart from the data, the intervention meetings and the project reports will be taken into consideration.

The Positive Report Card

This is given to pupils who find it difficult to stick to the school rules, e.g. who use completely inappropriate language, talk back to the teacher, distract other pupils, fail to bring along relevant materials, fail to keep up with work demands and show total disrespect for others. These pupils run the risk of being permanently excluded. The main aim of the Positive Report Card is to give school teams, individual teachers and pupils an instrument to achieve positive behaviour so that the pupil can stay in school. Experiments show that 7 out of 10 such pupils avoid permanent exclusion with the help of this instrument.

The Positive Report Card is a daily form that the pupil gives to his teachers at the beginning of the lesson. They will fill it in at the end of the lesson and hand it back to the pupil. At the end of the day the pupil hands it in to the head teacher. Once a week a 'Link Teacher' discusses the forms of the past week with the pupil and gives him an assignment for the next week.

The Positive Report Card consists of a list of elements of behaviour that the school team considers to be essential. Next to each item on the list there are a number of boxes in which teachers can place their signature if the student has behaved well. They do not write anything in the box if the behaviour was not good. The Positive Report Card is a 'mirror'. It shows the pupil how the teachers see his or her behaviour. It shows the teacher what her or his own personal values and demands are. And it shows how these values and demands relate to those of other staff members. It is an instrument of self-reflection for pupil and teachers alike.

Relevant case study: Learning to Study at Home (Hasselt)

This project does not directly aim at combating violence in school. Its purpose is to promote the chances of succeeding in school for youngsters from socially weak environments. Criminological research shows that a positive attitude towards the school will diminish delinquent behaviour (Vettenburg, 1988). For this reason, and also because of the structural changes that this project tries to achieve, we have included it as an example of 'good practice'.

The project has three objectives:

1   to give youngsters in socially weak environments better chances to finish their education. This is done by giving them advice on how to study at home and by informing their parents as to how they can be of support to their children in this respect;
2   to give future teachers an insight into the problematic situation of these families and to teach them skills which will help them to co-operate with the parents of pupils in socially weak environments;
3   to collect procedures which have been proved useful during the house visits, adjust them in collaboration with the future teachers and to make them available to other schools.

Secondary school pupils who have learning difficulties get special training in their homes from students who are studying to become teachers. Together with the parents, the schools and the Centres for the Guidance of Pupils, the student teachers help these pupils to acquire better studying skills. The student teachers also accompany the parents during teacher–parent meetings at school, and attend the special teacher meetings that are held at the end of every term to evaluate the progress of these pupils. Those students of the Teacher Training Colleges who wish to participate in the project receive tuition and guidance.

Over the past two years the project has been readjusted. The methods and procedures have been refined. The limited evaluation after two years shows an overall positive feeling from all parties concerned. The student teachers have learnt that 'studying at home' is not a matter of course for some pupils. Not all homes are quiet when homework has got to be done. Not all parents ask about homework to be done or lessons to be learnt. Not all pupils can rely on somebody to help them with a difficult subject. This way the future teachers learn to approach the most vulnerable pupils in a different way. The pupils spend more time and effort on their school task, they enjoy studying more and they get better results at school. The students were able to build a positive relationship with 'their' pupils after a few weeks. They managed to motivate them to work harder for school, to plan their school work, to talk to their tutor, etc. In school, awareness is heightened that some pupils need extra tuition. Efforts are made to reach out to them and motivate them to invest in learning how to study.

This project aims at a perfect combination of individual care and a structural approach to the problem. Giving the pupils tuition at home calls on their individual capacities and alleviates the learning problems to which they are vulnerable because of their background. The parents become responsible as well. The family visits give future teachers a better understanding of pupils with a different background from their own. This will lead them to question their own values and to let go of prejudices. Finally, by means of parent–teacher meetings and teacher meetings, the student teachers can share their experiences with the secondary schools as well as with the teacher training colleges.

References

Blomart, J., Timmermans, J., Caffieaux, C. and Petiau, A. (2000). Recherche-action, Devenir son propre médiateur. Programme de socialisation à l'école, comme défi à la violence. Rapport de recherche non publié commandité par le ministère de la Communauté Française de Belgique.

Buidin, G., Petit, S., Galand, B., Philippot, P. and Born, M. (2000). *Violences à l'École: Enquête de Victimisation dans l'Enseignement Secondaire de la Communauté Française de Belgique*. Liège (ULG)/Louvain-La-Neuve (UCL).

De Meyer, N. and Massel, A. (1998). *Het Schooladoptieplan*. Antwerpen: politie Antwerpen.

Depuydt, A. and Deklerck, J. (2000). *Project 'Linkedness' ('Reliance'), Secondary Schools, Belgium. Interim Report*. Leuven: K.U. Leuven, Department of Criminology.

De Wit, J. (1998). Geweld neemt niet toe in Antwerpse scholen. *Gazet van Antwerpen*, 3 Dec, p.3.

De Witte, H., Hooge, J. and Walgrave, L. (eds) (2000). *Jongeren in Vlaanderen: Gemeten en Geteld. 12- tot 18-Jarigen over hun Leefwereld en Toekomst*. Leuven: Universitaire pers.

Ganty, J. (1993). Violence scolaire: délinquance en milieu scolaire et/ou sociopathie institutionnelle. *L'Observatoire*, 18, 25–30.

Mertens, W. and Van Damme, J. (2000). De School. In H. De Witte, J. Hooge and L. Walgrave (eds). *Jongeren in Vlaanderen: Gemeten en Geteld. 12- tot 18-jarigen over hun Leefwereld en Toekomst*. Leuven: Universitaire pers. pp.81–149.

Ministère de l'éducation, de la recherché et de la formation (1996). *Le Système Éducatif en Communauté Française de Belgique*. Bruxelles: Secrétariat Général.

Olweus, D. (1991). *Treiteren op School*. Leuven: Acco.

Olweus, D. (1999). Sweden. In P.K. Smith, Y. Morita, J. Junger-Tas, D. Olweus, R. Catalano and P. Slee (eds). *The Nature of School Bullying: A Cross-national Perspective*. London: Routledge.

Scheys, M., Dupont, C. and Huylebroeck, K. (1999–2000). Antisociaal gedrag op school voorkomen en oplossen. Een actieplan vanuit onderwijs. *Tijdschrift voor Onderwijsrecht en Onderwijsbeleid*, 1/2, 17–30.

Stevens, V. and Van Oost, P. (1994). Pesten op school: Een eerst deelonderzoek naar het optreden van pesten en gepest worden bij kinderen tussen 10 en 14 jaar. *Tijdschrift voor Klinische Psychologie*, 3, 239–259.

Stevens, V. and Van Oost, P. (1995). Pesten op school: Een actieprogramma. *Handboek leerlingbegeleiding. Probleemgedrag aanpakken*, 15, 93–100.

Tielemans, J. (1996). *Onderwijs in Vlaanderen*. Leuven: Garant.

Vandersmissen, V. and Thys, L. (1993). Onderzoek naar de schoolbeleving in Vlaanderen. Omgang met medeleerlingen. *Caleidoscoop*, 4, 4–9.

Verduyckt, E. (2000). *Positieve Samenwerkingsinitiatieven Tegen Antisociaal Gedrag bij Leerlingen. Projectevaluatie*. Brussel: Koning Boudewijnstichting.

Vettenburg, N. (1988). *Schoolervaringen, Delinquentie en Maatschappelijke Kwetsbaarheid. Een Theoretisch en Empirische Onderzoek in het Beroepsonderwijs*. Leuven: K.U. Leuven, Onderzoeksgroep Jeugdcriminologie.

Vettenburg, N. (1999a). Belgium. In P.K. Smith, Y. Morita, J. Junger-Tas, D. Olweus, R. Catalano and P. Slee (eds). *The Nature of School Bullying: A Cross-national Perspective*. London: Routledge.

Vettenburg, N. (1999b). Violence in Schools. Awareness-raising, prevention, penalties. General report. In Council of Europe, *Violence in Schools, Awareness-raising, Prevention, Penalties*. Strasbourg: Council of Europe Publishing.

Vettenburg, N. and Huybregts, I. (2001). *Geweld op School. Onveiligheid en Onveiligheidsgevoelens. Eindrapport*. Leuven: K.U. Leuven, Onderzoeksgroep Jeugdcriminologie.

Chapter 4

Luxembourg

First official steps to deal with violence in school

Georges Steffgen and Claire Russon

Background

The country

Luxembourg lies at the heart of Europe, bordering on Belgium, France and Germany. It is the smallest state in the European Union (2,586 km²) with a total population of 441,300 on 1 January 2001. Luxembourg is a representative democracy in the form of a constitutional monarchy.

Within the European Union, Luxembourg has reached a high standard of living. Thus, the GDP at market prices (42,900 in Purchasing Power Standards in 2000) is the highest in Europe, above that of Denmark, Ireland and Holland. The unemployment rate is traditionally very low. Over the last few years, the rate has oscillated around 2.6 per cent (Statec, 2002).

After the first migratory movements from northern Italy to the south of Luxembourg (in the 1870s and 1880s with the emergence of the steel industry), a new immigration pattern emerging at the end of the 1960s has had a major impact on social life. Today the demographic balance is maintained only by the influx of foreign residents. The foreign population resident in Luxembourg exceeds 164,700, or almost 37.3 per cent of the population (compared with 17 per cent in the 1960s). The great majority (upwards of 90 per cent) are nationals of European Union Member States, mainly Portugal and Italy. Also, there are more than 87,400 frontier workers from France, Belgium and Germany today, compared with only 8,200 in 1975. Altogether, of a total working population of 262,300, more than 50 per cent are foreigners (i.e. immigrants and commuters). Since 1998, an important flow of refugees (5,324 persons between 1996 and 1999) has arrived in Luxembourg, the majority of whom come from the Balkans (2,791).

Luxembourg is officially a trilingual country. The national language is Lëtzeburgesch, a Franconian/Moselle dialect that is the vernacular for the entire Luxembourg population. Legislation is drafted in French, administrative and legal affairs are dealt with in French, German and Lëtzeburgesch. The three official languages are supplemented by those of the country's immigrant population (Portuguese, Italian, etc.).

The school system

The school system in Luxembourg is highly centralized, and the legislation is strongly based on the principle of free, universal (i.e. compulsory) education. Parents and pupils are essentially faced with four alternatives to the public school system in Luxembourg: religious schools, the private Waldorf School, international schools, and education in one of the neighbouring countries. The religious schools offer the same syllabus as the public system. The Waldorf School dispenses the official curriculum in accordance with its own teaching principles.

The school system comprises two years of pre-school education, six years of primary education and up to seven years of secondary education. Primary schools have a typical size of 50 to 300 pupils, and secondary schools of 500 to 1,500 pupils.

The philosophy of primary education in Luxembourg is very similar to that of other European Member States. Teaching methods and procedures are unique because of the linguistic particularity of the country. The hours are the same for primary and lower secondary education: 30 hours a week, including breaks. This relatively heavy workload is due in particular to the need to develop skills in the official languages to a satisfactory level. Lëtzeburgesch is the auxiliary teaching language for reading and writing during the first one-and-a-half years at school, but German is the language in which children first learn to read and write. Oral teaching of French starts in the second half of the second year; written French is introduced from the third year of primary school. German and French are both compulsory in schools in Luxembourg, and children seeking to avoid repeated exam failure in languages often attend schools in neighbouring countries, particularly Belgium, where there is only one main language taught.

The secondary education is separated into three main streams: general secondary education; technical secondary education; and the preparatory stream.

- Full general secondary education lasts seven years, being completed at the age of 19 at the earliest. There are three levels: a lower level (first, second and third years), a general upper level (fourth and fifth years), and a specialization (sixth and seventh years). In the specialization years, pupils choose between a literary (humanities) or scientific orientation. The studies of the general secondary education are completed with an exam that is held throughout the entire country.

- The technical secondary education prepares pupils for professional life and also offers the possibility of taking up higher education or university studies. The duration of schooling at this level depends on the stream and/or trade/profession chosen. The minimum school leaving age is 15 years.
- The preparatory stream is especially for students with low school performance. This modular stream, which lasts three years, gives these pupils the opportunity to be admitted either to a class of the inferior or middle level of the technical secondary education or to enter vocational training.

Brief history of the interest in the topic of violence in school

The international events of the 1990s relating to violent behaviour in schools, especially in the USA, France and Germany, made the Luxembourg authorities more sensitive to the topic. More official interest in violence in schools, and promotion of activities against it, came at the beginning of 1998 when a Member of Parliament, referring to a European conference on violence that had been held in the spring of 1997, requested information about activities against violence in Luxembourg schools. In March 1998, the president of the Global Security Council transmitted a first report about 'violence and adolescence' to the Ministry of National Education and Vocational Training (Thill, 1998).

In February 1998 the Director of the National Centre for Psychology and School Guidance (CPOS) was delegated by the Ministry of National Education and Vocational Training to represent Luxembourg in the European work group on violence in schools set up by the European Commission (DGXXII). The Ministry also set up a national working group to examine the problem of violence in Luxembourg schools. After producing a written report that analyses the theoretical and clinical aspects of the subject (Colling et al., 1998), the working group put forward a prevention plan focusing on teaching communication skills to everyone involved in school life, primarily by: (1) giving initial and continuing training to teachers and counselling staff, and (2) getting head teachers interested. All actions taken to prevent or diminish violence in schools are closely co-ordinated with the educational health and environment promotion programmes that the Ministry has been implementing actively since 1997.

In December 2000, the Ministry of Culture, Higher Education and Research founded the Research Centre for Conflict Resolution (CRRC). In the future, this commission aims to formulate recommendations for prevention and intervention to reduce social conflicts. The first topic of interest this commission is working on is the social aspects of violence in schools.

Definition of violence in school in legal texts and official reports

In school regulations and other official or legal texts, matters such as discipline, violence or aggressive behaviour are referred to as 'prevention of vandalism, aggression and spiteful acts' (modified law of 19 March 1988; Gouvernement du Grand-Duché de Luxembourg, 1988), violations of disciplinary rules or breaches of the peace, e.g. through

> insults, rudeness, refusal to obey, refusal to follow security measures, refusal to attend classes or to participate in an exam, unjustified lateness or absence, fraud, thieving or stealing, forgery of documents or signatures, incitement to disorder or disturbances, organization of unauthorized public demonstrations and meetings inside school buildings, damage or destruction of public or private goods, violation of good morals, consumption of alcohol during class hours or during breaks, drug consumption or dealing.

The class tutor is responsible in matters such as 'order, security, respect of others and good manners' (Grand-ducal regulation of 1 June 1994 fixing the tasks and remits of the class tutors; Gouvernement du Grand-Duché de Luxembourg, 1994).

The report by Thill (1998) stated that 'violence has to be understood as a brutal and illegitimate voluntary action that physically or morally offends a person that tries to resist it'. Further, this report defines psychological, moral and social aspects involved in violent behaviour.

The report of the ministerial work group (Colling et al., 1998) quotes different experts (Pain, Barrier and Robin, 1997; Olweus, 1996), and defines violence as the

> non-legitimate use of force by an agent (person, group, institution) in a position of abusive power through actions in which this agent exerts constraint on a victim (person, group, institution) that is abused and hurt. We insist on the fact that violence is not only physical: it can be moral, verbal, psychological and also symbolical, political and environmental.

Violence is understood in a broad sense that does not restrict violent behaviour to physical aggression but also includes verbal aggression, physical damage to property, institutional violence and vandalism.

Knowledge

Research on the prevalence and frequency of violence in school

There has been little systematic research on the specific topic of violence in schools in Luxembourg (Steffgen, 2000a). In 1994, an inter-regional study comparing 323 pupils from Luxembourg with 346 pupils from Germany and 315 from France showed that the various types of violence in schools are also common in Luxembourg (Scherer, 1996). In 2000, a survey on 'Health behaviour among school-aged children' – a cross-national survey by the WHO – was conducted for the first time also in Luxembourg schools. Among other topics, children of primary and secondary school level were asked questions about violence and bullying in school. The results of this survey were the first to address the question of violence in schools representatively. At the moment, we can only present results for the secondary school level from the cross-national survey (below); results for the primary school level are not available.

Findings from research in primary schools

In recent years, two empirical studies have been conducted with teachers of primary schools. The first study measured frequency of violence in school from the teacher's point of view (n=90; using a questionnaire from Schubarth and Melzer, 1994). To the question: how often did bullying (in the sense of persecuting other children) occur in the current school year? 3.3 per cent of the teachers answered very often, 12.2 per cent often, 17.8 per cent sometimes, 43.3 per cent rarely and 23.3 per cent never. The majority of teachers believed that the incidence of violent behaviour (59 per cent) and bullying (66.3 per cent) had remained the same over the previous five years. However, 28.9 per cent believed that violence and bullying had increased. Finally, 5.6 per cent of the teachers noticed violent behaviour from teachers (actor) to children and 14.4 per cent from children (actor) to teachers at school (Steffgen, 2000b).

In the second study, the role that teachers play in the occurrence of children's aggressive behaviour was examined (Steffgen, 2001). This work indicates that the way in which the teacher expresses anger can influence aggressive behaviour in the classroom. The self-report questionnaire (n=158; using a questionnaire from Humpert, Tennstädt and Dann, 1987) also provided indications on whether teachers had experienced aggressive behaviour in their classrooms. The comparison with the findings of the first study confirms that teachers at primary school level are confronted with a substantial level of aggressive behaviour at school; see Table 4.1.

Findings for the secondary school level from the first nationwide survey

Data from the nationwide survey referred to above were collected from 7,397 children of the secondary level (six grades, omitting the final seventh grade). This sample represents 26.5 per cent of the relevant school population. The sample was selected from all secondary level schools. Parents

Table 4.1 Teachers' perceptions of aggressive behaviour (per cent)

	Entirely true	Largely true	Partially true	Hardly true	Not at all true
Pupils' aggressive behaviour in class has become increasingly frequent recently.	10.1	26.6	29.7	28.5	5.1
The climate in class is often aggravated by aggressive pupils.	15.8	19.0	19.6	37.3	8.2
Pupils behave aggressively in class fairly frequently.	7.0	20.3	22.2	40.5	9.5
Pupils behave aggressively in class fairly rarely.	6.3	30.4	23.4	27.2	12.7

Table 4.2 Boys and girls who reported being hit by or hitting another child (per cent)

Answering categories	Being hit		Hitting others	
	Boys	Girls	Boys	Girls
It never happened	81.7	91.2	70.8	88.8
Happened once or twice this year	9.0	3.3	15.9	4.7
Sometimes, but not every week	2.6	1.2	3.7	0.9
About once a week	0.6	0.2	1.2	0.2
Several times a week	1.0	0.3	1.9	0.5
Missing values	5.1	3.9	6.4	4.9

were informed about the survey and had the option of declining to participate. Questionnaires were given to pupils in their regular classrooms by research assistants. Teachers were absent from the classroom, and anonymity was guaranteed. Eight questions were used to measure the frequency of situations in which the pupil was a perpetrator or victim of violence and instances of bullying in school.

The report from this survey has not yet been published. However, we have some findings from the Ministry of National Education and Vocational Training. This first set of data gives estimates of the frequency of violence in boys as compared to girls in different school types and in different grades. The gender difference is considerable in these statistics. Boys were more likely to be hit or to hit others than girls (see Table 4.2). Also, boys consistently bully other children more often than girls – 7.8 per cent of boys vs. 2.8 per cent of girls bully other children at least once a week. But there is little difference between boys and girls as victims of bullying or in the impression of feeling safe in school.

The types of school included in this study are divided into three categories: general, technical and preparatory. The study found differences between the three types, as much with regard to bullying and hitting

Table 4.3 Schoolchildren from different types of schools feeling safe in school (per cent)

Answering categories	General	Technical	Preparatory
Always	46.7	36.2	32.3
Often	34.6	30.6	23.9
Sometimes	10.6	18.7	19.4
Seldom	3.5	6.3	7.8
Never	1.5	4.4	7.5
Missing values	3.1	3.9	9.0

Table 4.4 Schoolchildren from the first and second grades who reported being a victim of bullying or bullying others (per cent)

	Victim of bullying		Bullying others	
Answering categories	First	Second	First	Second
It never happened	58.8	71.2	51.0	60.4
Happened once or twice this year	19.9	13.7	23.8	18.0
Sometimes	10.6	8.7	14.4	13.0
About once a week	2.3	1.0	1.9	1.7
Several times a week	3.0	1.1	4.0	2.7
Missing values	5.4	4.2	5.0	4.1

others as to being bullied or hit. 10.3 per cent of the children questioned said that they 'seldom or never' feel safe at school; 38.4 per cent reported that they 'always' feel safe at school. Children from general schools (with the highest academic requirements) reported being bullied less and bullying others less than their peers from the two other types of schools. Children from the preparatory schools (with the lowest academic requirements) yielded the highest percentages; see Table 4.3.

Secondary school children were split into two grades: first grade, the lower level (three years) and second grade, the upper/intermediate level, including the first year of specialization (three years). Bullying and being bullied are less frequent in the higher grades (see Table 4.4). The results confirm other studies (Smith et al., 1999) that find that bullying and being bullied decrease as children move upwards in school grades.

It is apparent that violence is a problem in Luxembourg schools also, and it affects a considerable number of pupils. The average results from some data of the first survey show that violence and bullying in schools appear to be less extensive in Luxembourg than in northern or southern European countries (Olweus, 1999; Fonzi et al., 1999; Ortega and Mora-Merchan, 1999). Nevertheless, we must recognize that more than a third of Luxembourg's schoolchildren do not feel safe at school and that a considerable number of children are confronted with the violent behaviour of peers.

The results also suggest that it would be advisable to support further research in which the various forms and degrees of violence should be differentiated thoroughly. There are a lot of gaps in our empirical knowledge about violence in school. At the moment no findings about the effects of specific risk factors or differences between ethnic groups are available in Luxembourg.

It is commonly agreed that the school system in Luxembourg is very selective: many pupils are faced with failure, orientation to less demanding courses or the need to leave the national system. Data on school failures for secondary schools in technical secondary education show that between 20 per cent and 25 per cent of pupils fail during the intermediate level and 18 per cent to 25 per cent in the first year of the upper level (Lévy, 2000). Especially for Luxembourg, it could be very useful to examine the relationship between school failure and violence in school.

Action

Current national policies regarding violence in school

As mentioned above, the Ministry for National Education and Vocational Training established a national work group to analyse the situation in Luxembourg. The group's aims were to create a greater awareness and understanding of violent behaviour and to provide advice, counselling and resource materials seeking to prevent and combat violent behaviour in school. This group undertook various initiatives:

- drawing up a document establishing the status quo in Luxembourg and the definition of violence in schools;
- organizing lectures by international experts on the topic of violence;
- offering training to teachers with the support of the Ministry for National Education and Vocational Training;
- starting research activities concerning violence and bullying in schools; and
- the publication, in 2000, of a booklet, 'Vers une école de la communication' – this booklet is distributed free of charge to all primary and secondary school teachers.

In addition, more psychological and socio-educational counselling staff are currently being recruited for secondary schools in order to react to social and school-related problems. The issue of violence in schools is also receiving more and more attention in national events for pupils organized or supported by the Ministry of Education, as in thematic one-day gatherings or youth film festivals. As yet, however, no clear guidelines exist, nor has any official anti-violence initiative been implemented.

Local initiatives

In parallel with the work undertaken on a national level, local authorities have been participating in the discussion about violence in schools, addressing the problem more specifically in terms of juvenile delinquency. The city of Luxembourg (about 80,700 inhabitants) in particular has been interested in the problem in view of its population of approximately 20,000 adolescents, to which must be added the thousands of secondary school children that travel into town every day. Local investigations concerning delinquency amongst young people have brought together representatives of the local authorities, city schools, the police force, legal authorities, social assistance services and parents' associations.

In this way, municipal policy on the prevention of violence in schools stresses the notion of partnership. This is the approach that has been pursued since the start of the school year 1998–1999 by distributing a document on committed partnership at school to parents, pupils and teachers. Moreover, while communication between teachers is crucial in solving problems, external aid, particularly in support of the victims of acts of violence (e.g. racketeering) is envisaged.

The most recent developments have been observed at a regional level: networks have been created between schools respectively from the south and the north of the country. These schools are making common efforts to organize and set up various information and prevention activities concerned with violence in school.

School initiatives to prevent and reduce violent behaviour

An exploratory study was conducted by Steffgen et al. (2001) to collect data about all current initiatives for the prevention or reduction of violence in Luxembourg secondary schools. All thirty-three secondary schools were contacted, and twenty-eight participated: 21 public national schools (9 general secondary schools, 12 technical secondary schools); 4 private national schools (2 technical secondary schools, 2 general and technical secondary schools); and 3 private international schools. A short telephone interview was carried out, with nineteen head teachers, one assistant head teacher, one direction assistant, one chief educational consultant, four psychologists, one teacher, and, for one of the schools, a head teacher and a psychologist.

The questionnaire drawn up beforehand was of a semi-structured nature, and the questions asked for information on all the measures that

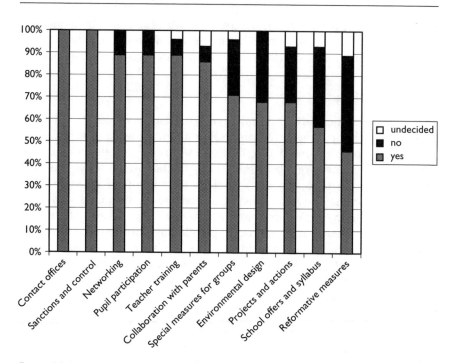

Figure 4.1 Percentages of schools having undertaken activities in different areas

had been taken so far to prevent or reduce the phenomenon of violence in schools directly (i.e. in direct relation to violence) or indirectly. Jäger (1999) has proposed a classification that roughly differentiates eleven areas of intervention; and the interviewees were asked to specify, from their personal point of view, the nature of any measures taken in each of these eleven categories. The various activities in different secondary schools are outlined in Figure 4.1. Following is an indication for each of these areas as to whether and in what manner violence has been the subject of direct or indirect measures in schools so far.

Contact office

All interviewees (100 per cent) indicated that they have a contact office at their respective school. The primary contacts were the members of the School Psychology and Orientation Service staff (SPOS), followed by the head teacher, teachers, form teachers and educational assistants. The educational counsellors, the Guidance Centres and classmates were also mentioned.

Sanctions and control

All interviewees (100 per cent) indicated that sanctions are the consequence of violent behaviour. The following procedure is adopted in such cases: a first contact with the aggressor is established by the form teacher, the teacher, the head teacher, the psychological service (SPOS), the chief counsellor, or the disciplinary representative. A clarification of the causes and circumstances of the situation is attempted. Classroom discussions are held by the teacher, the head teacher or the psychological service. Then, the parents are contacted by the head teacher, the SPOS or the teacher. The application of disciplinary measures (class and disciplinary council) is recommended in the majority of cases. Punishment and sanctions such as kitchen work, detention, object repair and cleaning are other options. The suspension or expulsion of re-offenders, the lodging of a formal complaint, or calling the police for an investigation are actions that were rarely mentioned. In one school, a working group was set up to revise disciplinary measures.

Networking

Eighty-nine per cent of the interviewees indicated that they have installed a network. Concerning direct measures (83.3 per cent of 54 measures mentioned), we noted a contact with the police in 47 per cent of the cases. Thirteen per cent of the cases consist of collaboration with special homes. A regular and close relation with another school was found in 11 per cent of the cases. In 29 per cent of the cases, there is contact with social workers, juvenile court judges, sixth year primary school teachers, the Ministry of National Education and relevant social and parents' associations. With regard to indirect measures, a great majority of people interviewed stressed the current lack of networking.

Pupil participation

Eighty-nine per cent of the interviewees indicated that pupils were allowed to take part in their school's activities. Concerning direct measures (26.3 per cent of 38 measures mentioned), pupils participated in several activities, such as the production of greeting cards, telephone cards, cartoon books and brochures related to projects against violence, the design of a questionnaire on verbal and physical violence directed at pupils (what type of violence, frequency, origin), the production of statistics and a brochure, the organization of round-table talks with class representatives, the psychological services and the head teacher on the subject 'How do pupils react to violence?', the production of a video against racism and xenophobia that was shown on cinema screens, an exhibition and conference on violence in African countries, and the organization by pupils and the teachers' committee of a petition against racism. Amongst the indirect measures (73.3 per cent) taken to actively involve pupils, most were discussion groups held by pupils' committees on the subjects of safety conditions in school and violence approached in an indirect way, and talks organized to give pupils the opportunity to voice their opinions on various subjects.

Teacher training

Eighty-nine per cent of the interviewees indicated that some of their teachers participated in vocational training courses. Of the direct measures (28.8 per cent of training courses of 80 measures mentioned) taken with respect to training courses, 48 per cent represent courses dealing with violence in schools taken by School Psychology and Orientation Service staff (SPOS). Twenty-six per cent of the training measures followed by teaching staff dealt with the question 'How to manage conflict', and 22 per cent consisted of conferences and educational activities on the subject of violence that were organized for teachers. Of indirect measures taken in respect to training, 35 per cent were courses given on relational communication and mediation, 12 per cent dealt with listening skills and interviewing technique and 33 per cent were training classes on the education of choice; all of these were followed by SPOS staff. Eight per cent of these measures were courses on the subject of communication and attitude to pupils, taken by teachers, and 2 per cent represent teachers who also followed training on the education of choice.

Collaboration with parents

Eighty-six per cent of the interviewees said that they established collaboration with parents. Of the direct measures (62.5 per cent of 40 cases), there is regular contact between the head teacher and pupils' parents in the case of a violent act in 76 per cent of cases. Twenty-four per cent of the measures taken consist of a close collaboration between SPOS and pupils' parents in the case of a violent act. Eighty-seven per cent of indirect measures concern regular contacts between SPOS and parents' associations.

Special measures for groups

Seventy-one per cent of the interviewees indicated that special measures are taken for problem groups. Of these, 97 per cent are of a direct nature: in 46 per cent of such direct measures, individual interviews with the aggressor and/or victim are conducted by an educational assistant, SPOS, the head teacher or educational counsellors. Discussion groups are held by SPOS and tutors in 26 per cent of the cases. SPOS also organizes class interventions following violent acts to discuss the situation (8.5 per cent). Collaboration with parents is established by SPOS, the head teacher and educational counsellors (11 per cent).

Environmental design

Sixty-eight per cent of the interviewees indicated that special environmental design activities have been organized inside their schools. In 28.1 per cent of cases (9 out of 32), these measures were in direct relation to the subject of violence. Direct measures undertaken are the putting up of posters in school corridors and classrooms. These posters are designed as part of campaigns dealing with the phenomenon of violence. Concerning indirect activities (71.9 per cent) that were mentioned most often, pupils are given the opportunity to decorate their classrooms with posters, pictures and paintings (39 per cent), or else they are free to decorate their school, i.e. with paintings and graffiti in school yards, stairwells and playgrounds (39 per cent). Apart from this, 13 per cent of activities consist in turning school grounds into a pleasant environment, for example by planting greenery or installing ponds and paths.

Projects and actions

Sixty-eight per cent of the interviewees indicated that specific projects are conducted in their schools. Of these, 36.6 per cent (26 out of 71) bear a direct relation to the subject of violence. The main part of such activities relate to the topic of violence only indirectly. Concerning direct measures, the main emphasis is on the organization of round-table talks, discussion groups in class and, especially, an artistic approach to the subject. Indirectly, the subject was treated via projects dealing with the working atmosphere inside the schools and those relating to the various types of communication. Other projects, in which the emphasis is put on artistic dialogue and physical activities, have positive effects on violent behaviour in schools.

School offers and syllabus

Fifty-seven per cent of the interviewees indicated that violence is a topic in their syllabus. In 96.9 per cent of the cases (31 out of 32), the subject of violence was dealt with directly. In the majority of cases (86 per cent), the subject of violence was treated regularly in mandatory classes. In only 7 per cent of cases, specific classes are held by SPOS staff and form teachers. Besides this, relaxation classes are offered to violent pupils and self-defence classes are proposed for female pupils.

Reformative measures

Forty-six per cent of the interviewees indicated that reformative measures were taken in their schools. Of these, 78.6 per cent (11 out of 14 cases) were related to the subject of violence indirectly. Amongst the indirect measures, the emphasis is put on the responsibility and the active and autonomous organization of pupils. In most cases, the importance of favouring communication between all involved, i.e. pupils, teachers, head teacher, SPOS and technical assistants, is mentioned.

Conclusion

With regard to violence at school in all its various explicit or implicit forms, the results of the exploratory study show that there are numerous and varied initiatives on different levels at secondary schools. It has to be pointed out that for some of the secondary schools there is still a need for action to undertake special measures, projects and actions as well as environmental design activities, and to deal with the subject of violence in the syllabus. Since schools find themselves in a permanent process of adjustment and change, more realization of reformative measures is also necessary. However, one should keep in mind that these findings are only based on the reports of the head teachers of the schools and do not address the depth, the duration or the efficiency of the actions undertaken.

Future recommendations

For Luxembourg we recognize four main tasks for handling the subject of violence in school in the near future:

1   *To formulate and to realize a nationwide policy against violence*
    Even if individual representatives from ministries support or try to initiate actions to tackle violence in schools, all in all a common concept or programme on this issue is still missing at government level. There is no straightforward political commitment to develop national resources (experts, budgets, intervention tools, research, etc.) nor to increase means to take action. Many projects and initiatives have been launched at different levels, but no academic or political reference or structure is available in Luxembourg to assess, develop and co-ordinate them.
2   *To carry out more systematic research on the specific topic of violence in schools*
    The state of knowledge about violence in school and on the effects of initiatives taken is still at an early stage. There is a growing emphasis on the topic that should be based on empirical evidence.

3 *To carry out scientific evaluation of projects and intervention programmes*
    In terms of concrete actions, we note that the policy of most decision
    makers in schools is still at the stage of empirical development, experi-
    mentation and reflection. A further need indispensable to handling
    the problem is a change at the 'school policies level' and the imple-
    mentation of project management and project evaluation activities.
    As yet, no systematic scientific evaluation of any intervention pro-
    gramme has been carried out in Luxembourg.

4 *To motivate more actors in the school field (especially teachers) to participate
    in training seminars on the topic*
    Considering the teachers' key role, and the fact that they are con-
    fronted with the problem of violence on a daily basis, they should be
    given tools to handle situations in an appropriate, pedagogic way.

Though first official steps have been taken in Luxembourg, it is now
necessary to go further!

References

Colling, P., Friedel, C., Khabirpour, F., Rolin, H., Schiltz, L. and Weber, M. (1998).
    La Violence à l'École. Luxembourg: Centre de Psychologie et d'Orientation
    Scolaires.
Fonzi, A., Genta, M.L., Menesini, E., Bacchini, D., Bonino, S. and Costabile, A.
    (1999). Italy. In P.K. Smith, Y. Morita, J. Junger-Tas, D. Olweus, R. Catalano
    and P. Slee (eds). *The Nature of School Bullying: A Cross-national Perspective*.
    London: Routledge. pp.140–156.
Gouvernement du Grand-Duché de Luxembourg (1988). Texte coordonné de la
    loi modifiée du 19 mars 1988 concernant la sécurité dans la fonction publique.
    Mémorial A, Journal Officiel du Grand-Duché de Luxembourg 14, 170.
Gouvernement du Grand-Duché de Luxembourg (1994). Règlement grand-ducal
    du 1er Juin 1994 fixant la tâche et les attributions des régents de classe dans les
    établissements d'enseignement secondaire et secondaire technique. *Mémorial
    A, Journal Officiel du Grand-Duché de Luxembourg* 52, 999.
Humpert, W., Tennstädt, K.-C. and Dann, H.-D. (1987). *Erfassung subjektiver
    Theorien von Hauptschullehrern, des Unterrichtsklimas sowie berufsbezogener Einstel-
    lungen*. Konstanz: Universität Konstanz.
Jäger, R.S. (1999). Gewaltprävention. In M. Schäfer and D. Frey (eds). *Aggression
    und Gewalt unter Kindern und Jugendlichen*. Göttingen: Hogrefe. pp.203–244.
Lévy, L. (2000). L'Enseignement Secondaire Technique (1998/99) *Statistiques
    générales et analyse de la promotion des élèves*. Luxembourg: Ministère de l'Educa-
    tion Nationale, de la Formation Professionnelle et des Sports.
Olweus, D. (1996). *Gewalt in der Schule*. Bern: Huber.
Olweus, D. (1999). Norway. In P.K. Smith, Y. Morita, J. Junger-Tas, D. Olweus,
    R. Catalano and P. Slee (eds). *The Nature of School Bullying: A Cross-national
    Perspective*. London: Routledge. pp.28–48.

Ortega, R. and Mora-Merchan, J.A. (1999). Spain. In P.K. Smith, Y. Morita, J. Junger-Tas, D. Olweus, R. Catalano and P. Slee (eds). *The Nature of School Bullying: A Cross-national Perspective.* London: Routledge. pp.157–173.

Pain, J., Barrier, E. and Robin, D. (1997). *Violences à l'École. Allemagne, Angleterre, France. Une Étude Comparative Européenne de Douze Établissements du Deuxième Degré.* Vigneux: Matrice.

Scherer, D. (1996). Gewalt in der schule. *AK-Beiträge,* 9, 1–199.

Schubath, W. and Melzer, W. (1994). Gewalt an Schulen. Ergebnisse einer Schulleiterbefragung zum abweichenden Verhalten an Schulen in Sachsen. Forschungsbericht der Forschungsgruppe Schulevaluation, Fakultät Erziehungs- wissenschaften, Technische Universität Dresden.

Smith, P.K., Morita, Y., Junger-Tas, J., Olweus, D., Catalano, R. and Slee, P. (eds) (1999). *The Nature of School Bullying: A Cross-national Perspective.* London: Routledge.

Statec (2002). *Le Luxembourg en chiffres 2001.* Luxembourg: Statec.

Steffgen, G. (2000a). Steigt die Gewalt an Luxemburger Schulen? In Centre de Psychologie et d'Orientation Scolaires (ed.). *Vers une École de la Communication.* Luxembourg: Ministère de l'Education Nationale. pp.71–75.

Steffgen, G. (2000b). *Violence à l'École. Rapport Intermédiaire du Projet de Recherche.* R. and D. MEN/IPE/00/002. Walferdange: Institut Supérieur d'Etudes et de Recherches Pédagogiques.

Steffgen, G. (2001). Influence de l'Expression Émotionnelle de l'Enseignant sur l'Agressivité des Élèves. In A. Flieller, C. Bocéréan, J.-L. Kop, E. Thiébaut, A.-M. Toniolo and J. Tournois (eds). *Questions de Psychologie Différentielle.* Rennes: Presses Universitaires de Rennes. pp.387–391.

Steffgen, G., Russon, C., Kieffer, T. and Worré, F. (2001). *Prévenir et Réduire la Violence à l'École. Catalogue d'Actions des Lycées au Luxembourg.* Luxembourg: Centre de Psychologie et d'Orientation Scolaires.

Thill, A. (1998). *Violence et Adolescence.* Luxembourg: Ministère de l'Education Nationale et de la Formation Professionnelle.

Chapter 5

From combating bullying and violence to fostering prosocial behaviour

A report from The Netherlands

Carolien Bongers, Frits Prior and Guido Walraven

Background

The country

The Netherlands has twelve provinces and nearly 16 million inhabitants. The population of The Netherlands is concentrated around the four 'big cities', Amsterdam, Rotterdam, The Hague and Utrecht. This high density area is called the 'Randstad' (with more than two million inhabitants).

Although The Netherlands has always been a country welcoming immigrants, today's Dutch society is much more heterogeneous than it has ever been. After World War II, The Netherlands experienced several periods with a strong influx of people from other countries. Currently 12 per cent of the population are ethnic minorities; three-quarters are first generation (people born in a country other than The Netherlands with one parent also born in a foreign country) and one-quarter second generation (persons born in The Netherlands but whose parents were both born in a foreign country).

Not all immigrants are officially treated as minorities. In Dutch policy, the following ethnic minority groups are mentioned: people of Surinam, Turkish, Moroccan, Antillian/Aruban or Tunisian origin, people from the Northern Mediterranean countries and the Cape Verde islands, as well as Chinese and Vietnamese people. Officially recognized refugees and asylum seekers who are allowed to stay in The Netherlands are also regarded as minorities. The number of people staying illegally in The Netherlands is difficult to estimate. Estimates for 1995 varied between 30,000 and 150,000.

The official language in The Netherlands is Dutch. There are regional dialects and in the province of Frisia people have Frisian as their first language. Ethnic minorities as a rule use their own languages at home and among themselves. For children and youth with Dutch as a second language that situation tends to create problems at school, especially since school language differs from colloquial language in many respects.

Those problems are found especially amongst Moroccan and Turkish youngsters from lower socioeconomic backgrounds.

The school system

Before school, there are many types of childcare, catering for children from the age of 6 weeks up to 4 years. For example pre-school playgroups are usually open two or three days a week, between $2\frac{1}{2}$ and 4 hours a day. The Education Act stipulates that education is compulsory for children in the age range of 5 to 16 years. From the age of 4 children are allowed to enter primary education and, in practice, most children (98.6 per cent) do so.

Primary education

This lasts eight years, and most primary schools are organised in eight separate year levels or 'groups'. In 1997–1998, there were 7,253 schools for primary education; the average number of pupils per school was 210. Only a proportion (33 per cent) of the primary schools in The Netherlands are public (i.e. accessible to all children and not bound to a certain orientation); the remaining schools are mainly of Catholic (30 per cent) or Protestant (30 per cent) affiliation. Some schools use classic reform pedagogies (like Montessori, Waldorf or Freinet) and recently there has been an influx of Islam oriented schools.

In The Netherlands all schools are publicly financed, but only the 'public schools' are also under public management; all other schools have private boards. This compromise is the outcome of a longstanding political battle on freedom of education, settled in 1918 but still a sensitive issue.

For young children, a school day may last $5\frac{1}{2}$ hours at the maximum, starting at 8.30 or 8.45a.m. The general aim of primary education is to enhance the development of children's intellect and creativity and the acquisition of adequate social, cultural and physical skills. Primary education is the same for all pupils, mixing together children of all abilities in the same group. To achieve the best results for all the pupils, adaptive teaching is required in these heterogeneous groups. In the final year of primary school, parents and children together decide which of the various types of secondary school to choose, informed by the advice of the head teacher and (in most schools) the yearly official assessment of mostly cognitive results of all eighth formers of primary schools (the Cito-test).

Secondary education

From the age of 12 upwards, there are several different types of secondary school or educational streams within a school, and each school/stream has its own teaching programme that matches the ability and work rate of the pupils. In 2001 there were 834 secondary schools, with an average 1,034 students each.

The types are: pre-vocational education and junior general secondary education (VMBO); senior general secondary education (HAVO); and pre-university education (VWO). However, every school begins with a two- or three-year period of basic secondary education. All pupils study a broad *core* curriculum that is the same at every school, although the level varies depending on the type of school. This allows a *transition period*, which postpones choosing a specific type of secondary education for a little longer. Schools differ widely in the way they group pupils into classes. Many schools put all the pupils who have been recommended for the same type of education, e.g. VMBO/HAVO or HAVO/VWO, in one class. Other schools, however, mix pupils together. No matter how the classes are organized, all pupils follow the same curriculum during the first year or so. Recent developments, however, are that some schools cater specifically for VMBO students and others only for HAVO–VWO students.

The following subjects are taught as part of the basic secondary education curriculum: Dutch, English, German or French, mathematics, physics and chemistry, technology, biology, economics, physical education, history and politics, life skills, IT studies, geography. A school may choose two creative subjects from drawing, handicrafts, photography, film, audio-visual studies, music, drama and dance. In the province of Friesland, Frisian is also taught, unless the school has applied for a dispensation.

Pre-vocational education and junior general secondary education (VMBO) (recently, pre-vocational education and junior general secondary education were merged and reorganized) lasts four years and prepares pupils to go on to some form of vocational training, basic, professional or middle-management. Departments include: building techniques, mechanics, electrical engineering, motor mechanics, fitting techniques, catering, caring occupations, beauty care and hairdressing, fashion and clothing, retailing, agriculture and the natural environment, and clerical work and commerce.

Senior general secondary education (HAVO) lasts five years and prepares pupils for higher professional education (HBO). A HAVO certificate also allows pupils to go on to pre-university education.

Pre-university education (VWO) lasts six years and is mainly designed to prepare pupils for university. There are two types of VWO school: the *atheneum* and the *gymnasium*. The gymnasium is similar to the atheneum except that pupils also learn Latin and Greek in the lower years and Latin and/or Greek in the upper years.

Major changes were implemented in the higher grades of the secondary education system in 1998 and 1999. All HAVO and VWO schools, for instance, introduced compulsory subject combinations. And, more importantly, a system of self-regulated learning was started in the last two or three years of education. The aim of these changes was to improve study behaviour and learning skills, also relevant for higher professional education, university and lifelong learning.

Preventive child health care is available for all schoolchildren (from 4 to 18 years old). Almost all school health services provide three examinations of all individual children between the ages of 4 and 14 years. Another service is the school social work, which focuses on the social well-being of children.

Special education

The Netherlands has an elaborate special education system. This system includes provision for vulnerable children, i.e. pre-school children with developmental difficulties. There are 965 schools for special education (primary and secondary), with 121,000 pupils who need special attention due to disabilities and/or disorders. About 5 per cent of all children of school age participate in special education.

Referral to a special school usually takes place after some years in primary education. Since the early 1990s a policy programme, *Going to School Together*, has been implemented to let as many different types of pupils as possible into regular education. Children with mild educational handicaps are placed in schools for regular education, and the schools involved are helped with extra care and support for these children.

Linguistic/definitional issues

In The Netherlands 'bullying' is widely known as *'pesten'*, a verb derived from the Dutch word for 'plague'. *'Pesten'* focuses on the epidemical way in which bullying tends to spread amongst children and youths. The most common definitions of *'pesten'* and 'violence' (used in studies of van der Meer, Mooij and Van der Ploeg) are based on the earlier works of Olweus and others and do not differ much.

Outside school, the word 'violence' means: vandalism, theft, the use of weapons, racism and sexual harassment – in other words criminal behaviour. If incidents of this kind occur in schools, they must of course be taken very seriously. But in daily school life, criminal acts such as these are far less frequent than other kinds of violent acts and disruptive behaviour: teasing, name-calling, laughing at others, gossiping, bullying, threatening with words, touching others offensively, damaging or taking away other pupils' possessions, starting arguments and fights. And, in relation to teachers: disruptive behaviour, disobedience, offensive and vulgar language, etc.

The Dutch campaign 'Safety at school' used a very simple definition. Violence comes down to 'crossing the line between "Yes" and "No" without invitation or permission'. Everybody can do what they like as long as they do not disrupt, annoy, hurt or endanger others. But if somebody crosses that line, his/her fellow pupils and teachers have the right to say: 'Stop doing that'. Those people have to accept criticism of their own behaviour. For victims, offenders, parents and teachers such a definition is far more workable than the complicated and abstract definitions researchers tend to use.

Relevant historical background

In The Netherlands systematic attention to school bullying and violence dates back to the early 1990s. Initially, surveys by Ton Mooij and influential books and promotion activities by Bob van der Meer succeeded in getting bullying and violence on the political and public agenda. Van der Meer's (1988) book *The Scapegoat in the Classroom* opened the eyes of many teachers and principals, and Mooij's survey *Violence in Secondary Education* (1994) was the first public acknowledgement of existing violence in schools. Almost parallel to these publications, and strongly linked to them, two consecutive promotion campaigns by the four main national associations of parents affected schools and school policy more directly; these were for a national *'Pestprotocol'* and a computerized *PestTest* (especially for primary schools). From 1995 the Dutch national campaign 'Safety at school' provided a practical guide to safety policy in schools and succeeded in breaking taboos on discussing violence in schools.

Mooij repeated his survey in 1999: *'Safe schools and (pro)social behaviour in secondary education'* (Mooij, 2001). Both surveys were instigated by the Ministry of Education, Culture and Sciences in order to inform the parliament in more detail. The new report:

- evaluates the five-year running national campaign 'Safety at school';
- compares his 1991 and 1993 survey data with the situation in 1999 involving 60 schools and some 10,000 pupils, 300 teachers and 60 head teachers;
- suggests new directions for schools fostering prosocial behaviour.

This was not easy, as educational policy and schools changed a lot over the last decade: larger schools, more immigrants (mostly second generation), changes in the role of local authorities and school boards, changes in school policy, curricular and didactical changes. But Mooij concluded that safety and security in Dutch secondary schools have not changed significantly in the 1990s, and that violence and bullying have not really changed between 1993 and 1999.

Possibly the focus on violence in the press and the media and the fact that many people no longer tolerate violence, can explain the feeling that everything is deteriorating nowadays. But this was not supported by the findings of the survey. For instance the percentage of pupils admitting to the possession of a weapon ('an object which could be used as a weapon') decreased from 25 per cent in 1993 to 21 per cent in 1999; and the percentage who admitted bringing a weapon to school decreased from 11 per cent to 8 per cent. Such results could be viewed as positive. But as the target of the five-year campaign was to get the rate of violent incidents in schools *significantly* down, this slight decrease was not enough for some commentators.

For even more positive results when it comes to less violence and a higher feeling of safety among pupils and staff, schools should focus more directly on providing the right learning environment for fostering prosocial behaviour. It is not accidental that in 2001 the Dutch Ministries of Education and Internal Affairs started a joint train-the-trainer programme focused on training teachers of several hundred primary and secondary schools to work with an empowering learning environment.

In addition to the *Pestprotocol* (pupils, parents and staff sign the same document against bullying) and the *PestTest* (surveying the bullying situation in schools) a new instrument will provide pupils, parents and teachers individually with tailor-made advice after filling in their story (of violent experiences). This *Guide to Bullying and Violence* has been published on the internet (www.pestweb.nl) and a version in English will soon follow.

In his recommendations Mooij underscored the need for a change of direction. His survey showed that focusing on policy, instruments and regulations does not really change things. It is necessary to opt for a comprehensive approach focused on prosocial behaviour (instead of only reacting to antisocial behaviour), not as part of extra-curricular activities, but integrated into daily teaching, guiding and supporting in the classroom. To achieve this we need to: discern between necessary reactions to antisocial behaviour and preventive actions to foster prosocial behaviour; focus more strongly on prosocial behaviour in daily teaching and in communication with parents as part of quality policy in school; create school and classroom conditions which foster prosocial behaviour in such a way that the effects can be evaluated properly; introduce transparent and supportive learning conditions for all pupils using proper materials, teaching skills and an effective pupil monitoring system; use diagnostic tests to support the pupils and not so much to disqualify them; assess the starting qualities (and deficiencies) of all pupils and provide them with all the preventive help they need; maintain specialist help outside the classroom or outside school, but also focus on well-chosen help in the classroom; co-operate with youth care and other specialist institutions to form a supportive network around school; give extra attention to examples of evaluated good practice; and continue longitudinal research in this field, especially with regard to children at risk.

Knowledge

Statistical information on school violence is relatively scarce in The Netherlands; a (secondary) analysis of all data from dispersed sources is also missing. We restrict ourselves here to the main research (Mooij, 1994).

Statistics

Bullying

Mooij (1992) reported on a nationwide random survey in April–May 1991, conducted in 30 mainstream and special primary schools (45 classes, 1,065 pupils aged 9 to 12 years), and in 36 mainstream and special secondary schools (43 classes, 1,055 pupils aged 13 to 17 years). This was a one-off survey examining variables at pupil, class and school level. At pupil level, 'bullying' was operationalized using the Olweus bully/victim questionnaire; the junior version for primary schools, the senior version for secondary schools. Table 5.1 shows for each possible answer and in each type of school the percentages of pupils who indicated that they were victims of bullying or themselves bullied others. In common with other findings, the incidence of reported victimization is less in secondary school. Data also collected about perceptions of classmates' social behaviour (sociometric data) validated this self-assessment data.

Violence and sexual harassment

Mooij (1994) reported the results of a nationwide random survey of violence by pupils in the third and fourth years of secondary education,

Table 5.1 Victims and bullies: percentage of pupils at primary and secondary school

	Victim of bullying		Bullying others	
	Primary	*Secondary*	*Primary*	*Secondary*
Not this academic year	39	71	30	44
1 to 2 times this year	38	23	50	40
Regularly	15	4	14	11
About once a week	4	0	3	2
Several times a week	4	2	3	3

Source: Mooij, 1994.

aged 15 to 17 years. Seventy-one schools, 100 classes and 1,998 pupils participated. Individual pupils were asked whether they had been the victim or perpetrator of bullying or violent behaviour (self-assessment), and whether they had experienced sexual harassment by boys or girls in school, in the period September 1992 to March 1993. At the same time, they were asked to assess the prosocial and antisocial behaviour of their classmates (sociometric information). Information of this kind was also provided about each pupil by the class teacher.

Pupil responses were assessed on two victim scales: 15 per cent were a victim of physical violence, and 43 per cent a victim of intentional damage to property or emotional violence. On three perpetrator scales, 51 per cent were a perpetrator of disruptive behaviour in school, 15 per cent a perpetrator of premeditated physical violence, and 7 per cent a perpetrator of intentional damage to property. Teacher reports indicated that 8 per cent of pupils were occasionally the victim of bullying or violence by other pupils; 7 per cent of pupils occasionally bullied other pupils or used violence towards them; and 18 per cent of pupils exhibited disruptive behaviour in class.

The survey also included items relating to unwelcome physical advances by male or female pupils. According to self-reports, 22 per cent of pupils had been the victim of sexual harassment by boys at least once; 14 per cent had been the victim of sexual harassment by girls; also, 8 per cent of boys and of girls had initiated sexual harassment.

Action

Current national/regional policies regarding violence in school

National policies

In the Ministry of Education, Culture and Science, emphasis is placed on 'the educational role' of school boards, staff and parents in putting into practice the values and norms to be imparted to the children. In 1992, the *Project for the Prevention of Sexual Harassment* was given the task of translating government policy into policy and practice within schools. Following a study on pupil violence in secondary schools, Tineke Netelenbos, Junior Minister Secretary for Education, appointed a committee in October 1994 to devise an action programme to combat violence in schools. In June 1995 this programme was published under the title *Voorkoming en Bestrijding Geweld in Scholen* (Preventing and Combating Violence in Schools); the Ministry simultaneously published a brochure on 'safe schools' (Ministerie van Onderwijs, Cultuur en Wetenschappen, 1995a, 1995b). The campaign on safe schools 1995–2000 and the follow-up are dealt with below.

At the end of the year 1999 the Ministry assigned a project to Sardes Educational Services to develop a programme for conflict management in all schools for primary and secondary education, including didactic materials, training and a format for peer mediation (Sardes, 2000). In May 2001 the Ministries of the Interior and Education assigned a four-year project for implementing this programme, in all schools for primary and secondary education who would like to participate.

The Ministry of Justice has researched the literature on the effectiveness of public education in the prevention of crime (Humbert, 1993). Effective, interpersonal, ongoing education and social control (rewards and punishments) are more effective than media campaigns. In 1994, the Ministry published a report by the Juvenile Delinquency Committee (Ministerie van Justitie, 1994) arguing for early, swift and consistent intervention and placing the emphasis on prevention, through schools and other establishments. Junger-Tas has stressed the need for the earliest possible preventive action, particularly in the family (Junger-Tas, 1996). The results of this type of research stimulated the Ministry to write a white paper on juvenile crime and crime prevention, with special emphasis on youth at risk. It was a paper in which the special risk of youth from ethnic minorities was highlighted.

As a follow-up on the Juvenile Delinquency Committee report of 1994, the Ministry of the Interior drew up agreements or covenants with twenty-five cities and large towns in 1994–1996. One of the key elements of these agreements is an emphasis on tackling the problems of high risk groups regarding vandalism, violence and (other) criminal behaviour. After 1996 a large programme regarding youth and safety continued under new agreements.

Four ministries, including the Ministry of Health, Welfare and Sport, commissioned a report concerning the background and characteristics of vulnerable youth and policies concerning them (Schuyt, 1995). There was an emphasis on early identification and effective support for such youngsters, emphasizing the necessity of continuous support along biographical lines, the co-operation of services and the building of a 'chain of responsibilities' between those services (Ministerie van Volksgezondheid, Welzijn en Sport and Ministerie van Onderwijs, Cultuur en Wetenschappen, 2000).

Additional national initiatives:

- The National Health Education Centre (NIGZ) compiles information for regular publication. Health organizations promote the implementation of a health policy in schools and focus on special health topics such as alcohol, tobacco and drug abuse and prevention of Aids.
- The Institute for Non-Commercial Advertising (SIRE) combats problems within society by means of propaganda and advertising campaigns. In 1995 this included a campaign against bullying.

- The confederation of National Parents' Associations has concentrated on tackling the problem of bullying and violence in schools since the early 1990s. An anti-bullying protocol (to be signed by pupils, parents and staff) and a bullying test (PestTest) are part of that campaign.
- The National Secondary School Pupils' Action Committee (LAKS) concerns itself with developing and promoting the interests and rights of schoolchildren (Landelijk Aktie Komitee Scholieren, 1999).
- The Netherlands Supply Teachers Fund and Staff Health Service has examined the levels of aggression, violence and sexual harassment encountered by people working in schools. It has published a manual, a 'Safe in school' questionnaire and an accompanying set of explanatory notes including an action plan (Kelder and Van Lemette, 1996).
- The Government has recently published a report giving a (rather positive) overview of work in the last six to seven years (Studulski and Hoogbergen, 2002).

A national campaign on safe schools and the Transfer Centre on Youth, School and Safety

This was launched in 1994 to improve safety in and around schools, after parliamentary debates on the Mooij research (Procesmanagement Voortgezet Onderwijs, 1996). The campaign aimed at public recognition of the disturbing findings and at stimulating schools to prevent and combat violence. The campaign had three main foci: improving social competence; preventing violence and dealing with violent incidents; and safety facilities and regulations. Each school makes its own choices, but results should be visible through increasing feelings of safety of both pupils and staff, and diminishing incidents of violence. Measures for schools included:

- the development of crisis support;
- the development of a simple analytical instrument making it possible to tailor solutions to the specific problem;
- the dissemination of information about models and successful examples of approaches;
- the development of a step-by-step strategy and the drafting of guidelines for discussion within schools;
- the drafting of a range of training and support measures;
- the drafting of a health and safety plan in accordance with the legislation (including the appointment of confidential counsellors, the establishment of complaints procedures and a four-yearly policy plan in schools).

Measures for pupils included:

- a symposium and a competition (video, photography, texts, comic strips, posters, music or drama);

for pupils, parents and schools:

- a national telephone helpline;

for local municipalities, school boards, welfare organizations, social services:

- agreements (covenants) with cities and large towns including a section on 'safe schools';

for national policies:

- assimilation into integrated policies on young people and on innovation.

Linked up with the campaign was a Project for the Prevention of Sexual Harassment. This has taken a number of steps, including the appointment in all schools of a confidential counsellor, the establishment of a complaints committee, the design of a complaints procedure, and the provision of public information. In an educational law of 1998 a complaints procedure and a confidential counsellor were made obligatory for all schools. The project has produced a self-help package designed to enable primary schools to identify and deal with sexual harassment (Visser, 1996). There are no available data on the reliability, validity or effectiveness of these ways of dealing with sexual harassment; however, the educational inspectorate reported on the matter in 2000.

The campaign was held over five consecutive years (1995–2000); it was crucial in keeping the issue of school safety on the agenda of both politicians and school professionals, and instrumental in making the issue into something all schools could discuss in the open (without fear of being labelled a problem school). However, after five years there was still a lot of room for improvement, so although the campaign had to stop, the co-ordinator got an assignment to set up a Transfer Centre on Youth, School and Safety. The national telephone helpline and the project on the prevention of sexual harassment are now an integrated part of this Transfer Centre. A code of conduct for youngsters has been developed, to be discussed at school, in sports, and in public areas such as discos and bars. In April 2001 a series of booklets on safety related issues were published, among other things about youth participation, conflict management, procedures for dealing with crises and safety policy plans.

Working on a code of conduct for behaviour in school at the start of a school year can help both pupils and teachers. Recently, a draft code of

Table 5.2 Safety-directed actions reported by schools in 1993 and 1999 (scores from 1: not present to 8: continually present/functioning)

Activity	1993	1999
Care for social bonding: learning and living together		
Active role of pupils in class and in school	3.8	4.9
Training and maintaining social attitudes and skills	2.7	4.5
Well-directed support in class and in school	5.5	6.5
Clear and widely supported school regulations	5.7	6.1
Well-planned and expert dealing with incidents		
Establishing and maintaining incident protocols	2.6	4.9
Training personnel to deal expertly with incidents	2.0	4.5
Establishing a complaints procedure in school		
(for sexual harassment, bullying and discrimination)	1.7	6.9
Care for a safe physical environment in and around *school and responsible use of the facilities*		
Updating facilities according to ARBO-regulation	1.6	5.6
Practical guidelines for the use of facilities on the premises	4.5	5.3
Good co-operation with police, justice, health and youth care	2.8	5.4

conduct has been formulated in The Netherlands, that might be used as a starting point for discussions in schools and school classes:

Respect: I respect my schoolmates and teachers.
No crossing lines: I try not to cross the lines and when it happens I correct this by stepping back.
No violence: I try to solve my conflicts without using any violence.
Accountable: Please tell me what I'm doing right or wrong.

Partly due to the national campaign, but surely also influenced by many other initiatives and the increased focus on violence in the press and the media, the taboo on discussing violence in schools has been conquered. An evaluation of the campaign has been made by Mooij (2001). He found that in most Dutch schools matters of safety and security are being discussed more openly now and there has been an increase in safety-directed actions (as reported by head teachers and teachers), which cover all three foci of the 'Safety at school' campaign (see Table 5.2). The most striking self-reported improvements (in complaints procedures and regulations) are due to recent legislation.

The report also shows increased attention to social competence. In many secondary schools, pupils in the first two grades get specific 'life-style' training, and issues like healthy food and drink, more physical activities, safe sex and prevention of addiction to smoking, alcohol and drugs are now being taught as part of the curriculum. Relatively new is the focus on self-directed learning, and sharing responsibilities with pupils in the learning process.

Local initiatives or programmes

Problems regarding safety should be tackled at a local level where, according to a central policy assumption, co-operation between relevant partners is easier to establish than it is at a national level. Therefore, national policy is aimed at offering conditions for local solutions and the governmental role concerning youth and safety policy has in part been decentralized. Municipalities and provinces are primarily responsible for funding and co-ordinating local and regional activities. Recently the focus has been on active participation and a responsible role for young people. Within individual regions and municipalities, there is co-operation between schools and agencies concerned with welfare work, cultural and social activities, child protection and services for young people, and with the regional institutes for mental welfare, the police and the courts. Between the different regions or municipalities, however, there may be new or traditional differences.

In 1994, the Education Department of the Municipality of The Hague published a report, *Effe Dimme* (Dienst Onderwijs, 1994), putting forward rules for teachers and school management concerning the physical and legal aspects of violence. Other cities and large towns followed suit with similar approaches, sometimes with slightly different emphases. At the same time, consultations have been stepped up and there has been co-operation between educational institutions and organizations in the welfare sector. Co-operation between schools and the police has produced initiatives such as crime-prevention lessons by police officers, on themes such as vandalism and rowdiness, theft and receiving stolen goods, abuse and victim support, the police station, police procedures, and addiction.

Local authorities are responsible for a local youth and safety policy. Special activities in schools can be part of this policy. In several cities in The Netherlands local authorities promote the Safety at school policy and give extra financial incentives. Local authorities and police promote regular contact between police and schools to prevent and combat vandalism, petty crime and violence. Agreements on co-operation are part of this policy. More recently a community approach for schools has been promoted. Local authorities, schools and local institutions combine forces to create a firm network of education, care and welfare to support children and parents together more appropriately.

In 1999 an inventory was made of all the local governments that had an active policy concerning safe schools. One of the outcomes was that some local authorities created covenants between parties around school safety. Covenants are presently in place in various municipalities between the municipality, police, the judicial authorities, HALT (an organization implementing alternative sanctions for first offenders), and the schools. The most important aspects are:

- schools, police and assistance services communicate with one another via permanent contact persons;
- schools register incidents and report suspicions of punishable acts to the police;
- schools inform students and parents of this (*inter alia* via the school regulations and school guide);
- the police and judicial authorities will deal with such matters swiftly and offer support where necessary;
- where possible, the school will co-operate with the enforcement of alternative punishments via HALT;
- the municipality must find a solution in respect of traffic safety and nuisance from young people who are playing or hanging out.

Municipal policies: the example of Utrecht

The city of Utrecht has, over the last few years, helped all schools to take part in safe school programmes. It started with a diagnosis of the safety situation in and around school, which identified points in need of improvement. In a safety improvement plan, each school could choose its own priorities to work on, varying from school climate and class management to improving playgrounds. The local school advisory board also identified a peer mediation programme (the New York Resolving Conflict Creatively Programme, evaluated in primary schools in the USA), translated it into Dutch and adapted it to the Dutch educational situation. Some pilot schools are working with this programme.

School policies

Although the direction of the Safety at school campaign is very clear, schools are free to make choices fitting their special situation. So the national campaign does not prescribe a safety policy as such. None the less, schools can be questioned by pupils, parents and staff and by school inspectors about the results of their own policy. School policies appear to be gradually taking shape. Mooij (1994) found that secondary schools have: appointed confidential counsellors (69 per cent); included clauses in school rules about the way in which pupils should treat each other (55 per cent); and drawn up crime prevention plans (7 per cent).

A growing number of schools make use of participatory schemes regarding safety and youngsters, such as peer education and peer counselling. This is one way of dealing with problems of social cohesion and social bonding within schools: making students more responsible tends to provoke more responsible behaviour. Schools are steadily learning that students are not only part of 'the problem', but can also be a constructive part of the solution.

As part of the national quality policy, schools will soon be required to include figures on safety in their annual school guide, and account for their policy in four-year school plans. A general complaints procedure will also be required for parents and students. Schools must also have one or more confidential advisers.

The campaign included instruments available to enable schools to make policy choices:

- a 'thermometer' which will allow the school to gauge feelings of security, and prevent incidents (see Table 5.3);
- material to enable schools to enlist the active involvement of students and parents when *making priorities* (such as a top ten list and discussion card game);
- a simple matrix for use by a policy group at school in order to make a *general diagnosis* (the matrix positions security in the broader context of school development);
- a *'guide' to education, materials, methods and successful examples* to help schools make choices that fit with their situation and development;
- a 'crisis spectrum' (computer programme) with the help of which schools can draft drills for crises and assess their effectiveness;
- *concise school regulations* against which schools can review their own often extremely complicated and almost incomprehensible regulations.

Table 5.3 The 'thermometer' available for school use

Course: Year: Class:	Date:			
This week I felt				
in the classroom	safe	not so safe	insecure	extremely insecure
at school	safe	not so safe	insecure	extremely insecure
around the school	safe	not so safe	insecure	extremely insecure
between home and school	safe	not so safe	insecure	extremely insecure
This week / this month				
I was teased and/or laughed at	never	sometimes	often	always
I was called names and/or threatened	never	sometimes	often	always
Something was stolen from me, or broken	never	sometimes	often	always
I was afraid of certain students	never	sometimes	often	always
I was harassed	never	sometimes	often	always
I suffered from physical violence	never	sometimes	often	always
I spoke about this to: This was/was not a help because:				

Violence and social competence

It is important that teachers possess the ability to strengthen the social and emotional skills of students within the context of the lessons and the school. Broadly speaking, this comes down to *learning to act with responsibility towards yourself, towards others and towards your surroundings.* Key words are *reflection* and *communication*. These are meta-cognitive skills that can be practised at school, in and outside classes. More attention than before will be devoted to fostering these skills in in-service training and teacher training programmes. For instance a reflective method for professionals in education, social work and care working on social competence of youngsters has been developed and is being implemented (Prior and Walraven, 1999).

More attention is being given to the active role which young people themselves can play in preventing and solving insecurity, both inside and outside the school. Such activity may involve having a say in and participating in decision making – a youth parliament, youth panels, student councils and membership of participation councils. Less formalized opportunities occur in schools, for example: involving pupils in drafting and observing codes of conduct; assigning them more responsibilities in the area of organization and management; training them as confidential advisers and to act as mediators in cases of teasing and bullying; involving them as mentors and in tutoring; involving them in the furnishing and use of the building and surroundings; and involving them in solving conflicts about nuisance and vandalism.

Conflict management and social competence in education

A new innovative programme in this area, developed by Sardes Educational Services, was ready for implementation in late 2001 in all primary and secondary schools that wanted to participate. It has a whole-school approach, a focus on a strong and safe learning environment, and a view of conflict management as part of social competence and, in consequence, part of the social competence curriculum.

What do we regard as 'a strong and safe learning environment'? Several definitions are possible: an environment that addresses all the needs of our desire to learn adequately – autonomy, connectedness and competence; or, an environment that facilitates the transfer of knowledge, skills, attitudes and behaviour to new situations; or, an environment that is active, fitting, authentic, and engaging. Since we aim at a whole-school approach, we also need to consider what skills and attitudes an educator needs to be able to create such an environment. Four are particularly important: to learn, to create conditions for learning, to support active learners, and to strengthen and deepen learning.

In November 2001 the first group of qualified professional school advisers and experts in conflict management finished their training. They are trained to support primary and secondary schools to implement the programme. The first schools started in January 2002.

References

Dienst Onderwijs (1994). *'Effe dimme'. Omgaan met agressie of geweld in en om school.* 's-Gravenhage: Gemeente Den Haag.

Humbert, M. (1993). *Voorlichting ten behoeve van criminaliteitspreventie; theoretische en empirische aspecten.* 's-Gravenhage: Ministerie van Justitie, Directie Criminaliteitspreventie.

Junger-Tas, J. (1996). *Jeugd en gezin. Preventie vanuit een justitieel perspectief.* 's-Gravenhage: Ministerie van Justitie, directie beleid.

Kelder, M.J. and Lemette, H.A. van (1996). *Agressie, geweld en seksuele intimidatie op scholen: vragenlijst, handleiding en toelichting.* Heerlen: Stichting Vervangingsfonds en Bedrijfsgezondheidszorg voor het Onderwijs.

Landelijk Aktie Komitee Scholieren (1995). *Checklist om een gouden school te worden.* Amsterdam: LAKS.

Landelijk Aktie Komitee Scholieren (1999). *Een leefbare school.* Amsterdam: LAKS.

Meer, B. van der (1988). *Het zwarte schaap in de klas* [The scapegoat in the classroom]. Den Bosch, Nijmegen: KPC-Berkhout.

Ministerie van Justitie (1994). *Met de neus op defeiten. Advies aanpakjeugdcriminaliteit.* Den Haag.

Ministerie van Onderwijs, Cultuur en Wetenschappen (1995a). *Notitie van de commissie 'Voorkoming en bestrijding geweld in scholen.* Den Haag.

Ministerie van Onderwijs, Cultuur en Wetenschappen (1995b). *De veilige school.* Den Haag.

Ministerie van Volksgezondheid, Welzijn en Sport and Ministerie van Onderwijs, Cultuur en Wetenschappen (2000). *Early Childhood Education and Care Policy in The Netherlands.* The Hague.

Mooij, T. (1992). *Pesten in het onderwijs.* Nijmegen: Katholieke Universiteit, Instituut voor Toegepaste Sociale wetenschappen.

Mooij, T. (1994). *Leerlinggeweld in het voortgezet onderwijs. Sociale binding van scholieren* [Violence in secondary education]. Nijmegen: Katholieke Universiteit, Instituut voor Toegepaste Sociale wetenschappen.

Mooij, T. (2001). *Veilige scholen en (pro)sociaal gedrag. Evaluatie van de campagne 'De veilige school' in het voortgezet onderwijs* [Safe schools and (pro)social behaviour in secondary education]. Nijmegen: Catholic University, Institute for Applied Social Sciences.

Prior, F. and Walraven, G. (1999). *Sociale competentie: zelf leren.* Utrecht: Sardes.

Procesmanagement Voortgezet Onderwijs (1996). *De veilige school: maat, toonsoort, instrumenten en uitvoering.* 's-Gravenhage: Procesmanagement Voortgezet Onderwijs.

Sardes (2000). *Veiligheid staat op de kaart: lokaal werken aan 'jongeren, school en veiligheid'.* Utrecht: Sardes.

Schuyt, C.J.M. (1995). *Kwetsbare jongeren en hun toekomst*. Rijswijk: Ministerie van Volksgezondheid, Welzijn en Sport.

Studulski, F. and Hoogbergen, M. (2002). *Veiligheid als voorwaarde: Werken aan een structureel veiligheidsbeleid op school, 1995–2001*. Utrecht: Sardes.

Visser, A. (1996). *Doe het zelfpakket basisonderwijs voor een themavergadering rond 'Herkennen en begeleiden van seksuele intimidatie in de schoolsituatie'*. Utrecht: Project Preventie Seksuele Intimidatie.

There is a website concerning safer schools, where examples of good practice are presented (www.aps.nl/transferpunt) and some information on the programme on conflict management and social competence in education is to be found at www.sardes.nl.

Chapter 6

The Austrian situation

Many initiatives against violence, few evaluations

Moira Atria and Christiane Spiel

Background

The country

In 2001, Austria had a population of 8,065,465 people living in an area of 83,859 km². Somewhat less than 10 per cent (730,000) of the residents are not Austrian nationals, with most of them coming from former Yugoslavia and Turkey. Austria is a federation of nine individual states – Burgenland, Carinthia, Lower Austria, Upper Austria, Salzburg, Styria, Tirol, Vorarlberg and Vienna (which is both the national capital and an individual state).

The school system

Responsibility for structuring and administering the education system is divided between the federal government and the states according to provisions in the federal constitution; the states are responsible for executing the national laws and regulations. Since the early 1990s the Austrian school system has changed in some aspects; currently, the intention of Austrian educational policy is to strengthen school autonomy and reinforce co-operation between teachers, parents, and pupils. As a consequence, schools can conduct projects, develop their own school profiles and establish behavioural rules autonomously.

Compulsory schooling starts during the September following a child's sixth birthday and comprises nine school years. In the first four years, attendance at a *Volksschule* (primary school) is mandatory. After the *Volksschule* pupils can either attend a *Hauptschule* (general secondary school; fifth to eighth grade) or an *Allgemeinbildende Höhere Schule* (*AHS*; academic secondary school; fifth to twelfth grade). Primary schools have a typical size of 60 to 234 pupils (average is 117), general secondary schools a typical size of 220 pupils, and academic secondary schools a typical size of 600 pupils.

Primary and general secondary school only cover eight years of compulsory education, and thus the ninth school year has to be completed at a *Polytechnische Schule* (polytechnic school) or at another school type. Other options include a *Berufsbildende Mittlere Schule* (vocational middle school; ninth to eleventh grade), a *Berufsbildende Höhere Schule* (*BHS*; higher technical or vocational college; ninth to thirteenth grade), or a transfer to the upper level of an academic secondary school.

Attendance at an *AHS* or a *BHS* depends on the pupil's success at his or her former school. Both school types terminate in the *Matura* (matriculation exam) that is the entrance exam for universities, higher technical colleges, and academies.

In the first four years, school usually lasts from 8a.m. to 1p.m. After the fifth grade, lessons also take place on Saturday and sometimes in the afternoon. Some schools offer additional afternoon supervision for the pupils.

Children with special educational needs either attend a *Sonderschule* (special needs school; ages 6 to 15) or can be integrated into *Volksschule* or *Hauptschule*. The organization of the Austrian psychological and social support system for pupils with behavioural or educational problems is very complex and, as a consequence, not always easy to access for parents. Within schools there are a variety of specialists who can be contacted (mostly teachers with special qualifications), and there are also a number of external support institutions (e.g. School Psychology) and telephone hotlines (e.g. *Kindertelefon, Rat auf Draht*).

Violence in schools: linguistic and definitional issues

In recent years, the term 'violence in schools' has been used in quite a broad sense in Austrian public discourse. It is used to describe direct and indirect aggression, verbal and physical aggression, and interpersonal aggression between pupils as well as between pupils and teachers. Unfortunately, in many of the empirical investigations no clear distinctions between various forms of violence or aggression were made. Most of the empirical studies refer to the concept of bullying, defined by Olweus as aggressive behaviour or intentional injury between pupils that is exercised repeatedly and over a longer period of time within relationships that are characterized by an imbalance of power (Olweus, 1993).

Relevant historical background

In the last ten years, several spectacular acts of violence by pupils have shocked the Austrian public, and violence in schools has begun to gain broad public attention. The *Ministerratsvortrag* of September 1997 was the first governmental declaration against violence in different social fields (violence in society, in families, against women, and in mass media, child maltreatment and sexual child abuse). As a result, information centres have been established, intervention projects have been financially supported, and information materials about violence have been distributed. Single projects have been developed in many individual schools, but no nationwide prevention programme has been set up. The current situation in Austria can be described as follows: (1) there is a lack of systematic empirical research on violence in schools; (2) there is a wealth of materials, project descriptions, and handbooks for teachers that are not based on the results of empirical research. Communication and co-operation between researchers and practitioners is insufficient, and due to this lack of exchange it is feared that 'the wheel will be invented again and again' (see also Jäger, 1999).

Knowledge

Information on violence in schools is based on empirical studies, mostly in the form of diploma or doctoral theses, conducted at the Universities of Vienna, Graz and Salzburg. The studies available address the prevalence of bullying, the personal characteristics of bullies and victims, and a number of specific questions. Unfortunately, hardly any of this information has been published, and thus it is not available in the scientific databases. Some aspects of the topic were investigated in the international project 'Health Behaviour in School-aged Children (HBSC)', organized by the World Health Organization (WHO) and in which Austria is participating. Empirical results are not easy to compare because of differences concerning measurement instruments, samples, and statistical methods.

Violence between pupils: frequency and types of bullying

Krumm and his colleagues (1997) surveyed 10,000 pupils aged 12 to 18, asking them to describe how often they had been involved in violence in the last month. Prevalence rates for physical violence differed depending on pupils' age. In the subsample of adolescents aged 12 to 14 years, 12 per cent described themselves as victimized by physical attacks and another 12 per cent used physical aggression. In the subsample of 17- to 18-year-old pupils, only 1 per cent described themselves as having been frequently physically attacked, and 3 per cent described themselves as frequent physical aggressors.

In the above-mentioned WHO study, a representative sample of 2,160 pupils were asked if they had ever acted as bullies or had ever been victimized. In the subsample of 11-year-old pupils, 35 per cent of the boys and 22 per cent of the girls answered this question affirmatively (Gesundheit und Gesundheitsverhalten bei Kindern und Jugendlichen, 2000).

Table 6.1 Verbal, physical and indirect aggression among pupils; results from two studies

	Survey by Krumm et al., 1997[a]	*Survey by Riffert and Paschon, 1998*[b]
Verbal aggression	25% bullies	10% bullies
	30% victims	19% victims
		35% bully-victims
Physical aggression	12% bullies	8% bullies
	12% victims	9% victims
		7% bully-victims
Indirect aggression	10% bullies	3% bullies
	9% victims	5% victims
		1% bully-victims

Notes
a. N = 5,000; pupils aged 12 to 14 years.
b. N = 632; pupils aged 10 to 18 years.

Results of a study conducted by Klicpera and Gasteiger-Klicpera (1996) on 1,594 eighth grade pupils identified 14 per cent bullies, 6 per cent victims, and 8 per cent bully-victims. Riffert and Paschon (1998) invest-igated 632 *AHS* pupils aged 10 to 18 and found 8 per cent bullies, 9 per cent victims, and 7 per cent bully-victims.

Comparisons of the different forms of violence showed consistent re-sults across studies: the highest prevalence rate was observed in verbal aggression, followed by physical aggression and indirect aggression (for details see Table 6.1). Generally, gender differences were observed in physical aggression, with male pupils more aggressive than female ones (e.g. Gasteiger-Klicpera and Klicpera, 1997; Riffert and Paschon, 1998; Singer and Spiel, 1998). Riffert and Paschon (1998), for example, found 14 per cent bullies, 13 per cent victims and 14 per cent bully-victims among male pupils but only 3 per cent bullies, 5 per cent victims, and 1 per cent bully-victims among girls. In contrast, no gender differences were found in verbal aggression and damage to property.

Substantive differences in the prevalence rates of violence depending on the school type were found; the higher the academic level of the school, the less bullying was present. In particular, prevalence rates of frequent physical aggression in academic secondary schools *(AHS)* were clearly lower than in other school types (e.g. Gasteiger-Klicpera and Klicpera, 1997). An exceptionally high rate of aggression (5 per cent bullies, 4 per cent victims, and 25 per cent bully-victims) was observed in voca-tional middle schools (Atria, Spiel and Krilyszyn, 2000).

Results concerning age effects are consistent with findings in other countries; in general, younger pupils were found to be victims more often than older pupils (e.g. Klicpera and Gasteiger-Klicpera, 1996; Singer

Table 6.2 Age and number of injuries resulting from fights among pupils, 1999

Age in years	6	7	8	9	10	11	12	13	14	15	16	17	18+
Injuries		15	65	83	108	122	189	230	221	204	117	45	13	7

and Spiel, 1998). Evidence of the relationship between age and physical violence can be inferred from statistical data on injuries resulting from fights among pupils: as shown in Table 6.2, there is a parabolic relationship between age and accident rate, with a peak at the age of 12 years.

Differences in pupils' violent behaviour depending on their country of origin were found in a study by Strohmeier and Spiel (2000; see also Strohmeier, 2001): 326 pupils with German mother tongue and 242 pupils with non-German mother tongue aged 11 to 13 were asked about their own and their classmates' behaviour. Peer ratings concerning physical aggression described pupils with German mother tongue as being more involved in violence than non-native speakers. In contrast, self-report data suggested that non-native speakers were more often subjected to verbal aggression and isolation than pupils with German mother tongue.

Characteristics of bullies, victims, and bully-victims

Results concerning personal characteristics associated with aggressive behaviour are relatively homogenous in various studies (e.g. Gasteiger-Klicpera and Klicpera, 1997; Klicpera and Gasteiger-Klicpera, 1996; Strohmeier and Spiel, 2000). Bullies and bully-victims exhibit more dissatisfaction with school than their non-bullying classmates; they are frequently poor pupils, have negative attitudes towards school and learning and frequently have problems with teachers. In general, their social information-processing mechanism seems to be disturbed. In conflict situations, bullies more often react impulsively and are more likely to escalate the conflict. However, their self-esteem is very high. Bullies describe themselves as being popular and part of cliques (e.g. Strohmeier, 2001).

Victims describe themselves as being unpopular and isolated in their classes. Like bullies, they have a negative image of teachers. Victims tend to have high scores in anxiety, dependency on others, and helplessness. In conflict situations, victims use similar strategies to pupils not involved in violent behaviour. They prefer problem-oriented strategies and seek social support. In peer-ratings, victims are always described negatively.

A negative family climate is a high risk factor for aggressive behaviour. A lack of cohesion, openness, independence and organization in the family increases the probability of aggression. While the education style

Table 6.3 Aggression by teachers against pupils in the previous month (per cent)

	Pupils aged 12 to 14 years				Pupils aged 17 to 18 years			
	Never	1x	2x	3x	Never	1x	2x	3x
Unjustly treated	54	16	8	22	63	17	9	11
Felt hurt	62	13	6	19	77	11	4	7
Made angry	49	15	8	29	64	13	7	16

Source: Krumm, Lamberger-Baumann and Haider (1997).

Note: Unfortunately the authors did not give any information about the absolute numbers of pupils in this survey.

in families of victims was found to be dominated by rigidity, bullies described a lack of parental supervision (Klicpera and Gasteiger-Klicpera, 1996) combined with frequent viewing of videos and movies. In particular, a positive correlation between the watching of horror movies and aggressive behaviour was found (Robier and Spiel, 1998).

Violence between teachers and pupils

There is a lack of studies investigating violence by teachers against pupils. Only Krumm and his colleagues addressed this topic in their surveys (e.g. Krumm, Lamberger-Baumann and Haider, 1997; Krumm and Weiß, 2000). Pupils were asked to assess how often teachers had treated them unjustly, hurt them and/or angered them in any way in the last month. Results are shown in Table 6.3.

The authors interpreted the pupils' answers as a clear indicator of violence by teachers against pupils. However, this study was criticized because of its 'weak' operationalization: Posch (1997) posed the question of whether the above-mentioned categories are precise enough to serve as indicators for violence; he argued that to feel 'angered in any way' is not necessarily a consequence of violence suffered. In spite of his critique, the author acknowledged the importance of this issue and proposed that it be investigated and discussed more precisely. In other studies, the same research group around Krumm observed teachers' use of unfair methods in evaluating pupils, for example a lack of defined performance criteria, and the use of unjustified evaluation factors (e.g. Krumm and Weiß, 2000). They also observed that 16 per cent of the 12- to 14-year-old pupils slandered their teachers three times or more per month. Age differences were again found: older pupils showed less aggression towards their teachers than younger pupils (Krumm, Lamberger-Baumann and Haider, 1997).

Table 6.4 Number of accidents in school breaks, from 1989/90 to1998/99

	School year				
	1989/90	*1990/91*	*1991/92*	*1992/93*	*1993/94*
Accidents	11,628	11,749	12,969	12,919	13,567
Total number of insured pupils	980,780	980,340	1,003,870	1,020,500	1,033,590
	School year				
	1994/95	*1995/96*	*1996/97*	*1997/98*	*1998/99*
Accidents	13,430	12,485	11,524	10,500	11,168
Total number of insured pupils	1,040,870	1,048,390	1,053,230	1,057,690	1,066,240

Trends over time and consistency across settings

To provide information on any increase of violence in schools, one study collected cross-generational data in three subsamples: adolescents aged 14 to 24, young adults aged 24 to 39, and middle-aged adults aged 40 to 59 were asked about the violence they had experienced during their schooling (Karamaz-Morawetz and Steinert, 1995). The results did not show any general increase in violence: while physical aggression decreased, psychological and verbal aggression showed a slight increase.

Additionally, some information can be drawn from the National Accident Insurance Company's pupil statistics regarding the number of accidents that occurred in schools during breaks. This data supports the results of the cross-generational study (see Table 6.4). No systematic shift in the number of accidents was seen over a ten-year period.

Atria, Spiel and Krilyszyn (2000) assessed the stability of aggressive behaviour among particular pupils in a study of 350 pupils aged 15 to 21 attending a vocational middle school. These pupils were investigated four times within a period of 1½ years. However, the stability of the four types (uninvolved, bully, victim, bully-victim) could not be established. A notable percentage of pupils changed roles during the school year; for example, less than 50 per cent of 'bully-victims' remained in this role between the first and second measurements. Additionally, comparison of the situation at the beginning and end of the school year showed an increase in aggression, illustrated by the shrinking of the 'uninvolved pupils' group from 75 to 60 per cent (in contrast, over the summer holidays a general decrease of aggression could be observed). A similar phenomenon of increasing aggression during the school year was also observed by Riffert (2000) in an academic secondary school.

The question of consistency across settings has been addressed by Aspalter and Spiel (2001; Spiel, Wagner and Aspalter, 2000), who compared the aggressive behaviour of 116 adolescents aged 9 to 15 in schools and in a summer camp. High consistency in victims and uninvolved subjects across settings was shown, but consistency of bullying behaviour was much lower: more than 50 per cent of bullies in schools described themselves as not having been involved in violence at summer camp.

Summary of knowledge base

In Austria the number of empirical studies on violence in schools is relatively small, and the heterogeneity of the measurement instruments used impedes the comparison of results. To date, public institutions have not systematically funded or commissioned nationwide surveys. However, findings consistently suggest that the division of pupils into four types of aggressive behaviour has proven its value. The largest group consists of pupils neither actively nor passively involved in violence (66 to 84 per cent). Pupils (bullies) who show frequent and intense aggressive behaviour have a prevalence rate between 3 and 16 per cent. Pupils who are repeatedly and massively subjected to violence are described as victims (3 to 16 per cent). The fourth group, with a prevalence rate of between 8 and 25 per cent, consists of pupils who are both bullies and victims.

Gender and age have been found to moderate aggressive behaviour. Empirical results suggest a parabolic relationship between age and physically aggressive behaviour, with a peak at the age of 12 years. Female pupils are less often physically aggressive than male pupils. In addition, violence varies systematically according to school type. There is an inversely proportional decrease in the rate of aggression as the academic level of the school increases. According to the results of a cross-generational study, there was little support for the frequently stated assumption that there has been an increase in violence among pupils over time.

A few pupil surveys have also provided information about violence between teachers and pupils, showing that there is violence by teachers against pupils and by pupils against teachers. Investigations concerning stability and consistency of aggression suggest that violence varies depending on time and setting.

Action

Austrian public institutions have defined their responsibilities in terms of fulfilling demand: offering training for teachers, distributing information materials, funding single projects for schools, counselling for interested schools and individuals. However, national programmes to prevent violence in school have neither been established nor are they currently planned.

The selection and presentation of the initiatives and projects for this paper were guided by the intention of explaining prevention as an educational process. Therefore, we tried to get information about the theoretical background of the initiatives, the procedure, and the relevant conditions. However, during data collection we were confronted by the problem that only a few of the projects were carefully documented and that there is a lack of evaluation. As a consequence, initiatives, programmes and projects can only be briefly described, but not evaluated concerning their effectiveness.

The first part presents a primary prevention project that intends to integrate social learning and subject knowledge by promoting social competencies. In the second part, secondary preventive initiatives are summarized; these programmes focus on coping with conflict situations. Third, the few intervention projects addressing violence reduction in schools or classes that have been systematically evaluated are reported. Finally, single initiatives and information material prepared for schools are briefly described.

Primary prevention

Social learning

This project started in 1984 as a pilot project, but within a few years it became one of the most frequently applied projects in academic secondary schools. According to the project's aims, educational goals comprise both subject knowledge and social learning processes. Teachers who are interested in participating attend a four-day preparatory training seminar where teacher teams are established to run the project in the schools. The programme consists of seven key steps: (1) self-reflection and self-presentation; (2) attention to and acceptance of others; (3) feedback and rule definition; (4) coping with conflicts; (5) establishing teams; (6) working in teams; and (7) evaluation of teamwork.

Development of class rules

This example shows a lesson focused on the social learning process (Mitschka, 1988). The unit starts with a presentation of the unit's specific goals and detailed instructions. Small groups of pupils are given the task of finding a fair way of distributing a limited quantity of resources. Then they discuss their experiences and talk about fairness and unfairness. Afterwards, the pupils look for informal rules within the class (democracy game) and try to set new rules for the class (parliament game).

Secondary prevention

Peer mediation

Since 1995, twenty-three Viennese academic secondary schools have participated in the project *Peer mediation*. In special seminars guided by school
psychologists, interested pupils are trained in how to intervene in conflict situations between their classmates. The seminar's topics are: (1)
basics of conflict management, e.g. knowledge about forms and causes
of conflicts, conflict analysis; (2) theory and practice of mediation, e.g.
staying neutral, differentiating between goals and wishes; (3) basics of
communication psychology, e.g. active listening, reaching agreements
(Banner, 2000).

School psychology

Every Austrian state has its own school psychology system, which offers
two types of support: (1) Individual support aimed at helping children
(and their teachers and parents) cope with specific problems (learning problems, behavioural problems, school career planning); (2) system
support including teacher training, pedagogical conferences, teacher
supervision and conflict management.

Intervention programmes: evaluation studies

Anti-aggression programme (Olweus)

A shortened version of this programme was applied and its effectiveness
was evaluated (Singer and Spiel, 1998). Four classes from two general
secondary schools participated in the programme; parallel classes from
two other schools functioned as controls.

The Olweus programme consists of three main parts: actions at the
school level, class level, and individual level. The shortened version (three
months' duration) concentrated on the following elements: development of class rules against bullying, systematic supervision during
breaks, literature lectures on violence, weekly social hour, regular discussions with parents, serious talks with bullies and victims.

In spite of the two intervention psychologists' high level of engagement, the programme evaluation did not show a reduction of violence
in comparison with the control classes. This result clearly contrasted
with the subjective impression of everyone involved in the programme.
Possible causes for the lack of effectiveness, such as an increased sensitivity to violence, which could have changed pupils' frame of reference,
are discussed by Spiel (2000).

Social training in school (Petermann, Jugert, Tänzer and Verbeek)

Riffert (2000) conducted a prevention project based on this programme developed by Petermann et al. (1997). The training combines Dodge's conception of social information processing (1993) and behaviour therapy methods. It consists of ten units, each having a very specific time structure: introduction (10 minutes), rule phase (3 minutes), recreation phase (12 minutes), work phase (60 minutes), and concluding phase (5 minutes). Each phase is devoted to a specific topic, for example self-reflection or change of perspectives.

In a four-day seminar, Riffert introduced the teachers running the project to the programme's methods. One class at an academic secondary school with twenty-two pupils participated in the project; a second class served as a control group. Riffert could demonstrate very encouraging training effects in several variables like pupils' aggressive behaviour and anxiety in various situations. Pupil and parent acceptance of the training was very high.

Social competency training for pupils (Atria and Spiel)

This programme was developed at the Department of Psychology, University of Vienna. The training is based on a social information-processing theory (e.g. Huesmann, 1988) and on the empirical results of research on bullying as a group process (e.g. Salmivalli et al., 1996). The integration of these two approaches yields the programme's two main principles: (1) Behavioural enrichment: adolescents act in an aggressive manner when they do not know how to cope with critical situations. Thus an enrichment of their behavioural repertoire can help reduce aggression. (2) Participation: whoever is present at an aggressive action is at the same time involved in it. People who accept this principle tend to take more responsibility for what is happening around them.

Based on this model, an intervention curriculum with thirteen sessions divided into three phases was specifically designed to train high-risk school classes: in the group dynamics unit (six lessons) the pupils are confronted with the group dynamics within their own school class. Through role-plays and work on examples of critical situations, the programme trainer helps them to accept that aggression and violence are poor strategies for coping with conflict. The reflection unit (one lesson) gives pupils an opportunity to reflect on what has been learned in the first part of the programme. In the last unit, action (six lessons), the pupils and the trainer elaborate a specific programme for the whole group: together, they define how they want to profit from the remaining lessons.

Two school classes of a vocational middle school (fifty-five pupils) participated in social competency training; parallel classes at the same school served as controls. Due to various factors such as the ethnically mixed population, the pupils' low academic level and their parents' low educational level, this school can be termed a high-risk school type. Comparison between the intervention and control groups showed significant effects in the fields of democracy (behavioural enrichment) and perceived aggression. Pupils who took part in the training saw more possibilities for participating in school life. They described themselves as less involved in aggression against peers, and pupil–teacher interaction showed especially positive development. Teacher ratings also showed significant differences in the field of work attitude, describing the participating classes as being more attentive and interested in their lessons (Atria and Spiel, in preparation; see also http://www.univie.ac.at/psychologie/bildungspsychologie).

Information materials

Several booklets and brochures have been published within the last few years. The booklet *Gewalt in der Schule – Informationen und Materialien* (Violence in School – Information and Materials; Aigner and Sedlak, 1999) summarizes selected prevention programmes and current literature. The National Accident Insurance Company has prepared a broad range of materials for schools about how to effectively prevent accidents (see also http://cool.down.co.at/). The Federal Ministry of Education, Science, and Culture has published a brochure *Vereinbaren statt Anordnen* (Reaching Agreement Instead of Giving Orders; Kisser, 1999). It includes theoretical and legal information, practical tips, and some model examples for agreements between pupils, teachers, and parents.

Regional programmes

In 2001, the European Museum for Peace was established in Stadtschlaining (Burgenland). It offers an exhibition entitled *War or Peace: From a cult of violence to a culture of peace*, which aims to reach school classes who are encouraged to visit it. A package for school classes and their teachers, including lesson outlines, stories, songs, etc., is provided for preparation of the museum visit (for more information see http://www.konfliktkultur.at/).

An introduction to 'The Viennese Counselling Model' has been presented in the context of another Connect project (fi-006) and therefore is only mentioned briefly here (Combating Violence in School – The Viennese Counselling Model, 2001). This model is based on co-operation between regular schools and centres for special educational needs. Counselling teachers, i.e. teachers who have completed a special two-year training programme, support other teachers and their pupils in coping with pupils' behavioural disorders. This system was designed to keep pupils with special needs integrated in regular schools.

Additional activities

Below we summarize some examples of other initiatives. Most were surveyed by the Federal Ministry of Education, Science, and Culture in 1999. In this survey, all state education councils (*Landesschulräte*) were asked to report on prevention activities carried out in their states (see also www.bmbwk.gv.at).

Structural activities

Institutionalized feedback culture for pupils

Special measures designed to identify problems at school have been established. For example, class councils are held or pupils are given various other opportunities to verbalize their concerns (bulletin board).

Behaviour rules

School rules and class rules are worked out and published at the beginning of the school year. Compliance is monitored and pupils are sanctioned if they do not behave according to the rules.

Activities at a group and individual level

Police in schools

During recent years, co-operation projects between police and schools have been conducted, where police officers visit classes and discuss violence and its legal implications.

Experience-related educational initiatives

To promote pupils' experience of community, outdoor activities (e.g. accompanied expeditions) are carried out, at which pupils learn to value team work and co-operation (see also Pawek et al., 1999).

Summary and discussion

Since the governmental declaration of 1997, public institutions have supported services for schools, held training seminars for teachers, distributed information materials, set up counselling institutions, and funded single projects in the area of violence in schools. However, in contrast to many other European countries (Smith et al., 1999), neither national nor regional (state) programmes against violence have been implemented. No minimum standards for projects and programmes have been defined; systematic co-operation between researchers and teachers has not been organized. In Austria, individual schools have considerable autonomy regarding whether or not to start initiatives against violence. As a result, there are many initiatives, but they are neither co-ordinated nor evaluated.

What are the consequences of this clearly unfavourable situation? In most cases:

- projects and programmes do not fulfil international quality standards;
- the terms 'violence' and 'aggression' are not clearly defined and project goals are imprecisely formulated;
- programmes are not always documented and reports are rarely published. As a consequence, previous experience is thus often not taken into consideration and the effectiveness of the programmes is not evaluated;
- the cost-effectiveness of the measures has never been analysed.

Perspectives

In this final section we will not focus on general problems concerning research on and initiatives against violence, because a concise description of conditions in Germany by Lösel and Bliesener (1999) is also applicable to the situation in Austria. We will concentrate on problems that are specific to Austria.

Although public awareness of violence in schools in Austria has increased, there is a lack of both systematic research and national policy against violence. As a consequence, no reliable nationwide prevalence rates of the various forms of violence are available. Austrian schools have a high degree of autonomy in setting initiatives against violence. Although the principle of autonomy and self-management often facilitates progress, the total lack of supervision and evaluation often yields unsatisfactory results.

Therefore, setting standards for programmes and projects against violence seems to be the most urgent task in Austria for the near future:

- scientific standards and knowledge should be presented in training seminars for teachers;
- funding of projects should depend on fulfilling minimum standards, e.g. theoretical basis, definition of goals, description of methods, analysis of effectiveness;
- proposals for projects and programmes should be evaluated by external experts.

Additionally, initiatives against violence should not only focus on the behaviour of pupils but also address teachers' and parents' behaviour. In general, co-operation between researchers, governmental institutions, and practitioners (school principals, teachers and parents) should be improved. Currently in Austria there is an intensive debate about disciplinary regulations in schools. Preventing violence between pupils and by pupils against teachers is a central point in this discussion. Here, the Federal Ministry of Education, Science, and Culture is actively engaged and willing to take the initiative. There is some hope that the needs and perspectives discussed above will be considered in the future.

In summary, since 1997 violence in schools has begun to gain broad public attention in Austria, and many media reports have addressed this topic. Although public awareness of school violence is high, only a few empirical studies have been initiated so far. In September 1997, a co-operative declaration of five federal ministries including the Ministry of Education and Cultural Affairs expressed the intention to establish initiatives for preventing violence in several social fields. So far the government has financially supported single intervention projects and distributed information materials about violence in schools, but no nationwide prevention programme has been established. Most initiatives against violence in schools were organized by individual teachers. So far, researchers have been involved neither in planning nor in organizing these projects and only a few of them have been evaluated. Therefore, this report can only summarize these initiatives but can hardly report on their effectiveness.

References

Aigner, H. and Sedlak, F. (1999). *Gewalt in der Schule. Informationen und Materialien.* Wien: Bundesministerium für Unterricht und kulturelle Angelegenheiten.

Aspalter, N. and Spiel, C. (2001). Violence Among Children – Consistency of Bully–Victim Behaviour. In W. Kallus and N. Posthumus (eds). *Psychological Research in Austria.* Graz: Akademische Druck- und Verlagsanstalt.

Atria, M. and Spiel, C. (in preparation). Social Competency Training for Pupils: A Violence Prevention Program and its Evaluation. Manuscript.

Atria, M., Spiel, C. and Krilyszyn, V. (2000). Aggressives Verhalten an berufsbildenden mittleren Schulen. Vortrag gehalten im 5. Workshop 'Aggression', Hannover. 17–18 November.

Banner, G. (2000). *Projekt: peer-Konfliktmediation an Wiener AHS.* Unveröffentlichtes Manuskript, Wien.

Combating Violence in School – The Viennese Counselling Model (2001). Connect fi-006. European Commission Initiative.

Dodge, K. (1993). Social cognitive mechanisms in the development of conduct disorder and depression. *Annual Review of Psychology,* 44, 559–584.

Gasteiger-Klicpera, B. and Klicpera, C. (1997). Aggressivität und soziale Stellung in der Klassengemeinschaft. *Zeitschrift für Kinder- und Jugendpsychiatrie,* 25, 139–150.

Gesundheit und Gesundheitsverhalten bei Kindern und Jugendlichen (2000). Bericht zur Gesundheit der 11-, 13- und 15-jährigen SchülerInnen in Österreich. Bundesministerium für Soziale Sicherheit und Generationen.

Huesmann, L.R. (1988). An information processing model for the development of aggression. *Aggressive Behavior*, 14, 13–24.

Jäger, R.S. (1999). Gewaltprävention. In M. Schäfer and D. Frey (eds). *Aggression und Gewalt unter Kindern und Jugendlichen*. Göttingen: Hogrefe. pp.203–244.

Karamaz-Morawetz, I. and Steinert, H. (1995). *Schulische und außerschulische Gewalterfahrungen Jugendlicher im Generationenvergleich*. Institut für Rechts- und Kriminalsoziologie im Auftrag des BMUK.

Kisser, C. (1999). *Vereinbaren statt Anordnen. Leitfaden zur Erstellung von Vereinbarungen zwischen den Schulpartnern*. Wien: Bundesministerium für Unterricht und kulturelle Angelegenheiten (BMUK).

Klicpera, C. and Gasteiger-Klicpera, B.G. (1996). Die Situation von 'Tätern' und 'Opfern' aggressiver Handlungen in der Schule. *Praxis der Kinderpsychologie und Kinderpsychiatrie*, 45, 2–9.

Krumm, V., Lamberger-Baumann, B. and Haider, G. (1997). Gewalt in der Schule – auch von Lehrern. *Empirische Pädagogik*, 11, 257–274.

Krumm, V. and Weiß, S. (2000). Ungerechte Lehrer – zu einem Defizit in der Forschung über Gewalt an Schulen. *Salzburger Beiträge zur Erziehungswissenschaft*, 1, 60–79.

Lösel, F. and Bliesener, T. (1999). Germany. In P.K. Smith, Y. Morita, J. Junger-Tas, D. Olweus, R. Catalano and P. Slee (eds). *The Nature of School Bullying: A Cross-national Perspective*. London: Routledge.

Mitschka, R. (1988). *Soziales Lernen, Sich Selbst Entfalten und die Kraft der Gruppe nutzen. Ein Arbeitsbuch für alle, die im Team Arbeiten Wollen*. Wien: Bundesministerium für Unterricht und kulturelle Angelegenheiten.

Olweus, D. (1993). *Bullying at School: What we Know and What we can Do*. Oxford: Blackwell.

Pawek, R., Böhm-Schöller, J., Handzel, G., Meisel, R., Kernstock, O. and Banner, G. (1999). *Vom ich – zum du zum wir. Unterrichtsprojekte zum Prosozialen Lernen*. Wien: Arbeiterkammer und Österreichischer Gewerkschaftsbund.

Petermann, F., Jugert, G., Tänzer, U. and Verbeek, D. (1997). *Sozialtraining in der Schule*. Weinheim: Beltz.

Posch, P. (1997). Kommentar zu Krumm, Lamberger-Baumann und Haider. *Empirische Pädagogik*, 11, 277–283.

Riffert, F. (2000). Sozialtraining in der Schule – Evaluation eines verhaltenstherapeutisch orientierten Präventionsprogramms. *Verhaltenstherapie und Verhaltensmedizin*, 21, 51–64.

Riffert, F. and Paschon, A. (1998). Psychische Gesundheitsprophylaxe: Beispiele zu den bereichen Selbstwirksamkeitsüberzeugungen, Aggression, Angst, soziale Integration. *Salzburger Beiträge zur Erziehungswissenschaft*, 1, 23–39.

Robier, C. and Spiel, C. (1998). Aggressionsbekämpfung in Hauptschulen. Zum Einfluß von Angst und Gewalt im Fernsehen. In J. Glück, O. Vitouch, M. Jirasko and B. Rollett (Hrsg.), *Perspektiven Österreichischer Forschung*. Wien: WUV Universitätsverlag. Vol. 2, pp.227–230.

Salmivalli, C., Lagerspetz, K., Björkqvist, K., Österman, K. and Kaukiainen, A. (1996). Bullying as a group process: participant roles and their relations to social status within the group. *Aggressive Behavior*, 22, 1–15.

Schäfer, M. and Frey, D. (eds) (1999). *Aggression und Gewalt unter Kindern und Jugendlichen.* Göttingen: Hogrefe.

Singer, M. and Spiel, C. (1998). Erprobung eines Anti-aggressionsprogramms an österreichischen Schulen – Erste Ergebnisse. In J. Glück, O. Vitouch, M. Jirasko and B. Rollett (eds). *Perspektiven österreichischer Forschung.* Wien: WUV Universitätsverlag. Vol. 2, pp.223–226.

Smith, P.K., Morita, Y., Junger-Tas, J., Olweus, D., Catalano, R. and Slee, P. (eds) (1999). *The Nature of School Bullying: A Cross-national Perspective.* London: Routledge.

Spiel, C. (2000). Gewalt in der Schule: Täter – Opfer, Prävention – Intervention. In E. Tatzer, S. Pflanzer and R. Krisch (eds). *Schlimm verletzt. Schwierige Kinder und Jugendliche in Theorie und Praxis.* Wien: Krammer, pp.41–53.

Spiel, C., Wagner, P. and Aspalter, N. (2000). In der Schule ein Bully – immer ein Bully? Vortrag gehalten im 5. Workshop 'Aggression', Hannover. 17–18 November.

Strohmeier, D. (2001). *Multikulturelle Freundschaften oder soziale Ausgrenzung.* Unveröffentlichte Diplomarbeit, Karl-Franzens-Universität, Graz.

Strohmeier, D. and Spiel, C. (2000). Gewalterfahrungen von Kindern unterschiedlicher Muttersprachen – Eine Studie an Grazer Hauptschulen. Vortrag gehalten im 5. Workshop 'Aggression', Hannover. 17–18 November.

Chapter 7

Germany

Numerous programmes – no scientific proof

Mechthild Schäfer and Stefan Korn

Background

Country, population and language

The Federal Republic of Germany is a federal State, consisting of sixteen (since 3 October 1999; previously eleven) *Lands*. Approximately 82 million inhabitants live in the Federal Republic. The spoken and official language is German. The foreign population living in Germany is more concentrated in large cities than in rural areas and is much smaller in the eastern *Lands* of the Federal Republic than in western *Lands* (approximately 2 per cent migrants in eastern large cities vs. approximately 20 per cent in the western large cities) (Münchmeier, 2000). Of the children and adolescents without a German passport, 936,693 (9.3 per cent) were in public schools in the school year 1998/99. Of these children 43.6 per cent had a Turkish passport. This proportion of foreign pupils corresponds approximately to the proportion of the foreign inhabitants in the total population in Germany (numbers: Federal Statistical Office, 2000).

The German educational system

From 3 years old, children can attend kindergarten; for the two prior years they can be in a crèche. There is compulsory schooling for children who are 6 years old in all *Lands* of the Federal Republic. Grades one to four (ages approximately 6 to 10 years) form the primary stage (*Primarstufe*), in primary schools (*Grundschule*). Grades five to ten (ages approximately 10 to 16 years) form the secondary stage I (*Sekundarstufe I*), grades eleven to twelve or thirteen (ages approximately 16 to 19 years) and the vocational schools (*Berufsschule*) form the secondary stage II (*Sekundarstufe II*). School size varies in the different *Lands*, averaging, for example, 280 pupils in Mecklenburg-Vorpommern, 360 in North Rhine-Westphalia and 400 in Hamburg; the largest schools in these *Lands* have 1,600, 1,800 and

1,500 pupils respectively (numbers from statistical offices of MV, NRW and HH).

There are different types of secondary school. Successful final examination of the *Gymnasium* (high school) is the general unrestricted qualification for university entrance; the *Hauptschule* (ordinary secondary school) is the basis for craft occupations. The *Realschule* (middle school) is a third main school type which prepares pupils for commercial occupations. Not all *Lands* of the Federal Republic have these three types of schools, and in some *Lands* the *Schulartunabhängige Orientierungsstufe* (school type orientation stage), which covers grades five and six, is attached to the primary stage. There is also the *Gesamtschule* (comprehensive school), which integrates the three school types mentioned above. All school types are part of the ordinary national educational system in Germany and are free. There is also the possibility of attending a private school with special educational methods (e.g. Steiner schools or Montessori schools). About 1 per cent of the students attend these schools.

For disabled pupils (impaired vision, hard of hearing or learning disabilities) there are special schools, or individual classes integrated into regular school operations. For delinquent adolescents and for adolescents classified as 'trainable with difficulty' there are special national education homes with psychological and medical care.

A usual school day lasts (e.g. in Bavaria) from 8 a.m. to 1 p.m., divided into six periods of 45 minutes with one or two breaks. There can also be lessons in the afternoon. Girls and boys are usually taught together.

Following the fall of the Berlin Wall (1989) and German reunification (1990), social transformation occurred particularly in the east of Germany. Lang (1994) reports some changes in eastern schools. School personnel (head teachers and teachers) were exchanged, often against the will of the students and their parents; thus persons in whom pupils had confidence – especially important in times of change – went away. Furthermore, the classes of the GDR secondary school (a unitary type) were altered in favour of the western two- or three-type educational system. Despite these serious modifications, only 8 per cent of 1,706 pupils interviewed in the 'new *Lands*' of the Federal Republic, when asked in 1992, felt that their life situation was somewhat or much worse than before reunification (Kuhnke, 1994).

Definitions: violence, aggression, deviant behaviour

For the purposes of this chapter, violence or violent behaviour is taken as physical aggression. Olweus (1999, p.12) defines it as 'aggressive behaviour where the actor or perpetrator uses his or her own body or an object (including a weapon) to inflict (relatively serious) injury or discomfort upon another individual'. Thus, violence refers to the use of physical force or power. It does not include purely verbal aggression, or relational/ indirect aggression. Physical bullying (in which the aggression is repeated, against a less powerful individual) would be a subset of violent behaviour. Fights between equals, which are not bullying, would also be included.

The classification of the term 'violence' depends on the discipline within which the studies were executed. The *psychological* approach [above] is to regard violence as a subset of aggression; *educational-scientific* work sees aggression the other way around, as a subset of violence (e.g. Vieluf, 1993), whereas *sociological* and *criminological* approaches regard violence as a form of deviant behaviour (for an overview of the implications of the different approaches see, for example, Tillmann et al., 1999; Schubarth, 2000).

Physical quarrels in schools are almost exclusively called 'violence' (*Gewalt*) in German investigations. Not all research publications report with equal clarity which behaviours are regarded as violence (see Krumm, 1999). Some attention should be paid to comparing results of research on bullying. Bullying is a group phenomenon, which can use physical means among others, which occurs repeatedly over time, and whose main intention may be to gain status in the group (see Schäfer and Korn, 2001); thus there are differences from violence. Sexual harassment among pupils or between teachers and pupils is usually treated as an independent issue and is only rarely associated with other forms of deviant behaviour (e.g. Marquardt-Mau, 1995).

Knowledge

We carried out an extensive database inquiry in order to survey the status of research on violence in German schools. No national study about violence in schools, with a uniform instrument, has yet been undertaken, so a report for the Federal Republic of Germany is not yet possible. There are, however, a multitude of studies from different regions in Germany.

Statistics about violence: methods

Assassination attempts on asylum seekers' homes and other violent, xenophobic-motivated incidents in Hoyerswerda, Rostock, Moelln and Solingen since the start of the 1990s are assumed to be the stimulus for increasing scientific endeavours to research violence in schools (e.g. Tillmann, 1997).

Different measuring instruments are used by different researchers: 'violence' is not operationalized uniformly (if at all), and Disagree–Agree response scales range from dichotomous (e.g. Dettenborn and Lautsch, 1993) to 1-to-7 scales (e.g. Rostampour and Schubarth, 1997). Thus reported results of the inquiries permit only very limited comparisons (see Krumm, 1999), which is true also for the examples given below. Furthermore, it seems surprising to us that we could not find references to other European countries, either concerning the instruments, or the comparison of prevalences.

Mainly, pupils are surveyed. In addition, school head teachers (e.g. Meier et al., 1995; v. Spaun, 1997), caretakers and secretaries (Schwind, Roitsch and Gielen, 1999) and also parents (e.g. Hanewinkel and Eichler, 1999a) are used as sources of information. While all informants can give statements about their observations, nevertheless, detailed information about violent behaviour of students and experiences with violence (e.g. 'to be hit' or 'to hit') can only be obtained from those students who are themselves involved (Jäger, 1999). 'Observations' can probably be used to compare the view of different groups, but they are not good for the description of the commonly shared 'reality' and can not therefore be considered to be objective accounts of the frequency of violence in schools (Tillmann et al., 1999).

Statistics about violence: findings

Before presenting an overview of the reported data, this statement seems central to us: 'serious, criminally relevant crimes occur very rarely and are actually not typical of violence at schools' (Fuchs, Lamnek and Lüdtke, 1996, p.9). Qualitative interviews with students acknowledge that serious acts of violence are an unusual exception (Tillmann et al., 1999). Also, sexual harassment is only rarely admitted to in (standardized) interviews (Funk, 1995).

The typical form of violence in German schools is verbal violence. Reported rates of verbal violence are found to be far above those of physical violence (two to three times higher: Wetzels et al., 1999). Between schools, however, quite substantial differences are found concerning the prevalence of violence (e.g. Hanewinkel and Eichler, 1999b).

Many studies assert that there is a rise in violence. This is especially the case when teachers or school head teachers are asked to make judgements; for instance, half of the school head teachers and two-thirds of the teachers described a rise in the frequency of physical violence in Bochum (Schwind, Roitsch and Gielen, 1999). In contrast Wenzke (1997) could not find a rise of violence over five sequential years. He surveyed 650 students in Berlin and actually found a decrease in violent behaviour, in a longitudinal study from seventh to tenth grade. Willems (1993) found a volatile rise of police-registered xenophobic acts of violence after the media reports on the riots in Hoyerswerda and Rostock, which would lead to an apparent rise in general violence. The rise of violence in German schools – found commonly in the media – is thus at least disputed by research findings (Hamburger, 1993; Krumm, 1997; Willems, 1993), particularly since the causes of the alleged rise remain obscure.

Available comparative investigations reveal no substantial differences between individual *Lands* of the Federal Republic concerning the occurrence of physical violence at schools. While significant differences are found (e.g. in comparison of cities: Wetzels et al., 1999), their practical relevance appears unimportant.

Differences in the reported prevalence of violence between east German (smaller prevalence) and west German schools have been reported in surveys of school head teachers in 1993/94, and two years later in surveys of pupils. Schubarth and colleagues (1999) could not find these differences six years later; they found some adjustment in the east to a higher aggression level in the west, caused by unfavourable effects of modernization (such as a rise in unemployment). Wetzels and colleagues (2000) propose that increasing individualism as well as increasing social disintegration are new risks in the life of east German young people (see also Tillmann et al., 1999).

Gender differences, age and school type

Direct aggressive behaviour seems to correspond to the male role rather than the female role. Regarding physical forms of violence, boys are more often involved than girls, both as perpetrators and as victims (Tillmann et al., 1999). These findings are found in all studies that refer to gender differences. The opposite, however, is true concerning sexual harassment, which sees girls as victims more often than boys (Wetzels et al., 2000). Nevertheless, girls as well as boys report that girls are also involved in physical conflicts (Popp, 1999). Thus, direct interventions against violence should not under any circumstances refer only to boys.

A survey of 3,540 students in Hesse (sixth, eighth and ninth graders) found that 11.1 per cent of males (only 4.2 per cent females) were 'continuous perpetrators' (more often than *once a week*) and 51.6 per cent males (only 28.6 per cent females) were 'opportunity perpetrators' (*once a week* or less) (Tillmann et al., 1999). In a representative sample of 1,163 students (seventh and eighth graders) in Erlangen and Nuremberg (Bavaria), 52.0 per cent of boys and 77.6 per cent of girls indicated *not* having been 'beaten or kicked by other students' during the past six months (Lösel, Bliesener and Averbeck, 1999).

Agreement also seems to prevail that physical violence increases with age and peaks at 13 to 16 years (corresponding to seventh to tenth grade – and thus to puberty and beyond in boys); at older ages it decreases again.

Across the entire educational system the highest violence rates are found in schools for learning assistance (*Sonderschulen*), whereas *Gymnasien* have the lowest rates. Prevalence of violence in *Gesamtschulen, Haupt-* and *Realschulen* was found to be in the middle range (e.g. Holtappels and Meier, 1997).

Ethnic group

Münchmeier (2000) states that the contact between German and foreign young people is limited almost exclusively to (big city) schools (or universities). This contact, however, predominantly takes place on a dyadic basis. In contrast to this, Wetzels and colleagues (1999) show that in Munich more than half of the peer groups consist of both German and foreign young people.

In a study in Schleswig-Holstein, Ferstl, Niebel and Hanewinkel (1993) did not find systematic connections between the proportion of non-German pupils in the class (up to 27 per cent) and the characteristic rates of violence. In a representative pupil and teacher survey in Bavaria, Fuchs (1999) compared statements about acts of violence committed by German and non-German students. He found that non-German pupils were slightly more violent than German pupils (except for verbal violence); these differences, however, were very small and took place at a low level (on a four-point scale, the violence rate was about 0.2). In agreement with Schwind (1995) Fuchs found higher violence values in classes with more than 30 per cent non-German pupils, and also showed that this rise was not explained by increasing violent acts by non-German pupils, but by those of German pupils. It should be stated again, that even so the violence levels remained very low.

Pupils against pupils

Schwind, Roitsch and Gielen (1999) compared a west German and an east German *Land* (Saxony, n = 3,147 and Hesse, n = 3,540, considered as representative for both countries) and found that the violence prevalence rates were only slightly different. Over the period of a year, about 9 per cent of students of sixth, eighth and tenth grade reported generally having 'beaten up others' several times a month or more frequently, about 7 per cent having 'something taken away from others by violence', about 4 per cent having 'beaten others up on the way to school' and about as many to have 'taken weapons to school'.

Pupils against teachers

Ferstl, Niebel and Hanewinkel (1993) found in their Schleswig-Holstein (Kiel) sample that 13.5 per cent of pupils (mean age: 12.6 years) reported observing violent acts against teachers once, but only 2.7 per cent often or very often (Hanewinkel and Eichler, 1999a). These data certainly do not permit a statement about how often teachers are actually attacked violently by pupils.

Adults against pupils

Investigation of violence used by teachers against pupils is not possible in Germany, because the authority which must approve such investigations is at the same time the proper authority of the teachers.

The findings reported by Wetzels and colleagues (1999) seem remarkable in this context. They found that one out of ten ninth graders (about 15 years) of their Munich and Rostock sample said they had been physically abused by their parents before their twelfth birthday. Also, 20 per cent said they had been punished heavily and frequently, including being hit with an object. This suggests that approximately one in three young persons in Germany has already experienced physical violence in the family.

Use of weapons

Fuchs (1995) asked 3,400 pupils in Bavaria which weapons they took to school. Twenty-three per cent reported taking a knife to school at least once; however, Fuchs admits that pupils possibly do not regard knives as, strictly speaking, weapons. Other weapons were indicated comparatively rarely (e.g. tear gas 6 per cent). About 2 per cent of the total sample, or one in five of those pupils who took weapons to school, took four or more weapons. Fuchs could find no characteristics which differentiated these 'heavily' armed children and the remaining owners of weapons. Ninety-four per cent never threatened a schoolmate with a weapon and 96 per cent reported never being threatened with a weapon.

The use of weapons in violent conflicts seems to be a rare exception (Schubert and Seiring, 2000) and furthermore is seen by pupils as a sign of weakness ('he can't even defend himself without weapons': Böttger, 1997).

Action

Handling of violence: laws and regulations

Article 1 of German constitutional law (*Grundgesetz: GG*) defines human dignity as inviolable; article 2, paragraph 2 guarantees physical safety. The higher regional court in Saarland laid down in a resolution (as regards compulsory schooling) that teachers have the obligation to protect schoolchildren against 'damage to health and opportunity, and also from violation of other legally protected rights' (OLG Zweibrücken, resolution of 05.06.97, 6 U 1/97).

The German Federal Constitutional Court (*Bundesverfassungsgericht*), which is responsible for compliance with the constitution, sees national education in schools as a fundamental right (BverfGE 34, 165, SPE I A I S.21-21v); it is equal to the right of parents to educate their children (as embodied in the 1949 constitution – article 6 par. 2 GG). Thus, there is a passage in all school laws of the *Lands* which imposes on every school (apart from the teaching of knowledge) educational functions such as teaching students the ability to compromise and to be tolerant in relations with people of different opinions.

In some *Lands* (e.g. in Brandenburg) there are legal regulations for schools which stipulate in detail measures such as conflict mediation and disciplinary procedures. The legal bases in the Federal Republic of Germany are so far unambiguous: schools are to guarantee that 'their' students are protected against psychological and physical violations and damage. Nevertheless no clear statement can be made about the handling of violence in German schools. In principle, the handling of violence in German schools does not seem to be determined explicitly in a written form. Thus the threatening of sanctions is not easily understood by students and each case must be treated and discussed individually. Schools that execute explicit interventions against violence and which fix behavioural rules, are not yet the norm in Germany.

Federal/national level

In 1987, the German Federal Government followed the model of the USA and France by appointing a 'violence commission', called the 'independent government commission for the prevention and fight against violence' (*Gewaltkommission des Bundestags*). One of the functions of this commission was to develop concepts against violence in schools that were both related to practice and relevant to further action (http://www.nibis.ni.schule.de/infosos/gewaltko.htm, September 2000). Some suggestions for tackling and preventing violence in schools were presented at the end of 1989:

- Smaller classes and no more '*Mammut*' schools (really huge schools). Pupils should be educated to accept joint responsibility concerning conflict and sanction regulations, common fines and action to repair damage, creating tutorial groups and peer-supported action (suggestion 30).
- Arrangements for improvement of the 'school atmosphere'. The 'educational function' of teachers should be strengthened by

embellishment of curricular arrangements, and basic and advanced training for teachers should be undertaken so as to provide contact persons for personal problems. Reduction of bureaucratic regulations (suggestions 32 and 33).

- Training of pupils to detect situations leading to violence as well as to defuse or avoid such situations. Introduction of new lessons in jurisprudence to provide violence-free solutions of conflicts (suggestion 34).
- Early introduction of 'lessons in sexual matters' with consideration of partner-related behaviours, because some violent acts have a sexual aspect (suggestion 36).
- Better training for teachers in dealing with delinquent, violent behaviour of pupils (suggestion 40).
- Less tolerance of acts of violence in school. Teaching staff to intervene rapidly (suggestion 41).
- Creation of counselling committees within each school for support in case of conflicts between pupils and teachers (suggestion 42).

Level of the Lands of the Federal Republic

The following summary is based on telephone calls with a random sample of experts about violence prevention in ministries for education and cultural matters in different *Lands* of the Federal Republic, concerning programmes against violence in schools:

- Only a few of the suggestions of the independent violence commission specified above have been tackled, ten years after their publication.
- In all *Lands* of the Federal Republic there have been increasing efforts (since the start of the 1990s) to design programmes to reduce violence among young people. Primarily these programmes are recommendations to schools, so that schools can create specific programmes to tackle violence.
- Teacher training about violence in schools and direct interventions in schools (e.g. peer support training in conflict situations) has been undertaken by many *Lands*.
- In some *Lands* a 'round table panel' was created, in which representatives of different groups came together to develop further solutions (including ministries for education, internal or public affairs, and representatives of the police).
- There was no information available concerning co-operation between *Lands* over arrangements against violence in schools.
- A scientific component to evaluate the effect of measures against violence at schools, is only required in exceptional cases. The usual

form of 'success check' in the *Lands* is an acknowledgement by the schools, which is not an evaluation according to scientific criteria.

Exemplary arrangements from some *Lands* are enumerated in the following, which were determined from telephone interviews.

Baden Württemberg

- Since 1994, curricula of all school types have been modified. Educational targets: consideration and attention, tolerance and attention for the personal values and beliefs of others.
- *Land*-wide programme 'challenging violence' (co-operation between Ministry of Internal Affairs and Ministry for Education and Cultural Affairs).
- Since 2000/01, contact office for schools for violence prevention. Co-ordination and support function: project starting up and maintenance. Cooperation with ministries, state criminal police agency and national head office for political education.

Bavaria

- New curriculum design (including ethical issues): 1990 for *Gymnasien*, 1993 for *Realschulen*, in progress for *Hauptschulen*. New lesson forms: 'the educating curriculum' – interdisciplinary project lessons, action-oriented and situation-referred lessons and learning.
- Working group (Ministries of Education, Internal Affairs and Social Affairs).
- Mediation: conflict mediation training (teacher training).

Brandenburg

- 1999: 'regulation on conflict conciliation, education and order arrangements'.
- Since 1993, co-operation programme between schools and sport clubs.
- Six schools participating in a project on 'violence prevention and intervention in conflicts' (conflict mediation project).

Hamburg

- Since 1993, first consulting centre (with two psychologists) of a school administrative board exclusively for violence prevention. Capacity to give immediate practical support with acute violence incidents. Support to schools to develop school policies.

- Project: 'prisoners help adolescents', co-operation with police and law. Young people prone to conviction can, accompanied by teachers, talk to people in prison about the consequences of delinquent behaviour.
- Gender-specific training: for example, girls taught self-defence are less likely to become victims.

Rheinland-Pfalz

- Guidelines: sports and play instead of violence, de-escalation, conflict mediation.
- Since 1994, a specific budget item (now (€500,000) for financial support (up to 50 per cent) of projects for violence prevention in schools. 2000: open awareness of schools about violence.
- Further plans: networking of projects like 'pupils as leisure assistants', 'sports and breaktime activities in schools'.

Saarland

- School head teachers are advised to tell the ministry about incidents of violence against persons.
- Ministry promotes school projects by subsidies.
- Different departments co-ordinate their work against 'violence in the school'.

Saxony

- Emphasis on the content-related design of lessons (education for democracy). A sensitization to violence is expected via reflection of norms and human values. Additional specifications to the curriculum in 1996 and 1997.
- Options for schools to organize round-table discussions with police assigned to violence prevention activities ('safety partnership school–police').
- Concept school youth work (so far 300 schools), financial budget: (€1,750,000; music competitions (to attract at risk groups).

Saxony-Anhalt

- Prevention arrangements as a topic (for a positive school climate: partnership of teachers and pupils is needed against school truancy).
- Since 1994, project: 'school stress-aggression-relaxation' (all the schools received movement devices), with scientific participation by Professor Knopf, Uni Halle Wittenberg.

- Mediation: twenty-four facilitators for conflict mediation were trained (co-operation with federations).
- School social work: sixty-four projects at seventy schools: co-operation of school and juvenile welfare service.

Schleswig-Holstein

- Controlled resources for violence prevention.
- Olweus project: 47 schools, 15,000 pupils.
- Prevention in the team (PIT), about 170 schools: 'preventing crime' lessons in secondary stage I; various training materials (e.g. 'eighty-eight ways forward to prevent violence').
- 1999: Conflict mediation: at thirty-six schools; seventy-five teachers trained as facilitators.

Interventions/evaluations

Bibliographic evaluation and information from the ministries for education and cultural affairs show that empirical studies to evaluate the effectiveness of the suggested measures are completely absent. Real improvement via behavioural modifications in schools is only reported for approaches that address not only perpetrators or victims but use a whole-school approach – and even then only in a few school situations (Nolting and Knopf, 1998).

Hanewinkel and Eichler (1999b) report on the largest intervention in Germany, based on the Olweus programme, carried out in Schleswig-Holstein in forty-seven schools (14,788 pupils) and evaluated at thirty-seven of these schools (10,600 pupils). The participating schools took part voluntarily. The second assessment was twelve months (two schools), eighteen months (five schools) or twenty-four months (thirty schools) after the first assessment. The second assessment took place with age groups matched to those in the first assessment, and thus did not measure changes in the same pupils. However, the analysis was not executed at the school level.

The arrangements included summoning a school conference, discharging a programme with school-specific arrangements at school level, an introduction of class rules at class level (this should form the basis of the intervention), regular class discussions and intensive discussions between teachers, bullies, victims and their parents at the individual level. Olweus's concept refers not just to physical forms of violence, but to bullying. However, with successful intervention physical violence should be reduced anyway.

The responsibility for the execution of the intervention (creating principles, temporal co-ordination and motivation of the teachers) was with the schools. Hanewinkel and Eichler (1999b) report substantial differences in fulfilling this responsibility, 'so that a uniform intervention can not be spoken of' (p.252) and they give this as a main reason for very varying success of the intervention.

Unfortunately they do not report prevalence rates for physical violence. For the victims (following Olweus's definition of serious bullying) they report direct bullying (including physical forms) in primary school (third and fourth grade) and in the lower levels of secondary school (fifth and sixth grade) an average reduction of about 2 per cent. Prevalence rates for victims in seventh, eighth, ninth and tenth grade remained almost unchanged, while in higher grades (eleventh and twelfth grade) an increase of around 6 to 10 per cent was measured. The authors suggest the latter may be a sensitization effect due to the interventions. They express their suspicion that the instrument might not be optimal for assessment either in the course system, nor for this (high) age-group. They expected the questionnaire to detect at least a reduction of physical violence.

Due to the mixed success of the intervention, Hanewinkel and Eichler suggest the following conditions as being necessary for further optimization of this programme (see also Busch and Todt, 1999):

- a functioning communication network has to be developed and maintained;
- successes must be made visible for the whole school;
- besides a motivated and motivating head teacher, all other teachers should support the educational concept.

This is confirmed by Nolting and Knopf (1997) who emphasize that consent between teachers on intervention or prevention arrangements can reduce violence at school. They report on an intervention also based on the Olweus programme, but which works primarily through regular discussions about rules of behaviour in all classes (such as supporting attacked schoolmates to stop aggressive behaviour and to encourage positive behaviour). However, they think that the extent and duration of the effects and the meaning of the individual interventions need further observation and clarification.

Verbeek, Petermann and Jugert (1998) implemented social training in third to sixth grades as preventive arrangement against violence in school. They found that a tendency to quickly become aggressive when faced with conflict could be reduced by this training. This effect was assessed in four schools in Bremen by an instrument developed by the authors. Training took place in ten sessions, where the whole class participated in discussing and dealing with the topic (e.g. self-perception processes, cooperative behaviour). The introduction was followed by getting consent about class regulations (e.g. 'everyone may dissuade from' and 'everyone may say something') and a relaxation phase, and then work started: role-playing and interaction plays were introduced to implement a certain tenor which pupils can easily transfer to their everyday life in the school. The sessions were terminated by feedback about keeping the communication rules valid, and finished with a play.

Summary

- A study across the *Lands*, representative for Germany, and validated by an internationally accepted instrument, is definitely missing. Therefore results can not be integrated into a larger framework.
- To deal with the differences reported on the occurrence of violence between schools, we recommend selecting 'school' as a level of analysis. It remains unclear why this has not been done.
- There are numerous and creative suggestions, projects and programmes against violence in schools, but as long as nobody cares about their scientific evaluation, any success remains 'miraculous'. Thus the ways to deal with violence are limited to what the *Lands* pronounce as political or ethical targets but are not accessible to scientific examination. Through goodwill and several interventions a lot is set into action, but the effect can be considered as remaining doubtful.
- Even if statements by some ministries for education and cultural affairs are taken seriously, serious doubts about the effect of the interventions are reasonable: on the one hand, the picture has developed that a great deal has already been done concerning violence at schools; on the other hand, there are (still) serious complaints about the increase in violence.

References

Böttger, A. (1997). Panikmache oder 'bittere Wahrheit'? Überlegungen und Forschungsergebnisse zum Thema 'Gewalt in Schulen'. *Empirische Pädagogik*, 11, 181–194.

Busch, L. and Todt, E. (1999). Aggression in Schulen. In H.G. Holtappels, W. Heitmeyer, W. Melzer and K.-J. Tillmann (eds). *Forschung über Gewalt an Schulen*. Weinheim: Juventa. pp.331–350.

Dettenborn, H. and Lautsch, E. (1993). Aggression in der Schule aus der Schülerperspektive. *Zeitschrift für Pädagogik*, 39, 745–774.

Federal Statistical Office (2000). <http://www.statistik-bund.de/basis/d/biwiku/schultabn.htm>(accessed July 2000).

Ferstl, R., Niebel, G. and Hanewinkel, R. (1993). *Gutachterliche Stellungnahme zur Verbreitung von Gewalt und Aggression an Schulen Schleswig-Holsteins*. Die Ministerin für Bildung, Wissenschaft, Kultur und Sport des Landes Schleswig-Holstein.

Fuchs, M. (1995). Waffenbesitz bei Kindern und Jugendlichen. In H.v. Alemann (ed.). *Mensch Gesellschaft! Lebenschancen und Lebensrisiken in der neuen Bundesrepublik.* Opladen: Leske and Budrich. pp.103–120.

Fuchs, M. (1999). Ausländische Schüler und Gewalt an Schulen. In H.G. Holtappels, W. Heitmeyer, W. Melzer and K.-J. Tillmann (eds). *Forschung über Gewalt an Schulen.* Weinheim: Juventa. pp.119–136.

Fuchs, M., Lamnek, S. and Lüdtke, J. (1996). *Schule und Gewalt. Realität und Wahrnehmung eines sozialen Problems.* Opladen: Leske and Budrich.

Funk, W. (ed.) (1995). *Nürnberger Schüler-Studie 1994. Gewalt an Schulen.* Regensburg: Roderer.

Hamburger, F. (1993). Gewaltdiskurs und Schule. In W. Schubarth and W. Melzer (eds). *Schule, Gewalt und Rechtsextremismus.* Opladen: Leske and Budrich.

Hanewinkel, R. and Eichler, D. (1999a). Gewalt an Schulen Schleswig-Holsteins. In M. Schäfer and D. Frey (eds). *Aggression und Gewalt unter Kindern und Jugendlichen.* Göttingen: Hogrefe. pp.53–64.

Hanewinkel, R. and Eichler, D. (1999b). Ergebnisse einer Interventionsstudie zur Prävention schulischer Gewalt. In M. Schäfer and D. Frey (eds). *Aggression und Gewalt unter Kindern und Jugendlichen.* Göttingen: Hogrefe. pp.245–264.

Holtappels, H.G. and Meier, U. (1997). Schülergewalt im sozialökologischen Kontext der Schule. *Empirische Pädagogik,* 11, 117–133.

Jäger, R.S. (1999). Gewaltprävention. In M. Schäfer and D. Frey (eds). *Aggression und Gewalt unter Kindern und Jugendlichen.* Göttingen: Hogrefe. pp.203–244.

Krumm, V. (1997). Gewalt in der Schule. *Empirische Pädagogik,* 11, 111–115.

Krumm, V. (1999). Methodenkritische Analyse schulischer Gewaltforschung. In H.G. Holtappels, W. Heitmeyer, W. Melzer and K.-J. Tillmann (eds). *Forschung über Gewalt an Schulen.* Weinheim: Juventa. pp.63–79.

Kuhnke, R. (1994). Der gesellschaftliche Umbruch und seine Folgen für die Befindlichkeit, Identität und Verhaltensorientierung. In W. Bien, U. Karig, R. Kuhnke, C. Lang and M. Reißig, *Cool Bleiben – Erwachsen werden im Osten.* München: Verlag Deutsches Jugendinstitut. pp.31–78.

Lang, C. (1994). Schule als Eintrittspforte in die Leistungsgesellschaft. In W. Bien, U. Karig, R. Kuhnke, C. Lang and M. Reißig, *Cool Bleiben – Erwachsen werden im Osten.* München: Verlag Deutsches Jugendinstitut. pp.113–136.

Lösel, F., Bliesener, Th. and Averbeck, M. (1999). Erlebens- und Verhaltensprobleme von Tätern und Opfern. In H.G. Holtappels, W. Heitmeyer, W. Melzer and K.-J. Tillman (eds). *Forschung über Gewalt an Schulen.* Weinheim: Juventa. pp.137–154.

Marquardt-Mau, B. (ed.) (1995). *Schulische Prävention gegen sexuelle Kindesmisshandlung.* Weinheim: Juventa.

Meier, U., Melzer, W., Schubarth, W. and Tillmann, K.-J. (1995). Schule, Jugend und Gewalt. Ergebnisse einer Schulleiterbefragung in Ost- und Westdeutschland. *Zeitschrift für Sozialisationsforschung und Erziehungssoziologie,* 15, 168–182.

Münchmeier, R. (2000). Miteinander – Nebeneinander – Gegeneinander? Zum Verhältnis zwischen deutschen und ausländischen Jugendlichen. In Deutsche Shell (ed.). *Jugend 2000.* Opladen: Leske and Budrich. pp.222–260.

Nolting, H.-P. and Knopf, H. (1997). Gewaltverminderung in der Schule: Erprobung einer kooperativen Intervention. *Praxis der Kinderpsychologie und Kinderpsychiatrie,* 46, 195–205.

Nolting, H.-P. and Knopf, H. (1998). Gewaltverminderung in der Schule: Viele Vorschläge – wenig Studien. *Psychologie in Erziehung und Unterricht*, 45, 249–260.

Olweus, D. (1999). Sweden. In P.K. Smith, Y. Morita, J. Junger-Tas, D. Olweus, R. Catalano and P. Slee (eds). *The Nature of School Bullying: A Cross-national Perspective*. London: Routledge. pp. 7–27.

Popp, U. (1999). Geschlechtersozialisation und Gewalt an Schulen. In H.G. Holtappels, W. Heitmeyer, W. Melzer and K.-J. Tillmann (eds). *Forschung über Gewalt an Schulen*. Weinheim: Juventa. pp.207–223.

Rostampour, P. and Schubarth, W. (1997). Gewaltphänomene und Gewaltakteure. Befunde aus einer Schülerbefragung in Sachsen. *Empirische Pädagogik*, 11, 135–150.

Schäfer, M. and Korn, S. (2001). Bullying – eine Definition. *Psychologie in Erziehung und Unterricht*, 48, 236–237.

Schubarth, W. (2000). *Gewaltprävention in Schule und Jugendhilfe*. Neuwied: Luchterhand.

Schubarth, W., Darge, K., Mühl, M. and Ackermann, C. (1999). Im Gewaltmaß vereint? Eine vergleichende Schülerbefragung in Sachsen und Hessen. In H.G. Holtappels, W. Heitmeyer, W. Melzer and K.-J. Tillmann (eds). *Forschung über Gewalt an Schulen*. Weinheim: Juventa. pp.101–118.

Schubert, B. and Seiring, W. (2000). Waffen in der Schule – Berliner Erfahrungen und Ansätze. *Praxis der Kinderpsychologie und Kinderpsychiatrie*, 49, 53–69.

Schwind, H.-D. (1995). Handlungsstrategien aus kriminologischer Sicht. In K. Hurrelmann, C. Palentien and W. Wilken (eds). *Anti-Gewalt-Report: Handeln gegen Aggressionen in Familie, Schule und Freizeit*. Weinheim: Beltz. pp.211–229.

Schwind, H.-D., Roitsch, K. and Gielen, B. (1999). Gewalt in der Schule aus der Perspektive unterschiedlicher Gruppen. In H.G. Holtappels, W. Heitmeyer, W. Melzer and K.-J. Tillmann (eds). *Forschung über Gewalt an Schulen*. Weinheim: Juventa. pp.81–100.

Spaun, v., K. (1997). Ausgewählte Ergebnisse zur, großen Gewalt aus der Erhebung an bayerischen Schulen im Schuljahr 1992/93. *Empirische Pädagogik*, 11, 107–110.

Tillmann, K.J. (1997). Gewalt an Schulen. Öffentliche Diskussion und erziehungswissen-schaftliche Forschung. *Die Deutsche Schule*, 89, 36–49.

Tillmann, K.J., Holler-Nowitzki, B., Holtappels, H.G., Meier, U. and Popp, U. (1999). *Schülergewalt als Schulproblem. Verursachende Bedingungen, Erscheinungsformen und pädagogische Handlungsperspektiven*. Weinheim: Juventa.

Verbeek, D., Petermann, F. and Jugert, G. (1998). Verhaltenstrainings in der Schule. *Verhaltenstherapie und Verhaltensmedizin*, 19, 253–269.

Vieluf, U. (1993). Gewalt an Schulen? Ergebnisse einer Schulbefragung in Hamburg. *Pädagogik*, 45, 28–30.

Wenzke, G. (1997). Gewalt und Fremdenfeindlichkeit an den Schulen. Ein Querschnittsvergleich über fünf Untersuchungsorte. *Empirische Pädagogik*, 11, 151–166.

Wetzels, P., Enzmann, D., Mecklenburg, E. and Pfeiffer, C. (1999). *Gewalt im Leben Münchner Jugendlicher*. KfN-Abschlussbericht. Hannover: KfN.

Wetzels, P., Mecklenburg, E., Wilmers, N., Enzmann, D. and Pfeiffer, C. (2000). *Gewalterfahrungen, Schulschwänzen und delinquentes Verhalten Jugendlicher in Rostock*. KfN-Abschlussbericht. Hannover: KfN.

Willems, H. (1993). Gewalt und Fremdenfeindlichkeit. Anmerkungen zum gegenwärtigen Gewaltdiskurs. In H.-U. Otto and R. Merten (eds). *Rechtsradikale Gewalt im vereinigten Deutschland.* Opladen: Leske and Budrich. pp.88–108.

Part II

Mediterranean countries

Chapter 8

Portugal

The gap between the political agenda and local initiatives

João Sebastião, Joana Campos and
Ana Tomás de Almeida

Background

The country

The Portuguese population in the 1991 Census was 9,862,540 and in 2001 grew to 10,318,084. There is a slow growth, which hides different tendencies: for decades, especially from the 1950s until the mid-1980s, this slow growth was the result of the difference between population growth and emigration. Nowadays it results from ageing and is one of the most reduced rates of population growth in the European Union.

Culturally Portugal has a unique trajectory in the European context (Barreto, 2000). During the last eight centuries the frontiers were stable and one common language was widely shared, so that it was possible to speak of a monocultural country. There were few cultural minorities, and until recently few foreigners (about twenty thousand in 1960, almost all of whom were European). This situation has changed in the last two decades. The long-lasting emigration that had been characteristic, greatly reduced, and at the same time Portugal became a point of arrival for significant numbers of Africans coming from ex-Portuguese colonies, and Brazilians, as well as Europeans.

School system

The 1986 Portuguese Basic Law of Educational System established its current organizational shape. The first level of the educational system is pre-school education from ages 3 to 6; it is not compulsory. The basic compulsory education is composed of three grades, and children must attend between the ages of 6 and 15. The amount and content of each curricular area is determined nationally, but every school does its own curriculum management (Ministério de Educação).

The first grade of basic compulsory education involves four years in a class with the same teacher. Second grade lasts two years, and has a regimen of multiple teachers, but keeping some aggregation of learning areas. The third grade lasts three years and the end of this marks the first point of exit from the educational system and entrance into the labour market. Evaluation in Basic Education has a progressive perspective, pupils' progress being evaluated by various means. At second and third grade some pupils who make poor progress may be retained in that grade.

Secondary education lasts three years and is not compulsory; there are three different paths. Regular and technological courses coexist in the same schools. Professional schools guarantee training for specific areas and result from partnerships between local and national educational agents. Finally, the second chance school, for those who could not finish their basic or secondary education, is organized according to a model of adult education. It has an after-work timetable and also gives professional and/or educational training for access to higher education or directly to the work market. At secondary education the grade retention scheme for poorly achieving pupils also operates.

First grade schools can be small – only fifteen to twenty pupils in rural areas – up to about 200 pupils in urban areas. Second and third grade, and secondary schools have from around 500 to 1,000 pupils.

Pupils with special educational needs can be placed in regular education, with the support of teams constituted by specialized teachers and psychologists. These teams must produce an individual plan of evaluation for each child. Pupils of compulsory education age who cannot be placed in regular education must attend special care schools.

Linguistic/definitional issues

To identify the terminology used to discuss violence in schools, various documents and statistics were analysed: a group of official documents produced during the genesis and the execution of the Safe School Programme (inter-ministerial protocols, school guards' regulations, questionnaires used to report deviant incidents and statistics) and the regulations for student national guides and for schools internally.

Official documents are characterized by little use of the term violence (*violência*) and a total absence of any kind of definition. Documents from the Safe School Programme systematically use the words (in)security (*insegurança*) or marginality (*marginalidade*) to describe all the situations considered deviant from the school norm. Within the same general category are situations as different as bomb scares, drug trafficking or thefts and assaults. This situation has been current in the questionnaires used to report deviant incidents by the Security Cabinet since 1986. The revision of these questionnaires came with the progressive understanding, by the authorities, that most of the registered situations were committed inside the school by students and were not the result of outsiders coming from problematic neighbourhoods. Words like bullying (this word does not exist in Portuguese; we use the English term) and violence (*violência*) appear for the first time, but still mixed with indiscipline, racism or sexual abuse inside the general category of actions against persons (*acções contra as pessoas*).

The national guide for students' rights and duties in the regulations for school, one main document for the production of local regulations, also never mentions violent situations. Its strategy is focused on the promotion of prosocial behaviour and students' civic and educational training instead of trying to categorize students' behaviour.

Relevant historical background

Violence in schools became an educational issue for the first time during the 1990s, mainly through the persistence of parental associations and teachers' unions. However, this was not the first time that violence appeared in Portuguese schools to a significant extent (Sebastião et al., 1999). For decades, during the dictatorship, police violence against students was common inside universities. After the democratization of 25 April 1974 the number of violent situations reached a peak at which the intense political debate in schools often ended in physical confrontations between students and even teachers. Nevertheless this was a politically socialized and framed violence, quite different from the kind of violence we can find today. Small theft, random or systematic physical aggression, bullying, destruction of school or teachers' property are realities which became common during the last decade.

It was only in 1992 that a political measure was taken for the first time specifically to control the rise of violent situations inside schools. Politically its origin and implementation was based on a protocol between the Ministry of Education and the Internal Affairs Ministry. This protocol was signed with the purpose of combining the efforts of school authorities and police forces; it was quite brief and excluded any pedagogical dimension. From it resulted the Safe School Programme, which was implemented in a progressive number of schools during the following years, co-ordinated by the Security Cabinet of the Ministry of Education.

The recognition of a gap between the pedagogical and the security dimensions led the political authorities to develop at local level the Educational Territories of Priority Intervention (ETPI), and later, at national level, the co-operation between the ministries of education, health, social security and internal affairs in order to promote new dimensions of intervention and research.

Knowledge

Statistics

The scientific research and the available data on violence in Portuguese schools is limited, being essentially made up of the reports of the Security Cabinet of the Ministry of Education (GS/ME) plus two empirical studies.

The information produced by the Security Cabinet of the Ministry of Education suggests that a significant part of the growing feelings of insecurity, revealed by school communities, has its roots in increasing media attention and has no strong support in data about violence in schools. This Security Cabinet data is based on the occurrences reported by executive committees and school security agents and it is characterized by its non-exhaustive nature. There are some other factors affecting the reliability of this data. The difficulty of defining violent situations, the dramatization of incidents in school daily life, and the belief that violent situations contribute to the degradation of a school's image contribute equally to the low level of reports of violence by some school executive committees.

A growth in reports of violent situations between 1995 and 1997 is shown by the Security Cabinet reports, across almost all the country, even if these represent only those reported. The unequal distribution of occurrences across the nation is considerable, the higher frequencies being found in Lisbon and Porto's metropolitan areas (Table 8.1).

The total numbers must be considered relative to the total of 10,000 schools, 1,500,000 students, 150,000 teachers and 50,000 employees in Portuguese schools. From the Security Cabinet point of view these are relatively low numbers, due to measures taken by schools, and by the monitoring of schools by security forces, for example the increasing

Table 8.1 Regional distribution of violent situations as reported by schools; frequency and percentage of the country total (1995–1998)

Regional Education Direction (DRE)	1995		1996		1997		1998	
	No.	%	No.	%	No.	%	No.	%
Lisbon	198	45.7	557	60.9	548	57.7	488	59.8
Porto/North	147	34.0	192	21.0	236	24.9	185	22.7
Centre	32	7.4	96	10.5	76	8.0	61	7.5
Algarve/South	48	11.1	45	4.9	58	6.1	58	7.1
Alentejo/South	8	1.9	24	2.6	31	3.3	24	2.9
Total	**433**		**914**		**949**		**816**	

Source: Security Cabinet of the Ministry of Education, 1999.

Table 8.2 Violent situations as reported by schools, by type, and by whether inside or outside school; frequency of occurrence and percentage (1995–1998)

	1995		1996		1997		1998	
Occurrences	No.	%	No.	%	No.	%	No.	%
Robbery/vandalism	248	62.5	408	44.6	376	39.6	258	31.7
Drugs	27	6.8	61	6.7	80	8.4	43	5.3
Shots fired	1	0.3	9	1.0	5	0.5	19	2.3
Bomb threat	18	4.5	312	34.1	238	25.1	81	9.9
Sexual abuse	5	1.3	10	1.1	26	2.7	43	5.3
Fire	4	1.0	2	0.2	1	0.1	5	0.6
Alcoholism	1	0.3	–	–	2	0.2	–	–
Racism	–	–	1	0.1	1	0.1	3	0.4
Violence inside school	57	14.4	58	6.4	117	12.3	161	19.8
Violence outside school	36	9.1	47	5.1	92	9.7	161	19.8
Others	–	–	6	0.7	11	1.2	41	5.0
Total	**397**	**100**	**914**	**100**	**949**	**100**	**815**	**100**

Source: Security Cabinet of the Ministry of Education, 1999.

protection of school buildings by police forces and school guards and the hire of night guards.

Another interesting aspect is the type of incidents and their place of occurrence (Table 8.2). Incidents occur more in the interior of school grounds, particularly in the less supervised areas: recreation zones, corridors, bathhouses and toilets. Of the appreciable number of bomb threats, about 80 per cent are given in learning periods coinciding with the school year beginning, the examination periods and the carnival holiday; however, in all cases these were just threats, with no bombs actually exploding.

In 1999 the Security Cabinet of the Ministry of Education tried to overcome the data difficulties that had been noted, by changing the data collection instruments and especially by introducing new categories. For this reason data before and after 2000 has different indicators, making a comparative perspective or a historical understanding of the phenomena impossible.

The Security Cabinet occurrences registration for 2000 is presented in percentage terms, and distinguishes between actions against goods and actions against people. The report considers *actions against people* as occurrences against the physical and psychological safety of any individual; see Table 8.3 for a breakdown. Bullying actions constitute 19.2 per cent of the total, actions against people inside school 28.6 per cent, actions against people outside school 23.7 per cent, and other actions against people 28.4 per cent. The information is also broken down by region, see Table 8.4, and by where it happened.

Table 8.3 Types of violent situations reported by schools in 2000

Actions against goods	Frequency
Equipment theft	269
Vandalism against equipment	158
Fire	17
Shots fired	8
Teachers' property stolen	24
Employees' property stolen	10
Students' property stolen	87
Total	**573**

Actions against people	
Bullying	179
Violence inside school	336
Violence outside school	238
Sexual abuse	20
Gangs	77
Illegal drugs	232
Legal drugs	42
Racist attitudes	9
Bomb threat	105
'Blade' weapons	56
Fire weapons	6
Total	**1,300**

Source: Safe School Programme final report, 2000.

Table 8.4 Violent actions against people as reported by schools, by region; frequency and percentage of the country total in 2000

Regional Education Direction (DRE)	Frequency	Percentage
North	1,195	37.7
Centre	213	6.7
Lisbon/Centre	1,569	50.4
Alentejo/South	34	1.1
Algarve/South	129	4.1

Source: Security Cabinet of the Ministry of Education, 2000.

In addition to this information produced by the Security Cabinet of the Ministry of Education and the Safe School Programme, two other studies developed by Minho University and the Educational Innovation Institute can be described. Despite limitations of regional focus or methodology, they contribute to filling some of the existing dearth of information.

The study developed by the Child Studies Institute of Minho University in 1994 consisted of a questionnaire given to 6,200 pupils of the first and second grades of basic education, in eighteen public schools in the Braga and Guimarães districts. Despite its regional character the sample was intended to be representative of rural and urban areas, gender and social classes. The study's main goals were: the identification of aggressors and victims; understanding the nature of aggression; and the types of aggression and where they occurred.

A profile of the aggressors and victims was established: aggressors were mainly found among male pupils, coming from lower social class backgrounds and attending first grade schools in suburban areas. A positive correlation was found between the years in delay (years of grade retention due to poor academic progress) and aggression. Victims were generally found among male pupils of urban schools from the early years of schooling; only about one-half told their parents of their plight (50.4 per cent) or teachers (46.1 per cent). The most frequent places in which aggression occurred were the playground (50.8 per cent), classrooms (21.6 per cent), corridors and stairs (18.0 per cent) and the canteen (3.6 per cent).

The Educational Innovation Institute developed the second research project, in 1998. They gave a questionnaire to a sample of 5,000 pupils in 144 schools of third grade basic education and secondary education. Analysis was by gender, age and school year (second year of third grade, and first year of secondary). The main findings point to more aggression among male pupils. Physical and verbal aggression occur more inside school limits. Outside school violent confrontations occur predominantly between groups. Thus, 17.0 per cent of the pupils say they have witnessed violent confrontations inside school limits, and 19.1 per cent outside. Physical aggression is most frequent against the youngest male pupils. Sexual aggression (touching and exhibitionism) has the highest incidence against the youngest girls. Aggressors are mainly acquaintances when the aggression is inside school, but strangers when it occurs outside school.

Current national/regional policies regarding violence in school

The presence of violent situations in Portuguese schools led, during the last one and a half decades, to a collection of political measures characterized by different understandings of their causes and basic philosophies of intervention (Teixeira, Delgado and Sebastião, 1996).

One view is based on the idea that youthful delinquents, coming from outside the school, provoke violence and create a climate of insecurity inside schools. This view stresses the idea of protecting schools from outside aggression, and led directly to the Safe School Programme. Another view is based on the idea that a significant proportion of the violent situations have their source in schools' failure to achieve their educational goals. We call this the pedagogical approach.

The Safe School Programme

From the mid-1980s to the mid-1990s, this programme remained the only policy to deal with school violence, and was based on a preventive policing view. This programme appeared after a number of violent acts (assaults, aggressions, destruction of property, sexual assault, etc.) occurred in schools; and it was thought that young outsiders, who came from problematic neighbourhoods, generally provoked them. More recently this conception has evolved, with the perception that students themselves provoke violence inside schools.

A non-systematic co-operation between the Ministry of Education and the Internal Affairs Ministry to make schools safer during the 1980s was followed by a protocol in 1992, which structured the co-operation under the name of the Safe School Programme. Its goal was the promotion of safety in schools so that freedom of learning and teaching could be made possible. The programme covers all the public schools directly managed by the Ministry of Education, which are classified into different levels of security.

The Security Cabinet of the Ministry of Education assures the co-ordination of the programme, and is also responsible for a company of security guards (school guards), recruited from among retired policemen. The school guards' activity is developed inside the schools, controlled by the Security Cabinet and the school board, and co-ordinated with local police, a night watchman and porters. Their main activity is the identification and prevention of potentially dangerous situations, but they cannot take part in school disciplinary action, unless requested by the school board.

The pedagogical approach

It is agreed that the Portuguese educational system should effectively guarantee access to all. However, the persistence of high rates of school failure and early dropout represents a problem far from being solved. According to the pedagogical approach, school failure and dropout are very significant factors in the origins of school violence. Many of the violent situations are seen as coming from students' frustration and result in the destruction of school equipment and teachers' property, and aggression to colleagues or school staff (teachers or others). The defenders of this point of view (a mixture of sociological and psychological ideas) mainly consider that it is inside the pedagogical field that violence can be solved or, at least, avoided, giving little importance to measures based on the use of policing inside school limits (except in very specific situations).

We can identify two different groups of measures arising from this approach. The first is composed of legislation about decentralized school management and Educational Territories of Priority Intervention. The second comprises measures such as flexible management of the curriculum (particularly its local adaptation); the possibility of having an alternative curriculum for underachieving students; changing the evaluation process of pupils; trying to reduce premature exclusion; supported study, which tries to promote individual skills and habits of study in students; and national guidance for school regulations of students' rights and duties, giving guidance for the promotion of prosocial behaviours.

Local initiatives and programmes

Research and intervention programmes led by the University of Minho

In this section, we outline the initiatives carried out in the northern part of the country, in the district of Braga, a region characterized by rapid socioeconomic development during the last two decades and with the highest proportion of young people under 18 in the European Union. Indeed, contrary to the majority of urban areas where the school population has been decreasing, Braga's schools are working above their capacity, overcrowded and normally multiplying the number of classes per level, in order to maintain an average of twenty-five students per class.

RESEARCH PROJECT I

At a local level, since 1993, researchers at the University of Minho have been conducting several studies and implementing programmes or encouraging schools to take action against bullying. According to a first survey (Almeida, Pereira and Valente, 1994; Almeida, 1999) carried out in the northern region of Portugal among 6,200 students from 6 to 17 years attending the first and second cycles of basic education (year one to year six), one in four boys and one in five girls reported being bullied more than three times in the last term.

Following the survey, the executive committees of the schools involved had access to the results and these were discussed in order to plan measures to reduce bullying. A massive information campaign took place through school meetings, seminars and conference days in schools, and at the university. In addition, two teacher training courses were organized. The selection procedure prioritized small groups of teachers from the same school to encourage teacher group work in planning interventions back in school.

RESEARCH PROJECT II

From 1997–2001, the research team at the University of Minho has been part of a European network whose major goals are studying the 'nature and causes of bullying and social exclusion in schools, and ways of preventing them', co-ordinated by Peter Smith (Goldsmiths College, London – www.gold.ac.uk/tmr). The aims of this European project are to promote conditions to develop research and short-term intervention programmes at national and cross-national basis through collaboration among teams.

DEFINITION OF TERMS STUDY

The terms used by children, adolescents and adults when referring to different types of aggression were studied to ascertain which were more appropriate to describe particular subcategories of aggressive behaviour (Almeida and Ólafsson, 1998; Smorti, Almeida, and Menesini, 1999). Focus groups, using cartoons as stimulus materials, elicited common words that describe different types of aggressive and bullying behaviour. Six terms were investigated (violence, abuse, to act superior or domineering, provocation, insult and rejection). Exploration of similarities and differences between the six terms show a marked overlap of terms at younger ages, but a clear differentiation of terms employed by adolescents and adults. The terms were most widely used with cartoons illustrating verbal aggression.

SCAN BULLYING – A SCRIPT-CARTOON NARRATIVE OF PEER BULLYING

A new assessment method has been designed to study children's and adolescents' understanding of bullying interpersonal relationships (Almeida et al., 2001). The method uses narrative cartoon material to elicit views of bullying, its causes and consequences, the emotional understanding of victims and aggressors and how they themselves would cope with it. Results from a validation study carried out in Braga (Portugal), Madrid (Spain) and Florence (Italy) using a sample of 180 children (age 9, 11 and 13 years old) have been positive.

OBSERVATIONAL APPROACH TO STUDY SOCIAL AND AGGRESSIVE BEHAVIOUR OF CHILDREN IN THE PLAYGROUND AND CO-OPERATIVE GROUP TASKS

This study is in progress and uses a combination of observational methodologies (ethological catalogues and Fogel's relational coding system) to analyse 9-year-olds' interactions with peers in a playground setting and in co-operative group tasks in the classroom (Costabile et al., 2000).

Preliminary results suggest that victims show increased difficulties in working constructively with others, and bullies spend more time alone or as onlookers in playground settings, without interacting in socially adaptive ways.

Building bridges to supportive school environments

This intervention study is being developed as part of a wider evaluation of anti-bullying programmes in Mediterranean countries, in Portugal, Spain and Italy, funded by the Comenius/Socrates programme (Almeida and Benítez, 2002). It focuses attention on the social and relational atmosphere of the school, and aims to implement structures of peer support and conflict mediation. It incorporates a programme of social and personal development in the school curriculum. The programme is based on the assumption that to create a respectful and co-operative educational environment it is necessary to enhance and support changes through curricular approaches and maintenance of a number of school services that sustain and give strength to the qualitative changes at a wider organizational level. Essentially, the programme is structured around three components: (1) personal and social skills training for tutors; (2) peer support models for pupils which integrate a befriending model at a class level and a peer support service at a school level; (3) a conflict mediation service held by teachers, school personnel, students and parents.

Case studies

The Alfornelos educational territory intervention (Lisbon)

This intervention started after a request made by the Alfornelos second and third grade basic school to the Centro Investigação Estudos Sociologia (CIES) team to see if, together, ways could be found to solve or avoid the degradation of school life which had occurred there. The school board and teachers referred to a vast and somehow confused range of factors that were preventing any possibility of effective teaching and learning. Among these, factors most referred to were a huge rate of school failure in certain groups of students, the increase in rates of dropout, the persistence of serious disciplinary problems, and several violent situations inside classrooms, schoolyards and in the neighbourhood. Later, the two schools of the first grade within the area joined the project.

The Alfornelos educational territory is situated in a very conflict-ridden urban area, divided between established white working and middle class housing and one-storey run-down homes, almost entirely inhabited by poor African immigrants or their Portuguese descendants. The initial intense discussions showed that the school had great difficulties in dealing with the social and cultural diversity of its students and the social problems that surrounded it.

The research team defined two main lines of action: the first was focused on interaction between educational actors present in the community; the second was centred directly on changing the internal school situation. The first asked for a strong mediation process, which enabled communication between the different institutional interventions, promoting their co-operation in the search for solutions for the problems detected. The second was based on the diversification of educational opportunities inside school.

The intervention process began with a meeting with wide participation, in which the opinions of about forty local institutions were heard. The structuring of a voluntary co-operation group, including two first grade schools in the area, two community associations working in the African neighbourhoods, the CIES team and the Alfornelos second and third grade basic school, gave a start and co-ordination to the process. This co-operation group worked in a democratic way, with one member one vote; decisions were always taken by consensus, even those affecting pedagogical projects inside the school. After some initial meetings it was decided that the 'pacification' of school life was the first main objective, being vital in order to achieve further changes. To achieve this, four measures were put in place:

- *Organization of a group of cultural animators*   These individuals attempted to establish contact with a significant group of children/ youths who, despite coming to school, did not attend classes, spending their time playing or provoking incidents with other children (aggression, small-scale robbery, intimidation), even invading classes. It is likely that for most of these children, school represented the only social and cultural resource present in their poor neighbourhoods. The policy of recruiting cultural animators from among young adults from the neighbourhoods of the most problematic children was based on the idea that someone was needed to mediate not only between peers, when conflict situations happened, but also between school and the children, and school and families. Their activity proved to be decisive, building bridges over cultural gaps and conflicts between students and school staff, and providing the possibility to initiate new educational opportunities.
- *Creation of new educational opportunities*   The objective was to create a richer educational environment through the promotion of new educational opportunities. This was especially important for children from families with poor school qualifications, for those in neighbourhoods where there was little to occupy their free time, and provided alternative ways of learning and teaching. A toys and games room, a

study room, a 'free time' area with cultural animators and a media archive open to all the educational community were put in place. Support for community associations was also provided so that they too could organize leisure time occupations for children. Another important measure was co-operation between associations and schools when disciplinary actions had to be carried out. Disciplinary sanctions were no longer a prize for deviant behaviour, which could mean some days without attending school and an increase of popularity among peers, but – when needed – were redefined in a more productive way, such as spending time doing community work in the associations, in the study room with personal learning plans, and in activities with the cultural animators.

- *Change of teacher and other professionals' practices* Most of the interventions depended, from the research team's point of view, on the possibility of promoting pedagogical practices that integrated the idea of social and cultural diversity. To achieve this, a training course in differential pedagogy was organized for teachers from the first and second level over two school years. Comprehension of and respect for the different cultural heritage of the students provided a basis for creating, by co-operation between groups of teachers of both levels, the pedagogical instruments that should be used in schoolwork by teachers and students. Simultaneously diverse pedagogical projects were put in place, promoting comprehension of cultural diversity and co-operation between the different school personnel.
- *Link between community and school life* Another of the project's starting points was the need to bring together schools, families and communities in the project. The traditional non-participation of families and the near-disappearance of the parents' association brought increased difficulty in understanding their needs and concerns about their children's school life. Community leaders and cultural animators performed a central role in establishing a link between teachers and parents, and progressively involving parents in the school.

After two and a half years, there have been both achievements and frustrations. The achievements were significant: mainly, a large reduction in violent situations, dropping out and absenteeism. There was also a general opinion that disciplinary problems showed a reduction, with complementary benefits in teacher–student relationships. Children were more integrated in school life by a net of different learning possibilities, and the idea that an adult would be always supervising reduced the space and opportunity for the appearance of violence.

Another important improvement was in the material and pedagogical enrichment of the school. Having been previously characterized by poor resources, the school now turned out to be more interesting for students, who could find there opportunities generally absent from their daily life. Several multicultural pedagogical projects were set up, trying to promote better involvement of all the school community. For the first time, some teachers participated in community activities or festivals, interacting directly with the parents.

Schools became more open; teachers from different schools co-operated for the first time in reducing problems in the students' transition between levels; and other educational partners, such as the community associations, started to be seen as active participants in the schooling process.

There were also some less successful outcomes, and some issues were only occasionally surmounted. The involvement of families was always restricted to a few initiatives, and never became a lasting tendency. Parents were more involved in their children's school education, but mainly through the mediation of associations. Complaints about different forms of discrimination and racism never disappeared among African parents. White parents complained about the 'excessive' attention given to African children, who were considered aggressive and responsible for the decrease of the school's overall learning level.

Another great disappointment consisted in the transformation of teachers' professional practices. Even though training in differential pedagogy was provided, and the group of teachers were really committed, its impact on school life was fragile. The causes for this failure can be found in organizational aspects. The project co-ordinator could not convince teachers to organize classes so that the trained teachers could work together with the same students.

Two-and-a-half years after the intervention started, a change of government coincided with the election of a new school board. In one of its first educational measures, the new government created the Educational Territories of Priority Intervention (ETPI), and Alfornelos was one of the first chosen, because of its mixed history of problems and the lack of community co-operation. The ETPI legislation brought some radical transformations to the status of each partner. The Territory Pedagogical Council was created, in which teachers from all scientific groups and schools were represented, and some community associations were invited if their aims were considered relevant for educational goals. This resulted in a dramatic change in the balance between the different partners. Community leaders were little by little turned away from schools. Under the argument of improving their training and the lower cost to the school budget, young unemployed psychologists or social workers coming from the public employment centre replaced the local cultural animators, and the animation activities were replaced by homework help. The CIES team was also turned away, and constrained to a more or less distant and brief participation in the Pedagogical Council, limited to academic research activities.

Gradually, the rate of early dropout picked up again; the serious disciplinary problems returned; violent situations became more and more frequent. School guards from the Safe School Programme and video surveillance of schoolyards came to 'help' control violence inside the school areas. Policemen from the local police station tried to prevent assaults outside.

Although this is an account of what, in the end, has been an unsuccessful experiment, it gives an opportunity for deep reflection about intervention methodologies in complex contexts. The diversity of strategies, the idea of a community network as a fundamental resource to fight back against violence, the change of a school's structure as a basis for pedagogical innovation, are conclusions which proved to have a large potential for change.

Final synthesis

As a first conclusion we can say that the excessive media attention, and the use of school violence as a political argument, makes the phenomenon appear larger than it really is and contributes to a growing feeling of insecurity, which is not really supported by data. Probably because of this context, large resources are being spent to combat violence, even if its management is questionable and reliable and extensive data are almost non-existent. Scientific research on the topic in Portugal is just beginning, and restricted to a few studies. Only a small number of researches and interventions were identified, based in three academic research centres. As a consequence, scientific publishing about conditions regarding school violence in Portugal is also minimal.

Two major intervention trends could be identified. The first trend is evidenced in extensive co-operation between the police corporations and the Security Cabinet of the Ministry of Education, based on the idea that school violence is brought to school by deviant students and outsiders (the Safe School Programme). Independent evaluations of the Safe School Programme were never published. The other trend is based on a set of pedagogical measures, whose ambition is centred in the reduction of school failure and dropout, seen as the major causes of violence.

References

Almeida, A. (1999). Portugal. In P. Smith, Y. Morita, J. Junger-Tas, D. Olweus, R. Catalano and P. Slee (eds). *The Nature of School Bullying: A Cross-national Perspective*. London: Routledge.

Almeida, A. and Benítez, J.L. (2002). Building bridges to supportive school environments (unpublished manuscript).

Almeida, A., Del Barrio, C., Marques, M., Gutierrez, H. and Van der Meulen, K. (2001). A Script-cartoon Narrative of Bullying in Children and Adolescents: A

Research Tool to Assess Cognitions, Emotions and Coping Strategies in Bullying Situations. In M. Martínez (ed.). *Prevention and Control of Aggression and the Impact on its Victims*. Dordrecht: Kluwer Academic/Plenum Publishers.

Almeida, A. and Ólafsson, R. (1998). Bullying definitions: a comparative study of children and adolescents. Presented at the IV Congresso Galaico-Português de Psicopedagogia, Braga.

Almeida, A., Pereira, B. and Valente, L. (1994). A violência infantil nos espaços escolares: dados preliminares de um estudo no 1° e 2° ciclos do ensino básico. In L. Almeida and I. Ribeiro (eds). *Avaliação Psicológica. Formas e Contextos*, 2, 225–262.

Barreto, A. (2000). *A Situação Social em Portugal 1960–1999. Indicadores Sociais em Portugal e na União Europeia*. Lisboa: Instituto de Ciências Sociais.

Costabile, A., Palermiti, A., Genta, M.-L., Bartolo, G., Laranjeira, J. and Almeida, A. (2000). *Observational Approach to Study Social and Aggressive Behaviour of Children in the Playground and Cooperative Group Work*. Online. Available HTTP: <http://www.gold.ac.uk/tmr>.

Ministério de Educação (1999). *Gestão Flexível do Currículo*. Lisbon: Departamento da Educação Básica, M.E.

Teixeira, L., Delgado, L. and Sebastião, J. (1996). Avaliar (n)a escola: quadros, modelos, práticas. *Sociologia, problemas e práticas*, 22, 95–107.

Sebastião, J., Seabra, T., Alves, M., Tavares, D., Martins, J. and Portas, M.J. (1999). A produção da violência na escola. *Revista da ESES*, Escola Superior de Educação de Santarém, 10, 123–135.

Smorti, A., Almeida, A. and Menesini, E. (1999). *Adults' Definition of Bullying and Social Exclusion in Children: A Cross-cultural Comparison*. Online. Available HTTP: <http://www.gold.ac.uk/tmr>.

Chapter 9

Working together to prevent school violence

The Spanish response

Rosario Ortega, Rosario Del Rey and Isabel Fernández

Background

The country

Spain is located in south-western Europe, occupying 80 per cent of the Iberian Peninsula. The Balearic Islands, the Canary Islands and, on the north coast of Africa, the autonomous cities of Ceuta and Melilla are also an integral part of the Kingdom of Spain. The Spanish kingdom occupies $504,750km^2$ and has a population of 40,202,160 inhabitants. Divided into seventeen autonomous communities, plus Ceuta and Melilla, which have their own governments, Spain is constituted as a social and democratic state of law. Its political form is a parliamentary monarchy and it has been part of the European Union since 1996.

Spain's strategic location, as an entrance to Europe, has resulted in a large influx of immigrants from Africa. Many of them do not come with the intention of settling down, although their numbers are increasing. The current number of immigrants is 719,647 or 1.8 per cent of the total population, although it is impossible to know the actual number because of illegal immigrants, a situation that new immigration legislation is intended to remedy. Gypsies, as a cultural group, are present in all of Spain, though in some areas in greater numbers than in others; despite being the object of racial discrimination, and despite problems in certain schools, they are integrated from an educational point of view.

The school system

The responsibility for the organization and administration of school education is shared by the national and regional governments. The national legislation establishes the right of all citizens to an education and makes education obligatory and free, but regional parliaments and governments have the administrative responsibility.

The state is required to provide facilities for pre-school education, but parents are not required to send their children. Compulsory education is from 6 to 16 years, and students have the right to remain in school until they are 18. The academic year begins in the middle of September and ends at the end of June; in primary school, students attend school twenty-five hours a week and in secondary school, twenty-eight to thirty. School size can vary from around 100 up to 1,500 pupils, although the usual range is 500 to 700; but classes have a maximum size of twenty-five pupils in primary and thirty in secondary education.

Public schools are maintained using state funds or funds from the autonomous communities; the obligatory levels of private subsidized schools are financed, through agreements, with public funds; finally, the non-subsidized private schools are maintained with their own funds. All the schools are required to teach along the general lines of the curriculum, or basic curricular design.

Although the state has designed a single curriculum, it can be adapted to the autonomous communities, to the school context, to each classroom and to each pupil. A certain level of academic performance is required, but if certain students do not reach these minimum objectives, there are programmes designed to give them the basic training necessary to become a part of the workforce. A main aim of the Spanish education system is the principle of integration in schools even for students with disabilities who, in the majority of cases, remain in ordinary schools.

Definitional issues: school violence as the opposite of convivencia

In Spain, the term *violencia escolar* or *school violence* is used by the media to refer to problems of aggression by students towards teachers and by students among themselves. Teachers tend to use the terms *conflict, lack of discipline, aggression* and *bad behaviour* to describe a series of behaviours that they are unable to control using traditional procedures. Students, on the other hand, use terms like *abuse, mistreatment, hitting, bothering,* and *making life impossible* to describe unjustified aggression.

In the last few years, it has become common to refer to these phenomena as problems of *convivencia*, or lack thereof, in order to show that the education authorities have an interest in adopting a positive vision of intervention in combating school violence. The Spanish term *convivencia* could be translated as coexistence, but it signifies not merely sharing time and space, nor merely tolerance of others, but also a spirit of solidarity, fraternity, co-operation, harmony, a desire for mutual understanding, the desire to get on well with others, and the resolution of conflict through dialogue or other non-violent means.

Following the Olweus (1999) concept of bullying and some details from the World Health Organization (Salomäki, 2001) definition, the term school violence will be defined here as any interpersonal activity or situation in which a member of the education community is being physically, psychologically or morally damaged (Ortega, 2001).

Relevant historical background

The 1985 Right to Education Law (LODE), modified in 1999, highlights the basic responsibility of students to respect the school's rules regarding *convivencia* and, in relation to the goals of education, emphasizes tolerance, respect for differences and personal development. In addition, it emphasizes the responsibility of the school board to 'resolve conflicts and impose disciplinary sanctions on students according to the rules that govern the students' rights and responsibilities'.

The regulations closest to the problem of lack of peaceful coexistence are the Decrees of Rights and Responsibilities of the students. The decree of 1995 (RD 732/1995) of the Ministry of Education regulates the rights and duties of students in a large number of autonomous communities. It states 'one of the main aims of education is the training of the students in the exercise of the rights and liberties within the democratic principles of *convivencia*'. It is established in some regions: Andalusia, Canarias, Cataluña, Navarra, País Vasco and Valencia. In the region of Andalusia, as an example, it states in Article 43.1 that 'the discipline to be applied for not complying with the rules of *convivencia* should be educational and rehabilitating in nature; it should guarantee that each student respect the rights of the rest of the students and bring about improvement in the relationships of all the members of the educational community'. Corporal punishment is completely prohibited in Article 43.2.

In Spanish educational culture, people are starting to understand the importance of *convivencia*, but the need to confront violence has still not been made explicit in the existing regulations. However, socially, there are numerous public debates in which some type of intervention is demanded in order to put an end to violent incidents that have recently taken place. These debates, in which researchers and experts are frequently asked to participate, take place in written and audio-visual media.

Knowledge

Only recently have researchers in Spain turned their attention to school violence; however, in the last ten years there has been considerable activity. Not only have studies been carried out by specific research groups, but also general surveys financed by state institutions and education ministries of some autonomous communities. We shall discuss these studies according to whether they were carried out at the national or regional level.

National studies

There are three national studies that in some sense deal with the problem of school violence. In an evaluation of secondary school teachers in 1995, of the 18,000 teachers surveyed, 72 per cent considered the lack of discipline at school a serious problem. Two years later, in a General Diagnosis of the Education System, 60 per cent of the teachers affirmed that there had been isolated cases of aggression among students in the previous three years, and in 7 per cent of the schools more than ten cases of serious aggression had occurred.

Finally, at the request of Parliament, the Ombudsman's Office (Ombudsman, 2000) carried out a national study on school bullying (Defensor del Pueblo, 2000). The aim, using a total sample of 3,000 secondary education students from 300 public, subsidized and private schools, was to determine the incidence of thirteen types of violent acts. Three hundred deputy head teachers were also surveyed, and their opinions can be compared with those of the students in relation to the same type of violent behaviour.

The results, although they do not provide a general index of violence, present very relevant data because they refer to a representative sample of the entire country. Table 9.1 highlights the most significant data;

Table 9.1 Type of school violence from the point of view of victims, aggressors and teachers (from the Ombudsman's report on school violence); percentages of respondents

Type of violence studied	Student victims (it happens to me sometimes)	Student aggressors (I do it sometimes)	Teachers (it happens sometimes)
Insult	33.8	40.9	76.7
Criticize	31.2	35.3	71.7
Ignore	30.1	35.1	67.0
Nickname	20.0	32.9	67.0
Hide things	14.0	12.2	66.0
Not allow to participate	8.9	11.7	63.0
Threaten	8.5	6.8	62.7
Hit	6.4	6.6	62.7
Steal	4.1	1.3	60.7
Break things	4.1	1.2	60.3
Sexual harassment	1.7	0.5	33.3
Threaten – weapons	0.7	0.3	15.7
Force to do things	0.6	0.3	10.0

insult, criticize, ignore and nickname are the most frequent in the Spanish secondary school, although teachers tend to give a high frequency for all of the types. The complete report gives detailed descriptions of gender, ages and places where students are most at risk; the results are generally in line with international studies and previous regional and local studies in Spain: boys and groups are more highly involved; the violent episodes are less frequent the younger the students; and verbal violence is more common than the other types.

Regional studies or studies from autonomous communities

Due to the decentralization of the Spanish system, most of the autonomous governments have recently been carrying out regional studies on *convivencia* in schools. Not all of them have been completed, but here we discuss those that have: Andalusia, Galicia, Navarra and Valencia.

In 1998, Andalusia undertook a descriptive study on school *convivencia*, abuse and peer violence, in which information regarding attitudes towards unjustified aggression is also presented. Ortega and Angulo (1998) studied 2,828 students of secondary education (12 to 16 years) from the eight Andalusian provinces, using self-report questionnaires. Table 9.2 shows the students' responses in relation to *convivencia*. In relation to school violence, 22.5 per cent stated they had been victims of episodic violence and 27.3 per cent had been aggressors, while 3.5 per cent considered themselves victims and 1.5 per cent aggressors of persistent violence. The gender and social group profile of the aggressors, in relationship to their victims, paints a picture that is described in many other studies: boys, acting in groups, are the ones involved in most episodes of violence (35 per cent of aggressors are boys who act in groups, as opposed to 4 per cent of girls who act in small groups).

A study on *convivencia* in schools was sponsored by the Galician School Board (Zabalza, 1999). Eleven types of aggression are described, and all the members of the education community commented on them: directors,

Table 9.2 Students aged 12 to 15 years who expressed satisfaction with *convivencia* in secondary schools in Andalusia (per cent)

Age	Satisfied	Indifferent	Unsatisfied
12	66	33	1
13	60	35	5
14	49	47	4
15	47	50	3

Note: Percentages rounded off.

Table 9.3 Type of violence experienced in the community of Galicia (per cent)

Types of violence	Principals	Teachers	Students	Families
Theft	5	5	20	13
Physical aggression	3	4	11	6
Destruction	4	9	19	12

Note: Percentages rounded off.

teachers, students and families. Table 9.3 shows a synthesis of the results in regard to the types of aggression experienced.

In Navarra, a study on violence and conflict (Hernández and Casares, 2002) found that 31 per cent of students were afraid to go to school at some time; of these, 11 per cent identified the cause to be one or several classmates and 5 per cent, a teacher. When asked if classmates had ever abused one another, 68 per cent answered that they had.

A study developed in Valencia (Gómez, 2000) is a part of a programme to encourage *convivencia* in schools, including several studies on violence, gangs and vandalism. Among the most relevant results, 32 per cent of the students have seen violent actions by teachers towards students, 46 per cent by classmates towards teachers, and 68 per cent among students. Of those sampled, 32.5 per cent said that there are gangs in the school that carry out violent acts; of these, 40.5 per cent have seen these gangs perform violent acts against classmates, 14.5 per cent say that they have seen gang violence against teachers and 6 per cent against administrative personnel from the school. Regarding acts related to vandalism, 66.5 per cent of the students say they have seen their classmates break, destroy or damage classroom materials or installations, and 31 per cent say the same about school materials.

Specific studies and research on bullying

University professors and research groups had to work on different aspects of school violence, in particular the phenomenon of bullying, for ten years before public institutions finally decided to finance general studies at the regional level. The first study on bullying was carried out by Vieira, Fernández and Quevedo (1989); they found that 17 per cent of students were bullies and 17 per cent were victims. Later, Cerezo and Esteban (1992), in a study done in Murcia, found aggressors comprised 11.4 per cent and victims 5.4 per cent of students; Ortega (1994b), in a study in very poor areas of the city of Seville, found that 16 per cent called themselves aggressors and 15 per cent, victims. These three studies used a similar definition of bullying, but different instruments; Vieira, Fernández and Quevedo (1989) and Ortega (1994b) used self-report questionnaires and Cerezo and Esteban (1992) a peer nomination proced-ure. Then, in 1995, Mora-Merchán and Ortega carried out an extension of the Seville study, defining four exclusive categories: victims, aggressors, victimized aggressors (ambivalent) and students unrelated to the prob-lem. The study found that 11 per cent of the students were victims (only reporting experiences of victimization and never intimidating others); 20 per cent, aggressors (only reporting experiences of intimidation and never of being victimized); 45 per cent, both aggressor and victim (reporting both experiences: intimidation and victimization) and 24 per cent, un-involved in the problem (reporting never having experienced either intimidating others or being victimized).

Recently a study by Ortega and Mora-Merchán (2000), financed by the General Programme for Research Aid (I+D), provided the most exhaust-ive analysis of peer abuse carried out so far in Spain. A sample of 4,914 students between the ages of 9 and 18, from twenty-six schools in Seville, was surveyed. Eleven per cent of students were highly involved (answering 'a lot of times' to the respective question): 3.5 per cent were aggressors; 6.5 per cent, victims; and 1 per cent, victimized aggressors. However, 43 per cent of the students occasionally (answering 'a few times' to the respective question) had bad relationships with others and/ or were occasionally aggressive. The questions did not include a specific time period to have in mind when answering.

It is difficult to compare these studies due to the different approaches and resources used. To attempt such a comparison and offer general information, we have used some general categories, presented in Table 9.4. The order among the types of violent behaviour from most to least frequent is: verbal, physical, social, psychological, and theft.

Table 9.4 Student responses to questionnaires (not equivalent) in the studies reviewed (per cent)

	Verbal	Physical	Psychological	Theft	Social
National studies					
Ombudsman (2000)	33	7	9	20	11.5
Regional studies					
Andalusia (Ortega and Angulo, 1998)	60	30	29.5	3.5	26.5
Galicia (Zabalza, 1999)	43	16	19	20	–
Valencia (Gómez Casañ, 2000)	57	43.5	36	–	39
Local or research group studies					
Vieira, Fernández and Quevedo (1989)	19	13	–	14	–
Ortega (1994b)	22	8	12	16	10
Ortega and Mora-Merchán (2000)	53	32	24	5	16

Note: Percentages rounded off.

The studies agree that boys are aggressors more often than girls; the same is not true in terms of the victim since some studies indicate that girls are more often the victim and others, the opposite. This may be because, although boys are more often both aggressors and victims, girls may be more frequent in the victim-only category when these are discriminated. Apart from gender, the studies tend to present an analysis by age or school year, and all of them show that the level of victimization decreases with age, so that the last years of primary school and the first years of secondary school are those in which the most frequent reported acts of violence take place.

Action

Initiatives to combat school violence

The General Education Law (1990) introduced some positive aspects regarding coping with violence in schools, and the most relevant is making obligatory the creation of a *convivencia* commission for each school, in which all the members of the education community – teachers, students and families – are represented. This commission is in charge of coming up with rules and tending to cases of school violence, disruptiveness, lack of discipline, interpersonal aggression or other types of aggression, and antisocial behaviour.

Government initiatives at the national level

In Spain, there is no general activity on the part of the government directed at preventing school violence. The Ombudsman's report is an initiative at the national level intended to raise the level of social awareness regarding this problem in order to stimulate preventive policies. But the current Conservative Government did not allude to it in its electoral programmes, nor are we aware of specific initiatives by the Spanish Ministry of Education and Culture aimed at combating school violence, although they are changing many other aspects of the education system.

Regional policies or policies of the autonomous communities against school violence

The councils of education of the autonomous communities have, in the last five years, been establishing violence prevention initiatives, especially by stimulating an improvement in *convivencia* and in the social climate in schools. The response by the regional governments is progressive; normally, there are plans regarding *convivencia* made concrete in institutional documents in which the schools' social problems are analysed and orientation is provided for how to deal with them. However, these have not been fully established, much less evaluated. We shall concentrate on the initiatives that have established specific programmes against school violence.

The regions implicated are: Andalusia (Educational Programme for the Prevention of Bullying); Aragon (Aragonese Plan for *Convivencia*); Asturias (Guide for Supervision of *Convivencia* Relationships and Discipline in Schools); Catalonia (Education Department Research Commission for Student Behavioural Problems in Schools); Castilla la Mancha (Plan for School *Convivencia*); Madrid (*Convivencia* is Living Programme); Castilla Leon (Variation of Madrid's *Convivencia* is Living Programme and Support Service for Students with Antisocial Behaviour); Murcia (Regional Plan for the Development of *Convivencia* in Schools); the Basque Country (*Convivencia* in Schools Programme); Valencia (Encouraging *Convivencia* Programme); Cantabria (Conflict Mediation Programme); Melilla (Commission for School Failure and Violence); Navarra (School Family Programme, which includes a course on domestic and school violence prevention); Castilla Leon (Support Service for students with antisocial behaviour); Extremadura (Caceres: Adolescent Social Competence Improvement Programme); Badajoz (version of Seville Anti-School Violence (SAVE) Project, Ortega, 1997); and Galicia (version of Tolerance Education Programme, Díaz Aguado et al., 1996).

Characteristics of educational programmes against school violence

In Spain, most of the intervention programmes developed to eradicate school violence are designed around two general objectives: first, a decrease in violent acts; and second, their prevention, through an improvement in or creation of a good atmosphere of interpersonal relationships in the school based on democratic principles and mutual respect. We shall describe these different forms of intervention as well as which programmes they have been used for.

The integration strategies can be grouped into four categories: those aimed at changing the organization of the school, those aimed at training teachers to design their own intervention models; specific proposals for the classroom; and specific programmes to be applied in situations of violence where students are involved or at risk.

Programmes aimed at innovation or changes in the organization of the school

These strategies are based on the idea that the school is a general system of coexistence that must be governed in a way that facilitates positive relationships and discourages negative ones. Along these lines, the SAVE model stresses the need to involve all the members of the education community in the design and development of the school's organization. This way, there is a good correlation between the educational values proposed by the school and those that are developed at home, providing for students a coherent way of dealing with interpersonal relationships, based on dialogue, co-operation and mutual enrichment. To achieve this, it is essential to establish places and times that allow this enrichment among the members of the education community. The programmes that include this proposal are from Andalusia (Ortega, 1997; Ortega et al., 1998; Trianes and Muñoz, 1994; Trianes, 1996), Madrid (Carbonell, 1999; Fernández, 1998a); Murcia (Murcia ECE, 2000), Basque Country (Basque Country DDE, 2000); and Leon.

Programmes aimed at teacher training

These programmes are aimed at making professional relationships among teachers more dynamic through the formation of work groups in which the teachers themselves are active in designing the courses of action to be taken. Some examples are presented by Carbonell (1999); Fernández (1998a); Ortega (1997); and Trianes and Muñoz (1994). Others, such as the Basque Country *Convivencia* Programme (Basque Country DDE, 2000) and the Tolerance Education Programme (Díaz, 1996), use an external teacher training model.

Two other methods have been used in the regional initiatives: occasional teacher training programmes through public courses about different topics around school violence, and those promoted by the Navarra Community Council of Education (Navarra DDE, 2000), which believes that there should be a combination of internal and external training activities.

Apart from these proposals, teacher training in all of its forms has been implemented throughout the country, with certain central themes: conflict resolution, social skills, coexistence, tolerance, discipline, violence and proposals for intervention, which has made *convivencia* a priority in regard to teachers' continual training.

Proposals for classroom activities

There are six different types of proposals in this area: management of the social climate in the classroom; curricular work in co-operative groups; values education activities; activities about feelings and emotions; activities related to the study of situational ethics; and drama activities. Some intervention programmes propose a concrete list of classroom activities, for example Díaz (1996) and Cerezo (1997). Others leave the choice as to which line of work to follow up to the teacher. The democratic management of *convivencia* (Ortega, 1997) in classroom meetings, where dialogue, participation and co-operation by everyone is necessary, includes an analysis of daily events in which students find themselves involved, an evaluation of and changes to the group rules, and an atmosphere of social relations in which the students learn to manage their lives in a non-violent way.

The proposal for curricular work in co-operative groups intends that curricular contents should be dealt with using a methodology that promotes co-operation, dialogue and reflection, thus establishing good social relationships and preventing violence. One important aspect here is that students learn that they should pool all their individual knowledge, compare and discuss until they reach more or less stable agreements about what they know and how things are advancing in their daily classroom work.

The activities geared towards values education and activities about feelings and emotions attempt to promote the internalization of the values of mutual respect, solidarity, and peace through activities of reflection and debate about the feelings, emotions and relationships of the students. Examples from real or imaginary situations offered by the students themselves are used, examples in which emotions and interpersonal feelings appear and where students become aware of the consequences that anti-social or violent behaviour has for all those involved and are helped to reflect on ethical criteria and behaviour.

The objectives when working with situational ethics are the same as those of feelings and values in education. This strategy is usually highly motivating because of the disagreements about morality that arise in the classroom given that discussions about situational ethics encourage critical thinking and reflection about social reality as something very complex.

Finally, other researchers have proposed the use of drama as a didactic resource to prevent violence and improve *convivencia*. Proponents of this strategy believe that drama can make violent experiences real to the students and thus cause them to consider the personal effects violence can have for the victims. Table 9.5 shows the proposals included in each programme.

Table 9.5 Classroom activities proposed by the various school violence prevention programmes

	Classroom management	Co-operative group	Values education	Affective education	Situational ethics	Drama
Ortega et al. (1998)	X	X	X	X	X	X
Ortega (1997)	X	X	X	X	X	
Carbonell Fernández (1999)	X	X	X			
Díaz Aguado (1996)	X	X	X		X	X
Trianes and Muñoz (1994)	X	X				X
Basque Country DDE (2000)	X		X			

Specific strategies for combating existing school violence

A group of specific programmes, often designed outside Spain, have been applied in the country. Some of these are:

- *Quality circle* strategies (Smith and Sharp, 1994): a group of people meets regularly because they are interested in identifying, analysing and solving common problems. Quality circles are very effective for any situation in which students need to be motivated to achieve specific goals, such as the problem at hand.
- *Conflict mediation* strategies (Fernández, 1998a; Aguado et al., 2000): a group of people accepted by the education community as mediators is trained to carry out certain functions in the resolution of conflicts, to facilitate a positive solution. They are usually used to re-educate people in conflict resolution skills when the situation is still not serious in regard to violence.
- *Peer help* strategies (Cowie and Wallace, 1998; developed in Spain by Ortega and Del Rey, 1999): a group of students counsel and help other students who have experienced or are experiencing violence, mistreatment or abuse and try to find a solution through talking to them and facilitating support.
- *Pikas method* (Pikas, 1989): a social intervention strategy used to undo the aggressive ties between the small groups of victims and aggressors. Based on knowledge about the structure of an aggressive group that attacks a defenceless victim, it is designed to modify the social relationships in such a way that the aggressors end up helping the victim that they had previously attacked.
- *Victim assertiveness* strategies (Ortega, 1998): carrying out social skill exercises that enable the victim to go through the entire sequence of a situation in which s/he has to make a decision, in such a way that self-esteem is maintained and strengthened. The objective is to establish an affective and emotional distance with regard to the aggressor or group of aggressors and to defend the privacy of the victims and their right not to be molested.
- *Strategies of empathy development for aggressors* (Ortega, 1998): educational processes that re-establish an emotional and affective sensitivity in boys and girls who have lived in violent or non-affective environments. They are useful in schools where an improvement in *convivencia* is sought and students have been identified as at risk, or there are students who are already involved in problems of violence.

Table 9.6 shows the strategies used in the different programmes.

Table 9.6 Specific strategies used in various programmes with students involved in violence and those at risk

	Quality circles	Conflict resolution	Peer help	Pikas method	Assertiveness programme	Empathy programme
Ortega et al. (1998)	X	X	X	X	X	X
Ortega (1997)	X	X	X	X	X	X
Carbonell Fernández (1999)		X				X
Trianes and Fernández-Figarés (2001)		X	X			
Trianes and Muñoz (1994)		X				X
Aguado et al. (2000)		X				
Basque Country DDE (2000)		X			X	X
Díaz Aguado (1996)		X				
Fernández García (1998a)	X	X	X	X		

Educational programmes for dealing with school violence

Seville Anti-School Violence Programme

Developed during the academic years 1996 through 1999, this programme has been employed in twenty-six primary and secondary schools and affected directly or indirectly nearly 5,000 students. The study of the problem of peer violence, the establishment of school profiles in regard to this problem and the involvement of teachers from ten schools in a peer abuse prevention project yielded an open, ecological and global model of educational work that has brought about benefits of improved *convivencia* and prevention of violence by means of an evaluation process (Ortega and Del Rey, 2001).

Educational Programme for the Prevention of Bullying

Since 1997, this programme (Ortega et al., 1998) has involved co-ordination between the Andalusian Council of Education and Science and the University of Seville's Psychopedagogical Research Team. It is based on five courses of action that are mutually enriching and complementary: information and promotion of awareness in the education community and society in general by means of information campaigns; research on indicators of violence and the climate for interpersonal relationships in pilot schools; training educators, from general inspectors to teachers, through courses and didactic materials designed for their support; and, finally, establishing a free telephone hotline to help pupils facing harassment and abuse from classmates.

Convivencia is Living

The Convivencia is Living Programme (Carbonell, 1999) began, thanks to the collaboration of several institutions, in 1997. Its objectives include inter-institutional co-ordination so that the schools and all the members of the educational community can work to achieve a high level of *convivencia* and, through education, bring about non-violence. It focuses mainly on training teachers and those in the education profession. It also includes training for families of students in the schools where the programme is in place, throughout the entire process. It is designed to be implemented over a period of two years.

Programme for Tolerance Education and Violence Education among Young People

This programme (Díaz, 1996) is the result of a research project carried out between 1994 and 1997. Making use of four handbooks and two videos, its goal is to adapt the intervention to the developmental characteristics of adolescence, reduce risks of violence and develop protective conditions, encourage human rights, promote an attitude of tolerance and rejection of violence, and teach how to detect and fight against the problems that lead to violence and intolerance.

Convivencia in Schools

The Basque Country's Department of Education, with its *Convivencia in Schools* programme, is trying to promote a climate within the schools where the entire educational community can participate and coexist in the most enjoyable and satisfactory way possible, and the students can move in an environment in which negotiation and mutual respect are the basic tools that can contribute to the building up of a more democratic society. It is based on an analysis of the areas in need of improvement: dysfunctional interactions between people and groups, situations of peer abuse, other drug-related problems, marginalization, underprivileged environments, position of ethnic minorities, socio-political problems, and students with disruptive or violent behaviours, or mental health related behaviours.

Social and Affective Education in the Classroom

The Social and Affective Education in the Classroom Programme (Trianes and Muñoz, 1994) is based on a hierarchy of objectives to be achieved in a three-year period, and consists of three modules about: communication and interpersonal understanding; the class as a developing human group; self-management in the running of the class; knowledge and inferences regarding emotions and feelings; learning reflective thought and negotiation; beginning to work in co-operative groups; learning skills to work in co-operative groups.

Anti-school violence programmes and models that have been evaluated

The evaluation of the SAVE project (Ortega and Del Rey, 2001) was carried out in two ways. A self-report questionnaire was given before beginning the intervention (1995–1996) and four years later (1999–2000) in some of the schools that had used the SAVE model; this showed that the proportion of 'non-involved' pupils had increased from 86 per cent to 92 per cent, while the proportion of victims had decreased from 9 per cent to 4 per cent, of aggressors from 4.3 per cent to 3.7 per cent, and of victim-aggressors from 0.7 per cent to 0.3 per cent. This study included a control group (without intervention) of three schools, though only assessed at one time point; in these three schools that had not used the SAVE model there were 6 per cent of victims, 4 per cent of aggressors and 2.3 per cent of victim-aggressors.

The second evaluation framework was the perception of the effectiveness of the interventions, from the point of view of the students. For this, there was a questionnaire with three questions, in which the students were asked what the teachers had done to improve relations between classmates, since when they had been working at this, and what the effects of these interventions were. Pupils rated work directly with victims as being the most effective interventions, although work on education of feelings and values and the activities based on a democratic management of social relations also got high ratings, and especially for improving the quality of relationships in the schools.

An evaluation of the Tolerance and Violence Prevention Education Programme (Díaz, 1996) was carried out by teachers and students. The instruments used were interviews and questionnaires indicating the teachers' assessment of the students in regard to the objectives of the programmes. Results were positive for development of tolerance and empathy, improvement of abilities to co-operate, to communicate and to reason, and students' interest in learning and their attitude towards teachers; regarding prevention of violence, the evaluation found a significant decrease between pre- and post-test for students' 'justification of violence' and an increase for 'alternatives to violence'. However there was no change for the 'disposition to behaviour in a violent way'.

The Social and Affective Education in the Classroom Programme (Trianes and Muñoz, 1994; Trianes, 1996) was evaluated both quantitatively and qualitatively by means of interviews, questionnaires, self-reports, and observations. The teachers reported that the level of *convivencia* among the students in the classroom and among the teachers as a whole had improved over the three years of the programme. They stressed that the programme was a great incentive for them. The students believed that authoritarian control by the teachers had decreased and that the rules and regulations are clearer. The evaluation specifically of outcomes related to violence is still in process.

Other types of action taken to combat school violence

The National Police Force, mainly through a working group on 'The problem of violence in schools and the relationship between academic failure, reintegration in the workplace and delinquency', has designed several courses: understanding of the environment, school for parents, parental conflict, prevention of both drug use and initiation of drug use, and the implementation of didactic units on school protection and student self-protection. The Juvenile Defender's Office for the Community of Madrid has published the project *One More Day* (Fernández, 1998b) which consists of didactic materials for values education in secondary school and a video created by students that dramatizes a day at school.

Also, the teachers' unions have organized many seminars and conferences, where a large number of students and teachers have reflected on the courses of action that should be taken to combat violence.

The Spanish Federation of Catholic Schools has created, among other initiatives, a *Quality and Freedom in Teaching* forum that has produced a document that analyses the current situation in schools, as well as the consequences, and offers suggestions for combating violence; all of the initiatives and intervention programmes analysed in the previous section are included in these suggestions.

To conclude, we could affirm a very optimistic trend, that Spanish society, worried about school violence, does not just see it as a concrete psychological problem, but as a lack of education to promote *convivencia* (coexistence) and tolerance.

References

Aguado, J., Fernández, I., Funes, S., López, J., Martínez, M., Torrego, J.C. and De Vicente, J. (2000). *Mediación de Conflictos en Instituciones Educativas*. Madrid: Narcea.

Basque Country DDE (2000). *Programa Convivencia en los Centros Escolares*. Basque Country: Office of Educational Innovation, Department of Education.

Carbonell Fernández, J.L. (Dir.) (1999). *Programa para el Desarrollo de la Convivencia y la Prevención de los Malos Tratos. Convivir es Vivir*. Madrid: Ministry of Education and Culture.

Cerezo, F. (1997). *Conductas Agresivas en la Edad Escolar. Aproximación Teórica y Metodológica. Propuesta de Intervención*. Madrid: Pirámide.

Cerezo, F. and Esteban, M. (1992). La Dinámica Bully-Victima entre Escolares. Diversos Enfoques Metodológicos. *Revista de Psicología Universitas Tarraconensis,* XIV, 2, 131–145.

Cowie, H. and Wallace, H. (1998). *Peer Support: A Teacher's Manual.* London: The Prince's Trust.

Defensor del Pueblo (2000). *La violencia, el maltrato entre iguales en la Educación Secundaria Obligatoria.* Comunidad de Madrid: Defensor del Pueblo.

Díaz Aguado, M.J. (1996). *Programas de Educación para la Tolerancia y Prevención de la Violencia en los Jóvenes. Vol.I. Fundamentación psicopedagógica.* Madrid: Ministry of Labour and Social Affairs.

Díaz Aguado, M.J., Royo, P., Segura, M.P. and Andrés, M.T. (1996). *Programas de Educación para la Tolerancia y Prevención de la Violencia en los Jóvenes. Vol.IV. Instrumentos de evaluación e investigación.* Madrid: Ministry of Labour and Social Affairs.

Fernández García, I. (1998a). *Prevención de la Violencia y Resolución de Conflictos.* Madrid: Narcea.

Fernández García, I. (1998b). *Un Día Más. Materiales Didácticos para la Educación en Valores en ESO.* Madrid: Juvenile Defender for the Community of Madrid.

Gómez Casañ, P. (2000). *Programa de Fomento de la Convivencia en Centros Educativos.* Valencia: Ministry of Culture, Education and Science.

Hernández Frutos, T. and Casares García, E. (2002). *Aportaciones teórico prácticas para el conocimiento de actitudes violentas en el ámbito escolar. Encuesta realizada al alumnado de ESO en Navarra desde una perspectiva de género.* Gobierno de Navarra: Navarra Women's Institute.

Mora-Merchán, J.A. and Ortega, R. (1995). Intimidadores y Víctimas. Un problema de maltrato enre iguales. Communicación. IV Congreso Estatal Sobre Infancia Maltratada. Sevilla. pp.271–275.

Murcia ECE (2000). *Plan Regional para el Desarrollo de la Convivencia Escolar.* Murcia: Ministry of Education and Science.

Navarra DDE (2000). *Programa Escuela de familias: la prevención de la violencia doméstica y escolar.* Navarra: Department of Education. Studies and Programmes Section.

Olweus, D. (1999). Sweden. In P.K. Smith, Y. Morita, J. Junger-Tas, D. Olweus, R. Catalano and P. Slee (eds). *The Nature of School Bullying: A Cross-national Perspective.* London: Routledge. pp.7–27.

Ombudsman (2000). *Informe sobre Violencia Escolar.* Madrid: United Nations International Children's Emergency Fund.

Ortega, R. (1994a). Violencia interpersonal en los centros educativos de educación secundaria. Un estudio obre maltrato e intimidación entre compañeros. *Revista de Educación,* 304, 253–280.

Ortega, R. (1994b). Las malas relaciones interpersonales en la escuela. Estudio sobre la violencia y el maltrato entre compañeros de segunda etapa de E.G.B. *Infancia y Sociedad,* 27–28, 191–216.

Ortega, R. (1997). El Proyecto Sevilla Anti-violencia Escolar. Un modelo de intervención preventiva contra los malos tratos entre iguales. *Revista de Educación,* 313, 143–158.

Ortega, R. (1998). Trabajando con víctimas, agresores y espectadores de la violencia. In R. Ortega, J.A. Mora-Merchán, V. Fernández, I.M. Gandul, R. Del Rey,

R. Palacios, H. Ríos, P. Prieto, A. Valverde, J. Ortega and B. Gómez. *La Convivencia Escolar: Qué es y Cómo Abordarla*. Sevilla: Ministry of Education and Science, Andalusian Government.

Ortega, R. (2001). Ecological and cosmopolitan approach to prevent school violence. From Ripples to Waves. Tackling Violence in School. International Conference organized by Connect 006-Fi.

Ortega, R. and Angulo, J.C. (1998). Violencia escolar. Su presencia en institutos de educación secundaria de Andalucía. *Revista de Estudios de Juventud*, 42, 47–61.

Ortega, R. and Del Rey, R. (1999). The Use of Peer Support in the SAVE Project. Paper presented at the Children Helping Children Symposium of the 9th European Conference on Developmental Psychology. Spetses, Greece.

Ortega, R. and Del Rey, R. (2001). Aciertos y desaciertos del Proyecto Sevilla Antiviolencia Escolar (SAVE). *Revista de Educación*, 324, 253–270.

Ortega, R. and Mora-Merchán, J.A. (2000). *Violencia Escolar. Mito o Realidad*. Seville: Mergablum.

Ortega, R., Mora-Merchán, J.A., Fernández, V., Gandul, I.M., Del Rey, R., Palacios, R., Ríos, H., Prieto, P., Valverde, A., Ortega, J. and Gómez, B. (1998). *La Convivencia Escolar: Qué es y Cómo Abordarla*. Sevilla: Ministry of Education and Science, Andalusian Government.

Pikas, A. (1989). The Common Concern Method for the Treatment of Mobbing. In E. Roland and E. Munthe (eds). *Bullying: An International Perspective*. London: David Fulton.

Salomäki, U. (2001). *The Proposal for an Action Plan to Tackle Violence in the School in Europe*. Report Finland. Finnish Centre for Health Promotion (Connect, 006-Fi).

Smith, P.K. and Sharp, S. (1994). *School Bullying: Insights and Perspectives*. London: Routledge.

Trianes, M.V. (1996). *Educación y Competencia Social: Un programa en el Aula*. Malaga: Aljibe.

Trianes, M.V. and Fernández-Figarés, C. (2001). *Aprender a Ser Personas y a Convivir: Un Programa para Secundaria*. Vizcaya: Descleé de Brouwer.

Trianes, M.V. and Muñoz, A. (1994). *Programa de Educación Social y Afectiva*. Malaga: Puerta Nueva, Office of Education and Culture.

Vieira, M., Fernández, I. and Quevedo, G. (1989). Violence, Bullying and Counselling in the Iberian Peninsula. In E. Roland and E. Munthe (eds). *Bullying: An International Perspective*. London: David Fulton.

Zabalza Beraza, M.A. (Dir.) (1999). *A Convivencia nos Centros Escolares de Galicia*. Santiago de Compostela: Ministry of Education and University Organization.

Chapter 10

A multifaceted reality

A report from Italy

Ersilia Menesini and Rossella Modiano

Background

The country

According to the last census, the 2000 population estimate for Italy is 57,679,955. Italy is divided into twenty regions; among them are five so-called 'autonomous regions' that benefit from a special statute giving them more autonomy (Friuli-Venezia Giulia, Sardegna, Sicilia, Trentino-Alto Adige and Valle d'Aosta).

The present incidence of legal immigration is 2.2 per cent of the resident population, of which 13 per cent comes from EEC countries and 8.8 per cent from other developed countries. The main communities present in Italy are: Morocco (131,406), Albania (83,807), Philippines (61,285), USA (59,572) and Tunisia (48,909) (Istituto Nazionale di Statistica, 2001).

The school system

Currently, the first sector of the educational system is called primary elementary school and covers a period of five years from ages 6 to 11. The second sector, called secondary middle school, covers a period of three years from ages 11 to 14; however from 1 September 1999 the age of compulsory schooling was raised by one year, to 15 years (Law No. 9/99), and the total duration of schooling is now nine years. Secondary education, articulated in humanistic, scientific, technical and professional high schools, lasts five years prior to university entrance at around age 19. Primary schools typically have 200 to 300 pupils, secondary middle schools 300 to 400 pupils, and secondary high schools 400 to 800 pupils.

A large majority of primary schools in Italy (85 per cent) work for twenty-seven to thirty hours a week, organized over six days with one or two afternoon sessions. Fifteen per cent of primary schools, mainly in Northern and Central Italy, have a schedule of thirty-six to forty hours a week, with a timetable from 8.30a.m. to 4.30p.m. for five days, and a lunch break taken at school. Most schools in Southern Italy (70 per cent) have a morning schedule of twenty-seven hours a week with no classes in the afternoon. Middle schools usually have a schedule of thirty hours a week, from 8.30a.m. to 1.30p.m., with no lunch break. Humanistic and scientific secondary schools generally have a thirty-six hours timetable per week, an average of six hours daily. Technical and professional secondary schools have a longer timetable, around forty-two hours per week, coming back to school in the afternoon twice a week. Break time is a short period of between ten and fifteen minutes once or twice a day, usually directly supervised by teachers.

As far as children with special educational needs are concerned, the Italian educational system grants them the same rights to education that other children have, but no special schools or sections exist to meet their needs. They attend normal schools, sharing the classroom with other children (Law No. 297/94), and receiving extra support from a specialist teacher assigned for every four such children in the school.

In 1996 a reformation process began that involved the structure of the educational system as well as the organization and curricula. Basically, the most important provisions concern school autonomy and the reformation of school cycles. In relation to school autonomy, since January 2001, local regional and provincial authorities have been abolished and schools acquired greater autonomy in managing funds and projects. Each school carries out its own educational policy through a document that states its goals and the services offered. In March 2000 a law concerning the re-ordering of school levels (Law 30/2000) was approved and is still the object of a widespread debate at political and professional level.

Linguistic/definitional issues

From a review of Italian literature and school documents, terms related to *violenza* (violence) have several meanings that can be grouped as follows:

1   We found documents and official statistics that refer to violence as a crime against the person. This concept of crime is related to the problem of school violence in terms of developmental risk pathways and the continuity of antisocial conduct.
2   At school level, one of the main approaches has been that of bullying, which includes a wide range of behaviours, from psychological to verbal and physical attacks (Smith et al., 1999). The term *'bullismo'* has entered in the professional language of teachers and school psychologists and it is often used as a synonym for school violence.
3   A third and more confused meaning can be traced on the basis of official and political documents where violence is used in a very

broad sense as students' physical, verbal or psychological constraints. Often these documents confuse specific terms like violence and bullying with related and broader terms like *'disagio scolastico'* (school malaise).

Relevant historical background

Recently, the problem of juvenile violence has been a relevant issue in the scientific and political debate in Italy and this increase of awareness has led scholars, politicians and professionals in the area to analyse the problem and to try to reduce and prevent it.

Historically, the awareness of violence among young people has grown recently in relation to the publications and the studies on school bullying. A first large-scale survey of this problem was published in a popular psychological magazine in 1995 by Ada Fonzi, followed by a book on the extent of the problem (Fonzi, 1997). In 1997 a group of researchers from Florence and Cosenza University obtained European Community funding to carry out research on bullying and ways of preventing it (*TMR Network Report*, 1997).

Another example of juvenile violence, often reported in the media, is the so-called 'baby gangs'. These are mostly pre-adolescents and adolescents, often friends or classmates, who rob or extort peers inside or outside schools just for economic and psychological gain. In order to tackle this phenomenon the Parliament nominated a Committee on Juvenile Group Violence that approved a resolution in March 2000 whereby the Government committed itself to enhance school activities and promote health education projects in order to reduce the problem. In spite of this general commitment at a political and ministry level, until now we have not registered any initiative specifically aimed at tackling violence in schools. In terms of school legislation, there are some Ministry directives with broad aims within which anti-violence initiatives and projects could be brought forth. They are:

- *Presidential Decree 567/1996* This aims to regulate complementary and extracurricular activities and is an attempt by the Italian Government to head off deviant behaviour and violence among young people by promoting longer school hours.
- *Law 285/97 'Promotion of rights and opportunities regarding childhood and adolescence'* This established the National Fund for Children and Adolescents within the Prime Minister's Office. Its purpose is to take action to promote rights, quality of life, development, individual fulfilment and social integration of children and adolescents.
- *Presidential Decree 249/98* ('Statute of Boy and Girl Students') This defines rights and duties of secondary school students, abolishing

the old sanction system and delegating to schools the choice of rules and sanctions to safeguard rights and duties.

Knowledge

Statistics

Given the above definition of violence, we present data at two different levels. The first is juvenile crime statistics; these give information on violent offences generally, not only in school. The second is information on bullying in school by physical means, and violence among students, obtained from different informants: students themselves, and head teachers.

Statistics on juvenile crime and illegal actions

Data from National Statistical Institute (Istituto Nazionale di Statistica, 2001) show that the total rate of juvenile delinquency in Italy in 1998 was 0.9 per cent (1.4 per cent boys and 0.4 per cent girls). In relation to gender, the statistics show a higher prevalence for boys, especially those above 14 years of age (2.3 per cent).

Despite some recent alarming news (family homicides committed by minors; robberies and violent acts perpetrated by 'baby gangs'), these statistics do not show a strong increase in juvenile delinquency during recent years; on the contrary, it seems to decrease at least as far as Italian minors are concerned. The trend of juvenile crime in Italy in the last decade is shown in Table 10.1. From 1990 to 1998 the number of juvenile crimes was fairly stable, with a slight peak in 1995 and a slight decrease from 1996, which is continuing.

Data from the last decade split by ethnicity show a clear decrease for Italian young people, which can predict a further decrease in the future. For foreign offenders, it is not possible to make the same prediction. The

Table 10.1 Number of juvenile crimes 1990–1998

Years	<14 years	14 to 17 years	Total
1990	8,756	32,295	41,051
1991	9,195	35,782	44,977
1992	9,213	35,575	44,788
1993	9,036	34,339	43,375
1994	9,739	34,587	44,326
1995	10,815	35,236	46,051
1996	10,452	33,523	43,975
1997	8,909	34,436	43,345
1998	7,657	34,450	42,107

Table 10.2 Number of personal crimes registered for young offenders 1990–1998

	1990	1991	1992	1993	1994	1995	1996	1997	1998
Murders	103	129	150	116	115	110	120	105	122
Personal damage	3,572	3,912	4,218	4,340	4,335	4,587	4,897	4,729	4,649
Rapes							329	453	519

Source: ISTAT, 2001.

proportion of juvenile delinquency by foreign minors is documented. During the period 1991–1998 the ratio of foreign minors involved first increased, from 17.6 per cent in 1991 to 27.6 per cent in 1996, then stabilized, being 25 per cent in 1998.

In relation to the type of offence, data from the 1998 statistics show that violent crime against the person is the second most frequent crime with a figure of 20 per cent, preceded by property crimes (58 per cent), and followed by crimes like drugs pushing and trading (14 per cent). The majority of violent offences (94 per cent) are committed by Italian (non-foreign) young people and usually consist of personal assaults and damages.

Analysing the trend of crimes against persons by young offenders in the last decade (see Table 10.2), we notice that the number of personal offences progressively increased, together with the number of sexual offences (rapes) for which data are not available until 1995. On the other hand we can see a certain stability for the category of murders.

Violent offences against the person have a higher percentage in the southern part of the country and in the islands (Sicilia and Sardegna), probably because in these areas young people are often involved in crime organizations such as the Mafia and therefore are more prone to be involved in violent and personal assaults. The ratio in the four regions (Campania, Puglia, Calabria and Sicilia) most at risk because of the presence of organized crime is worrying since in comparison to a national decrease of 4.3 per cent in the 1996–1998 period, the number of minors prosecuted in these areas increased by 9.8 per cent.

Statistics on bullying in school by physical means, and violence among students

In relation to bullying, the book *Il bullismo in Italia* (Bullying in Italy), edited by Fonzi (1997), presents several researches carried out on an overall sample of 7,018 students attending primary and middle schools in the following areas: Turin, Bologna, Florence, Rome, Naples, Cosenza and Palermo. All these studies made use of the Olweus bully/victim questionnaire (Olweus, 1993), translated and adapted to the Italian population.

Table 10.3 Children being bullied by physical means in primary and middle school, in different Italian cities (per cent)

	Turin	Bologna	Florence	Rome	Naples	Cosenza	Palermo
Boys (primary)	10.81	13.95	10.37	–	10.67	7.31	6.70
Girls (primary)	7.67	4.08	10.22	–	8.25	4.08	3.32
Boys (middle)	3.94	–	6.45	2.45	5.92	4.41	6.34
Girls (middle)	2.38	–	2.46	2.91	5.88	2.47	1.03

An important issue during the translation of the questionnaire was finding a clear word to connote 'bullying' for use with children. We considered a plurality of terms, and after some pilot studies the term *'prepotenza'* was selected as the best translation since it covers the multidimensional nature of bullying (physical, verbal and indirect).

From these data a rate of bullying by physical means was calculated, being the percentage of pupils who experienced physical forms of being bullied once or more often in the last two to three months. This new percentage gives a reliable index of the incidence of being bullied by physical means in different areas of Italy (see Table 10.3). Primary school boys reported an average of 9.97 per cent of being bullied by physical means in the last term; girls an average of 6.27 per cent. For middle schools the rate of being bullied by physical means is less: 4.92 per cent for boys and 2.90 per cent for girls.

Two other studies carried out in Central and North-East Italy give some insights on the rate of the problem in high school students (Belacchi, Benelli and Menesini, 2000; Menesini and Rossi, 2001). In these studies questionnaires were given to 1,047 secondary school students (629 from Central Italy, 418 from North-East), and an average incidence of being bullied by physical means in the last two to three months was found of 3.9 per cent for boys and 1.4 per cent for girls. Furthermore, in secondary schools relevant differences related to type of school were found; the highest incidence of bullying with physical means was in the professional and college schools.

In the study carried out in high schools of Central Italy (Ancona), specific attention was given to students with special needs and disabilities, who are integrated in normal schools. Twenty-eight disabled adolescents, just 4.5 per cent of the total sample, took part in the study. Within this specific subgroup, the incidence of being bullied was 25 per cent, double the incidence of being bullied in the normal population of this age. However, the large majority of bullying episodes were not physical attacks but mainly verbal and indirect aggression; physical victimization was reported by only two out of the twenty-eight disabled students.

Consistent figures on the rate of school violence from the teacher's perspective have been reported in a study on school climate carried out recently by Caprara and collaborators (Centro Interuniversitario and Ministero della Pubblica Istruzione, 2000a). They investigated eighty-one secondary middle schools distributed across the whole country. Head teachers answered a questionnaire aimed at evaluating the rate of violent attacks in their schools over the past year. The large majority estimated a low incidence of violence: only 7.4 per cent reported one or two episodes during the past year.

Another study using the same questionnaire collected data from ninety-eight high schools distributed over the whole country, participating in a national project on peer education (Centro Interuniversitario and Ministero della Pubblica Istruzione, 2000b). The rate of violence estimated by these head teachers is higher than in the middle schools of the previous study: 87 per cent of the high schools reported one to five violent episodes.

Age differences and nature of violence

The trend for bullying by physical means reported by students shows a decrease with age, from primary to middle and secondary schools. At the same time, data based on head teachers' questionnaires reported an increase of violent episodes from middle school to high school. Also, the statistics on the rate of crime in the country show an increase of offences during adolescence (14 to 17 years) as compared with the pre-adolescent years.

These contradictory findings have an equivalent status in the scientific literature. Findings on the development of aggression and antisocial behaviours (Coie and Dodge, 1998) and on general bullying (Smith et al., 1999) show a decrease of aggression with age from pre-school to adolescence. But other studies concerned with high risk populations show an increase of violence during adolescence, up to the point that in some cases aggressive behaviour can be accepted as a part of group culture (Coie et al., 1995).

Loeber and Hay (1997) tried to reconcile these contradictory findings by addressing different manifestations of aggression at different developmental stages. In the Pittsburgh Youth Study aggressive behaviours were classified as: minor aggression, aggression, or violence. There is a developmental ordering of the seriousness of aggression with age. Minor aggression emerged first from 3 to 10 years, followed by physical aggression which increased from 10 years onward. Violence had an onset around 10 years and increased from 11 up to 16 years. Therefore, while minor and physical aggression decrease in adolescence, the more serious violence tends to increase with age and follows the well-known age–crime curve, peaking in late adolescence.

The Italian data are consistent with this analysis, since the self-reported bullying data shows a decrease with age from pre-adolescence onwards, whereas crime statistics and head teachers' evaluations report an increase in violence from pre-adolescence onwards. Students' views report the developmental trend of minor aggressions (which much bullying consists of). Head teachers, on the other hand, reflect a view mainly related to the incidence of the most serious attacks in schools that need disciplinary interventions.

Gender differences

Data split by sex, either for crime or bullying, show that in girls the incidence of the problem is very low; specifically, the ratio between boys and girls for crime statistics is 4:1. This ratio becomes lower taking into account self-report measures of bullying with physical means; the ratio for probability of receiving a physical attack is 2:1. As an overall figure our data are in line with findings on gender differences related to aggression which show that physical attacks are more typical of boys, whereas girls are more commonly using indirect and verbal forms of aggression (Bjorqvist, Lagerspetz and Kaukiainen, 1992).

General consideration of the statistics on bullying and violence

The global measure on bullying reported in a previous international report (Fonzi et al., 1999) shows high figures in Italian schools. On average, 41.6 per cent of students in primary schools and 26.4 per cent in middle schools reported being bullied sometimes or more in the last two to three months. The majority of studies considered in this report show a certain consistency in finding a basically low level of the incidence of violence and physical aggression in schools (on average 8 per cent of primary school and 4 per cent of middle school students reported being bullied by physical means). Given the ratio between global bullying and bullying with physical means in Italy, this seems explained mainly by the higher incidence of verbal and indirect aggression, including what teachers and psychologists refer to as lack of politeness, problems of indiscipline, and disturbing behaviours which are typical especially of male students.

Action

National and regional policies

The institutional policies introduced to head off violence at school are essentially educational and formative rather than repressive. Within the reform process the most significant and innovative law is Law No. 59/1997 which sets out provisions on autonomy in matters of teaching, research, organization and administration of schools. This establishes a means for schools to find the most suitable solutions to any relevant problem concerning the school, including problems related to violence and bullying.

Each year a Ministry Directive in the area of health promotion and school malaise prevention is enacted. The intervention plan is usually focused on the general problem of school malaise with its multidimensional meaning, where issues such as drug addiction, depression or school dropout are included, together with violent behaviour.

The main projects funded in the last Ministry Directive (292/99) are the following:

- CIC (Information and Counselling Centres) set up in secondary schools, which aim to provide information and assistance at local level in order to prevent juvenile malaise and pathological behaviour.
- Family Project aiming at involving families to improve pupils' relational skills.
- School Autonomy, Life Skills and Peer Education, whose aims are to improve school climate and the level of communication between pupils and teachers, and to pilot peer education pathways that can promote students' participation and self-efficacy in the areas of learning abilities and psychological well-being. This project involves forty cities and around 150 high schools distributed across the country.
- *SPORA* Project (whose name is the acronym of the Italian words for experimentation, orientation and integration), aiming to promote and disseminate innovative curricular pathways to foster school success and to prevent school failures by means of specific attention to the student as a person.
- Training Project, addressed to teachers, school personnel and school heads in order to train them to help students at risk, or at a more general level, to tackle problems involving the juvenile malaise.
- Risk Area Project, aimed at tackling juvenile deviant behaviour and school failures, especially in the southern part of Italy where juvenile criminality is related to the presence of crime organizations such as the Mafia.

Among other national initiatives, a specific agreement against violence was taken in the area of education in May 1999 by the Ministry of Education and the Institute of Psychology of the National Research Council (CNR). Despite the relevance of this act, up to now it has not been translated into specific initiatives for schools at local level.

An important regional project was carried out in the area of Venice, under the title *Peer support: development and evaluation of a research-action in Veneto schools*. It has been funded by the Ministry of Education and co-ordinated by IRSSAE (Institute of Research and School Experimentation on Educational Activities) during 1999–2002. In the first two years it has involved two primary schools and four middle schools in different cities of the area. During 2001 the project was extended to three secondary schools, whose interventions are being evaluated at European level within a Connect project (<http://europa.eu.int/comm/education/connect/selection.html> or <http://www.gold.ac.uk/connect>).

Local initiatives or programmes

The picture so far highlights that the majority of ministerial projects address the general issue of school malaise and failure but are not focused specifically on the problem of violence. However, at local and school level, several specific initiatives against violence have been implemented and carried out in the last decade, both in terms of crime and of school bullying prevention.

Juvenile crime prevention

These projects were mainly based on co-operation between university research groups and local authorities. A noteworthy example is the project *Progetto Deta* carried out in Milan and lasting eleven years (De Leo, 1998). The focus was on the community and the prevention of juvenile delinquency in schools. The intervention was carried out at two levels: (1) in the community – teachers were recommended to send pupils showing some kind of malaise to the counselling centre created by the project and minors receiving judicial measures could profit from specific personal and professional support; (2) in schools – by specific interventions with parents, teachers and students. There were some limitations to this project, including conflicts and difficulties in collaboration between the university team co-ordinating the project, and the social service professional teams of the community. Also, since the beginning the model has lacked ongoing evaluation which could guide decisions and specific directions for the intervention.

Another project based on the prevention of juvenile crimes has been carried out in secondary middle schools in Turin. It aimed to inform youngsters about relevant social problems (related to delinquency) and to educate them through the presentation of real cases and experiences of detention (De Leo, 1998). A questionnaire given at the end of the year showed a clear change in the attitudes towards detention, and students expressed the will to commit themselves to some kind of voluntary service to help detainees.

A more widespread approach is that of 'education to legality', adopted by several schools as part of the educational policy or as a specific intervention. This aims to develop students' awareness of personal responsibility and to promote knowledge of and respect for the law. A survey made in Rome and its district (Provveditorato agli Studi di Roma, 2000) showed that 53.3 per cent of schools have carried out specific interventions using this approach as a preventive means to tackle deviant behaviours among students.

Besides school-based interventions, in the area of crime prevention several initiatives have been taken also at the community level, through projects co-ordinated by local authorities aiming to support youngsters at risk in the transition period from 15 years old to adulthood (De Leo and Malagoli Togliatti, 2000).

School bullying prevention

Given the high incidence of school bullying in Italy, a considerable number of local initiatives have specifically addressed the problem of school bullying as a relevant predictor and correlate of school violence. Several studies, action researches, in-service training for teachers and information activities have been carried out by university or professional teams in collaboration with schools. A collection of school interventions has been edited by Menesini (2000) in the book *Bullismo: che fare?* (Bullying: What Should be Done?). Other experiences are reported in the book *Giovani a rischio* (Youngsters at Risk), edited by Bacchini and Valerio (2001), which reports several studies carried out in the South of Italy.

The majority of school interventions characterized as action researches were carried out on a small scale in different areas of the country, and their efficacy was assessed over a short period of time. They usually followed a three-step scheme: (1) teacher training; (2) classroom interventions; and (3) pre-and post-test evaluation. Among them we can distinguish several types that exemplify the content and the main approaches used: curricular interventions, whole-school policy, peer support and clinical approaches.

Curricular interventions

This type of intervention usually consists of different integrated activities in several areas of the curriculum. Many proposals for Italian schools have been developed in the following areas: literature, history, audio-visual education, role-playing and drama, empathy training, communicative skills and mediation training.

The curricular approach is one of the most popular for teachers and schools when they first address the problem of violence. An example is a project carried out in Modena (Pignatti and Menesini, 2000) with an experimental group of 101 pupils and a control group of 76 pupils at the third elementary school grade. The intervention integrated activities from literature, empathy training and role-play, followed by discussion and sharing of experiences. To evaluate the efficacy of the intervention, Olweus' anonymous bully/victim questionnaire (1993), translated and adapted for an Italian population, and a peer nomination questionnaire to select bullies and victims, were used. The results showed a clear decrease of victimization and bullying in the experimental classes (respectively 2 and 4 per cent lower) as compared with the increase registered in the control group (on average 3.5 per cent higher on both measures), in the second data collection, after six months.

Another important curricular intervention is NOVAS RES, co-ordinated by the local educational authority of Turin (Prina, 2000). This project, still in progress, has been funded by the European Union within the Connect initiative and aims to develop and evaluate proposals for schools at different age levels (see <http://europa.eu.int/comm/education/connect/selection.html>).

Whole-school policy and peer support models

Interventions aimed to develop a positive school climate are also starting, although mainly at an experimental level. One relevant experience of whole-school policy development was carried out in a middle school in Lucca (Menesini, 2000) over a period of six years. Designing the educational policy on bullying followed the earlier involvement of a teaching group in some curricular interventions carried out in their classes since 1994/95. The need to disseminate involvement beyond this teaching group first led to the creation of a counselling space in the school and then to drawing up a whole-school policy against bullying, shared with students, parents and other teachers of the school. This was implemented at the class and the school levels.

The effects on rates of bullying have been evaluated by giving questionnaires to 170 students in the school year 1993/94 (before the start of the intervention); to 187 students in the school year 1996/97 (after two years of curricular interventions); and to 242 students in the school year 1999/2000 (after a total of six years' intervention and two years after the whole-school policy implementation). Altogether the data show a progressive decrease in bullying. From 1993 to 2000 there was a decrease of 59 per cent from the first to the third evaluation for the index 'being bullied sometimes or more', and a decrease of 66.5 per cent for the index 'bullying other children sometimes or more'. Also, the corresponding indexes of higher frequency ('once a week or more') show decreases of about 50 per cent.

In the same school a model of peer support has been active since 1998. These interventions are aimed at enhancing students' sense of responsibility in confronting bullying and improving the school climate. In studies carried out in several schools a 'befriending' model has been developed and adapted for Italian schools. For some of these studies evaluation results are now available that highlight how this type of intervention is able to reduce problems of violence escalation in the class and to promote responsibility and prosocial behaviour among students (Menesini and Benelli, 2000).

Clinical approaches

Two relevant interventions have been carried out in two cities in the South of Italy, Naples and Palermo (Bacchini et al., 2000; Di Maria and Piazza, 1998), in areas where the presence of criminal organizations and the Mafia are particularly high. In both studies, authors talk about 'Mafia-like feelings' which pervade the communities and people's habits and behaviours. Both interventions were characterized as clinical interventions making use of focus group techniques for teachers and students; there was a strong role for psychologists who intervened directly with the groups of teachers and pupils. During these sessions psychologists try to enhance cognitive and emotional awareness of participants. Results are not always positive, showing how the problems of these risk areas require multi-level efforts and approaches.

Awareness promotion activities

Given the scientific work on school bullying and the debate in the country, several awareness-raising activities like conferences, meetings and other initiatives have been undertaken in the last five years. In some conferences, relevant international scholars in the area of bullying and violence such as Olweus, Smith and Dodge were invited in order to promote a cross-cultural and comparative discussion. In recent years, two travelling exhibitions have been produced, one of them focused on school bullying (Bulli e Bulle) (boy bullies and girl bullies) and the other on conflict awareness and resolution (Conflitti litigi e altre rotture) (conflicts, quarrels and other disputes).

Conclusions

This report on school violence in Italy gives a contrasting picture of a prevalence of violent offences and behaviour that may be lower than expected, together with a prevalence of school bullying that is serious and worrying. Findings have been reported in relation to specific studies that often conflict with each other. The main factors that might explain inconsistencies across data can be related to specific characteristics of population, measures used and type of informants. The report shows a multifaceted reality where the incidence of violence is different in relation to deprived or non-deprived areas, to head teachers' and students' perspectives, and to types of persons (disabled or not, boys or girls, younger or older). Further investigations are necessary in order to have a more coherent understanding of the incidence of the problem and to reach a better agreement about how to define and to address the different manifestations of violence in schools.

Problems arise also from the use of general terms like *'disagio scolastico'* (school malaise), so frequent in professional and political documents. On the one hand this can have benefits, since it offers a comprehensive framework to encourage preventive interventions in schools; but on the other hand it might be misleading since it confuses different types of developmental symptoms and consequently different approaches to tackle them.

In terms of intervention there is a contrast between the interesting number of local studies reported and the absence of a specific national policy. The comparison between these two levels of analysis shows the need for better co-operation between different agencies working in the area: schools, universities and political committees.

In conclusion, the organization of a national agency of documentation is to be hoped for, in order to collect documents and information across the country and to give a new impulse to the research and intervention in this area.

Acknowledgements

Thanks to Dr. G. Boda and Dr. R. Anoé for their help in data collection, and Professor G.V. Caprara and Professor A. Fonzi for comments on an earlier draft of the chapter.

References

Bacchini, D., Amodeo, A.L., Comito, M. and Di Clemente, R. (2000). 'Pensare alle prepotenze, fare prepotenze': un'esperienza di gruppo con alunni e insegnanti. In E. Menesini (ed.). *Bullismo: che fare? Prevenzione e strategie d'intervento nella scuola.* Firenze: Giunti. pp.160–189.

Bacchini, D. and Valerio, P. (eds) (2001). *Giovani a rischio.* Milano: Franco Angeli.

Belacchi, C., Benelli, B. and Menesini, E. (2000). Il bullismo in età adolescenziale. Entità e caratteristiche del fenomeno dopo l'obbligo scolastico. Provincia di Ancona, Atti del convegno 15.12.2000.

Björkqvist, K., Lagerspetz, K.M.J. and Kaukiainen, A. (1992). Do girls manipulate and boys fight? Developmental trends in regard to direct and indirect aggression. *Aggressive Behavior*, 18, 117–127.

Centro Interuniversitario per la ricerca sulla genesi delle motivazioni prosociali ed antisociali, and Ministero della Pubblica Istruzione (2000a). Primo rapporto del progetto 'Percezione del clima in ambito scolastico' (Direzione generale della scuola media).

Centro Interuniversitario per la ricerca sulla genesi delle motivazioni prosociali ed antisociali, and Ministero della Pubblica Istruzione (2000b). Rapporto sul programma 'Autonomia, Life Skills e Peer education', Fase I e II.

Coie, J.D. and Dodge, K.A. (1998). Aggression and Antisocial Behavior. In W. Damon (Series ed.) and N. Eisenberg (eds). *Handbook of Child Psychology: Vol.3, Social, Emotional and Personality Development.* New York: Wiley. pp.779–862.

Coie, J.D., Terry, R., Zakriski, I.A. and Lochman, J.E. (1995). Early Adolescent and Social Influences on Delinquent Behavior. In J. McCord (ed.). *Coercion and Punishment in Long-term Perspectives.* New York: Cambridge University Press. pp.229–244.

De Leo, G. (1998). *La devianza minorile.* Rome: Carocci.

De Leo, G. and Malagoli Togliatti, M. (2000). Il rischio della delinquenza e la sua prevenzione. In G.V. Caprara and A. Fonzi (eds). *L'età sospesa.* Firenze: Giunti. pp.179–196.

Di Maria, F. and Piazza, A. (1998). Oltre la violenza. Una ricerca/intervento sul bullismo, Parte terza: la ricerca empirica. I dati concernenti gli insegnanti. *Psicologia e Scuola,* 18, 17–26.

Fonzi, A. (ed.) (1997). *Il Bullismo in Italia. Il fenomeno delle prepotenze a scuola dal Piemonte alla Sicilia.* Firenze: Giunti.

Fonzi, A., Genta, M.L., Costabile, A., Menesini, E. and Bacchini, D. (1999). Italy. In P.K. Smith, Y. Morita, J. Junger-Tas, D. Olweus, R. Catalano and P. Slee (eds). *The Nature of School Bullying: A Cross-national Perspective.* London: Routledge.

Istituto Nazionale di Statistica (2001). *Annuario Statistico Italiano 2001.* Roma: ISTAT.

Loeber, R. and Hay, D. (1997). Key issues in the development of aggression and violence from childhood to early adulthood. *Annual Review of Psychology,* 48, 371–410.

Menesini, E. (2000). *Bullismo: che fare? Prevenzione e strategie d'intervento nella scuola.* Firenze: Giunti.

Menesini, E. and Benelli, B. (2000). Responsabilizzazione degli alunni e forme di supporto tra coetanei. In E. Menesini (ed.). *Bullismo: che fare? Prevenzione e strategie d'intervento nella scuola.* Firenze: Giunti. pp.116–127.

Menesini, E. and Rossi, F. (2001). Bullying in high-schools: comparison between teachers' and students' perspective. Internal Report, Department of Psychology, University of Florence.

Olweus, D. (1993). *Bullying at School: What we Know and What we can Do.* Oxford: Blackwell.

Pignatti, B. and Menesini, E. (2000). L'approccio curricolare. In E. Menesini (ed.). *Bullismo: che fare? Prevenzione e strategie d'intervento nella scuola.* Firenze: Giunti. pp.88–99.

Prina, F. (2000). Il Progetto NOVAS RES. In C. Baraldi, T. Mancini, E. Menesini and P. Prina (eds), *Ragazzi a scuola: regole, conflitti e prevaricazioni.* Atti del Convegno 10 ottobre 2000, Modena.

Provveditorato agli Studi di Roma – Ufficio Studi e Programmazione (2000). 'La cultura della legalità nella scuola romana' – Rapporto 2000.

Smith, P.K., Morita, Y., Junger-Tas, J., Olweus, D., Catalano, R. and Slee, P. (eds) (1999). *The Nature of School Bullying: A Cross-national Perspective*. London: Routledge.

TMR Network Report: Nature and Prevention of Bullying (1997). Online. Available HTTP: <http://www.gold.ac.uk/tmr>.

Website pages:

<www.arpnet.it/~smaurodd/bullismo.htmwww.censis.it/censis/ricerche/1999/010399.html>

Chapter 11

Tackling violence in schools

A report from Greece

*Anastasia Houndoumadi, Lena Pateraki and
Maria Doanidou*

Background

The country

Greece currently has a population of about 10,578,000 people spread over 131,957 km². The country is divided into ten geographical regions. The Greek language is spoken by 95 per cent of the population. There are two groups of people acknowledged as minorities: the Muslim minority, which resides in Thrace in northern Greece, and the Roma minority, which is not limited to any geographical region. Adding to the diversity of the population are economic immigrants who officially amount to approximately 500,000. This figure, however, rises to almost 800,000 when illegal immigrants are included. More than half of these people come from Albania, and the remaining come mainly from Bulgaria, Romania, Pakistan, Ukraine, Poland and Georgia, with fewer from the Philippines and other countries in Asia, Africa, and the Middle East. Most of those immigrants are concentrated in the two large urban centres of Athens and Thessaloniki.

The recent waves of economic immigrants have affected the school population in significant ways because, as pointed out by Mitilis (1998), although there is an estimated 3 to 4 per cent annual decrement of the total school population, the rate of increase for the minority students amounts to about 50 per cent. The children of immigrants, who attend school, experience a number of learning difficulties due to the problems they face with the Greek language. The Greek school retains its identity as monocultural and monolinguistic even though the student population in many areas of the country is no longer culturally homogeneous and speaks more than twenty different languages (e.g. English, French, German, Russian, Arabic, Polish, Kurdish, Bulgarian, Serbian, Romanian and Philippino).

Indicative of a climate of xenophobia in which these students have to adjust culturally and socially are the findings of a recent poll of 2,343 people done on behalf of UNICEF by Kappa Research and reported by Mastoras (2001). Almost half (42 per cent) of the parents asked, reported that they considered the presence of non-Greek children in school as a rather negative and threatening event, whereas 62 per cent want the 'non-necessary' and illegal immigrants to leave the country. Only 38 per cent of the teachers surveyed believed that children of immigrants should be able to enrol in any school, while the remainder believed that they should attend special schools set up for these children. In view of the increasing number of immigrants' children attending schools, it is alarming that seven out of ten teachers reported that they believed they do not have adequate training to face the demands of teaching those children. In general, primary school pupils appear to be more tolerant and accepting of children coming from different cultures, while they tend to become less accepting as they grow up.

The school system

Educational policy in Greece is centrally regulated by the Ministry of Education and Religions, a situation that frequently hinders or discourages local initiatives. Even though there are both public and private schools offering educational services, the educational principles, curriculum and structure are common to both types of schools and determined by the Ministry of Education and Religions. However, there are differences in the methods of teaching, the facilities offered, as well as the extracurricular activities. The private schools are found mainly in the three large cities of Athens, Thessaloniki and Patra.

Primary school is compulsory and consists of six grades with children graduating at the age of 12. A typical school day begins at 8.15a.m. and ends at 1.15p.m., allowing for a twenty-minute break after the second hour and a ten-minute break between hours thereafter. The total number of class hours amounts to twenty-five per week in the first grade, rising up to a total of thirty class hours per week by the fifth grade.

The total number of students enrolled in primary school for the academic year September 1999 to June 2000 was 609,315. Out of these, 45,597 were immigrants and 19,949 were children of repatriated Greeks of the diaspora with at least one Greek parent. This amounts to 7.5 per cent of the student population being non-Greeks and 3.2 per cent being partially Greek.

Having successfully completed the sixth grade, students enter junior high school (*gymnasium*). This consists of three grades, at the conclusion of which compulsory education is completed at the age of 15 years. All grades have a total of thirty-five class hours weekly. A typical day will commence at 8.30a.m., allow for a fifteen-minute break every second hour and finish at 2.30p.m. It has been estimated that about 7 per cent of the students drop out of school before completing their gymnasium studies, even though completion is a legal requirement.

Upon completion of the nine years of compulsory education there is a choice to be made. Students may choose to join the labour force or some public or private educational programme acquiring a specific trade such as that of an electrician. Most students, however, continue their studies in senior high school (*lyceum*). The lyceum studies last three years and students graduate by the time they are 18 years old. In the first grade of lyceum students have a total of thirty-one class hours, finishing at 1.30p.m. four days a week and at 2.30p.m. on the fifth. In the second grade students complete a thirty-three hour weekly programme. At this point students may choose from three directions, which will determine the subjects they study: 'theoretical' (including literature, history, and classics), 'positive' (including mathematics and natural sciences) and 'technological'. In the third grade students continue their studies according to the direction chosen. According to the latest law, entry to university is based on Panhellenic examinations taken at the end of the second and third grades of lyceum.

Of the almost 600,000 students at gymnasium and lyceum levels for the academic year September 1999 to June 2000, 16,475 were non-Greeks and 11,192 were children of repatriated Greeks of the diaspora with at least one Greek parent.

Schools both at the primary and secondary level (gymnasia and lycea) differ in size, but in urban areas are typically around 200 pupils. The maximum number of students per class is about seventeen students at the primary level and twenty-seven students at the secondary level. In the private sector, however, numbers tend to be higher. Most large schools are found in the urban centres of Athens and Thessaloniki, where shortage of space has forced schools to share premises in shifts. Thus some schools may operate either in the mornings or afternoons on a fixed basis or alternating every other week. Each school is a complete independent entity consisting, in addition to the student body, of a head teacher, and teaching as well as supportive staff. The sharing of school buildings is fraught with problems, as there tends to be less of a feeling of belonging and commitment associated with a particular school or classroom.

There are three intercultural primary schools as well as two gymnasia and two lycea, in the greater Athens area. The number of intercultural schools across all educational levels around the country is presently about twenty and will soon rise. These schools, originally created to cater to the needs of the children of repatriated Greeks, are now serving students of economic immigrants, refugees and repatriates alike. The curricula followed by all intercultural schools are similar to those of the regular public schools adjusted to the cultural, social and learning needs of the students. Additionally, there are a number of primary schools in Thrace in northern Greece where students are taught both in the Greek and Turkish languages.

Linguistic/definitional issues

References to phenomena of violence on school premises made in the Greek language use terms such as 'βία' (violence) 'επιθετικότητα' (aggression) and 'βανδαλισμός' (vandalism). It is interesting that up to 1998 there was no corresponding word in Greek for the term 'bullying', although the phenomenon existed and as revealed by research was recognized as such by both students and teachers. Following recent research the term 'εκφοβισμός' (bullying) has been introduced and is increasingly adopted by researchers, practitioners, and the general public. Less frequently, bullies are referred to in the popular press as 'ψευτοπαληκαράδες', and 'νταήδες'.

Historical background

The phenomenon of school violence has not yet been the focus of extensive empirical research, and there are no special provisions at the state level regarding appropriate policies to prevent and deal with incidents of violence in schools. Schools themselves usually lack a clear policy on bullying and school violence, while media attention is attracted only when an extraordinary event takes place. It is indicative that there has been no corresponding word in Greek for the term 'bullying', as mentioned above.

Knowledge

Findings of research on physical violence have not given us a uniform picture. This can be accounted for by the different methodologies employed in various studies (student self-report questionnaires, selected student home interviews, questionnaires completed by school principals) and the different ways in which physical violence was defined, or grouped with other types of behaviours such as cheating or use of drugs. The results we could tease out from the reports are presented in this section grouped by educational level. We have tried to report only evidence that clearly refers to physical violence, avoiding data that do not allow the differentiation of physical violence from other forms of violent or antisocial behaviours.

Primary education

Pateraki and Houndoumadi (2001), using self-report questionnaires, focused on bullying behaviours among 1,312 primary school pupils between 8 and 12 years of age in the greater Athens area. They reported that 14.7 per cent of the pupils self-identified as victims of bullying, 6.3 per cent as bullies, and 4.8 per cent as both bullies and victims. Significantly more boys than girls self-identified as bullies and bully/victims. The number of self-reported victims tended to decrease with increasing age; in contrast, older pupils were more likely to admit bullying others, though in more indirect ways. Similar sex and age differences were also observed by Boulton et al. (2001), who explored the incidence of self-reported aggressive behaviours (hitting/kicking others, calling them names, and purposefully socially excluding others) in a sample of 664 pupils aged 8 to 11 years old. Physical aggression was found to decline with age among girls, while the reverse was observed among boys, who reported greater involvement in incidents of verbal or physical aggression. Additionally 10- to 11-year-old boys reported greater physical victimization than girls did. A higher incidence of reported involvement in aggressive behaviours predicted a more positive and open attitude towards aggression as well as a stronger belief that aggressive behaviour can lead to positive results. These attitudes may play a crucial role in shaping the school climate and affecting the expression of violent behaviours. It is in this context that we should view indications of peer pressure as revealed by Pateraki and Houndoumadi (2001), who found that 35.5 per cent of pupils reported feeling forced to join in bullying others.

Related to school climate, Petropoulos and Papastylianou (2001) reported that on the basis of primary school principals' responses to questionnaires, antisocial behaviour (including physical violence between pupils) was negatively related to sociability among teachers and positively related to the number of schools sharing the same buildings. The existence of a positive social climate among teachers was reflected in an overall positive atmosphere where violence was unwelcome, while overcrowding and sharing of premises in shifts was related to a climate of lesser involvement in the school community facilitating and/or not inhibiting the expression of physical violence.

According to a country-wide sample of primary school principals (Petropoulos and Papastylianou, 2001) the frequency of violence (beatings resulting in injury) between pupils received a rating of 1.59 on a Likert scale varying from 1: never to 5: very often, while violent confrontations with pupils from other schools received a rating of 1.06. The low incidence reported might be indicative of the lack of awareness on the part of teachers and principals of the true extent of physical violence in schools. This lack of awareness was documented in another study conducted in primary schools in the Athens region (Houndoumadi and Pateraki, 2001).

Papastylianou (2000), using a country-wide stratified sample of 2,926 students from different educational levels, found that primary school pupils gave very low ratings both of the frequency of use of violence by teachers against pupils and of the incidence of physical violence between pupils. Furthermore, pupils' physical victimization was found to be positively related to the use of violence against others and negatively related to reported fair treatment by the family. In other words, pupils who experience physical violence tend to retaliate by using the same means, while pupils who feel that their family does not treat them fairly are more likely to exhibit violent behaviour towards other pupils.

Secondary education (gymnasium and lyceum)

The earliest data on the expression of violence between pupils, not necessarily on the school grounds, was collected in 1984 by Bésé (reported in 1998) in a country-wide sample of 3,795 students aged 14 to 17 years. According to students' self-reports, 60.9 per cent had slapped others or engaged in a fistfight, 19.9 per cent had fought using a weapon (a piece of wood, stone, knife) and 12.7 per cent had participated in a fight resulting in injury.

Fakiolas and Armenakis (1995), conducting research in 153 high schools in the municipality of Athens, distributed self-report questionnaires to 3,774 students aged 12 to 19 years. They found that 4.4 per cent of the students reported beating others seldom and 2.5 per cent reported beating them many times, while 6.0 per cent engaged in both physical and verbal violence many times. Across all categories of violence between pupils, girls exhibited lower levels of violence than boys did at all ages (25 per cent versus 42 per cent).

Gotovos (1996) carried out an extensive study on a sample of 2,545 high school students aged 12 to 16 years, attending schools in the city of Ioannina and the island of Corfu, both in north-western Greece. A total of 40.2 per cent of students reported being aware of violence in their school, while more specifically, 23 per cent reported having been hit on the school premises, or on their way to or from school. In another set of questions analysing further the frequency of reported violence, 52 per cent of the students reported hitting, beating or attacking others that are weaker than themselves often or sometimes, while 57 per cent reported being involved in physical fights with other students with the same frequency. More boys than girls were aware of violence in schools, were victims of violence and carried weapons for protection against that violence. Violence was also found to be related to age, with younger students being more frequently victimized than older ones.

Doanidou and Xenaki (1997) studied the phenomenon of bullying in a major private school in the area of Athens. They administered the junior high school version of the Olweus questionnaire to 149 students aged 12 to 13 years and 143 students aged 14 to 15 years. It was found that

22 per cent of the 12- to 13-year-olds and 19 per cent of the 14- to 15-year-olds reported being victimized, while 10.1 per cent of the former group and 13 per cent of the latter admitted to bullying other students. Both victimization and bullying were reported to take place from 'sometimes' to 'several times a week'. Unfortunately the data were not reported separately for physical and verbal violence and the incidence reported refers to both kinds of violence.

The phenomenon of violence in school life was also studied by the General Secretariat for Youth and National Youth Council for Hellas (1999), through structured home interviews conducted with 350 lyceum students who formed a stratified sample drawn from the mainland and the island of Crete. According to the findings, 82 per cent reported that they had witnessed incidents of violence between same-age students, and 69 per cent between students of different ages. More specifically, 57 per cent reported witnessing beatings among students and 12 per cent reported witnessing attacks, where some form of weapon was used. Age differences were identified, as twice as many first graders as second and third graders (18 per cent vs. 9.1 per cent and 8.9 per cent respectively) reported witnessing such incidents. Additionally, three times as high an incidence was reported in urban areas compared with semi-urban and rural areas (16 per cent vs. 5 per cent and 6 per cent respectively).

Any reference to violence in the subsequently reported findings from the above study includes both physical and verbal violence, which was considered as one variable by the researchers. Inquiring about students' victimization experiences, 11.6 per cent reported having been victims of violence. More boys than girls reported that they had been victimized (16.8 per cent vs. 6.6 per cent) and more low achievers than high achievers (22.7 per cent vs. 3.5 per cent). With respect to being violent, 23 per cent admitted that they had participated in episodes of violence in schools. More boys than girls reported participating (36.5 per cent vs. 10.4 per cent), and more low achievers than high achievers (26.1 per cent vs. 10.2 per cent).

Concerning the characteristics of those involved in violent episodes, 6 per cent reported that violence was directed against students with special physical characteristics, while 29 per cent reported that violent episodes were observed between Greek and non-Greek students. Those violent incidents between Greek and non-Greek students were more frequently reported in urban areas (especially in Thessaloniki, 58 per cent and Athens, 39 per cent) compared with semi-urban (15 per cent) and rural (19 per cent). Episodes of violence among non-Greek students were reported by 26 per cent of the students, most of them in urban areas (in Athens the frequency of reporting reaches 84 per cent). Additionally, over a third of the students (35 per cent) reported observing (at least once) violent episodes between students and teachers, while 22 per cent reported the occurrence of violent episodes between students and people who were not teachers but part of the general school staff.

A substantial number of the students questioned in that study (69 per cent) reported witnessing episodes of violence between students and youth not attending school, while 64 per cent witnessed outbreaks of violence between gangs in the Athens region and to a lesser extent in the rest of the country.

Contrary to the above evidence, the following three studies report a low incidence of violence among high school students. Petropoulos et al. (2000b), using a Likert scale indicating frequency of engaging in various behaviours (0: never to 4: very often), found that students rated as 0.43 their engagement in violent behaviours towards other students. Reporting their own victimization, they rated the frequency of being physically victimized by students as 0.68 and by teachers as 0.21. Boys reported that they were more frequently victimized than girls, while victimization was found to be positively related to frequency of punishment by parents and negatively related to the perception of fair and just treatment by classmates, teachers, parents and siblings.

Papastylianou (2000), using the same sample, reported that in addition to victimization, boys more frequently than girls also reported expressing violence directed at other students. Furthermore, victimization and violence directed at others were found to be positively related to each other, as well as to unjust treatment by the teachers. It appears that the same students tend to be both recipients and perpetrators of violence, which flourishes more in cases where the school ethos is characterized by perceived unjust treatment by the teachers.

Petropoulos et al. (2000a), in their sample of school principals, found that the frequency of violence between students involving beatings resulting in injury, received a rating of 1.42 on a Likert scale varying from 1: never to 5: very often, while violent confrontations with pupils from other schools received a rating of 1.13. On the basis of the responses given by the principals, it was found that perceived frequency of pupil victimization was again related to school ethos. The higher the sociability among teachers, the lower the victimization between students, while the higher the number of students attending a school, the higher the reported violence.

Manoudaki (2000), who has documented the expression of violence through gang participation, indicates that 16.6 per cent of lyceum students reported having participated more than once in group violent behaviour, while 7.1 per cent admitted to being members of a gang. A knife or a dagger, and once a gun, were reported to have been used in 33 per cent of the attacks. It should be noted that while 52.3 per cent of students reported having been victims of such group attacks, none reported the incident to the teachers or the police!

Overall, considering findings from both primary schools and high schools, the results clearly support the existence of a sex difference, with more boys engaging in violence than girls, at all ages. There is also a distinct age trend, with the younger pupils experiencing more violence than the older ones. Furthermore, school climate, as reflected by the quality of relationships among teachers and the number of schools housed in the same buildings, was related to violence. Lastly, the findings suggested that violence in schools appeared to be a phenomenon that mostly occurred in urban areas.

It should be mentioned at this point that a form of violence that has attracted considerable research attention in Greece is that against school property. Thus, school principals (Petropoulos and Papastylianou, 2001) reported a higher incidence of destruction and/or theft of school property (books, maps, computers, instruments) than physical violence between persons. This extensive form of vandalism has been of great concern (e.g. Kalabaliki, 1995) as it is widespread and in essence interferes with the smooth or effective functioning of the instructional process, eventually causing discomfort and irritation to all parties involved (teachers and students). It is possible that this form of violence towards objects is more frequently reported and researched because of the ease with which it can be observed. Students do not express violence either towards others or towards property while teachers, directors or researchers are watching, but the expression of violence towards property leaves undeniable traces behind. Additionally, this violence expressed against the school is considered by many researchers (e.g. Panousis, 1995; Papaharalambous, 1995) to be an expression of a 'just retaliation' by the students who report experiencing the school as the perpetrator of violence against them. Students frequently perceive the educational system as unduly harsh, involving extensive amounts of homework and demands that force them to resort to attending tutoring schools in addition to their regular school hours. The school is a place of frequent examinations, and limited social and creative activities that would promote genuine communication between students and teachers, who frequently resort to authoritarian practices.

Action

Current national/regional policies regarding violence in school

This section of the report is based on the information provided by Koralli (1999). Interest in and concern about the issue of violence in schools has been rather recent in Greece. Even though some policies have been developed to address the problem of violence and school bullying, these policies do not seem to form a unified whole and are at different stages of implementation. Some of the initiatives and actions taken by the Ministry of Education and Religions, the Institute of Education and the Ministry of Health and Social Welfare involve the following:

- Development and publication by the Institute of Education of an information pamphlet to be distributed to all teachers and students. This pamphlet describes the phenomenon of violence in schools and discusses prevention and treatment in a school environment.
- Publication of educational materials aiming at the creation of an anti-bullying and anti-racist attitude through the teaching of subjects such as mathematics, geography, history and literature; funded by the Ministry of Education and Religions and the Greek Federation of Teachers working at public schools.
- A number of actions developed by the Ministry of Education and Religions and the Ministry of Youth in order to combat racism, prejudice and xenophobia, which might lead to violence in schools. These actions include the development of programmes in multicultural education, special TV programmes and after-school activities in arts and sports.
- A number of actions developed by the Ministry of Health and Social Welfare on issues related to violence in schools, such as health education, drug abuse prevention programmes, and training on psychosocial issues for different age groups of students.
- A teachers' training seminar on the theme of violence and aggression in schools organized by the Institute of Continuing Adult Education (IDEKE).

A more detailed description and evaluation of the aforementioned teachers' training seminar organized by IDEKE will be presented. During the period 1997–1998, two rounds of seminars were organized by IDEKE. The 580 participants were in-service teachers from all over Greece selected on the basis of the frequency of violent incidents in their schools and the location of the schools (priority was given to areas with a multicultural population).

Based on a post-seminar evaluation, it was concluded that it contributed to:

- the development of a new 'point of view' and realization that aggression and violence concern both the adolescent student and the teacher;
- the provision of an impetus to acquire a discourse, which does not depend on ready-made answers and solutions but rather faces human behaviour in a more flexible way;
- the broadening of both the knowledge and perspective of teaching staff as far as the theme of violence and aggression in school is concerned.

Unfortunately no systematic data were obtained regarding the impact of the training upon the students and the school community at large when the teachers returned to their schools.

Recently, in the framework of a larger educational reform undertaken by the Ministry of Education and Religions, supportive programmes have been introduced targeted at students with learning difficulties, while 'second chance' schools have been established for youth above age 18 who dropped out of school early and wish to complete their education. Additionally, special measures have been taken aiming at the social adjustment of immigrants, refugees, and repatriates as well as minority Roma and Turkish speaking students. To meet this goal, instructional materials and audio-visual aids sensitive to their cultural characteristics and educational needs have been developed.

Nevertheless, as Artinopoulou indicates, 'we do not recognize school violence as a social phenomenon, but only as a case study or individualized behaviour of some deviant juveniles, or we do not even mention it, so as not to suggest that schools are places of conflict rather than places of consent in everyday life' (Artinopoulou, 1997, p.16).

Relevant case studies

The Moraitis School

The information in this section is based on an unpublished report by Doanidou and Xenaki (1997) and concerns the case of Moraitis School. This is a large private school in the Athens area with over 2,000 pupils enlisted in all grades from kindergarten to lyceum (ages 4 to 18 years). In the beginning of 1995, the psychology/counselling department of the school started dealing with bullying problems in a more systematic manner.

Initially, the frequency and types of school bullying cases were studied using the junior high school version of the Olweus questionnaire. Based on the results obtained, and advice sought from Professor Smith, the formulation and implementation of a whole-school anti-bullying policy began. The first step was to raise the awareness of teachers and non-teaching staff in the school. Special meetings were organized and carried out by the psychology department for this purpose. A booklet was also written explaining the nature of bullying, the frequency of its occurrence in the school and what one could do to prevent and tackle specific cases.

Awareness raising among the pupils was a second step. The aim was to promote prosocial and supportive behaviour among pupils and to change the existing ideas surrounding school bullying, like 'it is "cool" to bully others', that 'one can do nothing to stop it', or that 'one is not supposed to ask an adult for help'. Awareness raising is a continuous process and different activities to support it are organized within the curriculum. Those activities include reading and discussing relevant material, classroom discussions facilitated by one of the counsellors and presentations in the school auditorium.

In parallel, there is an organized system of referral and coping with specific bullying cases. It includes:

• counselling both the victims and the bullies involved;
• informing and counselling the families when necessary;
• enforcing consequences and punishment for the bullies whenever required.

A particularly successful approach is the Lyceum Student Assistance Team (SAT), which has been operating for two years. It is composed of school personnel, including people from administration, the counselling department and teachers. Its purpose is to identify pupils who are at risk or in crisis, to assess the nature and extent of their problem and provide them with counselling and follow-up services.

A third step in the whole-school policy was to raise the awareness and gain the collaboration of parents. This was achieved by sending every family a special booklet describing the problem of bullying, explaining the school's approach in preventing and dealing with bullying, and suggesting parental actions in case they suspect or know that their child is involved in a bullying situation. Furthermore, an open invitation was extended to all parents to attend a presentation on bullying and take part in the ensuing discussion.

Although the effectiveness of the programme has not yet been formally evaluated, there are obvious changes in the school's climate and perception concerning the issue of school bullying.

Lyceum of Kallithea

This case study, which illustrates an initiative taken at the local level, is based on information provided by Artinopoulou (1998). In an attempt to cope with problems arising from defiance of school rules, physical violence between students, student apathy, vandalism and signs of drug abuse, the school principal of Kallithea (a municipality in the greater Athens area) and the local teachers' association sought help from a local family counselling centre. The centre professionals followed school life closely for two weeks, interviewing teachers and students. The initial findings revealed that the school problems stemmed from a lack of communication between students and teachers as well as between students and students, lack of leisure time, the authoritarian practices of some teachers, and the substandard physical environment where the school operated (old buildings, unattractive classrooms and insufficient school yard space).

On the basis of those findings, a three-month intervention programme was designed aiming at the provision of:

- space where students could meet and hold activities;
- opportunities for joint student–teacher participation in the planning and carrying out of recreational and sport activities;
- opportunities for students' participation in finding solutions to the school problems;
- regular meetings between teachers and the counselling centre's professionals to provide psychological support for problems arising from within and outside the school;
- individual counselling for senior students;
- drug awareness campaigns;
- career advice.

At the conclusion of the intervention phase, an evaluation was carried out through input provided by students and teachers. The reported effects can be summarized as follows:

- a significant reduction in vandalism and acts of violence;
- an improvement in the students' communication skills and self-awareness as a result of added opportunities for self-expression;
- increased awareness among teachers regarding problems faced by the students both inside and outside the school;
- expanded knowledge among teachers regarding different ways of handling student violence.

Conclusion

In the last five years Greece has witnessed the beginnings of empirical research regarding the phenomenon of school violence. This has led to some initial realization of the existence of the problem. It has become apparent, however, that a lot of work remains to be done with respect to sensitization at all levels, from students and teachers to families, society and state policy.

Intervention programmes designed to combat violence are still few, and isolated. They lack systematic internal and external evaluation so that the reports we have frequently restrict themselves to descriptive data, glossing over problems and possible inadequacies. Additionally, it is essential at this initial stage to co-ordinate and disseminate accumulated knowledge to all interested parties, so that innovation and long-term continuity can be ensured. Any training seminar addressing school professionals and sharing knowledge about violent behaviour in school settings as well as principles of successful intervention should be presented in a way that ensures its implementation when the training programme ends. The diversity of problems usually encountered by professionals who try to use the knowledge acquired may frequently discourage application. Experience has shown over and over again that nothing proceeds in the smooth, predictable fashion it is presented as in training seminars, where model intervention programmes are introduced.

Teachers should be provided with extensive supportive resources, which they can use in case of problems, while active efforts should be taken to ensure a positive school ethos, which will not support the expression of violence between students, between teachers and students, or between teachers.

Finally, measures have to be taken to help minority students, whose numbers are steadily increasing, deal with difficulties in adjusting to school. Problems experienced might lead to intercultural conflict and pave the way to an escalation of alienation and racism. Schools need to develop beyond the oppressive homogenization that characterizes them today, towards respect for heterogeneity in the background interests and abilities of students, of Greek and non-Greek origin alike.

Acknowledgement

We acknowledge the assistance of Pania Laskaratou in the collection of the information included in this report.

References

Artinopoulou, V. (1997). School violence: actual trends in research and coping strategies. Paper presented at a conference on 'Education and Social Exclusion', Athens, Greece. 7 December.

Artinopoulou, V. (1998). Promoting prosocial behavior as a school violence prevention policy: the case of Greece. Paper presented at the workshop: Prosocial Pupil Development. Nijmegen, ITS, The Netherlands. 26–27 June.

Bésé, L. (ed.) (1998). Βία στο Σχολείο, Βία του Σχολείου [Violence at School, School Violence]. Athens: Ελληνικά Γράμματα.

Boulton, M.J., Karellou, J., Laniti, J., Manoussou, V. and Lemoni, U. (2001). Aggression and victimization among pupils of Greek primary schools. [επιθετικότητα και θυματοποίηση ανάμεσα στους μαθητές των Ελληνικών Δημοτικών σχολείων]. Ψυχολογία, 8, 12–29.

Doanidou, M. and Xenaki, F. (1997). Frequency and forms of bullying at Moraitis School. Unpublished manuscript.

Fakiolas, N. and Armenakis, A. (1995). Εμπλοκή μαθητών και χρηστών τοξικών ουσιών σε βιαιότητες [The involvement of students and illegal substance users in violent incidents]. Σύγχρονη Εκπαίδευση, 81, 42–50.

General Secretariat for Youth and National Youth Council for Hellas (1999). Φαινόμενα Βίας στη Σχολική Ζωή (Οκτ. 1999 – Νοεμ. 1999) [Phenomena of violence in school life (October 1999 – November 1999)]. Unpublished manuscript.

Gotovos, A.E. (1996). Νεολαία και Κοινωνική Μεταβολή: Αξίες, Εμπειρίες και Προοπτικώς [Youth and Social Transformation: Values, Experiences and Perspectives]. Athens: Gutenberg.

Houndoumadi, A. and Pateraki, L. (2001). Bullying and bullies in Greek elementary schools: pupils' attitudes and teachers'/parents' awareness. Educational Review, 53, 19–26.

Kalabaliki, F. (1995). Καταστροφικότητα, σχολική εμπειρία και πολιτική συμπεριφορά [Destructiveness, school experience and political behavior]. Σύγχρονη Εκπαίδευση, 81, 32–41.

Koralli, L. (1999). Report on policies/activities by Member States 1997/99 by the Expert Group on Violence in School. Brussels: European Commission.

Manoudaki, T. (2000). Νέες μορφές παραβατικότητας ανηλίκων στο χώρο του σχολείου [New Forms of Juvenile Delinquency in Schools]. In N. Petropoulos and A. Papastylianou (eds). Προκλήσεις στη Σχολική Κοινότητα: Έρευνα και παρέμβαση. Athens: Παιδαγωγικό Ινστιτούτο. pp.142–148.

Mastoras, N. (2001). Φοβού τους φτωχούς ξένους [Beware of the poor foreigners]. Daily newspaper TA NEA 21 March.

Mitilis, A. (1998). Μειονότητες στη Σχολική Τάξη: Μια σχέση αλληλεπίδρασης [Minorities in the Classroom: An Interactive Relationship]. Athens: Οδυσσέας.

Panousis, G. (1995). Η βία στα σχολεία: Double Face [Violence in schools: Double Face]. Σύγχρονη Εκπαίδευση, 84, 79–81.

Papaharalambous, T. (1995). Η βία δεν έχει θέση στο νέο σχολείο. Ο ρόλος του Δασκάλου [Violence has no place in the new school. The role of the teacher]. Σύγχρονη Εκπαίδευση, 84, 88–92.

Papastylianou, A. (2000). Μαθητές-θύτες και μαθητές-θύματα: Κοινωνικο-ψυχολογική προσέγγιση [Student-perpetrators and student-victims: a socio-psychological approach]. In N. Petropoulos and A. Papastylianou (eds). Προκλήσεις στη Σχολική Κοινότητα: Έρευνα και παρέμβαση. Athens: Παιδαγωγικό Ινστιτούτο. pp.115–133.

Pateraki, L. and Houndoumadi, A. (2001). Bullying among primary school children in Athens, Greece. Educational Psychology, 21, 169–177.

Petropoulos, N. and Papastylianou, A. (2001). Μορφές Επιθετικότητας, Βίας και Διαμαρτυρίας στο Σχολείο [Types of Aggression, Violence and Protest in School] Athens: Παιδαγωγικό Ινστιτούτο.

Petropoulos, N., Papastylianou, A., Harisis, K. and Katerelos, P. (2000a). Βία και Διαμαρτυρία στα Σχολεία της Πρωτοβάθμιας και Δευτεροβάθμιας Εκπαίδευσης [Violence and Protest in Schools of Primary and Secondary Education]. Athens: Παιδαγωγικό Ινστιτούτο.

Petropoulos, N., Papastylianou, A., Katerelos, P. and Harisis, H. (2000b). Αντικοινωνική Συμπεριφορά Παιδιών και Εφήβων [Antisocial Behaviour of Children and Teenagers]. In A. Kalantzi-Azizi and H. Bezevekis (eds). Θέματα Ψυχικής Υγείας Παιδιών και Εφήβων. Athens: Ελληνικά Γράμματα.

Part III

Scandinavia

Chapter 12

Tackling violence in schools

A report from Finland

Kaj Björkqvist and Viktoria Jansson

Background

The country

Finland is a Scandinavian country, located on the eastern side of the Baltic and bordering Sweden and Russia. Although the area of the country is relatively large, the inhabitants number only 5.2 million. Finland has two official languages: Finnish (spoken by the majority) and Swedish (spoken by a minority of roughly 6 per cent, with schools and two universities in their own language). In Lapland (northern Finland) lives a small ethnic group of Saami people, having schools in their own language. Recent years have witnessed increased immigration from Russia and Estonia, but also refugees from the Balkans, Somalia, the Middle East and central Asia.

Since gaining her independence as a nation in 1917, Finland has been a multi-party democracy of Western European type. Finland had a period of swift urbanization after World War II, but about 30 per cent of the inhabitants are still living in the countryside. Citizens are guaranteed free education (even universities are not permitted to demand fees for enrolment, and private universities are not allowed), free health care, and a high level of general social welfare. However, in recent years, a trend towards privatization of previously government funded enterprises may be discerned. In an attempt to cut foreign debts, funds for (among other things) education have been cut, a fact that has affected the educational system somewhat negatively, resulting in bigger classes and increasing stress among teachers – probably making the schools less safe than they used to be.

The school system

In Finland, school is free of charge at all levels, and government funded. Private schools are not prohibited, but not encouraged either. In major cities, a few private schools may be found, typically Waldorf schools (based on Rudolf Steiner's educational philosophy) or Montessori schools. These are rare, however.

The Ministry of Education makes decisions pertaining to nationwide requirements about curricula and teacher education. The curriculum includes personal and social education, as well as education for citizenship, but only approximately one to two hours a week are reserved for these activities. In order to become a teacher at any level within the Finnish school system, one must earn the degree of Master of Education, which takes between five and six years of university level study.

Children attend compulsory comprehensive school from ages 7 to 16. Comprehensive school, in turn, is divided into two parts: primary school (grades one to six), and junior secondary school (grades seven to nine). After age 16, those who wish may continue at senior secondary school (grades ten to twelve). Primary schools usually have 100 to 500 pupils, but in remote areas, they may have as few as twenty to fifty pupils. Secondary schools may vary in size from approximately 200 to 1,000 students, but larger schools also exist in urban areas. A typical class size is twenty to thirty pupils.

Children with special educational needs, such as pupils with behavioural disturbances and disabilities, are provided for in special classes with specially trained teachers. These classes are usually located with regular primary/secondary schools, rather than being separated from them. In some cases, children with special needs may attend normal classes but be aided by specially appointed educational assistants.

Linguistic/definitional issues

The Finnish word for 'violence' is *väkivalta*, and school violence is called *kouluväkivalta*. The Swedish equivalents are *våld* and *skolvåld*. Bullying is referred to as *kiusaaminen* and school bullying as *koulukiusaaminen* (actually, 'harassment at school') in Finnish, and *mobbning* (in Swedish). *Väkivalta (våld)* refers to physical violence only, while *koulukiusaaminen (mobbning)* also includes psychological harassment and indirect bullying. These terms are used both in research and legislation (see below). In Swedish, however, the legislative term for bullying is *kränkande särbehandling*, which literally translates into English as 'abusive special treatment', implying that an individual is treated differently from others in the class or in the work group, and that the treatment in question is offensive and abusive.

In Finnish research, *koulukiusaaminen (mobbning)* is usually defined as negative activity or aggression exerted by one or more individuals (the bully/bullies) towards one or more individuals (the victim/s), and these activities are of a kind that the victim/s find painful, either in a psychological or physical sense, and would like to avoid. There is usually a power imbalance between bully and victim, with the consequence that the victim is not fully able to defend him/herself. In order to classify as bullying, these activities must be repeated and ongoing for at least a period of time; singular incidents do not count (Lagerspetz et al., 1982). In legislation, however, singular incidents of *kiusaaminen* or *kränkande särbehandling* do count, if severe enough. Also in everyday language, in contrast to research, singular incidents may be referred to as *kiusaaminen (mobbning)*.

Relevant historical background

Although teacher education includes no obligatory training in how to tackle problems of violence in schools, the new school legislation of Finland, effective from the beginning of 1999, emphasizes safety in schools. The legislation states that every student has the right to a safe school environment. According to the new policy, the provider of education must make sure that students will not experience acts of violence or bullying during school hours or in any other school-related activity. The legislation covers all official education (Veijola, 2000).

Corporal punishment of pupils was prohibited by law as early as 1890. However, when the senior author of this report went to school during the 1960s, he still witnessed teachers striking pupils on several occasions, either with their hand or with an object, usually on the head. Nowadays, corporal punishment is extremely rare in Finnish schools, and is likely to result in the expulsion of the teacher in question. It may be noted that in present day Finland – as in other Scandinavian countries – corporal punishment is prohibited by law not only at school, but also within homes.

Knowledge

Violence in schools

No official statistics with respect to the prevalence of violence in schools exist in Finland. Severe violence is rare in Finnish schools, and homicides have not occurred during the last two decades. The most recent case took place twenty-five years ago, when a junior secondary school pupil in the city of Turku killed a teacher with a spade.

In the following, we briefly summarize the eight worst cases of violence in Finnish comprehensive schools reported during the last three years, incidents of violence so grave in character that they became news items in all major media (Markkula, 2001):

- *Case 1*: in Vehkalahti in 1998, a 15-year-old attempted to kill a 13-year-old peer with a baseball bat. The teacher present did not dare to intervene. Luckily, the boy changed his mind in the middle of the assault, and no severe damage occurred.
- *Case 2*: in February 1998, in the city of Kemi, five 14- to 15-year-old boys tied a 14-year-old peer to a chair, assaulted him by beating and kicking, also hitting him with a baseball bat. They filmed it with a video camera: the assault took place during an ordinary school lesson when the class was supposed to learn about movie making. The teacher was, for an unknown reason, not present, and the boys decided to make a violent film – an enterprise which got completely out of hand.
- *Case 3*: in September 1998, in the city of Haukipudas, a 10-year-old and an 11-year-old boy tried to hang an 11-year-old peer with an electric cord, during a school break. Luckily they failed.
- *Case 4*: in April 1999, in Eurajoki, a 15-year-old boy stabbed a ninth grade peer with a knife. It was a close case: the victim nearly died due to loss of blood.
- *Case 5*: in April 2000, in Saarijärvi, four 8- to 12-year-old boys assaulted a 10-year-old peer in the school yard: while the victim was lying on the ground, the boys repeatedly kicked him and jumped on his chest. The victim luckily survived.
- *Case 6*: in January 2001, in Hollola, a 15-year-old boy stabbed a 14-year-old peer in the back with a knife. It was a question of revenge: the 14-year-old was a bully, who had terrorized him for a long period of time. The victim survived.
- *Case 7*: in January 2001, in the city of Espoo, a severe fight between two 11-year-old boys of different ethnic/racial background took place; although no weapons were used, the fight was so severe that the police had to be called to the school in order to stop it.
- *Case 8*: also in January 2001, in the city of Jyväskylä, a 13-year-old boy got into a fist fight with his teacher. He left school, went home to collect two knives, and returned with the intention of killing the teacher. The police managed to stop the incident.

Summing up these eight cases, the following conclusions may be drawn:

- only one incident was a case of pupil–teacher violence; seven of the eight were cases of conflicts between pupils;
- of these seven, all incidents were cases of male-to-male violence: only boys were involved, both as perpetrators and as victims;
- four cases of seven were dyadic conflicts; only three incidents involved group violence with more perpetrators than one;

- the age range for perpetrators and victims varied between 8 and 15. Cases involving weapons such as knives or baseball bats involved 13- to 15-year-old boys;
- the following weapons/aids were used: knives three times, baseball bats twice, a rope for tying up the victim once, and an electrical cord for hanging once. Only two cases of eight involved no weapon. These were incidents involving younger boys;
- only one case had the character of an ethnic/racial conflict.

Although most of these cases were life-threatening, such incidents are relatively infrequent.

As a contrast, bullying is seen as a far worse (at least, more far-reaching) problem in Finnish schools than is violence *per se*. For instance, in autumn 2000, a girl attending junior secondary school committed suicide as a result of psychological bullying. Five of the cases mentioned above (cases 2, 3, 5, 6, and 7) were in fact also bullying-related (four were cases of bullying, and one was a case of revenge of bullying). Thus, it appears to be incorrect to make a strict distinction between bullying and violence in schools in Finland. Rather, in most cases, severe violence appears to be the tip of the iceberg of bullying-related problems.

According to a variety of studies (e.g. Lagerspetz et al., 1982), bullying in schools involves 10 to 12 per cent of all Finnish pupils, if bullies as well as victims are included. In the Lagerspetz et al. study, the first of its kind in Finland, the frequency of bullying was investigated in urban and rural schools in children aged 12 to 16 years. There was a significant difference in frequency of bullying between boys and girls, bullying being a more prevalent problem among boys (8 per cent of victims) than among girls (2.2 per cent of victims). It should be noted, however, that at this point, indirect bullying was not yet recognized, and bullying was mostly seen as physical. No difference in frequency between urban and rural schools was found, neither could any difference due to school size be recognized. Bullying decreased by age, being more frequent at age 12 than at age 16.

Salmivalli et al. (1996) investigated not only the roles of bullies and victims, but also the roles of reinforcers, assistants, defenders, and out-siders in bullying situations. They found assistants of bullies to form 6.8 per cent of the class, and reinforcers as many as 19.5 per cent. That is, when these roles are taken into account, bullying involves far more pupils than previously thought. Salmivalli et al. also found bullying to be a more frequent problem among boys than among girls. Furthermore, reinforcers and assistants to bullies were far more often boys than girls, while defenders and outsiders were more often girls.

In a recent study by Rimpelä, Orre and Jokela (2002) and funded by STAKES, the Finnish National Research and Development Centre for

Welfare and Health, comprising 57,385 adolescents between the ages of 14 and 17, it was found that at age 14, 5 per cent of all boys and 4 per cent of all girls said that they had been bullied at least once a week; at age 15, the percentage was 3 per cent for both boys and girls, and at both ages 16 and 17, the percentages were 1 per cent for boys and 0 per cent for girls.

Action

Prevention and intervention programmes: general aspects

Measures intended to tackle violence in schools in Finland have in general been combined with anti-bullying measures. These have a fairly long tradition, because Olweus' works in Swedish (e.g. Olweus, 1973) became known in Finland during the 1970s. Olweus' book *Bullying among School-children: What we Know and What we can Do* was published in Swedish 1986 and translated into Finnish 1992. His methods, suggesting a number of possible measures at three levels – individual, class, and school levels – became the most well-known and applied anti-bullying programme. The Kempele programme (see below) was partly based on Olweus' ideas and provides an evaluation of them in a Finnish context.

Pikas' book on how to counter bullying was published in its original Swedish version in 1975 but not in Finnish until 1990. However, Finland being a bilingual nation, Pikas' methods became well known long before that. A central idea in Pikas' method is an effort to get the bully to commit him/herself to active assistance in the rehabilitation of the victim. If the bully accepts, s/he in turn is promised that his/her parents will not be informed about his/her previous bullying behaviour. (In this sense, the method differs drastically from that suggested by Olweus (1986, 1992), according to which parents always should be informed. In Scandinavia there has been an at times quite intensive and heated debate about which system is to be preferred.) The focus in Pikas' method is on how to talk to the bully. No evaluation of the method has been published in Finland, but it is popular among many teachers and schools.

A third anti-bullying programme, called the Farsta method (named after a city in Sweden), was developed by Ljungström, based partly on Pikas' principles, and his manual was translated into Finnish in 1990. A typical feature of the Farsta method is that each school has a trained team of two to four teachers who intervene immediately in cases of bullying. When dealing with bullies, they use the Pikas method. Peer support systems are often also included. This system is applied in many Swedish-speaking schools in Finland. A large-scale anti-bullying project based on the Farsta method is about to begin this year (2002) in Swedish-speaking schools in Finland, perhaps also in a number of Finnish-speaking schools, and one of the present authors (Björkqvist) will make a quantitative evaluation of it.

Several organizations have been involved in intervention and prevention programmes against school violence and bullying, such as *Mannerheimin Lastensuojeluliitto* [Mannerheim's Association for the Protection of Children], *Kiusattujen Tuki* [Victims' Support Organization], the Finnish Red Cross, *Hem och Skola* [Home and School], and *Folkhälsan* [People's Health]; the last two among Swedish speakers only. Besides organizations, a number of private persons and individual schools have been active in this respect. It would be impossible within the present report to present all programmes and initiatives, and, in the following, we concentrate on a selection of four programmes which have been evaluated to at least some extent, and which appear promising.

The alarm bracelet

One of the most innovative measures of intervention in Finland was presented in a study by Lahtinen and Sankala (1998). The principle was ingeniously simple and easy to apply.

A general problem in bullying situations is that teachers in the school yard either do not notice what is going on at all, or intervene too late. Accordingly, there is an urgent need to alert teachers immediately when a bullying situation is about to begin. Modern technology offers help, in the form of alarm systems originally developed for elderly people, for the purpose of alerting medical personnel in sudden situations. Similar alarm systems may be used to alert teachers or guards in bullying situations. Individuals prone to be victimized may wear a message 'sender' in the form of a bracelet resembling a wristwatch, and the teacher or individual on guard has a cellular phone on. When the victim notices that his/her tormentor is approaching, s/he presses a button on the bracelet, and a signal is immediately sent to the guard's mobile phone, making it possible to intervene quickly.

The system used by Lahtinen and Sankala was named Tele-Alert, and offered by the teleoperator Sonera (a Finnish company), but similar alarm systems are likely to be provided by other operators in other nations as well. The evaluation by Lahtinen and Sankala (1998) was a Master's thesis at the University of Oulu, and as such rather limited; more research is needed to assess its usefulness as an aid in anti-bullying programmes.

Nuutinen's victim slide show

Timo Nuutinen, who had worked for years in a department at a polyclinic, was shocked to find how frequently young victims of other adolescents' violent behaviour were admitted, and how easily severe injuries were inflicted: tripping a victim in the school yard, a snowball aimed at the eyes, or a single blow to the nose. Seemingly harmless bullying often caused broken teeth, damaged eyes, broken noses, concussion or even irreversible brain damage.

Nuutinen compiled a slide show, presenting photographs and X-rays of real-life cases of injured young victims. The slides were quite shocking. He presented this slide show to pupils in schools, accompanied by lively descriptions of how the injuries were produced. Nuutinen's slide show became very popular, in fact so popular that it has been shown in practically every comprehensive school in Finland. Everywhere he went, the pupils appeared impressed by the pictures and his vivid descriptions. The slide show seemed to have an almost shocking effect. Nuutinen has now extended his work and developed films as well (Nuutinen, 2001).

Björkqvist and Österman (1999) measured 12- to 16-year-old pupils' attitudes to violence on three occasions: before, and four days after they had been exposed to Nuutinen's slide show, and then again five months later. The results are presented in Figure 12.1. As the figure shows,

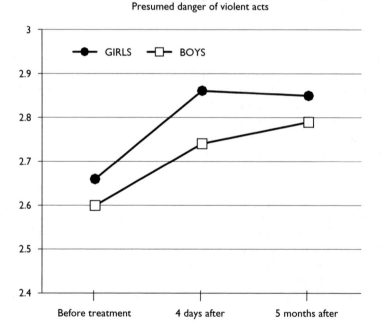

Presumed danger of violent acts

Figure 12.1 The level of presumed danger of violent acts among comprehensive school-children, before exposure to the victim slide show, four days after, and five months later. The presumed danger of violent acts was measured by use of a five-item scale ($\alpha = .92$)

Source: Adapted from Björkqvist and Österman (1999).

even a short treatment of this kind has some effect, at least on attitude. We did not expect long-term effects, but significant long-term effects were indeed found. Although the study was limited in the sense that only attitudes, not behaviour, were measured, the results were quite encouraging.

In our view, the effect of Nuutinen's slide show may be explained in two ways:

1   The viewing schoolchildren gained very clear information about the consequences of real-life violence, of a type which could easily happen to them themselves. Since young people watch so many movies in which violence is glorified, and the consequences of violence, to a large extent, are understated or totally ignored, they do not usually have a proper understanding of what the consequences really are for victims. The slide show very effectively gave them such information.
2   While watching the photos and X-rays of victims, the pupils were likely to feel increased empathy towards the victims. Empathy has been found to be an effective antidote to aggression (see for instance Björkqvist, Österman and Kaukiainen, 2000).

Kempele longitudinal study

In Kempele, a large-scale project, based mainly on Olweus' principles, was started in 1990. The prevalence of bullying was investigated among three cohorts: pupils of grades four, six and seven of comprehensive school. Measurements were repeated four times with two-year intervals, the last time in 1998, and 2,729 pupils participated in the study (Koivisto, 1999).

Some of the measures taken to counter bullying concerned intervention, others prevention. A basic principle was that bullying was not to be tolerated. The schools established rules with respect to bullying. When bullying occurred, measures to stop it were to be taken immediately. In single cases, groups of pupils were involved to discuss cases of bullying, while in other cases, only the involved parties were engaged in discussions with teachers and parents. When needed, external experts were called in. The school yards were also better guarded than before. Co-operation between school and homes was encouraged and enhanced. Measures were taken to increase the feeling of cohesion in schools, with positive input like trips, school parties, etc.

According to both self-estimations and peer evaluations, bullying was reduced to one-third, by these measures (see Table 12.1). The strongest reduction occurred during the first two-year period. The Kempele study, therefore, was extremely successful (Koivisto, 1999).

Table 12.1 Victims of bullying, according to both peer and self-estimations, at the start and end of the Kempele longitudinal study (per cent)

	Peer estimations		Self-estimations	
	Boys	Girls	Boys	Girls
1990	9.3	7.3	5.3	2.3
1998	3.6	2.0	0.7	0.7

Source: Based on data from Koivisto, 1999.

The Salmivalli–Kaukiainen intervention programme

Salmivalli and Kaukiainen (2000) developed an anti-bullying intervention programme based on teacher training. The rationale was simple and straightforward: if teachers do not know how to tackle bullying, intervention cannot be successful. Teachers from eight schools attended seminars and received information. Two seminars were attended during autumn 1999, and two during spring 2000. The teachers were given modern, up-to-date information based on research on bullying and how to counter it. Between the seminars, the teachers were supposed to apply what they had learned, and then report to Salmivalli and Kaukiainen, who served as their trainers.

Altogether, 625 pupils from twenty-four classes and eight different schools participated in the intervention programme. In addition, twelve classes from four other schools served as controls. Based on Olweus' principles, the intervention techniques were categorized as being either at school, class, or individual levels. At the individual level, principles based on Pikas and on the Farsta methods were also applied.

The intervention programme will be longitudinal and is still ongoing. The first phase is finished, however, and has been reported (Salmivalli and Kaukiainen, 2000). The results were less promising than expected. Observed (peer-rated) physical and verbal bullying did decrease (physical bullying only marginally), but observed indirect bullying increased, and self-assessed experience of bullying of all types actually increased. The pupils were also tested with Salmivalli's participant roles model (Salmivalli et al., 1996). The hypothesis was that the programme should lead to changes in the pupils' participant roles, with a decrease in the number of bullies, reinforcers, and victims – but that did not happen.

Legal measures

Bullies may be fined, despite their young age. In a case that set a precedent, in the city of Raahe in September 1995, two 15-year-old pupils were fined for systematic bullying of a same-aged peer over an extended period of time. The bullying consisted of both physical and psychological harassment. Interestingly, fines for inducing mental pain were greater than fines for physical abuse of the victim: one of the bullies was fined 10,000 FIM (about €1,200) for psychological harassment, but only 1,000 FIM, or €167, for physical harassment (Simonen, 1995).

Besides being fined, bullies may be given a restraining order by the court of law, just as battering ex-husbands may be forbidden to come near their ex-wives. In another precedent setting case in spring 2000, two 16-year-old boys in the city of Varkaus were given a restraining order and forbidden to approach a peer that they had been bullying. Not only bullies, but also responsible school authorities may be fined for neglect in cases of bullying and school violence. According to §29 of the Finnish Code of Law concerning comprehensive schools, every pupil has the right to a safe school environment. The same is stated in §21 in the Code of Law for senior secondary schools, and in §28 in the Code of Law for vocational schools. These paragraphs are interpreted to cover not only physical safety, but also the right not to be bullied or exposed to violence at school. In a third precedent setting case in autumn 1999, the city of Huittinen was fined 72,500 FIM, equalling about €12,000 (with an additional €5,000 in fees) in compensation to a former pupil who had been exposed to bullying for a number of years. The former pupil was already 22 years old at that time, but the retrospective evidence was considered binding enough, and it was ruled that the city had not been able to guarantee his safety as it should, in accordance with the paragraphs mentioned above.

Conclusions

The Salmivalli–Kaukiainen programme is probably the intervention programme that has been most thoroughly tested in Finland so far. It has proper control groups, and it measures bullying on many levels. Its meagre results, at least in the early phases, indicate how difficult intervention really is. However, the programme continues, and it is too soon to establish success or failure as yet.

The Kempele longitudinal study suggests that intervention really is possible, and that levels of bullying clearly were reduced, and kept low, during a ten-year period in Kempele, due to the measures taken.

Nuutinen's victim slide show has successfully affected attitudes towards violence and bullying, even on a long-term basis. However, it has not been tested whether violent behaviour decreased as a result.

Finally, the alarm bracelet seems to provide a promising addition to intervention techniques. We suggest that it would be well worth trying it out on a broader basis and in more schools, perhaps in countries other than Finland as well.

References

Björkqvist, K. and Österman, K. (1999). Finland. In P.K. Smith, Y. Morita, J. Junger-Tas, D. Olweus, R. Catalano and P. Slee (eds). *The Nature of School Bullying: A Cross-national Perspective*. London: Routledge. pp. 56–67.

Björkqvist, K., Österman, K. and Kaukiainen, A. (2000). Social intelligence – empathy = aggression? *Aggression and Violent Behavior*, 5, 191–200.

Koivisto, M. (1999). Koulujen mahdollisuudet vähentää ja ehkäistä kiusaamista: seurantatutkimus koulukiusaamisesta Kempeleen peruskouluissa vuosina 1990–1998 [The possibilities for schools to reduce and prevent bullying: a longitudinal study of school bullying in the comprehensive schools of Kempele during the period 1990–1998]. Project report. Oulu University.

Lagerspetz, K.M.J., Björkqvist, K., Berts, M. and King, E. (1982). Group aggression among school children in three schools. *Scandinavian Journal of Psychology*, 23, 45–52.

Lahtinen, P. and Sankala, A. (1998). Tekniikasta apu kiusatulle? Hälytinkokeilu Salmelan ala-asteella [Can technology be an aid to victims of bullying? An alarm experiment at the Salmela primary school]. Master's thesis. Oulu University.

Ljungström, K. (1990). *Mobbaus koulussa. Käsikirja mobbauksesta ja sen selvittämisestä Farsta-menetelmällä* [Bullying in Schools: A Handbook on Bullying and its Treatment by use of the Farsta Method]. Kauniainen, Finland: Jessica Lerche F:a.

Markkula, H. (2001). Kouluväkivalta peruskoulussa [Violence in comprehensive schools]. *Ilta-Sanomat*, 26.1, 9.

Nuutinen, T. (2001). Vaaratonta iskua ei ole [There is no such thing as a non-dangerous blow]. Online. Available HTTP: <http://netti.fi~timonuut/timo.htm>.

Olweus, D. (1973). *Hackkycklingar och översittare* [Bullies and Whipping-boys]. Kungälv, Sweden: Almqvist & Wiksell.

Olweus, D. (1986). *Mobbning i skolan – vad vi vet och vad vi kan göra* [Bullying among Schoolchildren: What we Know and What we can Do]. Stockholm, Sweden: Liber.

Olweus, D. (1992). *Kiusaaminen koulussa* [Bullying among Schoolchildren: What we Know and What we can Do]. Helsinki, Finland: Otava.

Pikas, A. (1975). *Så stoppar vi mobbning!* [How to Counter Bullying]. Lund, Sweden: Berlingska.

Pikas, A. (1990). *Irti kouluväkivallasta* [How to Counter Violence in Schools]. Imatra, Finland: Weilin & Göös.

Rimpelä, M., Orre, S. and Jokela, J. (2002). Kouluterveyskysely 2001 – Valtakunnalliset tulokset [School health questionnaire 2001 – national results]. Online. Available HTTP: <http//: www.stakes.fi/kouluterveys/2001/kiusaaminen01. htm>.

Salmivalli, C. and Kaukiainen, A. (2000). *Kiusaamisen vähentäminen opettajien koulutuksen kautta: seurantatutkimuksen ensimmäinen vaihe* [Reducing bullying through teacher training: the first phase of a longitudinal study]. City of Helsinki Publication Series A11.

Salmivalli, C., Lagerspetz, K.M.J., Björkqvist, K., Österman, K. and Kaukiainen, A. (1996). Bullying as a group process: participant roles and their relations to social status in the group. *Aggressive Behavior*, 22, 1–15.

Simonen, M. (1995). Kahdelle pojalle sakkoja koulukiusaamisesta [Two boys fined for school bullying]. *Iltalehti*, 29 September, p.9.

Veijola, E. (2000). Preventing bullying and violence at school. Finnish Ministry of Education. Unpublished manuscript.

Chapter 13

'Taking back adult control'

A report from Norway

Erling Roland, Gaute Bjørnsen and Gunnar Mandt

Background

The country

About 4.5 million people live in Norway, giving a population density of only 13.7 per km^2. The capital city of Oslo has almost 500,000 inhabitants. The country is divided into nineteen counties and 439 municipalities, of which forty-seven are towns. Besides Norwegian, a relatively small Sàmi population in the north, estimated at approximately 20,000 people, has its own language and its distinctive culture, and is centred mainly in the northernmost county of Finnmark. Otherwise, there are a large number of immigrant groups, but most of them are rather small in number. For the country as a whole, 6.3 per cent of the citizens have an immigrant background. However in Oslo, this rises to one out of five citizens (Statistics Norway, 2001). Pupils with an immigrant background have the right to receive tuition to keep up and develop their mother tongue.

The school system

Universal schooling for children was introduced in Norway 250 years ago. From 1889, seven years of compulsory education were provided. In 1969 this was increased to nine years and in 1997 to 10 years. Compulsory schooling in Norway now starts at the age of 6 years. Primary and lower secondary education in Norway is founded on the principle of a unified school system that provides equal and adapted education for all on the basis of a single national curriculum. All young people share in a common framework of knowledge, culture and values. The municipalities are responsible for primary (grades one to seven) and lower secondary schools (grades eight to ten). These schools typically have 100 to 300 pupils, although in rural areas many schools are very small, with less than 100 pupils. The counties are responsible for upper secondary schools (grades eleven to thirteen). These typically have 500 to 1,200 pupils. Since autumn 1994, everyone between the ages of 16 and 19 has a statutory right to three years' upper secondary education leading either to higher education or to vocational qualifications or partial qualifications.

According to the Education Act, all public education is free, and it shall be adapted to the background and abilities of all pupils. Pupils with special needs should as far as possible be integrated in ordinary schools.

Coping with children with behavioural disturbances

All persons associated with the school or with training establishments should make efforts to ensure that pupils and apprentices are not injured or exposed to offensive words or deeds. The principles of integration of pupils with special needs in ordinary schools apply also to children and adolescents with behavioural disorders. The national and centralized special schools were in principle removed from the school system during 1991–1992. The most severe cases are given tuition at institutions administered under the social and medical healthcare system. A number of schools, however, organize alternative tuition, often linked to outdoor life and/or practical skills for violent and aggressive pupils in more or less segregated environments and contexts – creating 'time-outs' of various durations, for the pupils themselves as well as for their surroundings. A pupil can be moved to another school against the will of the parents in extreme cases of antisocial behaviour.

Definitional issues

In this report, violence is taken as physical aggression, which inflicts injury or discomfort upon another individual. In cases where referred statistics concern relevant behaviour that is not covered by this definition, the behaviour in question will be explained.

Physical violence as a phenomenon in itself has only been focused to a limited degree, as the majority of surveys have looked into the prevalence of bullying, both physical and psychological. The majority of surveys dealing with violence in schools in Norway therefore have given a picture of the prevalence of physical violence in the context of bullying. This has naturally been reflected in most programmes and approaches to counteract and prevent aggressive behaviour, as they have been launched under the bullying label.

Relevant historical background

A new trend concerning aggression in schools emerged at the beginning of the 1990s, when several severe incidents of violence occurred in school yards. In the public opinion of today, one might say that the general impression is that 'things are getting worse'; there is an impression of an escalation of aggression and violence among young people and in society in general, and there is a growing awareness of the new challenges related to racism and ethnic conflicts.

The first national programme to counteract bullying was conducted in 1983, and was initiated by the Ministry of Education. A main focus in this campaign was on what to do when bullying became a problem. The main preventive approach was for the teacher and the pupils to use some material, e.g. literature, and discuss the problem in class. The preventive perspective of the campaign, then, was rather limited, and bullying focused (Olweus and Roland, 1983; Roland, 2000; Roland and Munthe, 1997).

This first programme in Norway has been described and discussed by several researchers (Olweus, 1991, 1993; Roland, 1993; Roland and Munthe, 1997). Follow-up studies found that the campaign had a very positive effect over one or two years, in Bergen schools, where further support to schools was also initiated (Olweus, 1991, 1993); but a limited effect over three years in schools in Rogaland (Roland, 1993). The Rogaland schools got no support from the researchers. The rather weak result in Rogaland was explained by difficulties in maintaining the activities in most schools (Roland, 1993; Roland and Munthe, 1997).

A second wave of anti-bullying work in Norway, initiated by the Ministry of Education and headed by the Centre for Behavioural Research, started in 1996. This programme comprised a much broader preventive perspective than that of 1983, as well as additional methods of intervention. This preventive perspective is not very bullying focused. In the booklet for teachers, it is recommended they adopt a general management approach to improve both social interactions and on-task activities in the class, as well as co-operation with parents about this. There was no funding for evaluation of this programme.

Knowledge

Police records on juvenile violence

Norwegian official statistics on violence refer to the number of persons charged by the police for violence. Persons reported to the police by victims or others are not part of the statistics, unless the investigation of the police leads to a charge. Therefore, the real number of offenders and victims cannot be estimated from these statistics. Changes over a period of time may, however, be identified.

From 1990 to 1998, there has been a doubling of the number of persons charged for violent offences, in the age categories 5 to 14 years, 15 to 17 years, and 18 to 20 years. The increase is most significant for the age group 15 to 17 years (Ministry of Children and Family Affairs, St. melding nr. 17, 1999–2000).

Some statistics and research are available to evaluate whether the escalation in violence outside schools in Norway is also present in schools. In Oslo, a total of fifty, forty-nine and fifty pupils were reported to the police for violence in 1997, 1998 and 1999, respectively. These figures are stable, then, but the police suspect that many of the incidents are not being reported.

In the early 1990s, steps were taken in Oslo to enforce on all primary and lower secondary schools in the community a routine report system on incidents of violence. The schools are instructed to report to the Oslo Community School Administration 'any action that has an intention of inflicting physical damage/injury, including threats of violence' (Skram, 2000, p.68). Statistics from the three years of 1996, 1997 and 1998 reveal a stable number of reported incidences of violence in the Oslo primary schools; 126 incidents in 1996, 118 in 1997, and 128 in 1998. Based on these figures and background data, there was no good reason to conclude that there has been an increase in the level of violence or a development of more serious or dangerous actions of violence from the pupils, nor to conclude that the injuries had become more severe during a five-year period (Skram, 2000).

In Skram's report, the figures reveal that only half of the schools in Oslo had reported incidents of violence during the whole period 1993–1999. In addition, the level of reported incidents in the Oslo schools strongly contrasts with the results of other scientific studies in the 1990s (Skram, 2000). The reliability of the information from the reporting system can clearly be questioned, as discussed by Skram (2000, pp.69–74).

Levels of violence inside and outside school

In Norway, there is no established reporting system on incidents of violence in schools on a national basis, outside Oslo. Data monitoring the general level of violence in Norwegian schools are therefore not available. Large-scale research programmes on this specific topic are few, and there are questions regarding research methods and treatment and interpretation of data that prevent us from drawing a clear conclusion regarding the level of violence in Norwegian schools. One problem is that some studies do not differentiate clearly between violence inside and outside schools.

Hegg, Myhr and Ringheim (1995) conducted a survey in spring 1995 on different perspectives of violence among 3,000 pupils aged 14 to 15 years, living in larger and smaller Norwegian towns. In this survey, violence was defined as physical aggression, and not limited to a bullying context.

The results refer to violence in general, not only in school. Twenty-three per cent of the pupils (two-thirds of them boys) confirmed that they had been the victims of violence, and 7 per cent of these needed medical attention from a doctor. Twenty-nine per cent reported having been violent themselves (of which 72 per cent were boys, 28 per cent girls). Sixty-six per cent of the incidents of violence that the pupils reported having witnessed took place in school.

Haaland (2000) recently conducted a questionnaire survey among 4,702 foundation course pupils (aged 15 to 17 years) at upper secondary schools in four of the largest cities in Norway. More than 30 per cent said that they had been the victims of violent acts, or threats of violence, over the course of the past twelve months. Comparing his findings with those of other studies from the early 1990s (Hagen, Djuve and Vogt, 1994; Gautun, 1996), Haaland finds that the proportion of young people injured by direct violence, or threats of violence, has increased. While threats were the most common form early in the decade, violence resulting in visible marks or injuries has become the most prevalent category in 1999. Compared with the earlier figures, it is clear that girls are increasingly the victims of violence. While the ratio between assaulted girls and boys about ten years ago was 1:6, at the end of the decade it is 1:2. Twenty-three per cent of the reported incidents of violence occurred at school, or on the way to/from school. Youths from immigrant families are involved slightly less than youths from a Norwegian background – but young immigrants who do experience violent behaviour, do so far more frequently, and the type of violence is more serious than when young Norwegians are the victims.

Harassment of teachers

A survey of 2,367 teachers in primary and lower secondary schools (grades one to ten) showed that 47.7 per cent of the teachers reported having experienced violence, harassment and/or criminal damage in the period of the last three years (Kile, in progress). The number reporting having experienced physical violence over this period was 22.1 per cent, of whom just over one-half had experienced physical violence during the school year 1999/2000. The most prevalent acts of violence were blows and kicks.

The School Environment Study: Centre for Behavioural Research

The Centre for Behavioural Research (CBR) is a research institute at Stavanger University College and a national competence centre, appointed by the Norwegian Parliament to assist pre-schools and schools to prevent and cope with emotional and social problems among the pupils. It has twice carried out a School Environment Study at a national level. In 1995 a study covered two samples of pupils, in grade six (1,049 pupils) and grade nine (1,071 pupils). The investigation was conducted again in 1998 in grades five (1,801 pupils), six (1,822 pupils), eight (2,083 pupils) and nine (2,002 pupils). Grades five and six represent primary schools and grades eight and nine lower secondary schools. The schools were selected according to the classification system for municipalities and schools recommended by the Norwegian Bureau of Statistics, and the schools are regarded as representative for primary and secondary schools in Norway. All data were obtained by questionnaires given to pupils. The response rate was between 80 and 90 per cent for all samples. This design makes it possible to compare the data obtained from grades six and nine in 1995 and 1998, to estimate changes over a period of three years, and to analyse prevalence of physical violence among girls and boys at four age levels in 1998.

A main focus of the studies was to estimate bullying among the pupils. In the questionnaires, bullying was described for the pupils according to common standards (Roland, 1998).

> We call it bullying when one pupil or several together are unfriendly or nasty towards another pupil, who can not easily defend him or herself. This can be done by *kicking, hitting* or *pushing*. It is also bullying when pupils are *teased* a lot or when pupils are *excluded* from being with the others.

The two items concerning physical violence are in the context of bullying. Although the use of physical violence in different contexts probably correlates, the overall prevalence of physical violence by pupils in schools is clearly underestimated in these investigations.

The analysis of the data and the results are reported by Roland, Bjørnsen and Westergaard (2001). Regarding the change over a three-year period, the estimates for perpetrating and for being victimized, separately for boys and girls in grades six and nine, show that physical violence in the context of bullying seems to have increased slightly from 1995 to 1998. The negative tendency is very consistent for the different estimates, although only a minority of these are significant.

Examining the results for prevalence, more boys than girls are victimized by physical means in bullying interactions, and boys conduct substantially more physical violence than girls in all grades. These differences between boys and girls exist at primary level and increase as the pupils get older.

Regarding the mean prevalence rates for victims, there is a decreasing tendency with increasing age for both genders, but stronger for girls than for boys. The percentage for frequent (once a week or more) victims falls strongly for girls with increasing age; for boys, the tendency goes in the opposite direction, but it is not systematic or significant.

For perpetrating physical violence in bullying interactions, the changes with increasing age go in clearly different directions for girls and boys. With increasing age, the mean level decreases significantly for girls, while it increases significantly for boys. Both effects are quite linear. The most remarkable change is for frequent offenders among boys. In primary schools, only a very small minority of the pupils, about 1 per cent, engaged in bullying related violent behaviour regularly (weekly or more often), while about 2.5 per cent do so in secondary schools. The difference between girls and boys is great at both primary and secondary level, and the difference increases with increasing age. In grade nine, about 5 per cent of the boys are frequent offenders. This means that boys in secondary schools conduct the majority of regular physical violence in the context of bullying.

An overall tendency with increasing age, then, seems to be that the target group of those frequently victimized by physical means gradually comprises more boys relative to girls, and that the number of frequent offenders increases strongly for boys but not for girls. At secondary level, physical violence in bullying interactions has predominantly become an issue for boys, and the target group of boys is more limited than at primary level. Also, with increasing age, the number of *frequent* boy offenders increases. This means that the interactions in physical violence become specialized in certain ways. For schools, it seems very important to note that the percentages of boys that persistently conduct physical violence in interactions in bullying increase from 1.2 in grade five (11 years) to 4.9 in grade nine (15 years). The pre-puberty period, then, seems critical for preventing a dangerous development for some boys.

Physical violence in Norwegian schools: a concluding remark

Although the developmental tendencies are difficult to estimate because of weak statistics and somewhat different results, it seems that use of physical violence in society has increased slightly among children and adolescents during the last decade. The data indicate that this escalation in physical violence has been stronger outside school than within school. The School Environment Study revealed that bullying related physical violence in schools probably has increased slightly from 1995 to 1998. The tendency was very consistent for all estimates, although statistically significant for only some of them. This study did not confirm the finding by Haaland (2000) that the percentage of girl victims increased more strongly than the percentage of boy victims. One explanation might be that the School Environment Study was conducted among primary and lower secondary pupils, while Haaland investigated pupils in upper secondary schools. Also, most incidents of violence in the latter study referred to out of school situations.

Action

Current national policies regarding violence in schools

In December 1999 the Storting (Norwegian Parliament) passed a *Programme for action on crime among children and youth* (Report no.17 to the Storting, 1999–2000). This report presents a comprehensive national programme for action on violence, bullying, crime, intoxication and racism among children and youth, co-ordinating the work of all the ministries dealing with questions related to the education and adolescence of children and youth. The programme comprises forty ongoing and new initiatives, within six main areas, of which the school area is one.

Under this programme, one section concerns actions in schools. In this section several national programmes that are related to tackling violence in schools are identified, of which peer mediation and social and cognitive skills training approaches are central. Two major programmes are designed to train key personnel and teachers in preventing and tackling antisocial behaviour among the pupils: the Samtak programme and the Olweus programme.

Samtak

This is a development programme designed to provide staff in the educational/psychological service and school head teachers with increased competence in the area of reading and writing difficulties, social and emotional difficulties and multiple learning difficulties (Roland and Fandrem, 2000). The programme covers a three-year period, and started in January 2000. The programme for social and emotional difficulties is designed and led by the Centre for Behavioural Research, and is to a large extent based on the experiences gained from the national programmes of 1983 and 1996 to counteract bullying, mentioned earlier. The thematic plans of the Samtak programme for social and emotional difficulties comprise five central topics, of which bullying and severe behavioural problems are two.

Aspects of the Samtak programme were selected for evaluation and dissemination in the UK-001 Connect programme, funded by the European Commission (www.gold.ac.uk/connect). Following this, the Ministry of Education has funded a long-term programme to develop the principles for reducing antisocial behaviour in school adopted in the Connect research. These principles are briefly described in the case study on page 208, Gran school in Oslo. This further work was started in autumn 2001, and will continue for three-and-a-half years. A considerable number of schools will be involved and the results will be evaluated. The programme is also led by the Centre for Behavioural Research.

Olweus' programme against bullying and anti-social behaviour

This was developed in Bergen during 1983–1985. Its principles, and evaluation in Bergen, have been fully described elsewhere (Olweus, 1991, 1993). The programme consists of the following core components:

- General prerequisites: awareness and involvement on the part of adults;
- Class level: class rules against bullying; regular class meetings with students; class PTA meetings;
- School level: questionnaire survey; school conference day; better supervision of students during recess and lunch time; co-ordinating group;
- Individual level: serious talks with bullies and victims; serious talks with parents of involved students; teacher and parent use of imagination.

A new edition of the Olweus programme, in the form of a programme pack, is being brought into use during the autumn of 2002. The programme is part of the Ministry's national strategy to reduce bullying and antisocial behaviour, and is implemented through the Norwegian Board of Education. The intention is to offer the programme pack to all primary and secondary schools in Norway. The initial phase, starting spring 2002 at 150 schools in nine of Norway's nineteen counties, consists of preparational work and the selection and initial training of key personnel. No evaluation is yet available for this new edition, although a report from the Olweus group on the activity and progress in the year 2001 is due to be presented to the National Board of Education during 2002.

In addition to these initiatives, a range of programmes concerning aggression, violence and crime are used in schools around the country. The Norwegian Ministry of Education is working on a 'master plan' aiming at the integration of all elements and programmes into coherent whole-school strategies for an improved learning environment.

Case study: Gran – a combined primary and lower secondary school in Oslo

In 1997, the Centre for Behavioural Research was called upon by a large, multi-ethnic, combined first to tenth grade school in Oslo, which reported alarming behavioural problems among the pupils. The school leadership were in no way novices in dealing with violence and disruptive behaviour. Resource persons at Gran were instrumental in working out the earlier mentioned reporting system on incidents of violence in Oslo schools, as well as in developing a comprehensive resource book for schools, called 'Stopp Volden' ('Stop the Violence') (Oslo kommune, Skolesjefen, 1993). In spite of all their competence, the school leadership and teachers lost control of the situation.

The Centre for Behavioural Research was already aware of the severe problems at that school. In January 1997, the *Evening Post*, a conservative national newspaper, had published a very critical article describing alarming conditions at Gran School. The article described how violence, the use of weapons, threats towards pupils and teachers, disruption and vandalism had become part of everyday life at Gran. Groups of pupils controlled the school with terror, and the leadership and staff at the school were in desperate need of help, as the situation had got beyond their control.

The Gran school is located in the suburban area of Furuset outside Oslo. Its 450 pupils are recruited from lower socioeconomic groups, with a high degree of mobility, and a large and growing percentage of immigrant and refugee families. Of the pupils at Gran, more than 60 per cent (in 1998) had a mother tongue other than Norwegian, with Urdu prevailing due to a large Pakistani population in the local community of Gransdalen.

The impression from our first visit to Gran was that the school suffered from many different and interrelated problems, and that physical violence conducted by a number of pupils was an integrated part of this. This social context of physical violence had been observed by the Centre for Behavioural Research before, and in particular at a medium to large rural school that comprised both primary and secondary levels. Although the rural school and Gran were very different in their surroundings, architecture and population of pupils and their parents, the general social pattern seemed to be quite similar.

The most alarming aspect in both cases was that the head teacher and the staff had lost control. The social power in these schools was apparently in the hands of a rather large group of pupils, which was controlled by a hard core composed of pupils from several classes with connections to even more deviant and experienced young adults outside. Simultaneously, the head teacher, the staff and the parents were generally not a co-operating group of adults, but disorganized, confused and frightened. Subgroups and conflicts among the adults were part of this. The majority of the pupils in these schools were uncomfortable with this situation, but they were mainly afraid and passive. Sometimes, however, some or many could support or even take part in minor deviant behaviour.

Social structures at school level, including confused and fatigued leadership, limited co-operation and low consensus about professional matters among staff, are related, and so are weak classroom management, social structure in the class and deviant pupil behaviour (Galloway, 1983;

Galloway et al., 1998; Mortimore, 1996; Mortimore et al., 1988; Roland, 1998; Rutter et al., 1979; Teddlie and Stringfield, 1993). Furthermore, different kinds of deviant behaviour are also related (Olweus, 1993; Roland, 1998). Probably, physical violence to the amount and degree that was demonstrated at the two schools and others that the Centre for Behavioural Research has worked at, could not be possible without a breakdown of adult control, and destructive power structures and much minor deviant behaviour among a great minority of the pupils. Therefore, major problems of physical violence have to be coped with by a broad approach that includes many different and related elements. The approach that can be offered to schools by the Centre for Behavioural Research comprises such elements.

The programme at Gran: a joint approach

Together with the leadership at Gran, the Centre started an empowerment process for the school staff and leadership. Several staff meetings involving Centre representatives and all staff at the school were run, with the aim of creating a common understanding of the situation and the principles for further work to regain control. Following this, courses were run for all teaching personnel on classroom management, peer counselling groups for teachers, co-operation with parents, intervention, breaking up deviant subgroups, and attractive activities. Integrated in this programme is a strong element of *support for the head teacher and the deputies*. This support is vital in the demanding process of creating common attitudes and a will to change things, both fundamental conditions for further action.

The strong concern about the situation communicated from the school to the local and community authorities – signals that were enforced by the media focus at the beginning of the year – also resulted in a project starting in August 1997, entitled 'Home/school/local environment'. The project was assigned a full-time project leader, and the mandate of the project was to work out a project plan, focusing on four central areas: school environment, co-operation with parents, interaction with the local environment and interdisciplinary approaches within the local municipality. In this phase, the guidance role of the CBR was ended.

To start with, a survey was conducted on well-being among the pupils. This survey was the basis for selecting many of the initiatives and activities that were then tried out in a pilot project of three months, primarily focusing on groups at risk. The pilot project was very fruitful. Positive effects were noticeable after only three months. These clearly indicated that this initial approach was promising, and the full-scale project was established, with considerable attention and some economic support from the Oslo community, as well as from the Ministry of Child and Family Affairs.

The main goal was formulated as: to contribute to making the Gransdalen a secure and positive area of adolescence. To achieve this, the project identified the following sub-goals:

- to develop the Gran school into a dynamic force in the local environment;
- to strengthen the co-operation between the school and the parents;
- to develop co-operation with the voluntary organisations and establish a variety of leisure activities in the local environment;
- to co-operate with the local authorities on upgrading the outdoor areas of the school.

As part of the project, the project leader and the leadership at Gran worked out a plan of action for the school, called 'School without borders' (Indrevær et al., 1998). This plan built on the empowerment approach and the Centre principles, and systematically pointed out goals for further work.

The head teacher of Gran put it this way at a national conference recently: 'It was not one, single and genius thing that made the great difference, but the sum of many small moves'. This seems to be very true for Gran, and is in accordance with much research (Griffiths, 1993; Mortimore et al., 1988; Sharp and Thompson, 1994). Furthermore, there is a close, positive relationship between prevention and intervention (Kounin, 1970), and between teacher authority and responsibility of the pupils (Roland, 1998).

The multitude of actions can be divided into these categories:

- actions to strengthen the school and the teachers (the empowerment part);
- changing school routines and teaching methods;
- changing the attitudes of the pupils to school by opening the school outside school hours, offering attractive activities;
- breaking up the hard-core gang using sports and attractive outdoor activities;
- the aesthetic perspective: upgrading and renovating the school interior and exterior, including focusing on keeping the premises tidy. Consequently use the pupils' handicraft products for decorating the interior of the school;
- building confidence and improving relations with the parents of pupils with immigrant backgrounds; i.e. by recruiting teachers, counsellors and a peer mediator with an immigrant background.

Results at Gran

At least from the outside, setting up attractive activities seemed to be the most successful and visible approach. Indeed, the leader team and the teachers were very good at the sports and cultural approach, and this work has been presented at several national conferences and regarded by authorities and teachers as the main reason for the success. It would not have been possible, however, without the empowerment approach that was taken on beforehand. Otherwise, the teachers would not have been in a position to handle difficult groups of pupils during sessions of sports and cultural activities in the way that they did.

Much effort was put into positive profiling of pupils, i.e. exposing positive pupil behaviour and activities, and drawing attention to pupils' products from the art and handicraft lessons. Otherwise, the school adopted most of the elements from the Centre programme that was briefly described above. Gradually, the school was changed: not without frustrations and disappointments, but steadily, to be a safer and more interesting place for both teachers and pupils. In particular, it was impressive to observe how smoothly many of the multi-ethnic problems disappeared, and how different cultures were appreciated instead of being a constant source of conflict. A very strong and clear leadership of the school, demonstrating will and ability to fight racism and prejudices, and giving room and attention for the individual, is probably one central factor of success in the building of bridges and confidence between the school and the parents of immigrant pupils, and reducing the general level of tension among the pupils.

Initially, the intention was to run an external evaluation. In 1999, however, the steering group decided on an internal evaluation, based on the annual project reports and questionnaire surveys among pupils, parents and staff. Surveys were conducted in 2000 among parents and the staff of the school in the form of questionnaires. According to the background data, major improvements on all issues measured among the staff were identified. The mean trend for the parents' answers was also positive. The following main results can be seen in 2000, at the end of the three-year project, according to the project report (Suzen, 2000):

- peace and quiet in the classrooms;
- fewer 'problem pupils';
- pupils have a more positive attitude towards the school;
- pupils are more active in their leisure time;
- parents are interested in having contact with the school;
- a very low rate of vandalism;
- teaching staff report a high degree of job satisfaction and well-being;
- teachers from other schools wish to be transferred to Gran.

Perspectives for further work

Physical violence in school is a very serious problem when it occurs, and the prevalence seems to be slightly increasing in Norway. It is tempting but probably not very fruitful to try to reduce this problem by adopting a too narrow and naive approach.

The project report from Gran says that their approach to stop the violence ten years ago was rather too narrow, but it was in accordance with what the Norwegian authorities recommended at that time, and often still recommend (Suzen, 2000, p.6). In principle, such approaches or methods seem to be very focused on the particular problem, for example violence among the pupils. By using this approach, the problem is only superficially attacked, but for politicians and the audience, action seems to have been taken. Such narrow campaigns have been introduced again and again towards many different problems in Norwegian schools during previous years, but the results seem to be meagre at best (Nordahl et al., 2000; Roland, 2000; Roland and Munthe, 1997, Sørlie, 2000). One reason is probably the limited scope that overlooks historical causes and the wider context. Another problem is that very problem-focused programmes are difficult to maintain, often because new programmes or reforms demand attention from schools and teachers (Roland, 2000; Roland and Munthe, 1997).

In future years, the Centre for Behavioural Research will concentrate on further developing the CBR programme to reduce social and emotional problems in schools, and evaluate the effects of this programme. There are two main principles of this programme:

1 The preventive approach will be broad and include leadership at school level, systems for learning and co-operation among staff, co-operation with parents and classroom management.
2 The approaches for intervention will be different according to the problem in question.

Efforts will be made to evaluate how effective each main component of the programme is, in reducing different kinds of social and emotional problems. Furthermore, the whole programme will be put in operation and its effects will be evaluated.

References

Galloway, D. (1983). Disruptive pupils and effective pastoral care. *School Organization*, 3, 245–254.

Galloway, D., Rogers, C., Armstrong, D. and Leo, E.L. (1998). *Motivating the Difficult to Teach*. London: Longman.

Gautun, H. (1996). Voldens ansikt. *Fafo-rapport* 189. Fafo.

Griffiths, C. (1993). A Systemwide Approach to Changing Attitudes Towards the Acceptability of Bullying or Harassment in Schools and Reducing its Prevalence. In D. Evans, M. Myhill and J. Izard (eds). *Student Problems: Positive Initiatives and New Frontiers*. Sydney: Australian Council for Educational Research.

Haaland, T. (2000). Violence – conflict and gang formation. A study among youth in four cities. NIBR Project Report 2000:14.

Hagen, K., Djuve, A.B. and Vogt, P. (1994). Oslo: den delte byen? *Fafo-rapport* 161. Fafo.

Hegg, A., Myhr, K.I. and Ringheim, G. (1995). Stopp volden. *Dagbladet*, Special print issue, August.

Indrevær, G., Myhrvold, A., Naustdal, G. and Finvold, K.-O. (1998). *Prosjekt grenseløs skole. Gran skole som et helhetlig og inkluderende miljø*. Internal Plan Document, Gran school.

Kile, L.K. (in progress). Kartlegging av trakassering og vald mot pedagogisk personale i Møre og Romsdal. Utdanningsforbundet i Møre og Romsdal.

Kounin, J.S. (1970). *Discipline and Group Management in Classrooms*. New York: Holt, Reinhart & Winston.

Mortimore, P. (1996). Theme 1. High performing schools and school improvement. *School improvement internationally*, 7, 4–5.

Mortimore, P., Sammons, P., Stoll, L., Lewis, D. and Ecob, R. (1988). *School Matters: The Junior Years*. Wells: Open Books.

Nordahl, T., Egelund, N., Samdal, O., Sørlie, M.-A., Brunstad, P.O. and Bø, A.K. (2000). *Vurdering av program og tiltak for å redusere problematferd og utvikle sosial kompetanse*. Innstilling fra faggruppe oppnevnt av Kirke- utdannings- og forskningsdepartementet og Barne- og familiedepartementet.

Olweus, D. (1991). Bully/victim Problems among School Children: Basic Facts and Effects of a School Based Intervention Program. In D. Pepler and K. Rubin (eds). *The Development and Treatment of Childhood Aggression*. New Jersey: Lawrence Erlbaum Associates.

Olweus, D. (1993). *Bullying at School: What we Know and What we can Do*. Oxford: Blackwell.

Olweus, D. and Roland, E. (1983). *Mobbing – Bakgrunn og tiltak*. Oslo: Kirke-undervisnings-og forskningsdepartementet.

Oslo kommune, Skolesjefen (1993). *'Stopp Volden'* ['Stop the Violence']. Booklet on preventive work in schools, August.

Roland, E. (1993). Bullying: A Developing Tradition of Research and Management. In D.P. Tattum (ed.). *Understanding and Managing Bullying*. Oxford: Heinemann Educational.

Roland, E. (1998). School influences on bullying. Unpublished PhD thesis. School of Education, University of Durham.

Roland, E. (2000). Bullying in school: three national innovations in Norwegian schools in 15 years. *Aggressive Behavior*, 26, 135–143.

Roland, E., Bjørnsen, G. and Westergaard, E. (2001, in progress). Physical violence in school, and an emerging approach of prevention and intervention. Stavanger, Centre for Behavioural Research.

Roland, E. and Fandrem, H. (2000). Strategier for lokalt utviklingsarbeid i Samtak. *Skolepsykologi*, 5, 19–32.

Roland, E. and Munthe, E. (1997). The 1996 Norwegian program for preventing and managing bullying in schools. *The Irish Journal of Psychology*, 18, 233–247.

Rutter, M., Maughan, B., Mortimore, P. and Ouston, J. (1979). *Fifteen Thousand Hours*. London: Open Books.

Sharp, S. and Thompson, D. (1994). The Role of Whole-school Policies in Tackling Bullying Behaviour in Schools. In P.K. Smith and S. Sharp (eds). *School Bullying: Insights and Perspectives*. London: Routledge.

Skram, G. (2000). *Alvorlige atferdsproblemer i Osloskolen*. En kartleggingsstudie av voldsepisoder i perioden 1994–1999 og en intervjuundersøkelse om erfaringer med alvorlige utageringsepisoder.

Statistics Norway, Statistisk årbok 2001. Online. Available HTTP: <http://www.ssb.no/aarbok/fig/f-020220-087.html>.

Suzen, E. (2000). *Prosjekt Hjem/skole/Nærmiljø*. Prosjektrapport 2000.

Sørlie, M.-A. (2000). *Alvorlige atferdsproblemer og lovende tiltak i skolen*. Praxis forlag.

Teddlie, C. and Stringfield, S. (1993). *Schools Make a Difference*. New York: Teachers College Press.

Chapter 14

Tackling violence in schools

A report from Sweden

Robert Svensson

Background

The country

Sweden has a population of approximately nine million, 85 per cent of whom live in the southern half of the country, concentrated around three cities: Stockholm, the capital (1.8 million inhabitants, suburbs included), Gothenburg, on the west coast and Malmo, in the south. Around 20 per cent of the population has an overseas background, having either been born outside Sweden themselves or having at least one parent who was born abroad. The largest immigrant group comprises Finns, who make up approximately 20 per cent of all those with an immigrant background. Other large immigrant populations include those from the former Yugoslavia, Norwegians, Danes and Germans.

The school system

The state school system in Sweden comprises both compulsory schooling and non-compulsory forms of education. Nine years of compulsory education are obligatory for all children between the ages of 7 and 16 years. Approximately 96 per cent of children begin their schooling prior to age 7, in a pre-school class.

The majority of pupils concluding their compulsory education continue into further education. The sixth-form system (age 16 to 18/19) offers a total of seventeen three-year national programmes, whose objective is to provide a broad education and the general competence needed to study further at the university level. Alongside these national programmes there are specially formulated and individual programmes. Approximately one-quarter of students who complete a sixth-form programme continue their studies at a university.

Primary schools in Sweden have an average of 200 pupils. A small number of schools in the larger metropolitan areas have slightly over

1,000 pupils. In certain rural areas, on the other hand, school size may be as low as 20 pupils. In general, the number of pupils is somewhat higher at sixth-form colleges.

The Swedish Education Act states that all Swedish children and youths shall have access to an equivalent education. The Swedish Government specifies curricula, national objectives and guidelines for the state school system. Special assistance is provided for pupils with learning difficulties of one kind or another. For the most part, these pupils are included in mainstream classes at the primary, secondary and sixth-form levels. In certain cases, separate teaching groups are provided for pupils with physical disabilities and for those with social and emotional problems.

Definitional issues

In Sweden, violence is defined in different ways depending on who is conducting the research. The use of different definitions in different studies causes problems in relation to the comparability of findings. It is also extremely difficult to decide where the line is to be drawn between bullying and violence, or as Farrington (1993, p.384) has put it, 'there is no universally accepted operational definition of bullying.' Farrington also points out that 'a major problem is to decide where teasing ends and bullying begins' (p.385), and it is also difficult to know where violence starts and bullying ends.

The Swedish Education Act specifically states that schools are to actively combat all forms of offensive behaviour in school. The National Inspections carried out by the National Agency for Education define offensive behaviour in the following way (Skolverket, 1999, p.12) 'offensive behaviour includes such acts as psychological harassment, abusive language (defamation), threats of physical violence (threatening behaviour), physical violence (assault, causing physical injury or illness, using unlawful force), harassment, racial discrimination (racial agitation), sexual discrimination, exclusion and others.' This relatively wide definition includes both bullying and violence.

Studies conducted in Sweden tend to distinguish between levels of seriousness in the violence studied. The concept 'non-serious violence' often refers to acts of violence not requiring medical attention, whilst 'serious violence' refers to acts which give rise to a need for medical attention (BRÅ, 2000; Lindström, 2001). Weinehall (1999) employs the following definition: milder physical violence (for example a clip round the ear, a push or a mild slap with an open hand), serious physical violence (for example kicks, hits, punches, strangling or the use of a weapon), psychological violence (for example insults or bullying), sexual harassment (for example unwelcome advances, sexual innuendo), sexualized violence (for example making sexual use of someone else's body without their consent, sexual assault and rape) and material violence (for example destroying property in order to frighten or injure someone, stealing or misappropriating another's property).

Relevant historical background

Offensive behaviour at school, such as physical and psychological violence, bullying and harassment, including acts of a racist nature, attracted increasing attention during the 1990s (Lindroth, 1994). National policy instruments such as the Education Act and the National Curriculum have been tightened and now specify that all those working in schools are required actively to combat all forms of offensive behaviour such as violence and bullying. The responsibility of schools in this area has thereby been clarified. The National Curriculum also directed head teachers to introduce action plans to deal with this type of problem (see *Action*, page 223).

In the context of the ongoing debate on violence and bullying in schools, much attention is focused on the social climate in schools, and on its importance for reducing the risk of violence and bullying. The social climate in a school affects the conditions in which work is carried out to develop the democratic competence of children and young people, which in turn will affect the incidence of offensive behaviour and violence. The National Agency for Education contends that 'a good social climate that ensures that children and young people are content in school also affects the occurrence of offensive behaviour . . . there is much to suggest that bullying and other offensive behaviour constitute the most important reason that children are unhappy at school' (Skolverket, 2000, p.21).

Knowledge

The exact number of students being victimized in Swedish schools is very difficult to pinpoint and it is also difficult to say whether violence in schools is on the increase. Prevalence rates will differ depending on how the data are collected. Two of the most common data collection methods are the self-report study and the use of police records.

The majority of studies examining violence and bullying in schools are based on self-reports (cf. Farrington, 1993). Such data are prone to a number of problems, e.g. non-response, under- and over-reporting. The majority of researchers contend nonetheless that this method produces reliable results (e.g. Elliott, Huizinga and Menard, 1989; Hindelang, Hirschi and Weiss, 1981; Huizinga and Elliott, 1986; Junger-Tas and Marshall, 1999). Another methodological problem that ought to be discussed and which may affect the results produced by different studies and their comparability relates to the use of different definitions across different studies. Similar problems also arise in connection with the use of different recall periods and variations in sampling procedures. Using police records involves other problems, since youths under the age of 15 years are not registered in connection with criminal offences. The 'dark figure' (crimes that do not come to the attention of the police) also presents problems when police data are used (e.g. Wikström, 1985). In this chapter, the focus will be on self-report data, but certain findings relating to school violence reported to the police will also be discussed.

Prevalence

The following results are taken from one of the first national surveys looking at violence in Swedish schools, from 1995. Youths in year nine were asked whether they had been victims of violence in school during the preceding term, and whether they had sustained any injuries as a result. Four per cent of boys, and 1 per cent of girls, reported having been victimized over the course of the previous term to the extent that they suffered some form of injury. However, 14 per cent of boys and 5 per cent of girls had been victims of violence that did not require medical attention (Andersson and Hibell, 1995).

A nation-wide questionnaire survey of youths in year nine has been conducted in Sweden on three occasions during the 1990s (1995, 1997 and 1999). Approximately 5,000 pupils participated in each survey (BRÅ, 2000; Ring, 1999). The question illuminating the issue of exposure to violence in school is somewhat limited and is formulated as follows: 'Has anyone intentionally hit, kicked or in some other way used violence against you at any time during the last twelve months so that (1) you had to seek medical attention, (2) it hurt but did not require medical attention?' If the pupils answered in the affirmative, they were asked to state where the most recent violent incident had taken place.

Approximately 20 per cent of pupils reported having been the victim of non-serious violence in 1999, and 6 per cent reported experiencing more serious violence. Of these, 47 per cent of the most recent incidents of non-serious violence and 42 per cent of the most recent cases of serious violence had taken place in school. The findings indicate that a large proportion of those experiencing violence are exposed to this violence in school or on school grounds. In total 9 per cent of respondents had their most recent experience of non-serious violence at school, compared with 2 per cent of respondents whose most recent experience of serious violence occurred at school. About 12 per cent of the boys had fallen victim to less serious forms of violence as compared to 5 per cent of girls. Approximately 3 per cent of boys and 1 per cent of girls had been exposed to more serious violence. There were no marked differences across the three years of the study.

Table 14.1 Pupils who have been victims of violence at school, and who have perpetrated violence against others at school, by sex; years seven, eight and nine (per cent)

	Year seven		Year eight		Year nine	
Behaviour	Boys	Girls	Boys	Girls	Boys	Girls
Hit someone causing injury	25	6	25	7	17	4
Been hit and required medical attention	7	2	8	2	5	1
Been hit no medical attention	18	8	23	9	17	6

Note
Sample sizes: year seven: boys 1,057, girls 1,044; year eight: boys 976, girls 924; year nine: boys 879, girls 893.

Questions were also asked about violence in schools in the context of the DARE programme (see page 226). Four surveys were conducted among pupils in years seven, eight and nine. These included questions on whether the youths had committed acts against other persons in school that caused serious injuries, and whether they had been hit in such a way that they required medical attention, or hit in a way that did not require medical attention. The recall period was limited to the previous term. The results show that boys more commonly hit others in a way that caused injury (Table 14.1). Boys were also more often than girls the victims both of acts that required medical attention and acts that did not require medical attention. In addition, the proportion of both boys and girls reporting having hit someone, or having themselves been the victims of violence, were greater among the younger pupils. Lindström (2001) contends that the high proportion of boys and girls reporting that they have been the victims of violence is largely a result of the fact that the schools in the study are located in urban areas.

Weinehall (1999) studied violence at home, at school and during leisure time among 6,596 sixth-form students at fourteen schools. Weinehall's questions covered both whether the respondent had been a victim of various forms of violence, and whether the respondent had perpetrated various types of violent acts on others. In a follow-up question, the students are asked to specify *where* the most recent of the incidents of violence occurred (no distinction is made here between different types of violence). Twenty-four per cent of boys and 9 per cent of girls reported having perpetrated violence and 24 per cent of boys and 17 per cent of girls reported being victims of violence at school. These constitute relatively large proportions. This might be because the students were asked whether they had *ever* been the victim of violence in school, and being sixth-formers, they had been in school for many years. The other studies cited in this report focus on youths in years eight and nine, and have a recall period commonly limited to one year or the previous term. Younger pupils more often reported having committed acts of violence against others at school.

Different forms of violence

Few Swedish studies have examined who perpetrates violence on whom. Weinehall (1999) found, however, that 2 per cent of pupils had experienced an act of violence perpetrated by an adult at the school, and approximately 20 per cent of pupils had experienced an act of violence perpetrated by another pupil. Further, one in four pupils had witnessed violence at school. Three per cent had witnessed violence against an adult and 36 per cent violence against a pupil. Three out of ten youths had seen a pupil commit a violent act.

As part of the DARE programme, a study was conducted of all crimes reported to the police by twenty-six Swedish secondary schools (Granath, 1998). The acts of violence most commonly registered consist of single punches, or a series of punches, kicks or head-butts. Injuries most often take the form of bruises, swelling, or no injuries at all. In a small number of cases, the injuries sustained were more serious, with teeth having been knocked out, for example, or cuts or gashes requiring stitches. None of the reported crimes involved life-threatening injuries or required admission to an intensive care ward in hospital, however. Granath states that it is difficult to draw the conclusion, as is often done in the media, that the violence perpetrated in schools is of a serious nature.

Estrada (1999) studied police-registered assault offences among 7 to 14 year olds in Stockholm between 1981 and 1997. Of the 768 incidents examined, 331 (43 per cent) occurred on school premises. Weapons were used in 12 per cent of these incidents. The most common weapons were blunt objects, sticks, clubs and knuckle-dusters, and guns. The study shows that two-thirds of the incidents went no further than scuffles; only a very small proportion resulted in really serious violence. Reports of serious assault have decreased over the years. The most common type of violence results in visible injuries such as swelling and bruises. In two-thirds of cases, no medical attention was sought by the victim. The results indicate that the less serious the violence, the larger the increase in the number of incidents reported to the police. Estrada draws the following conclusion:

> one interpretation might be that violence in schools, contrary to the prevailing image, is not becoming 'more and more serious' but rather 'increasingly mild'. This explanation presupposes that there is no given positive relationship between mild and more serious violence.

A more reasonable interpretation . . . is therefore that there has been an increase in the propensity to report.

(Estrada, 1999, p.118)

Other relevant factors

Research shows that crime patterns vary between different schools and that the school can have some effect on offending behaviour (e.g., Lindström, 1993). Relatively little research has been conducted in this area in Sweden. Results from those Swedish studies that do exist show that students in urban schools are victimized more often than students in other schools, but research also shows that prevalence rates differ within urban areas. The results in Table 14.2 show that in Sweden, the proportion of schools reporting violence, as well as the level of violence reported, is higher in areas with low social status. Research also shows that schools with high or low prevalence rates of violence reported to the police also present similarly high and low levels of victimization over time, as evidenced by self-report data from students (Lindström, 1997; Lindström, 2001).

Table 14.2 Crimes of violence reported to the police, broken down on the basis of the schools' catchment area

Catchment area's social status	Number of schools	Per cent of schools reporting violence	Number of violent offences	Average number of violent offences per school
High	23	22	13	2.6
Medium	54	41	72	3.3
Low	19	47	43	4.8

Source: Lindström, 1995.

Characteristics of perpetrators, victims and those who are both perpetrators and victims

Perpetrators

Among the characteristics that distinguish perpetrators of violence from other young people is their aggressive behaviour not only towards their friends, but also towards both teachers and parents. In a Swedish study of 2,000 youths in year seven, Lindström (2001) found that perpetrators have a relatively positive view of themselves, whilst others have found bullies to suffer from low self-esteem (O'Moore, 1991 cited in Farrington, 1993). Perpetrators tend to come from families where relations with parents are poor (Lindström, 2001; Stattin, 1995). The international literature also includes examples of studies that have found perpetrators/bullies to have poorer relations with parents (for a review see Smith and Myron-Wilson, 1998). Perpetrators' attitudes towards schoolwork and teachers are negative, their school performance is relatively poor and they tend also to have a number of delinquent friends and to run a higher risk of themselves becoming delinquents and alcohol abusers (Lindström, 2001; Olweus, 1991; Stattin, 1995).

Victims

Victims of violence and bullying are more anxious and insecure than students in general. Lindström (2001) found that victims have lower self-esteem than children in general and that they were not satisfied with themselves. The victims also tend to have closer relations with their parents. Other studies have found that boys exposed to violence have closer contacts with their parents, and with the mother in particular (Farrington, 1993; Olweus, 1991). Lindström (2001) also found that the victims have better relations to school than other children. In addition, it is rarer for victims to engage in shoplifting, to have delinquent friends or to use drugs than it is for perpetrators.

Both perpetrators and victims

In the bullying literature there is often talk about bullies and victims, and research has indeed gone further and defined subgroups of individuals among those involved in violence and bullying. Lindström (2001) found that 10 per cent were only victims, 10 per cent were only perpetrators and 6 per cent were both perpetrators and victims. Those who are both perpetrators and victims are more likely than other groups to have a poor relation with their parents, to show less interest in school, and to be involved in other deviant behaviours (Lindström, 2001). These results correspond very well with Svensson's (1999) findings based on comparisons of bullies, victims, and bully/victims using Swedish data. The international research literature also contains examples of studies indicating that bully/victims have a poorer relation with parents and Bowers, Smith, and Binney (1994) conclude that they form a distinctive subgroup relative to the two other groups.

Action

There is no doubt that violence and bullying among schoolchildren is a widespread and serious problem. But what can be done to counteract violence and bullying in schools? A number of different methods aimed at combating violence and bullying have been developed in Sweden, for example the Österholm model, the Farsta method and the DARE programme.

Since 1994, all schools have been required by law to formulate a planned response to bullying and other forms of offensive behaviour. The policy states that the head teacher is to take special responsibility for the action programmes and measures formulated by the school to combat bullying and other offensive behaviour at school.

Current national/regional policies dealing with violence in schools

The policy of creating a safe environment in Swedish schools has a long tradition. In Sweden, information on the prevention of bullying and violence in schools has been widely disseminated. These issues are regarded as very important and the National Agency for Education works with them on a nation-wide basis. The Agency produces publications, organizes conferences and sponsors research projects around the prevention of bullying and abusive behaviour in schools (see also BRÅ, 2001). The objective of this work is to create as positive and safe an environment in schools as possible. An important element in this work is the non-tolerance of bullying and violence in any form. The National Agency for Education states that:

> in a long term perspective, abusive behaviour must be regarded as a warning sign that not only tells us something about the children involved, but also something about the atmosphere and the social climate of a school. By improving the conditions for the development of good social relations, it is possible to combat offensive behaviour.
>
> (Skolverket, 2000, pp.21–22)

The principal goals and values of the school system are defined in the Education Act and National Curriculum. At the national level, the Education Act from 1 January 1998 (Education Act Chapter 1, paragraph 2) states that:

> Activities in school are to be formulated in accordance with fundamental democratic values. Everyone active in school is to promote respect for every person's self-worth and for our common environment. In particular, those who work in schools are to
> 1 promote equality between sexes and
> 2 actively combat all forms of offensive behaviour such as bullying and racism.

The curriculum for the compulsory school system, pre-school classes and the after-school centre (Lpo94), and (Lpfö98) curriculum for pre-school states the following:

The normative foundation and the role of schools
Schools are to promote an understanding for other people and the capacity to empathize. Nobody is to be subject to bullying in school. Tendencies towards harassment are to be actively combated. Hostility towards foreigners/immigrants and intolerance must be met with awareness, open discussion and active measures.

... Schools are to strive to be living social communities that provide a safe environment and instil the desire to learn.

... Schools are to promote the pupils' belief in themselves and provide faith in their future.

Lpo94 The responsibilities of head teachers
The head teacher has particular responsibility to ... establish, carry out, follow up and evaluate the school's strategy for preventing and combating all forms of offensive behaviour such as bullying and racism among pupils and employees.

Lpfö98
Concern for the individual child's well-being, security, development and learning should characterize the work of the pre-school.

Stimulate interaction between children and help them to resolve conflicts as well as work out misunderstandings, compromise and respect each other.

Develop their ability to function individually and in a group, to handle conflicts and understand rights and obligations as well as take responsibility for common rules.

The National Agency for Education was commissioned by the Government to inspect the quality of the work carried out by schools in this area (Skolverket, 1999). The Agency's examination of the work done to combat bullying and offensive behaviour was based on eighty-three reports from schools with pupils aged 6 to 19. A majority of the schools have established an action plan to deal with bullying and offensive behaviour. The schools have also shown awareness of the bullying problem.

The report identifies three types of school:

1   those that have formulated multifaceted and holistic measures and action plans which are integrated into the work of the school;

2   schools where the action plans are focused on problems, i.e. specific cases of bullying, and where they include preventive measures only to a limited degree;

3   schools where the focus is completely limited to measures taken in acute situations and where preventive efforts are not well articulated.

One conclusion drawn by the study is that 'too many of the schools inspected appear to base their approach on the assumption that victimization of this kind probably won't occur' (Skolverket, 1999, p.47) and that the majority of the schools ought to overhaul their action plans relating to bullying and offensive behaviour. They continue by stating that:

> the lack of knowledge relating to the occurrence of bullying is also a result of the fact that no systematic work is carried out to detail and follow up cases of victimization. The schools need to develop steering instruments and to formulate clear objectives for this work.
>
> (Skolverket, 1999, p.47)

Programmes

The DARE ('VÅGA') programme

This was introduced in Sweden as a drug and violence prevention project. The Swedish DARE programme constitutes a translation of the American programme of the same name. The objectives are to prevent drug use and crime among schoolchildren in the long term. Thus the primary focus is on the prevention of drug use among youths in school, but the formulation states further that the intention is also to prevent violence and bullying among these youths. The Swedish DARE programme is directed at youths in year seven. The project has been extensively evaluated in Sweden using measurements taken before the programme was started, together with post-programme measurements. The results show that 15 per cent of pupils in the thirteen control schools, and 17 per cent in the thirteen DARE schools reported having fallen victim to violence at school in year seven. A measurement that was taken directly after the programme showed that approximately 20 per cent reported having fallen victim to violence in both schools. Two years after the first measurement was taken, 12 per cent reported having fallen victim to violence in school. The most interesting aspect of these findings is the lack of any significant difference between the pupils participating in the DARE programme and those in the control group (Figure 14.1). Similar results were recorded in the analysis of those reporting that they had hit someone else. The

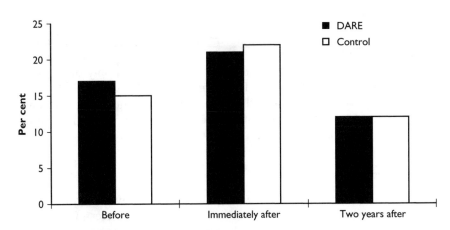

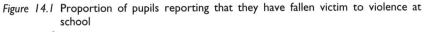

Figure 14.1 Proportion of pupils reporting that they have fallen victim to violence at school

Source: BRÅ, 1999.

evaluation concludes that 'the elements of the programme aimed at violence prevention were thus not observed to be effective judged by the pupils' responses' (BRÅ, 1999, p.36).

However, the report from the National Council for Crime Prevention (BRÅ, 1999, p.36) makes the point that 'while the assistance of the police in the teaching programme does not appear to have any measurable effect on youths' social problems, the presence of police in schools may nonetheless be of some significance . . . [B]y allocating resources to those schools most in need of police efforts, the work could probably be made more effective'. There was nothing to suggest that fewer offences were reported from those schools that had implemented the DARE programme.

The Österholm model

A number of different methods aimed at combating bullying have been developed in Sweden. One such is known as the Österholm model (Lagerman and Stenberg, 1999). This package aims to prevent, discover and stop bullying at an early stage and to encourage co-operation to this end between pupils and parents. The idea is to discuss the bullying problem with the bully at an early stage. It is also important to get the parents involved quickly in the work of prevention. The model also aims at ensuring that school staff will intervene in the case of any negative behaviour. An adult anti-bullying team works with cases of bullying, and support pupils are chosen in each class for peer support activities and to work together with adults to reduce bullying levels.

The Farsta method

This was developed by Karl Ljungström (see Ljungström, 2000), based on a model outlined by Anatol Pikas (1975). It employs a technique of structured dialogue with the bully, and action is taken only once a case of bullying has been identified. The parents are not involved in the first phase of the work. The anti-bullying team often includes pupil welfare staff and teachers. The team should meet on a regular basis and should also maintain contacts with groups in other schools.

The Olweus method

For Olweus, it is important to create a warm and positive environment in the school, and also one of involvement and positive interest. Clear lines should be drawn identifying behaviour that is considered unacceptable. It is important that preventive work be carried out at three different levels: the level of the school, the class and the individual pupil. The programme has four goals: to achieve an improved understanding of the bullying phenomenon (e.g. by carrying out surveys and dispelling myths about bullying), to get teachers and parents actively engaged in the project, to develop clear rules prohibiting bullying and to give protection and support to the victims (Olweus, 1991, 1993, 1999).

Friends

The Friends are a foundation with no political or religious affiliations who give lectures at schools around the country and train staff, pupils and parents in methods of preventing bullying and other offensive behaviour. They achieve this by: getting staff and pupils to accept responsibility and show they are not afraid to intervene, training *Friends* representatives (peer support workers chosen from among the pupils), developing action plans for schools, training anti-bullying teams and parents and helping companies and other organizations to understand the mechanisms of bullying. The implementation is begun by choosing one or two pupils from each class for peer support activities. It is then their job to attend to the problems that exist in the class. This is done together with other peer support assistants and a group of adults (school counsellor, school nurse and senior school staff) who work together to actively reduce problems associated with bullying and other offensive behaviour.

Discussion of the different methods

The Österholm model, the Farsta method and the Olweus method differ from one another on a number of points. The Österholm model includes the principal focus of the Farsta method, i.e. the initiation of a structured dialogue with the bully, aimed at resolving the problem. In both the Österholm model and the Olweus method, however, the parents are included in the work and a strategy of co-operation developed from an early stage. The literature has included some discussion of the focus of the Farsta method, and also that of Olweus (Ljungström, 1994; Olweus, 1994). These two programmes differ on two levels. The Farsta method focuses on teachers and bullies discussing the problem and thereafter informing parents. Olweus, on the other hand, contends that it is important to inform and activate parents at an early stage of the preventive work.

Neither the Österholm model, Farsta method or Friends has been evaluated to my knowledge; indeed, all forms of empirical study on the violence and bullying problem are something of a rarity in Sweden. There is a considerable need for longitudinal research into a number of aspects of violence and bullying. And perhaps most importantly, anti-violence and anti-bullying packages should be systematically and scientifically evaluated, something that has up to now been completely lacking in Sweden. The Pikas method has been evaluated in England (Smith and Sharp, 1994). The Olweus model has been scientifically evaluated in Norway and seen to have an effect on the level of bullying (see Olweus, 1993, and Norway chapter in this book). No such evaluations have as yet been conducted in Sweden, however.

Summary

Violence and bullying in schools is a social problem with consequences for both the perpetrator and the victim, and for society. Reducing the size of this problem is an important and pressing task. Preventive work in schools is generally accepted as an important means to this end. Results from Swedish studies indicate that approximately 15 per cent of schoolchildren have perpetrated acts of violence against others in school, whilst approximately 7 per cent have fallen victim to violence at school. Boys are more commonly perpetrators and victims. Results tend to vary a little between different studies, probably as a result of the way the questions are formulated and the length of the recall period. Violence in schools tends to be more common among younger pupils and certain schools experience more violence than others. The question of whether the level and seriousness of violence has increased is a difficult one to answer. Register studies indicate nonetheless that violence has not become more serious but there has rather been an increase in the propensity to report violence.

It is clearly stated in the Education Act that schools are to work actively to prevent all forms of offensive behaviour at school. The National Curriculum states that schools are to formulate action plans against violence and bullying at school, and that the head teacher is to be responsible for this. A study carried out by the National Agency for Education showed that the majority of schools had such a programme in place, but these programmes were seldom followed up and evaluated. It is important that programmes against violence and bullying at school exist, and that the follow-up phase is developed.

The lack of systematic scientific evaluations means that there is a lack of understanding of which measures are most likely to produce a position effect. If crime prevention programmes in school are to be effective, it is important that they are implemented in a spirit of co-operation between staff, pupils, parents and other groups (Lindström, 1996; Stattin, 1995). Lindström (1996) also suggests that co-operation is especially important in the case of schools with high levels of delinquency. The objective should be the introduction of well-designed programmes in those schools where the problems are most pronounced, whilst at the same time using 'control' schools to evaluate whether the measures used have had a significant effect.

References

Andersson, B. and Hibell, B. (1995). *Skolelevers Drogvanor 1995*. Rapport nr 47. Stockholm: Centralförbundet för alkohol- och narkotikaupplysning.

Bowers, L., Smith, P.K. and Binney, V. (1994). Perceived family relationships of bullies, victims, and bully/victims in middle childhood. *Journal of Personal and Social Relationships*, 11, 215–232.

BRÅ (1999). *Ungdomar, droger och polisens insatser*. BRÅ-rapport 1991, 1. Stockholm: National Council for Crime Prevention. Fritzes. (Authors: P. Lindström, A. Pauloff and R. Svensson).

BRÅ (2000). *Stöld, våld och droger bland pojkar och flickor i årskurs nio*. BRÅ-rapport 2000, 17. Stockholm: National Council for Crime Prevention. Fritzes. (Author: J. Ring).

BRÅ (2001). *Brottsförebyggande arbete i skolan*. BRÅ-rapport 2001, 9. Stockholm: National Council for Crime Prevention. Fritzes. (Author: K.B. Andersson).

Elliott, D.S., Huizinga, D. and Menard, S. (1989). *Multiple Problem Youth. Delinquency, Substance Use and Mental Health Problems*. New York: Springer-Verlag.

Estrada, F. (1999). *Ungdomsbrottslighet som samhällsproblem. Utveckling, uppmärksamhet och reaktion*. Auhandlingsserie Nr 3. Department of Criminology, University of Stockholm.

Farrington, D.P. (1993). Understanding and Preventing Bullying. In M. Tonry (ed.). *Crime and Justice. A Review of Research*. Chicago: The University of Chicago Press. Vol. 17. pp.381–458.

Granath, S. (1998). Våld i skolan polisanmäls men har det blivit grövre? *Apropå*, 5–6, 10–12.

Hindelang, M.J., Hirschi, T. and Weiss, J.G. (1981). *Measuring Delinquency*. Beverly Hills: Sage Publications.

Huizinga, D. and Elliott, D.S. (1986). Reassessing the reliability and validity of self-report delinquency measures. *Journal of Quantitative Criminology*, 2, 293–327.

Junger-Tas, J. and Marshall, I.H. (1999). The Self-report Methodology in Crime Research. In M. Tonry (ed.). *Crime and Justice. A Review of Research*. Chicago: The University of Chicago Press. Vol. 25. pp.291–367.

Lagerman, A. and Stenberg, P. (1999). *Att stoppa mobbning går*. Förlagshuset. Gothia.

Lindroth, J. (1994). Pressens bild av våld i skolan. Unpublished. Department of Sociology, Stockholm University.

Lindström, P. (1993). *School and delinquency in a contextual perspective*. BRÅ-report 1993, 2. National Council for Crime Prevention. Stockholm: Fritzes.

Lindström, P. (1995). Våld i skolan. I Forskningsrådsnämnden (eds). *Det obegripliga våldet*. Källa 46. Forskningsrådsnämnden.

Lindström, P. (1996). *Närpolisen och Skolan: Ett Brottsförebyggande Team?* Forskningsgruppen 1996, 1. Polishögskolans forskningsenhet. Solna. Stockholm.

Lindström, P. (1997). Patterns of school crime. A replication and empirical extension. *British Journal of Criminology*, 37, 121–130.

Lindström, P. (2001). School violence: a multi-level perspective. *International Review of Victimology*, 8, 141–158.

Ljungström, K. (1994). Till försvar för Farstametoden. *Lärartidningen*, 14, 27.

Ljungström, K. (2000). *Mobbing i skolan*. Ordkällan/Pedaktiv.

Olweus, D. (1991). Bully/victim Problems among Schoolchildren: Basic Facts and Effects of a School Based Intervention Program. In D.J. Pepler and K.H. Rubin (eds). *Development and Treatment of Childhood Aggression*. Hillsdale, N.J.: Erlbaum. pp.411–448.

Olweus, D. (1993). *Bullying at School: What we Know and What we can Do*. Oxford: Blackwell.

Olweus, D. (1994). Farstametoden är otillräcklig. *Lärartidningen*, 16, 22.

Olweus, D. (1999). Sweden. In P.K. Smith, Y. Morita, J. Junger-Tas, D. Olweus, R. Catalano and P. Slee (eds). *The Nature of School Bullying: A Cross-national Perspective*. London: Routledge. pp.7–27.

Pikas, A. (1975). *Så stoppar vi mobbning!* Stockholm: Prisma.

Ring, J. (1999). *Hem och skola, kamrater och brott*. Auhandlingsserie Nr 2. Department of Criminology, University of Stockholm.

Skolverket (1999). *Nationella kvalitetsgranskningar 1999*. Skolverkets rapport nr 180. Stockholm: Liber distribution.

Skolverket (2000). *Med demokrati som uppdrag*. Skolverket. Stockholm: Liber distribution.

Smith, P.K. and Myron-Wilson, R. (1998). Parenting and school bullying. *Clinical Child Psychology and Psychiatry*, 3, 405–417.

Smith, P.K. and Sharp, S. (eds). (1994). *School Bullying: Insights and Perspectives*. London: Routledge.

Stattin, H. (1995). Våld bland 15-åringar i en svensk stad. I Forskningsrådsnämnden (eds). *Det obegripliga våldet*. Källa 46. Forskningsrådsnämnden.

Svensson, R. (1999). Mobbare, offer och mobbare/offer: Deras relationer till familj, skola och kamrater. *Nordisk Psykologi*, 51, 42–58.

Weinehall, K. (1999). *Gymnasieelevers möten med våld – i hemmet, i skolan och på fritiden*. Rapport nr 59. Department of Education, University of Umeå.

Wikström, P-O.H. (1985). *Everyday violence in contemporary Sweden*. Report no. 15. National Council for Crime Prevention. Stockholm: Allmänna Förlaget.

Chapter 15

Denmark

Short-term non-preventive solutions in the absence of statistical research

Ebbe Ebbesen and Niels-Jørgen Jensen

Background

The country

Denmark covers an area of 43,094km² with a coastline of 7,314km. Denmark is a constitutional monarchy ruled by the unicameral Parliament or *Folketinget*. Administratively Denmark is divided into fourteen *amter* (counties) and two *kommuner* (boroughs). In addition there are 275 *local kommuner* (municipalities) of various sizes ranging from 5,000 to 250,000 inhabitants. The Faroe Islands and Greenland are parts of the Danish kingdom but have their own home rule (self-governing administration) (World Factbook, 2000; Danmarks Statistik, 2000).

The total population is 5,336,394 with an age structure as follows: 0 to 14 years: 18 per cent; 15 to 64 years: 67 per cent; 65 years and over: 15 per cent. The population growth rate is 0.31 per cent; total fertility rate is 1.73 children born per woman. Religion is predominantly Evangelical Lutheran (97 per cent). The unemployment rate is 5.7 per cent, inflation rate 2.5 per cent. Labour force, by occupation, is services, 71 per cent; industry 25 per cent; agriculture 4 per cent.

Languages spoken are Danish, Faroese, Greenlandic (an Inuit dialect) and German (a small minority in Southern Jylland). English is the predominant second language. Ethnic groups are Scandinavian, Inuit, Faroese and German. Since the 1960s there has been a rather marked increase in immigration from other countries; about 378,165 (by 2000) immigrants and descendants from countries such as Turkey (48,773), former Yugoslavia (39,879), Germany (25,448), Lebanon (19,011), Norway, Sweden, Iraq, Iran, Pakistan, and Somalia. The percentage of immigrant children in Danish schools is slowly but steadily growing, having reached 7 to 8 per cent in 1997, with a projected number of about 10 per cent by the end of the decade.

The school system

Because of a low unemployment rate and the large employment rate of women, Denmark has one of the highest rates of young children in kindergartens and daycare arrangements, run by the local municipalities. Children start school at the age of 6 to 7 years. The public school (*folkeskole*) covers primary and lower secondary education, starting with a non-obligatory kindergarten class (pre-school class) in which normally about 90 per cent of all school beginners participate. Education in primary and lower secondary levels is compulsory, from first grade to seventh grade (primary) and eighth and ninth grades (lower secondary). A tenth grade must be offered and a large proportion of the pupils continue in this grade. Some pupils transfer after the ninth or tenth grade and participate in upper secondary education (gymnasium, high school or vocational education). The size of the *folkeskoler* ranges from 100 to 800 pupils, typically being 300 to 400.

There are about 2,000 schools. Of these, 1,734 are the *folkeskoler* (public schools) controlled and run by the local school authorities in the municipalities. The schools are guided – not governed – by a board, where parents have the majority of influence within certain topics. The remaining schools are privately organized. The total number of Danish pupils is about 800,000, with 88 per cent in the public school system (World Health Organization, 1996).

A typical school day would start at 8 or 8.15a.m. Lessons last forty-five minutes. The maximum class size differs from municipality to municipality but would normally be about twenty-eight pupils. Each class has a base room where pupils get most of their lessons, and a main teacher, often the teacher taking the Danish lessons. This teacher is also responsible for the social welfare of the pupils and contacts with parents, special arrangements, etc. Ordinary subjects in schools are Danish, maths, society, geography, biology, physics, sport, English, German, French. The so-called 'timeless subjects' include health care, sexuality, traffic, crime. These subjects are to be taught during the year at appropriate times. The teaching process is quite often subject and project organized, going across two or three subjects over a period of time.

Special education must, according to the Act of Public Schools, be offered if the pedagogical psychological counselling office (PPR) in agreement with parents and the head of the school finds evidence of a special education need. The service is provided in each of the 275 municipalities in Denmark.Some 13 per cent of all pupils receive some kind of special education during a school year. This Act has been changed a number of times, most recently in 1997. Together with the Act, recommended curricula have been given to the municipalities (Oersnes, undated, *c.*1999; Dueholm, 1999). In serious cases and after actual incidents, disruptive pupils are suspended from school for up to a week. During this time the parents are consulted in order to find some kind of solution, possibly in collaboration with the municipal social department. In most cases they come back to school after this suspension.

Linguistic/definitional issues

We focus primarily on violence in schools according to the Olweus definition: aggressive behaviour where the actor or perpetrator uses his or her own body or an object (including a weapon) to inflict (relatively serious) injury or discomfort upon another individual. However, other aspects of aggression, including bullying, are included when needed to try to complete the picture of violence in schools. This is seen as essential for understanding the actions or the lack of actions being taken to prevent bullying or violence in school.

In Denmark bullying in more academic surroundings is normally defined as originated by Olweus and used by the Danish Ministry of Education: a student is being bullied or victimized when he or she is exposed, repeatedly and over time, to negative actions on the part of one or more other students (Oersnes, undated, c.1999). The Danish Govermental Board of Children, used by the Danish Government to advise in matters of children and family, gives the following definition of bullying: a repeated, systematic persecution or exclusion of an individual within a social context where this person is 'forced' to live (Rabøll Hansen, 2000). In common speech and in the common language of pupils this definition is broadened quite a lot, so that the term bullying covers all kinds of negative actions between persons. The Danish word for bullying is 'mobbe', which in fact is a rather new term in Denmark. Presumably the term *mobbe* was first widely known among pupils in the 1980s. Before then the words 'tease' and 'aggressive behaviour' were used, depending on the kind and degree of offensive behaviour. The term *mobbe* is not used to describe racial offences, or offensive behaviour to other ethnic groups, and it is generally not regarded (or used) as an appropiate word where ethnic or racial elements are in the foreground.

Bullying behaviour is not seen as a specifically social problem as such in Denmark. In the public as well as in more academic circles the understanding of bullying behaviour could, according to Niels Dueholm, Ministry of Education, be described as:

* normal developmental behaviour in learning and mastering social behaviour;
* behaviour caused by malfunctioning, low self-esteem and poorly developed group behaviour skills;

- as a symptom at a more general level, indicating non-specific problems of vigorous development;
- in severe (and rare) cases as a symptom of antisocial behaviour caused by deviant psychosocial development (Dueholm, 1999, p.52).

This means that bullying behaviour should be seen as a natural thing that everyone goes through at some time. Being bullied will strengthen you and help you overcome crises and in the end make you a strong and self-confident person. This also means that even if anyone would agree with the fact that bullying causes a lot of trouble – for example damaging your self-esteem and turning your daily life into a hell – the same people would consider bullying as something that you would have to go through and that would not last longer than a certain period of time. If systematic and long-term bullying takes place to such a severe extent that a person has to be moved from the class, you would not move the perpetrator but the victim instead; so the victim will be punished once more, moving to another school environment.

Relevant historical background

Systematic collecting of statistics on violence and bullying is almost non-existent so far as incidents of bullying and violence in schools are concerned. There has been little systematic research on the specific topic of bullying in Denmark. There have been several examples of local development projects including questionnaires on bullying, most of which lack sufficient basis of generalization. The only example of genuine research on bullying is the 1996 World Health Organization publication, *The Health of Youth – A Cross-national Survey*, in which bullying behaviour is one of the topics covered. According to this study, Denmark has a rather high score on students' bullying behaviour, coming in the top three for 'taking part in bullying others' out of the twenty-four countries surveyed, and in the top half for students who reported being bullied.

Interest in the topic of bullying has varied over time. The first newspaper articles and TV features focused on the area in the late 1980s. In the 1990s there was a decrease of interest in the topic among the public, in research and from the central authorities. During 1995–1998, interest grew again, assisted by rather 'sensational' newspaper articles. Suicides have in a few instances been mentioned in some newspapers as caused by bullying. As Denmark still has one of Europe's highest suicide rates, this might be an interesting subject to study (Jensen and Ebbesen, 1996). No studies have been carried out yet.

In 1988 a former Danish Minister of the Ministry of Education and Research took an initiative to deal with the topic of violence and bullying as seen from the pupils' point of view. He sent a letter to all pupil boards in the country and asked them to help in preventing antisocial behaviour, and improving social behaviour (all schools have a board of pupils, some of whom are the pupils' representatives on the general school board). He also asked for information on how pupils regarded bullying, how much bullying behaviour took place, what kind of bullying was most prominent, and finally what had been done and what could possibly be done to avoid bullying behaviour in future. The definition of bullying used was: *whenever one or two pupils treat a specific child or group in an unpleasant, negative way bullying is taking place.* Some 10 per cent of all schools responded to this letter by including a lot of materials on the above-mentioned questions. According to this 'pilot study' it was estimated that some 10 per cent of all pupils in schools were victims of bullying.

In 1994 the Inter-Ministerial Committee (fifteen representatives from the different ministries in the central administration) suggested a focus of initiatives for children at risk in Danish society. (This committee corresponds to a board at the political level: the Governmental Board of Children. The underlying idea is that in a highly developed and organized society like Denmark, it is necessary to develop co-operation between different ministries, all of which have something to do with children.) As far as the schools were concerned, there was agreement on the need to develop and strengthen pupils' social relationships in school in order to reach the above-mentioned goals. The 'intervention' was implemented in two ways:

1   A project to obtain pupils' own opinions, participation and ideas about 'well-being' in school (the Danish title *'Ha' det godt i skolen'* is difficult to translate but might be translated to 'Have a nice day in school').
2   A project utilizing the PPR services. In principle, every parent, pupil, teacher, etc. is in a position to receive information and guidance concerning pedagogical/psychological questions and problems. This should investigate such problems and develop answers and ideas as to how to cope with bullying situations.

A secretariat for the prevention of violence was formed on 1 January 1998. For a three-year period it was to safeguard the interests and tasks of the inter-ministerial committee made up of the Ministers of Justice, Social Affairs and Education. The secretariat was national, and was continuously to monitor the initiatives laid out in the Government's anti-violence packages and present new proposals to combat crimes of violence, especially those committed by young people.

The secretariat was closed down on 31 December 2000. Former tasks were to be continued by the Danish Criminal Preventive Board, which had been founded in 1971. It had been established because of a massive increase in criminality in the 1960s. It was necessary to put prevention efforts into focus and not just repair damages that had already happened. The goals are within the current acts of law to act preventively in relation to criminality by implementing safety promoting measures by informational activities or in other suitable ways (www.folketinget.dk; www.boerneraadet.dk; www.crimprev.dk; www.voldssek.dk; Dueholm, 1999; Hygum and Olesen, 1999).

Boerne- Ungdomsparlamentet [The Children's/The Youth parliament]

In 1999 the *Folketing* (Danish Parliament) held a *Boerneparlamentet* [Children's parliament] day on 22 March as a contribution to the 150-year jubilee of the Danish constitution. The idea was to offer young people from Denmark, the Faroe Islands and Greenland a chance to achieve a greater understanding for and wish to engage in democratic processes, by being a part of working out proposals for acts and discussing them in committees and in the parliament hall. The parliament day was made as similar as possible to a normal working day in the Danish Parliament, both in relation to content and organization. The children were also given the possibility of addressing questions to the ministers of the government – Ministers of Work, Environment, Energy, Justice, Social Affairs and Education. The topics had been planned and discussed ahead through a process in the public schools. At the end of the day nine proposals were decided (Boerneparlamentet, 1999).

One of the results of this parliament day was that the government put up a proposal for an Act, including a statement that the educational environment in schools and educational institutions should promote abilities for development and learning and therefore also include the mental and aesthetic environment. The proposal was introduced by the Minister of Education in October 2000, approved by the Danish parliament in February 2001 and started to operate in August 2001 (Lov om elevers og studerendes undervisningsmiljoe, February 2001, www.folketinget.dk).

The *Boernerådet* (Danish Children's Board) has commented that this proposed Act lies far from the recommendations given by the Children's Board in the consultation process. It lacks economic resources, and does not include any qualitative goals for what is meant by a safe and healthy environment in good conditions. There is no mention of common standards to be achieved, so that the proposal might have the opposite effect – that the process of developing a better educational environment comes to a halt. Because of the comments the Children's Board did not as a whole recommend the proposal in its present form (Boernerådet, 2000); however, the proposal went ahead, with some modifications.

Another youth parliament day was held in February 2001. At the end, eight out of twelve proposals were decided by the youth parliament, but none concerned violence in schools or bullying. However, one proposal about bullying was rejected by the youth parliament with 19 votes for, 133 votes against and 21 abstentions (Ungdomsparlamentet 2001).

Knowledge

Statistics

According to the *Rigspolitiet* (Danish State Police), acts of violence are only registered according to the character of the act. This means that questions about where and who committed the crime cannot be answered; also, statistical data about school violence cannot be found. According to the Danish Ministry of Justice, partial data about victim statistics and scenes of crime have already been and still are registered by the police for internal use. Discussions about a better statistical approach to personal crime statistics are taking place. However, lack of resources means that decisions have not yet been taken in order to start the necessary work (programming tools, implementation, etc.).

The best data about the extent of violence in schools has been gathered from *Arbejdstilsynet* (Danish Work Supervisonal Agency). According to a newsletter in November 2000, more than 2,187 employees reported an accident at work because of violence in 1997. This is an increase compared with previous years, for example 1,462 in 1993. It is stated that this is probably due to an increased awareness that violence leading to absence must be reported. It is also stated that you have to be careful in interpreting the figures as meaning that Danish workplaces are getting more violent. It is emphasized that the *Arbejdstilsynet* probably only receives a minor part of the accidents that should have been reported. Violence is one of the psychosocial areas where the *Arbejdstilsynet* prosecutes most cases, making orders or giving guidance to companies. About a third of the reports come from areas of home care service, and 24-hour institutions for adults (see Table 15.1). The figures steadily increased during the years 1993–1997. Some additional breakdown for the area of education and research is given in Table 15.2.

When all teaching tasks similar to those done in public school are added together, 71.8 per cent of the total violent accidents within the area of education and research happen in public schools. When educational tasks including working with people with a disability are included, this increases to 78.1 per cent. It is clear from these figures that severe problems of violence are present in public schools, even if proper statistics are not available. We still lack information about the dimensions of

Table 15.1 Number of working accidents related to violence, reported by type of work

Type of work	Year of accident					Total
	1993	1994	1995	1996	1997	
Transportation of passengers	125	181	139	145	197	787
Office and administration	114	185	226	209	323	1,057
Hospitals	191	189	180	219	196	975
Home care and institutions for adults	481	508	570	608	692	2,859
Institutions for children and young people	148	158	199	237	229	971
Education and research, including public schools	78	93	103	111	123	508

Source: <www.arbejdstilsynet.dk.>.

Table 15.2 Reported working accidents caused by violence (1993–1998) within the area of education and research – groups having tasks similar to those in public schools

Position	Year of accident						Total
	1993	1994	1995	1996	1997	1998	
Teaching in public and training schools				1		1	2
Teaching children and young people	50	61	61	60	73	86	391
Teaching small children			3	6	6	4	19
Taking care of children below school age	4	7	9	8	15	11	54
Teaching and taking care of people with a disability	6	2	1		2	5	16
Other teaching and care work	1	2	7	3	3	2	18
Teaching disabled children/adults	1	2		3	1		7

Source: Arbejdstilsynet, 2000.

violence – pupil/pupil, pupil/teacher, teacher/pupil, etc. – and about sex differences, age differences, etc.

In autumn 1993 a questionnaire study was carried out, analysing the mental working environment among the member organizations of the community board of salaried employees and officials. The study was performed by CASA (Centre for Alternative Social Analysis, 1994). The largest organizations include the Danish Association of Teachers, as well as nurses, salaried employees, etc. The purpose was to map the mental working environment by illustrating working tasks and working demands, and strains according to work and health conditions. Only the results relating to violence and threats of violence will be mentioned here. It was asked whether participants had been exposed to violence or threats of violence in their job during the last year. Overall, 11 per cent answered yes; the figure for education was about 9 per cent. It is not possible to get more detailed information in the public school area.

In summary, lack of statistical information and research studies makes it very difficult to give information about different types of violence, different dyads (pupil/pupil, pupil/teacher, teacher/pupil, etc.), age trends, sex differences, factors of ethnic groups, socioeconomic status, disability, special needs, school types, school ethos. However, it should be evident from the few statistical data and information given, that there is a problem of violence and threats of violence within the school area (see www.jm.dk; www.arbejdstilsynet.dk; www.politi.dk; Centre for Altemative Social Analysis, 1994).

Action

Current national/regional policies regarding violence in school

As mentioned earlier, the former government finished an Act about pupils' and students' educational environment. The Act does not include special attention on topics like violence or bullying in school. Nor does it include staff members like teachers. It also states that implementation of the Act will mean no further costs.

The *Arbejdstilsynet* [Danish Work Supervision Agency] started up a special activity plan in January 2001 for the area of education and research. The plan, covering the entire country, is about the mental working environment in certain jobs. The plan is running for the period 2000–2002 under the name: *Mental working environment – everyone's responsibility*. The plan follows a similar plan implemented in 1998. The implementation will be done by detailed inspection in relation to chosen establishments' mental working environment. The establishments are chosen from hospitals, education and research and public transportation; according to *Arbejdstilsynet*, employees in these jobs have a documented risk of being exposed to mental strain during their work. During the first and second quarter of 2001 efforts were made within the area of education and research.

The *Arbejdsmiljøinstituttet* [National Institute of Occupational Health] carried out a *projekt 3-dækker projektet* (project covering three areas) about the mental working environment, starting 1 January 1997 and ending 31 December 2000. Its purpose was to develop and test a questionnaire that could be used to measure a number of factors within the mental working environment. Looking at the analysis for teachers in public schools, the percentages reporting various characteristics are: qualitative demands 46.3; sensory demands 39.8; emotional demands 87.9; demands to hide feelings 58.8; insecure working 33.0; role conflicts 59.9. The figures, especially for emotional demands, hiding feelings, insecurity and role conflicts add to the overall picture of a school environment in deep crisis.

The *Amternes og kommunernes forskningsinstitut* [Research Institute of Counties and Municipalities] works with questions of interest to the public authorities and their users, especially problems of importance for counties and municipalities. The research deals with the citizens and their interaction with public services and institutions, and with the public use of resources or the public organization, efficiency, leadership and management. Its report (Amternes og kommunernes forskningsinstitut, 2000) states that the main problem in the public schools is that some teachers do not find it a professionally inspiring workplace and generally find the requirements of the Act on the public school too onerous. The overall picture is that there are some schools that are very active in the school development area, and in which there is a high level of job satisfaction among both head teachers and teachers, and some schools without the same high level of activity and job satisfaction.

Det Kriminalpraeventive Raad [The Criminal Preventive Board] is producing different kinds of materials and information campaigns related to children and young people (Det Kriminalpraeventive Raad, 2000). The Board is also responsible for running and developing the SSP (School, Social Services and Police) co-operation countrywide.

Some of the most important public and private organizations should be mentioned. These organizations try to influence politicians, parliament, organizations, etc. in very different ways by taking initiatives on national, regional or local levels. The *Boernerådet* [Danish Children's Board] is a consultative independent organization that is used for advising the Danish Government on issues of importance about children and young people; *Skole og Samfund* [School and Society] is a parental private organization trying to co-ordinate the efforts of the school boards in Denmark, which distributes its own materials and carries out studies individually or in co-operation with other organizations; *Boerns Vilkaar* [Children's Conditions] is an independent social organization working to take care of the interests of children and young people in Denmark (Boernenes arbejdsvilkaar, 2000).

No specific and systematic efforts (long-term action or plans, research studies, etc.) are currently being made about violence or bullying in schools at a national level – either related to statistics or to prevention (Arbejdstilsynets, 2000; Forslag til lov om elevers og studerendes undervisningsmiljø, 2000).

Local initiatives or programmes

Several schools do something to prevent violence. However, actions taken usually depend on the actual incidents. Actions are then taken to deal with the present problem and solve it. Perhaps a short-term plan will be made for preventing another incident. It should be emphasized that long-term prevention projects are non-existent. Most resources are used to deal with emergency problems.

However, one local initiative, 'Zippy's Friends', should be mentioned. In fact the project is of international interest as well. The project was, and still is running at a number of Funen public and private schools. 'Zippy's Friends' (formerly 'Reaching Young Europe') is a twenty-four week school-based project which focuses on coping with life emotionally, teaching children in kindergarten, pre-school, and first and second grade classes the necessary skills to cope with everyday life and adversities. The project includes six modules of four lessons each. Each module includes a short story about a cartoon stick insect ('Zippy') and a group of children around this insect, together with teacher's notes of guidance for different activities about the actual theme of the module. The six module themes are: feelings; communication; making and breaking relationships; conflict resolution; saying goodbye; we cope. The project is conducted by teachers who have been trained in the project on a two-day workshop, and who also attend follow-up days and are able to ask for further advice. The project was originally piloted in Denmark from October 1998 to April 1999. It was then revised and further piloted in Denmark and Lithuania, between October 2000 and April 2001. During 2001/02 it is being run as another pilot in Denmark and Lithuania after complementary improvements have been added. Evaluation tests have been made during all three pilot studies by independent international scientists using experimental and control groups, and standard international questionnaires for the teachers involved, as well as qualitative approaches such as oral and written evaluations during follow-up days on the first two pilots, in collaboration with the teachers involved.

The evaluation established that the programme had been successfully implemented in both countries, with few problems. Appreciation and participation levels for each of the sessions were remarkably similar in Denmark and Lithuania, suggesting that the programme can be successfully implemented in different languages, different grade levels and very different types of school environments. The short-term significant effects of the programme were remarkably similar in Denmark and Lithuania, and showed clear improvements in children's abilities to cope with adversities. Children who participated in the programme were observed by teachers to have used more coping strategies after participation;

reduction in school violence was not a specific target and no information is available on this (Vold som udtryksform, 2000, Mishara and Ystgaard, 2001; Befrienders International, 2001).

Closing remarks

Consideration about how to write this report left two options. The first one would have made a very brief report. At the present time no systematic and long-term initiatives in the areas of violence or bullying in schools have taken place; nor are any statistical data available in the area. The other option was that chosen here – to try to offer some kind of background insight in the area. This should be seen as an attempt to get behind the Danish way of thinking, acting and dealing with daily life. Because of the lack of systematic long-term planning and action, all resources are used in a temporary fashion, for 'repair and maintenance'. Of course this is not satisfactory in a long-term perspective.

In Denmark we are very familiar with research studies going on in other Scandinavian countries, primarily Norway, Sweden and Finland (e.g. Olweus, 1975, 1978, 1984; Björkqvist, Ekman and Lagerspetz, 1982; Lagerspetz et al., 1982; Pulkkinen and Tremblay, 1992; Smith et al., 1999). However, in spite of a close social and cultural community between the Scandinavian countries and in spite of the fact that their research studies are without any doubt essentially valid in Denmark too, Danes behave differently with this problem. Actually, we do not accept that this is a problem to deal with. Not even if, according to the UN convention on children, we are committed to ensure children a safe and secure environment.

In spite of the scientific research materials given, we do not see violence or bullying in schools as a problem arising between children with the poorest qualifications. Neither do we see that being the perpetrator of bullying in early childhood develops the criminals of today, and that being a victim of bullying in childhood may lead to depression and mental illness in adulthood. Of course no country can survive like this long-term – at least no democracy.

Summary

The Danish approach to bullying in schools is very much that being bullied is a somehow natural thing that everybody experiences at some time. Being bullied will strengthen you. On the other hand, anyone would officially agree that bullying is bad and anyone would know that it should be dealt with in order to avoid it. Nevertheless, the lack of systematic and long-term governmental initiatives is evident. The World Health Organization stated in 1996 that Denmark was in the top three for 'taking part in bullying others' by students. Figures from the Danish Work Supervision Agency indicate that figures of working accidents related to violence in Education and Research have almost doubled during the years 1993–1997. The problem of bullying and violence in schools is evident. The lack of statistics in the area makes it very hard to get an overall view of the extent and character of the problem. Most resources are used for short-sighted emergency repairs instead of prevention on a long-term basis. However, special attention should be paid to the project 'Zippy's Friends' (formerly 'Reaching Young Europe'). Independent international scientists have been testing the project, which has yielded remarkably good results.

References

Amternes og kommunernes forskningsinstitut (AKF) [Research Institute of Counties and Municipalities] (2000). Online. Available HTTP: <http://www.akf.dk/dk/forsk.htm>, Arbejdsmiljoeet i folkeskolen, Jill Mehlbye og Svend Kreiner, Juni 2000 AKF [The working environment in primary and lower secondary school – English summary. Online. Available HTTP: <http://www.akf.dk/dk2000/arbmiljoe_folkeskolen.htm>.

Arbejdstilsynet [Danish Work Supervision Agency] (2000). Online. Available HTTP: <http://www.arbejdstilsynet.dk>. Arbejdstilsynets emneindsats om psykisk arbejdsmiljø i udvalgte brancher 2000–2002 [DWSA's efforts of topics about mental working environment in chosen lines 2000–2002], 17 May.

Befrienders International (2001). Evaluation of the Revised Reaching Young Europe Programme in Denmark and Lithuania. E-mail: mishara.brian@uqam.ca, or mettey@psykiatri.ui. See also B.L. Mishara and Mette Ystgaard (2001).

Björkqvist, K., Ekman, K. and Lagerspetz, K. (1982). Bullies and victims: their ego picture, ideal ego picture and normative ego picture. *Scandinavian Journal of Psychology*, 23, 307–313.

Boernenes arbejdsvilkaar (2000). Boerns vilkaar nr. 3/august 2000, Boenenes arbejdsvilkaar, skal vi indfoere forbud mod mobning? + Boerns vilkaar nr. 4/November 1999, Kassetaenkning kan hindre boerns trivsel, praesentation af materialer om mobning, Boerns vilkaar. Online. Available HTTP: <http://www.bvdk.dk>.

Boerneparlamentet [Children's parliament] (1999). Online. Available HTTP: <http://www.ungdomsparlament.ft.dk/bp1999_baggrund.htm>.

Boernerådet [Danish Children's Board] (2000). Online. Available HTTP: <http://www.boerneraadet.dk>.

Centre for Alternative Social Analysis (CASA) (1994). Psykisk arbejdsmiljø – nu og i fremtiden [Mental Working Environment – Now and in the future: a study of FTF-members mental working environment]. March. Online. Available HTTP: <http://www.casa.dk>.

Danmarks Statistik [Statistics of Denmark] (2000). Statistisk Tiaarsoversigt 2000 – tema om børn og deres familier [Statistical survey of 10 years, 2000 – theme on children and their families]. Online. Available HTTP: http://dst.dk/dst@dst.dk>.

'Denmark' Microsoft®, Encarta® Online Encyclopedia (2000). Online. Available HTTP: <http://encarta.msn.com>.

Det Kriminalpraeventive Raad [The Crime Prevention Board] (2000). Overgreb mod børn, ser du det? Gør du noget? Rigspolitichefens trykkeri 2000; Dit liv – dit valg? Scanprint 1999; Etniske Grupper, kriminalitet og forebyggelse, Rigspolitiets trykkeri 1998; Samtale i stedet for vold, ideer til kriminalpraeventivt samarbejde mellem skole og politi, FGM Repro 1998. Kriminalpraeventiv undervisning, en vejledning, Rigspolitichefens trykkeri January 1998. Online. Available HTTP: <http://www.crimprev.dk>.

Dueholm, N. (1999). Denmark. In P.K. Smith, Y. Morita, J. Junger-Tas, D. Olweus, R. Catalano and P. Slee (eds). *The Nature of School Bullying: A Cross-national Perspective*. London: Routledge.

Forslag til lov om elevers og studerendes undervisningsmiljø [Act proposal about pupils' and students' education environment] (2000). Online. Available HTTP: <http://www.folketinget.dk/Samling/20001/lovforslag_som_fremsat/L40.htm>.

Hygum, E. and Olesen, S.G. (1999). *Introduktion til paedagogisk teori og praksis* (Introduction to pedagogic theories and practice). Viborg: PUC.

Jensen, N.-J. and Ebbesen, E. (1996). Relationer and Suicidal adfærd. *Den sociale Kandidatuddannelse*, Hold 93, Aalborg Universitet, May.

Lagerspetz, K.M., Björkqvist, K., Berts, M. and King, E. (1982). Group aggression among school children in three schools. *Scandinavian Journal of Psychology*, 23, 45–52.

Mishara, B.L. and Ystgaard, Mette (2001). Online. Available HTTP: <http://www.befrienders.org>. features the 'Zippy's Friends' project (formerly 'Reaching Young Europe') and the evaluation report 'Evaluation of the Revised Reaching Young Europe Programme in Denmark and Lithuania'. Contact the Director, e-mail: rye@befrienders.org. See also Befrienders International (2001).

Oersnes, B. (undated, c.1999). Country Report on Violence in Schools in Denmark. Educational Adviser in Ministry of Education, National Education Authority.

Olweus, D. (1975). *Hakkekyllinger og skoleboeller*. Gyldendals, Copenhagen: Gyldendals pædagogiske bibliotek.

Olweus, D. (1978). *Aggression in the Schools: Bullies and Whipping Boys*. Washington DC: Hemisphere Press (Wiley).

Olweus, D. (1984). Aggressors and their Victims: Bullying in School. In N. Frude and H. Gault (eds). *Disruptive Behavior in Schools*. New York: Wiley. pp.57–76.

Pulkkinen, L. and Tremblay, R.E. (1992). Patterns of boys' social adjustment in two cultures and at different ages: a longitudinal perspective. *International Journal of Behavioral Development*, 15, 527–553.

Rabøll Hansen, H. (2000). See ref. Boenerådet.

Smith, P.K., Morita, Y., Junger-Tas, J., Olweus, D., Catalano, R. and Slee, P. (eds) (1999). *The Nature of School Bullying: A Cross-national Perspective*. London: Routledge.

Theilgaard, L. (1999). Mobning – et overset problem eller en overdreven bekymring? Danmarks Laererhøjskole, Forskningscenter for Miljoe- og Sund-hedsundervisning. Online. Available HTTP: <http://www.dpb.dpu.dk/bogsalg>.

Ungdomsparlamentet 2001 [The Youth Parliament 2001]. Online. Available HTTP: <http://www.folketinget.dk>.

Vold som udtryksform [Violence as a way of expression] (2000). Kommunernes Landsforening (KL) og Dommunale Tjenestemaend og Overenskomstan-satte (KTO) [Danish Association of Municipalities (KL) and the Association of Municipal Public Servants and Employees appointed on a group contract basis (KTO)]. Online. Available HTTP: <http://www.ki.kl.dk>.

World Factbook (2000). Online. Available HTTP: <http://odci.gov/cia/publications/factbook/index.html>.

World Health Organization (1996). *The Health of Youth – A Cross-national Survey. WHO Regional Publications*, European Series No. 69, Canada.

Useful websites

Aahs, O. (2000). Uden konflikter i skole og boernehave, om at udvikle boerns sociale kompetence. Kroghs Forlag A/S 2000, <http://www.kroghsforlag.dk>.

Aarsberetning (1999). *Det kriminalpraeventive Raad*. Aabenraa trykkeri marts 2000, <http://www.crimprev.dk>.

Arbejdsmiljoeinstituttet (National Institute of Occupational Health) (2000). AMI's spørgeskema om psykisk arbejdsmiljoe (NIOH's questionnaire about the mental working environment) <http://www.ami.dk/research/apss/3daekker/index.html>.

En skole uden mobning (1999). Foraeldreorganization Skole og Samfund 1999, <http://www.skole-samfund.dk>.

Job med vold (Jobs with violence) (2000). Vold som udtryksform 2000 (Violence as a way of expression 2000) <http://www.vold-som-udtryksform.dk>.

Mobbedreng, en haandbog om mobning (1999). Boerneraadet, Saloprint a/s 1999, <http://www.boerneraadet.dk>.

Rigspolitiet (Danish State Police) (2000). <http://www.politi.dk/polkreds/rigspolitiet.htm>.

RisikoUngdom, ungdomsundersoegelse (1999). Af Flemming Balvig. Udgivet i samarbejde mellem Koebenhavns Universitet og Det kriminalpraeventive Raad, Rigspolitichefens krykkeri 1999, <http://www.crimprev.dk>.

Skole og Samfund (School and Society) (2000). <http://www.skole-samfund.dk>.

Skolens mobbemappe (1999). Mobbemateriale udsendt i et samarbejde mellem Danmarks Laererforening, Skole og Samfund, Kommunernes Landsforening og Undervisningsministeriet, Elbo Grafiske Hus, <http://www.uvm.dk>.

SSP-samarbejdet, Udvikling og perspektiver – Udgivet i samarbejde mellem Voldssekretariatet, narkotikaraadet og *Det Kriminalpraeventive Raad*, Rigspoliti-chefens trykkeri 2000, <http://www.crimprev.dk>.

Vold som kommunikationsmiddel (Violence as a communication tool) (2000). Pulje til konkrete udviklingsaktiviteter i forhold til uddannelses- og eller praktiksteder (Sum of money that can be applied for certain development projects (preventing violence) for educational and practice work places). <http://www.vold-som-udtryksform.dk>.

Chapter 16

Tackling violence in schools
A report from Iceland

Ragnar F. Ólafsson and Sólveig Norðfjörð

Background

The country

Iceland is the most sparsely populated country in Europe, with 2.7 inhabitants per square kilometre. The population is 283,000, of which about half lives in the capital Reykjavik and towns and villages in its immediate surroundings. The centre of the country is mostly uninhabited. The main agricultural area is in the south-west of Iceland.

The population is rather homogenous in culture and origin. The main language is Icelandic, spoken with hardly noticeable regional differences. The country was populated mostly from Scandinavia, especially Norway, in the ninth and tenth centuries, with some from Ireland and the Scottish islands. Only in the latter half of the twentieth century have there been immigrants to speak of: the majority of immigrants come from the Nordic countries, Western Europe and North America, and more recently also from Asia (e.g. Philippines, Thailand, Vietnam) and Eastern Europe (e.g. Poland, Yugoslavia, Russia) (Statistics Iceland, 2000).

The largest religious denomination is the Evangelical Lutheran Church to which 90 per cent of the population belongs, and among other denominations are Buddists, Muslims and Catholics. Literacy is 99.9 per cent. Life expectancy is 77 years for men and 81.5 years for women (Iceland Practical Information, 1999/2000).

The school system

Education is mandatory from 6 to 16 years of age, grades one to ten, and takes place in close to 200 schools around the country. There are forty schools and colleges at upper secondary level. The normal age for entering university is 20 years. Higher education is offered at eight establishments in Iceland and 39 per cent of Icelanders aged 20 to 24 are studying at university or a comparable institution, in Iceland or abroad (Ministry of Education, Science and Culture, 1995, 2000, 2002).

Compulsory education

There is no division between primary and lower secondary education. In general, pupils attend the school which is nearest to their home in the school district where they live. Most schools at this level cover the entire span from 6 to 16 years. There is no charge to pupils for compulsory schooling, and the government provides materials and textbooks free of charge. The largest urban schools have up to 1,000 pupils, but about half the schools in the country have fewer than 100 pupils. All these schools are co-educational.

The school year lasts for nine months and starts late August. There are at least 170 school days each year. Classes are held five days each week and school hours vary. The number of hours teaching varies, according to the age of the pupils, from thirty to thirty-five teaching hours per week. Icelandic, mathematics, natural sciences, social and religious studies and physical education are subjects which all pupils study from grade one through grade nine. In the tenth and final grade, all pupils study Icelandic, mathematics, English, Danish, natural sciences, social studies, life skills and physical education. Other subjects and electives vary, e.g. arts and crafts, information and communication technology, and home economics.

At primary level (grades one to seven), the same teacher instructs a class in nearly all subjects. At lower secondary level (eight to ten), teachers usually teach one or more subjects to a number of classes. Teachers may or may not follow the same class from one year to another. To qualify as a compulsory school teacher, a three-year course at a teacher-training college is required (Ministry of Education, Science and Culture, 1998).

Provisions for special needs

Pupils are generally expected to cover the same subject material at approximately the same speed. Pupils having difficulty are provided with remedial teaching, primarily in Icelandic and mathematics, but remain with their class for most of their lessons. There are provisions for the rights of immigrant children in the law on compulsory education which states that all children whose mother tongue is not Icelandic shall receive help to learn Icelandic as a second language. Such students shall, as far as possible and with the agreement of the local municipality in question, receive instruction in their mother language.

Pupils that have academic or social difficulties are offered a considerable amount of remedial instruction, after their difficulties have been diagnosed. Either the remedial teacher works with the class teacher in the classroom, where he or she assists the pupil, or the pupil is tutored by the remedial teacher on an individual basis or in a small group. Some schools have individual departments for students with severe learning disabilities. There are also some special schools for children with special educational needs (Eurybase, 2000).

Upper secondary school

Lower secondary school ends with nationally co-ordinated examinations. Although all pupils are legally entitled to upper secondary education regardless of their achievement in primary and lower secondary school, there are varied admission requirements to different programmes of study. The largest upper secondary schools have around 1,500 students, while the smallest have fewer than 50. The school year is nine months and divided into autumn and spring terms. Students usually attend thirty-two to forty lessons per week, where each lesson lasts forty minutes.

Courses of study at the upper secondary level can be divided into academically and vocationally oriented courses. Upper secondary schools generally offer educational counselling which often includes helping pupils with their personal problems. According to the law on upper secondary schools, disabled students should get instruction according to their needs and be given special support in their studies. If it is possible, they are to be integrated into mainstream education, attend regular classes and follow the same subjects as other pupils, but with special assistance.

Teachers of academic subjects must have completed at least four years of university education. Teachers of vocational or other technical subjects must be qualified in the field they teach or be a master craftsman in the trade in question and have at least two years' experience working in the field. Additionally, they are required to have completed a one-year programme of study in education and instruction methodology (Ministry of Education, Science and Culture, 1998).

Funding

Education in Iceland has traditionally been organized within the public sector and there are very few private schools. Only about 2 per cent of primary and lower secondary pupils are in private schools. Local municipalities pay almost the entire cost of compulsory education. The operating costs of upper secondary education are funded by the state. Compulsory education, including textbooks and materials, is completely free, but at upper secondary level and in state-run higher education only the tuition is free of charge (Ministry of Education, Science and Culture, 1998).

Linguistic/definitional issues

The usual term to describe violence is *'ofbeldi'*, referring to physical violence unless otherwise stated, as in *'andlegt ofbeldi'*, which means 'mental violence'. Most of the material reported below concerns physical violence. The type of definition and questioning used by researchers is important, as the reported incidence of violence is likely to vary depending on the words used to assess it.

To take into account these definitional issues, some researchers have adopted multiple questioning, i.e. asking for the incidence of violence with more than one question, using different words to identify various types of violence or aggression (see studies page 251). Answers are, for example, likely to differ depending on whether participants are asked if they have been 'subjected to violence' or if they have been 'kicked'.

'Einelti' is the term most commonly used to refer to bullying. It is a very recent addition to the language, but has been adopted by researchers, the media and the general public. Children's understanding of the meaning of the term *'einelti'* is very similar to the English term 'bullying' (Smith et al., 2002).

Knowledge

Statistics

According to police reports in 1999, the frequency of violence in Iceland as a whole (excluding sexual violence) was 50.6 incidents for every 10,000 inhabitants. Of perpetrators, 91.4 per cent were male, 8.6 per cent female; and of victims, 75.2 per cent were male and 24.8 per cent female. Of perpetrators, only 3.2 per cent were younger than 15 years old, but 35.7 per cent were 15 to 20 years old – the highest proportion of all age groups. Of victims, only 4.9 per cent were younger than 15 years old, but 25.5 per cent were 15 to 20 years old – again, the highest proportion of all age groups. Of all the incidents reported to the police in 1999, 2.5 per cent happened at schools (Ríkislögreglustjórinn, 2001).

A few studies have been conducted relatively recently in schools, which address at least indirectly the issue of violence. Individual questions in studies conducted with other main objectives can also provide some information. These are studies which have been conducted in schools and with pupils as participants. However, the violence being assessed has not been specifically limited to violence *in* the schools, but refers to violence in general. The relevant parts of these studies will now be summarized.

In a recent international study conducted in primary and lower secondary schools in thirty-seven countries, pupils were asked about whether they feared violence within their school. The results showed that about a quarter of Icelandic pupils aged 12 to 14 years said that during the last month they had feared being subjected to violence within the school (TIMSS, 1999, cited in Bjarnason et al., 2000). There are also indications that the general public's perception of violence as a problem is increasing. Gunnlaugsson (1996, cited in Bjarnason et al., 2000) showed that in 1989 only 14 per cent of Icelanders thought that crime and violence were a big problem, but in 1994, this proportion had gone up to 30 per cent.

A questionnaire study of violence among Icelandic adolescents (Þórlindsson and Bernburg, 1996) was conducted among pupils in the last year of compulsory school (15- to 16-year-olds). The questionnaire was administered in schools and was answered by 87 per cent of all youths in this age group (N = 3,810). The questionnaire addressed issues of social relationships, academic progress, smoking, alcohol and drug use – and whether they had been subjected to or subjected others to violence. There were also questions about criminal activities/behaviours. Pupils were asked whether they had been involved in violence (as victims and/or perpetrators); it was left to them how to define violence ('ofbeldi'). Additionally, to provide a more objective indication of 'violence', participants were asked whether they had been punched, kicked, threatened with a knife, etc.

The prevalence of violence (where the understanding of ofbeldi was left to the pupil) was that about 15 per cent of pupils in tenth grade said they had been subjected to physical violence once or more during the last twelve months, and 3.7 per cent reported that this had happened three times or more during this period. Considerably more boys than girls claimed they had been subjected to violence (18.2 per cent and 11.5 per cent respectively). However, 65.2 per cent of boys in this age group said they had been punched, kicked, hit or head-butted at least once during the past twelve months; the corresponding number for girls was 38.9 per cent. About 36 per cent of boys had been subjected to at least one of these behaviours three times or more and about 8 per cent nine times or more over the same period. The corresponding figures for girls were 12.9 and 1.8 per cent (Þórlindsson and Bernburg, 1996).

Thus, the incidence of violence is highly dependent upon whether violence (ofbeldi) is left undefined, or whether pupils are asked about specific types of behaviours and experiences. For example, there were about twice as many boys who reported having been punched (36 per cent) as those who reported having been subjected to 'violence' during the same twelve months (18.2 per cent). This indicates that participants employ a relatively narrow definition for the term 'ofbeldi' (Þórlindsson and Bernburg, 1996).

The percentage of participants who reported having subjected others to various types of violent behaviour indicates that two-thirds of boys and one-third of girls have subjected others to violence of the types listed above. There is thus a roughly equal proportion of perpetrators as there are victims.

Factors associated with violence

The authors link the violent behaviour with various other indicators of a more general lifestyle and show that violence is associated with antisocial behaviour such as alcohol and drug use, burglary and theft. A total of 1.2 per cent of boys and 0.4 per cent of girls had employed violence with the objective of stealing during the last twelve months (Þórlindsson and Bernburg, 1996).

Adolescents who show antisocial behaviour are more likely to have looser ties with traditional social institutions such as the family and schools. Þórlindsson and Bernburg (1996) found that those who do not employ violence find it easier to receive warmth and care from their parents. This relationship is stronger among girls than among boys ($r = .20$ and $.12$ respectively). Of those girls who found it 'almost never' easy to find warmth and care from their parents, about 55 per cent had subjected others to violence two times or more during the last twelve months. This percentage dropped to 31 per cent for those who found it 'sometimes' easy to find warmth and care from their parents. Violence is also associated with lower academic achievement ($r = -.21$), and with absence from school ($r = .18$). In a complementary analysis, Bernburg and Þórlindsson (1999) show that there is a significant relationship between using violence and having friends that use violence. This relationship holds when ties to family and school are controlled for.

Another study on school age adolescents, aged 15 to 16 years, was conducted in 1997 (Þórlindsson et al., 1998). The study covered the whole country and was given to all pupils present at school on the day of the study. A questionnaire was distributed in two versions, and one of those contained detailed questions about violence. The total sample was 7,785 pupils, which was 91 per cent of the population of pupils in this age group; about half of those took the questionnaire which covered violence.

Almost half of these pupils claimed that they had punched, pushed, kicked or hit someone during the last twelve months (Bjarnason et al., 2000). These figures were much higher for boys, 27 per cent, than for girls, 6 per cent. The number of pupils who claimed to have subjected someone to *ofbeldi* (violence) was much lower than the figures on individual behaviours like kicking and punching. This again shows that the pupils have a narrower definition of violence which does not include, for example, all kicking and punching.

The authors suggest that the discrepancy between the figures on *ofbeldi* (violence) and individual behaviours such as kicking and punching may indicate that part of the kicking and punching takes place in violent games and/or is seen as a minor incident or pure accident. The judged suitability of the term *ofbeldi* (violence) may be dependent on the situation. It is also likely that the definitions and use of *ofbeldi* is different between adults and adolescents (Bjarnason et al., 2000). Events which adults would classify as violence may not be looked at that way by adolescents.

It appears that the reported violence takes place first and foremost between the adolescents themselves. Around 20 per cent of pupils said they had been subjected to violence by their 'friend'. Thirty-two per cent had been subjected to violence by 'other adolescents'. About 6 per cent of adolescents had suffered violence from a 'close adult' and about 5 per cent from 'other adults' (Bjarnason et al., 2000).

About 17 per cent of boys are both victims and perpetrators of violence, 16 per cent are perpetrators only and 6 per cent are victims only. The respective figures for girls are 5 per cent, 4 per cent and 6 per cent. The authors point out that girls and boys seem to be equally likely to be 'only victims' while perpetration is more likely at the hands of boys. Within the female 'only victim' group, about half of the victimization is by adults, while only 13 per cent of boys who are only victims, have suffered violence from adults (Bjarnason et al., 2000).

The perpetration of violence was examined in relation to various other variables such as regional areas, educational level of parents and marital status of parents. Regional area explained relatively little of the variability in violence. Violence is somewhat higher among children who live with a step-parent than among those who live with both genetic parents (40 vs. 32 per cent for boys; 14 vs. 7 per cent for girls). There are no differences according to educational status of parents (Bjarnason et al., 2000). This indicates that in Iceland, the social status of parents accounts for little of the incidence of violence perpetration.

The relationship between academic record and violence was also examined by Bjarnason et al. (2000). Pupils were asked how often they felt studying was pointless. The correlation between this and the perpetration of violence was $r = .20$ for boys and $r = .18$ for girls. Similarly, the more often pupils said they were not prepared for classes, the higher the incidence of violence perpetration ($r = .23$ for boys; $r = .20$ for girls). The relationship between violence perpetration and academic achievement is somewhat weaker, but in the same direction ($r = .13$ for boys and girls) (Bjarnason et al., 2000).

Analysing the same data, Bernburg and Þórlindsson (2001) found a relationship between perpetration of violence and the perceived prevalence of such activities and attitudes among friends. Using multivariate methods, they found that the relationship between violent behaviour and perceived violent behaviour and attitudes among friends holds even when academic record and ties with the family are controlled for.

Table 16.1 Percentage of 10-, 12- and 14-year-old pupils who report having been involved in various violent behaviours as victims and/or perpetrators two to three times or more per month during last winter

	Victim					Perpetrator				
	Age			Gender		Age			Gender	
	10	*12*	*14*	*M*	*F*	*10*	*12*	*14*	*M*	*F*
Involved in fight	15	10	5	17	3	12	10	6	16	3
Beaten or hit	11	6	5	11	4	(not measured)				
Pushed or kicked on purpose	14	10	8	15	6	9	11	13	18	3
Violence	8	5	3	8	3	3	6	8	10	1
Hurt on purpose	15	8	7	14	6	7	9	11	15	3

Physical violence and bullying

In a study of bullying among children aged 10, 12 and 14 in Icelandic schools (N = 1,777), some questions pertained to physical violence, both as perpetrator and victim (Ólafsson, Ólafsson and Björnsson, 1999a). The results show a marked decrease in being subjected to various violent behaviours with age. On the perpetrator side, there is an increase with age in all behaviours (especially 'subjecting to violence'), but a decrease in 'involvement in fights' (see Table 16.1). Both victims and perpetrators are much more often boys than girls.

Broadly, these findings indicate a proportional shift of roles with age from victim to perpetrator. There is a decrease with age in involvement in fights, but 'violence' becomes more prominent. The term 'violence' (*ofbeldi*) has more serious connotations than any of the types of violent behaviour described in the other items. The results may indicate a decrease with age in playful fighting among equals, and an increased capacity in older children to subject younger ones to one-sided violence.

Physical violence can also be a part of bullying. The relationship between physical violence and bullying-victimization was examined by Ólafsson, Ólafsson and Björnsson (1999a). The experience of bullying as victim and perpetrator was measured using forty-four and thirty-five items respectively. No definition of bullying was provided. Pupils were asked to rate on a five-point scale how often they had suffered or subjected someone to a range of behaviours and experiences related to bullying and victimization. The items were derived mostly from earlier group interviews with children, who had been asked to define bullying and to give examples of it. A 'principal components' analysis revealed clear but correlated victimization factors. Among those were *physical victimization* (e.g. 'someone hurt me on purpose', 'I was beaten or hit'), *negative emotional experiences* (e.g. 'I felt bad because of how the other kids treated me', '. . . was scared', '. . . cried'), *verbal attacks* (e.g. 'someone made fun of my clothes', '. . . laughed at me cruelly'), *indirect bullying* (e.g. 'someone spread out stories about me', 'someone pretended to be my friend and then betrayed me') and *social exclusion* (e.g. 'no one wanted to speak to me', 'everyone was against me').

There were significant correlations between the physical victimization factor and the other victimization factors, showing that being subjected to physical violence is associated with various other types of bullying experiences. However, the correlation between physical victimization and self-reported bullying-victimization (i.e. answers to the question 'How often have you been bullied this winter?'), is only .37, while it is .47 for the negative emotional experience factor and .43 for the social exclusion factor. Thus, physical victimization is linked to a lesser degree with self-reports of being bullied than the other traditional victimization elements, as measured by the above victimization factors.

Interestingly, among the victimization factors, physical victimization also had important correlations with factors measuring bullying as a *perpetrator*. Correlations between the physical victimization and four perpetrator factors were between .31 and .54, while the respective correlations of the other victimization factors (e.g. social exclusion and negative emotional experience) with these perpetrator factors ranged only from .03 to .17. Thus, it seems that being subjected to physical violence is almost as much associated with being a bully, as it is with being a victim of other types of victimization experiences such as social exclusion and negative emotional experience.

The link between physical victimization and bullying as perpetrator is further evidenced when one looks at the way pupils cope with bullying experiences. There is a correlation of .26 between being subjected to physical violence and actively seeking revenge or responding by counterattack. There is, however, hardly any correlation between the physical victimization factor and passive responses such as showing submission and feeling helpless. These latter responses are more associated with other types of victimization, such as social exclusion. The choice of coping tactics of victims of physical violence is in that way similar to the responses that bullies exhibit, when/if they are subjected to bullying themselves.

A study conducted among Icelandic teachers, with the collaboration of teacher associations, indicated that teachers find it difficult to tackle bullying. Results showed that teachers feel they lack training in the area and claim that there is not enough time available to deal with these complicated issues (Ólafsson and Þór, 2000).

Racism

No study has been conducted on violence against children of foreign origin in Iceland. Pétursdóttir (2001, private communication), at the Intercultural Centre, is under the impression that open physical violence against immigrants is still at a minimum level in Iceland, but that prejudice and mental harassment are most certainly taking place. The centre has, however, heard of incidents where physical violence was used and racist comments made, but Pétursdóttir points out that to date there is no formal body or institution where it is possible to report harassment or discrimination because of origin or race, unlike in many other European countries. Thus it can be said that even if violence took place because of origin or race, then it is very likely that this information would not become apparent. Equally, the police point out that race or immigrant status is not reported systematically when charges are pressed for violence (Valsson, 2001).

Action

Current national policies regarding violence in school

Curriculum

In response to a number of international agreements that Iceland is party to, and to demands on schools to take on an increased role with respect to the general upbringing of the pupils, a special discipline has recently been established called Life Skills (*Lífsleikni*), that addresses issues such as human rights, gender equality, the protection of the environment, etc. The curriculum contains various elements that are relevant to tackling violence in schools. The discipline is to be taught for at least one class hour per week from fourth grade to tenth grade (i.e. between 9 and 15 years); the schools can, if they choose, increase this time. Below are paraphrased some of the aims of this programme as described in the curriculum provided by the Ministry of Education (www.mrn.stjr.is).

The discipline aims to enhance the general development and maturity of children, their physical health and psychological strength. It should increase their social maturity, moral values and respect for themselves and others. It also aims to increase their initiative, creativity and ability to adapt to demands and challenges in daily life. The main responsibility for these topics is seen to lie with the children's parents/guardians, and the school is seen to assist them in achieving these goals for their children. An emphasis is put on creating a positive and safe educational environment characterized by support and co-operation from all the school, pupils and staff alike. Life Skills is meant to provide an opportunity for the social development of pupils. The curriculum deals with factors linked to participation in a democratic society, being a member of a family, having friends, working with others and being able to see things from other people's point of view. It addresses issues such as social skills, expressing ideas, arguing one's case, setting goals and taking the initiative. The discipline also provides a forum to address current issues that can arise pertaining to the well-being of pupils and their feelings in general.

Pupils are encouraged to understand that uncontrolled emotions can result in violence or other negative and thoughtless action. It is seen as important that they learn to follow complicated rules in play and work, alone or with others, and to realise that each person has personal and emotional limits that are possible to break with negative behaviour.

The pupil is encouraged to develop empathy and respect for other people's opinions and values, and to increase their ability to have rich interactions with others regardless of gender, race, nationality, religious beliefs and physical or mental ability. It is seen as important that the pupils acquire a social vision that enables them to understand and respect the rules of society and thus develop the strength and responsibility to affect and improve their environment through democratic means and discussion.

This discipline is new in the curriculum and still in the developmental stage. It is, however, the forum which would be most suitable to tackle violence in schools.

An action plan for schools

In response to the increased concern and public debate regarding bullying in schools, and in light of the results of the two studies discussed above funded by the Ministry of Education, the Ministry established a committee with broad representation to prepare an action plan against bullying which would be applied in schools at compulsory school level. The committee recently published its suggestions (Morthens et al., 2001). They address prevention, an action plan for schools, and suggestions for a programme to increase education and information about the issue.

Prevention includes the following suggestions: an emphasis on a positive and democratic atmosphere in schools; a positive school ethos; a clear statement from schools that bullying is not acceptable and will be tackled; open discussions about bullying; school regulations should be clear about acceptable behaviour; teachers are provided with added support in the form of education and information; an emphasis on co-operation between homes and schools from the beginning of school attendance; and a strong collaboration with various associations and youth centres. It is emphasized that the school organization should not offer opportunities for bullying to occur in isolated places on the school grounds and in changing rooms, and finally that schools should investigate systematically situations, attitudes and work practices that affect prevention work and the action plans of each school.

The *action plan* includes the following suggestions: a bullying policy should be clear so that everyone knows what to do when bullying takes place and the plan should be published in the school curriculum. Each school should establish an anti-bullying team, with a professional grounding, and it should be clear to everyone who belongs to it what role they play. Bullying should not be viewed as the teacher's private problem, and finally, communication networks inside and outside school should be well defined.

Regarding suggestions for a *programme to increase education and information about the issue*, the committee suggests that the ideas of Dan Olweus should be implemented, and a conference was organized in the autumn of 2001 to introduce his ideas. In addition, a course based on his theories was made available for teachers during the summer of 2002. The committee also suggests that more education about bullying be provided in the general education of teachers (Morthens et al., 2001).

Local initiatives or programmes

The Red Cross in Iceland has spearheaded an initiative for young people against violence. The aim of the project is to make people more aware of different types of violence and of ways to tackle them, both with reference to the perpetrator and the victim. The project encourages people to be active in the battle against violence. As part of this, Red Cross representatives have travelled around the country on educational tours and published a brochure in collaboration with other parties. The Red Cross has also organized a photography competition on the topic and implemented many other initiatives (Kristjánsson, 2001, private communication).

Parent Management Training (PMT) is a specific therapy for parents who have children with behaviour problems. The method has been developed by Gerald Patterson and colleagues. The town of Hafnarfjörður has the goal of preventing serious behaviour problems in children by intervening while the problems are minor, by using PMT therapy and counselling. The aim of the therapy is to help parents to deal with all kinds of behaviour problems including violence, and direct children away from behaviour that is likely to develop later into antisocial directions. The method is seen to be most effective with children between 5 and 9 years old. The method is less suitable for children with a very unstable or weak social background, e.g. with poor family back up. After an appropriate and thorough training in PMT, the trainees will be able to educate more people in the implementation and practice of this programme and in the near future, the main offices in Hafnarfjörður will be able to use this method to help parents of children with behaviour problems (Sigmarsdóttir, 2001, private communication).

The Youth and Sports Council of Reykjavík has been active in tackling bullying. They have published educational materials both for their counsellors and for children. The project for the children consists of a two-hour educational visit in classes of 13-year-olds and includes a survey about the experience of bullying. Later they return to the classes and administer the survey again to evaluate the effectiveness of the programme. A preliminary evaluation of this programme has given encouraging results (Ólafsson, Ólafsson and Björnsson, 1999b). The council is now planning a similar project to suit 9- and 10-year-olds.

The Children's Ombudsman in Iceland held a conference about bullying and published a report that was distributed widely in the country. She has appeared on TV to draw attention to violence among children. There is also information about bullying in the Ombudsman's website (www.barn.is).

There are a few self-help groups for victims of bullying and some victims or former victims have come forward and talked about their experiences in the media and elsewhere. These include media personalities, actors, etc. A wealth of information about bullying is accessible in brochures and books, both original and translated (e.g. Smith and Sharp, 2000; Ólafsson, 1996; Roland and Vaaland, 2001). Novels for children have been published recently, which address bullying issues. The media is active in publishing interviews and articles on the issue.

Conclusions

There is relatively little information available on violence in Icelandic schools and little systematic data have been collected on the issue. A few studies provide percentage data on the incidence of violence in general which pupils aged 10 to 15 years have experienced, and links with various other variables, such as family relationships, academic achievement, drug use, etc. have been established. Physical victimization has been linked to other forms of bullying-victimization, and also to bullying as perpetrator.

A new discipline, Life Skills, has been introduced to the national curriculum, and seems to provide a suitable forum to tackle violence in schools. The Ministry of Education has also put forward guidelines to schools with suggestions on prevention, an action plan to tackle bullying and suggestions for increased education and information to be made available on the topic. Various initiatives against violence in schools have been run by the Red Cross in Iceland, the Reykjavik Youth and Sports Council has made available an anti-bullying programme pack for schools, and the town of Hafnarfjörður has provided training opportunities that will be useful to tackle violent behaviour. A variety of new materials have become available to facilitate interested parties in tackling bullying and/or violence in schools. The Children's Ombudsman has made available various materials in the area, and has initiated activities to tackle bullying.

British and Scandinavian material has been translated and adapted. Individual teachers and psychologists have also taken initiatives on their own. Thus, the issue of bullying and violence in schools is very much in the public domain and there is a steadily increasing activity to tackle these issues at all levels.

References

Bernburg, J.G. and Þórlindsson, Þ. (1999). Adolescent violence, social control and the subculture of delinquency: factors related to violent behavior and non-violent delinquency. *Youth and Society*, 30, 445–460.

Bernburg, J.G. and Þórlindsson, Þ. (2001). Routine activities in social context: a closer look at the role of opportunity in deviant behavior. *Justice Quarterly*, 18, 543–567.

Bjarnason, Þ., Ásgeirsdóttir, B.B., Þórlindsson, Þ., Sigfúsdóttir, I.D. and Bernburg, J.G. (2000). *Ofbeldi meðal íslenskra skólabarna og félagslegir skýringaþættir*. Reykjavík: Rannsóknir og greining.

Eurybase (2000). The Information Database on Education Systems in Europe. The Education System in Iceland. Online. Available HTTP: <http://www.eurydice.org>.

Gunnlaugsson, H. (1996). Empiri og ideology i kriminology. *Nordisk tidsskrift for kriminalvidenskab*, 83, 14–26. Cited in P. Bjarnson, B.B. Ásgeirsdóttir, Þ. Þorlindsson, I.D. Sigfúsdóttir and J.G. Bernburg (2000). *Ofbeldi meðal íslenskra skólabarna og félagslegir skýringaþættir*. Reykjavík: Rannsóknir og greining.

Iceland Practical Information. The official guide for business visitors (1999/2000). Reykjavík: Export Publication.

Kristjánsson, K. (2001). Private communication.

Ministry of Education, Science and Culture (1995). *The educational system in iceland*. Reykjavík: Ministry of Education, Science and Culture.

Ministry of Education, Science and Culture (1998). *The educational system in iceland*. Reykjavík: Ministry of Education, Science and Culture.

Ministry of Education, Science and Culture (2000). *Tölfræðihandbók um háskólastigið*. Reykjavík: Ministry of Education, Science and Culture.

Ministry of Education, Science and Culture (2002). Online. Available HTTP: <http://www.mrn.stjr.is>.

Morthens, M., Sighvatsson, G., Thoroddsen, J., Snævarr, S., Kristjánsdóttir, U. and Helgason, Þ.H. (2001). *Tillaga starfshops um einelti í grunnskólum*. Reykjavík: Ministry of Education, Science and Culture.

Ólafsson, G. (1996). *Einelti*. Reykjavík: Rannsóknastofnun uppeldis-og menntamála.

Ólafsson, R.F., Ólafsson, R.P. and Björnsson, J.K. (1999a) *Umfang og eðli eineltis í íslenskum grunnskólum*. Reykjavík: Rannsóknastofnun uppeldis-og menntamála.

Ólafsson, R.F., Ólafsson, R.P. and Björnsson, J.K. (1999b). *Mat á áhrifum fræðslu til að stemma stigu við einelti*. Reykjavík: Rannsóknastofnun uppeldis-og menntamála.

Ólafsson, R.F. and Þór, Ó.H. (2000). *Úrræði skóla við lausn á eineltisvandamálum.* Reykjavík: Rannsóknastofnun uppeldis- og menntmála.

Pétursdóttir, G. (2001). Private communication.

Ríkislögreglustjórinn (2001). *Brot gegn lífi og líkama.* Reykjavík: Ríkislögreglustjóri.

Roland, E. and Vaaland, G. (2001). *Saman í sátt: leiðir til að fást við einelti og samskiptavanda í skólum.* Translated and adapted by Elín Einarsdóttir and Guðmundur I. Leifsson. Reykjavík: Námsgagnastofnun.

Sigmarsdóttir, M. (2001). Private communication.

Smith, P.K., Cowie, H., Ólafsson, R.F. and Liefooghe, A.P.D. (2002). Definitions of bullying: a comparison of terms used, and age and sex differences, in a 14-country international comparison. *Child Development*, 73, 1119–1133.

Smith, P.K. and Sharp, S. (2000, English original 1994). *Gegn einelti: handbók fyrir skóla.* Translated and adapted by Ingibjörg Markúsdóttir. Reykjavík: Æskan.

Statistics Iceland (2000). Reykjavík: Hagstofa Íslands.

TIMMS (1999). Niðurstöður fjölþjóðlegrar samanburðarrannsóknar í stœrðfrœði og náttúrufrœðigreinum. Unpublished; cited in P. Bjarnson, B.B. Asgeirsdóttir, Þ. Þórlindsson, I.D. Sigfúsdóttir and J.G. Bernburg (2000). *Ofbeldi meðal íslenskra skólabarna og félagslegir skýringapættir.* Reykjavík: Rannsóknir og greining.

Valsson, K.S. (2001). Unnið gegn fordómum og fáfræði. *Daily-DV*, 30 January.

Þórlindsson, Þ. and Bernburg, J.G. (1996). *Ofbeldi meðal íslenskra unglinga.* Reykjavík: Rannsóknastofnun uppeldis- og menntmála.

Þórlindsson, Þ., Sigfúsdóttir, I.D., Bernburg, J.G., and Halldórsson, V. (1998). *Vímuefnaneysla meðal ungs fólks: umhverfi og aðstœður.* Reykjavík: Rannsóknastofnun uppeldis- og menntamála.

Part IV

United Kingdom and Ireland

Chapter 17

School violence in the United Kingdom

Addressing the problem

Helen Cowie, Dawn Jennifer and Sonia Sharp

Background

The country

The United Kingdom (UK) consists of Great Britain (England, Wales and Scotland) and Northern Ireland; it has a mid-1999 population estimate of 59,500,900 (National Statistics, 2000). England, the largest country, has nine regional areas: North East, North West, Yorkshire and Humberside, East Midlands, West Midlands, East, London, South East and South West. As of 1998, ethnic minority populations make up 7.5 per cent of the population of England, and about 1.5 per cent of the population of Wales and Scotland. In London, the proportion rises to 25 per cent. Greater London contains over 80 per cent of the total Black African population, nearly 60 per cent of the Black Caribbean population, almost half of the Bangladeshi and over 40 per cent of the Indian population. Nearly half of the Pakistani population lives in the metropolitan counties of Greater Manchester, West Yorkshire and the West Midlands (National Statistics, 2001).

The school system

The Department for Education and Skills (DfES) (until recently the Department for Education and Employment, DfEE) is the government department responsible for policy on education and training in England; the National Assembly for Wales is the devolved administration responsible for policy development in education and lifelong learning in Wales; the Department for Education and Training in Northern Ireland is responsible for policy on education and training in Northern Ireland; and the Scottish Executive is the devolved government for Scotland, responsible for education.

In Great Britain education is compulsory between a child's fifth and sixteenth birthdays (Department for Education and Skills, 2002). Most children of this age group attend school, although a small minority is educated by private tuition or by their parents/carers at home. In England and Wales, many primary schools operate an early admission policy whereby they admit children under 5 into reception classes. Arrangements in Scotland are broadly similar, although there are differences in detail (for example, there are no reception classes, and planning systems differ). In Northern Ireland, compulsory schooling begins at age 4.

Over 90 per cent of pupils attend publicly funded state schools, of which there are a number of different categories. In most areas, children aged 5 to 10 attend primary school, moving on to secondary school at age 11, for education up to age 16 and beyond. Primary schools are usually co-educational; secondary schools are also generally co-educational but a small minority are single sex. Primary schools typically have between 200 to 400 pupils, and secondary schools approximately 1,000 to 1,200 pupils. About 7 per cent of pupils in England and Wales attend independent schools, of which there are approximately 2,270. In Scotland about 4 per cent of pupils go to independent schools, of which there are approximately 114. Independent schools are funded from fees paid by parents and income from investments. Some of the larger independent schools are known as public schools (see Department for Education and Skills, 2002).

According to the National Curriculum (2000), all subjects provide opportunities to promote pupils' spiritual, moral, social and cultural development. Explicit opportunities to promote pupils' development in these areas are provided in religious education and the non-statutory framework for personal, social and health education (PSHE), and citizenship at Key Stages 3 and 4 will become statutory in 2002 (National Curriculum, 2000).

Within mainstream schools, the methods for coping with pupils with emotional and behavioural difficulties include the early identification and assessment of children with special educational needs, and effective communication systems between education, health and social services (Department for Education and Employment, 2000a). Sometimes this leads to specialist teachers working with the school to identify pastoral support programmes or other interventions. For a small number of pupils (2 per cent), special provision is offered to supplement the school's resources. Management of pupils includes strategies such as short-term target and goal setting, the implementation of a broad, balanced and relevant curriculum, the prevention of older disaffected pupils from influencing younger ones, and the implementation of behaviour management policies that are positive, establishing firm boundaries of behaviour and allowing for development. An extremely small number of pupils with special educational needs are placed in residential special schools.

Linguistic/definitional issues

An extensive literature search yielded little in the way of definitions or descriptions of violence in either statistics or school regulations. However, definitions and descriptions from other sources include the following:

> An incident in which an employee is abused, threatened or assaulted by a student, pupil or member of the public in circumstances arising out of the course of his or her employment.
>
> (National Association of Head Teachers, 2000)

> . . . behaviour which causes physical or psychological harm.
>
> (Varnava, 2000)

> Youth violence is defined as behaviour that is intended to cause, and that actually causes, physical or psychological injury, and that is committed by persons aged roughly between ages 10 and 21.
>
> (Farrington, 2001)

It is clear that these definitions include verbal and often psychological, as well as physical, harm to another person. The term 'bullying' is related to violence but is generally taken as implying repetition and an imbalance of power.

Relevant historical background

The 1989 Elton Report (Department of Education and Science, 1989) argued that school experiences, including relationships with adults and peers, have an influence on attitudes to and involvement in violence. In particular, schools with consistent behaviour policies and good systems of pastoral care, and which placed value on home–school relationships, were more effective in promoting good work and behaviour. Schools that adopted punitive regimes were associated with worse standards of behaviour. It was concluded that schools play an important part in reducing the risk of children becoming violent.

This finding is confirmed by Farrington and his colleagues (Farrington, 1998; Farrington and Welsh, 1999), who document successful prevention programmes that target risk factors to reduce aggression and violence in young people. These programmes focus on the risk factors of antisocial child behaviour, including troublesomeness in school, hyperactivity–impulsivity–attention deficit, low intelligence and poor school attainment, family criminality, family poverty and poor parental child-rearing behaviour. Evaluation research has demonstrated that many of these programmes are effective in reducing offending (Farrington, 2001).

In 1993 a Commission on Children and Violence was convened by the Gulbenkian Foundation to review what we know about why children become violent, and the extent of violence to and by children. In the context of education, the commission concluded that 'schools can either be a force for violence prevention, or can provide an experience which reinforces violent attitudes or adds to the child's experience of violence' (Gulbenkian Foundation, 1995, p.139). One recommendation of the commission was that education services and individual schools should adopt a commitment to non-violence and work towards a non-violent society. A key principle was that all discipline should be positive and children should be taught prosocial values and behaviour, including non-violent conflict resolution. Following the commission's report, the Forum on Children and Violence was founded in 1997, and is involved in a range of projects that are aimed at ensuring that children are protected from violence.

There have also been programmes designed to reduce school bullying. The Sheffield Anti-Bullying Project (funded by the then Department for Education), and a project in London and Liverpool funded by the Home Office, both ran from 1991 to 1994. Both reported some success in reducing rates of victimization (Smith and Sharp, 1994; Pitts and Smith, 1995). Other initiatives include, for example, ChildLine, a free telephone helpline for children and young people in trouble or danger. In 1999/2000, ChildLine (2000a) counselled over 126,000 children, of whom over 22,000 spoke about bullying.

Regulations for managing school exclusions were updated in 2000 to require all schools to develop individual pastoral support programmes to ensure appropriate early intervention in time to support pupils at risk of developing disruptive or violent behaviour. Additionally, a £3,000 payment was available to support pupils at risk of disaffection or exclusion when they transfer to another school (Department for Education and Skills, 2002).

A review of discipline in schools was launched in 1996 by the Department of Education Northern Ireland (DENI), with the aim of promoting and sustaining good behaviour in schools. The report informed the development of a strategy outlined in a publication entitled *Promoting and Sustaining Good Behaviour: A Discipline Strategy for Schools* which identifies a framework for providing a consistent, co-ordinated and coherent approach to promoting good behaviour in schools (Department of Education Northern Ireland, 1999).

In Scotland, the Scottish Executive Education Department and the University of Edinburgh jointly established the communication service, the Scottish Schools Ethos Network in 1995. The aim of the network is to facilitate schools getting in touch with each other to share approaches, methods of consultation, good ideas and action for improvement of school ethos. Developing a positive ethos programme involves a number of different activities including promoting positive discipline, involving parents in school development planning, promoting a sense of identity and belonging in all pupils, and developing an anti-bullying policy (Scottish Schools Ethos Network, 2001).

Further government initiatives include the Management of Safety at Work Regulations (1992), the Education Act (1996), the Crime and Disorder Act (1998), the Protection of Children Act (1999), and the Education (Restriction of Employment) Regulations (2000). Implementation of these Acts will have an influence on our current understanding of violence in schools, our actions towards violence in schools and our subsequent policy and strategy development.

Knowledge

Statistics

While violence in schools is reported anecdotally in the media and on telephone helplines such as ChildLine, there is no central register of violence in schools statistics available from either the then-DfEE (Department for Education and Employment, 2000b) or the Home Office (Home Office, 2000). With the exception of one or two surveys, most research over the last decade has focused on the related issue of school bullying (see Cowie and Smith, 2001; Mellor, 1990; Smith and Shu, 2000; Whitney and Smith, 1993). Currently, the best indicators for violence in schools are available in the form of school exclusion statistics from the DfES and DENI, violence in schools statistics taken from the British Crime Survey (Budd, 1999) and a study commissioned by the National Union of Teachers (NUT) (Neill, 2001).

Trends in permanent exclusions

Table 17.1 shows the number of permanent exclusions for England gathered by the DfES (Department for Education and Skills, 2002) for the four years for which data are available, the percentage of all permanent exclusions and the percentage of the school population excluded from each type of school and for all schools. (For comparable statistics for Wales, Scotland and Northern Ireland, see www.wales.gov.uk, www.scotland.gov.uk and www.deni.gov.uk respectively.) In each of the years 1995/96, 1996/97 and 1997/98 the total number of exclusions was over 12,000, representing about 0.17 per cent of the number of children in school. In 1998/99 the number of permanent exclusions fell to under 10,500, about 0.14 per cent. Even with the changes in the overall figures, the proportion of all exclusions in each type of school remained nearly the same each year:

Table 17.1 Permanent exclusions by type of school; 1995/96 to 1998/99

	1995/96	1996/97	1997/98	1998/99
Primary schools				
Number of permanent exclusions	1,608	1,573	1,539	1,366
Percentage of all permanent exclusions	13	12	13	13
Percentage of school population	0.04	0.04	0.03	0.03
Secondary schools				
Number of permanent exclusions	10,344	10,463	10,187	8,636
Percentage of all permanent exclusions	83	83	83	83
Percentage of school population	0.34	0.34	0.33	0.28
Special schools				
Number of permanent exclusions	524	632	572	436
Percentage of all permanent exclusions	4	5	5	4
Percentage of school population	0.54	0.64	0.58	0.45
All schools				
Number of permanent exclusions	12,476	12,668	12,298	10,438
Percentage of all permanent exclusions	100	100	100	100
Percentage of school population	0.17	0.17	0.16	0.14

Source: Adapted from Department for Education and Skills, 2002.

about 83 per cent of exclusions were from secondary schools, 13 per cent from primary schools and 4 per cent from special schools. The reasons for exclusion, according to Hallam and Castle (1999), tend to be related to general disobedience or physical aggression against staff and other pupils. Eighty-three per cent of permanent exclusions were male. Sixty-six per cent were of pupils aged 13, 14 or 15 at the start of the school year. Rates of permanent exclusion are highest in special schools, lowest in primary schools.

In 1998/99 the overall permanent exclusion rate of the total school population was 0.14 per cent; the exclusion rates for Black Caribbean, Black African and other Black pupils were 0.58 per cent, 0.21 per cent and 0.49 per cent respectively; the exclusion rates for Indian, Pakistani and Bangladeshi pupils were 0.04 per cent, 0.10 per cent and 0.07 per cent respectively; the exclusion rate for Chinese pupils was 0.03 per cent; and the exclusion rate for white pupils was 0.15 per cent (Department for Education and Skills, 2002). The over-representation of African–Caribbean pupils in school exclusions is a major cause for concern (Wright, Weekes and McGlaughlin, 2000). The Mental Health Foundation (1999) report, *Bright Futures*, recommends that special attention should be given to the position of cultural minorities through, for example, mentoring schemes.

Violence against teachers

With regard to violence experienced by teachers, the British Crime Survey (Budd, 1999), the most comprehensive and reliable to date on the extent and nature of violence at work in England and Wales, suggests that 3.2 per cent of teachers in primary schools and 4.2 per cent of teachers in secondary schools are victims of violence. Offence descriptions given by teachers suggest that pupils and their parents are the two main sources of violence. According to the report, teachers in secondary schools are most at risk of assault (2.2 per cent), whereas those in primary schools are most at risk of threats (also 2.2 per cent).

In response to recent concern about disruption in schools, the NUT commissioned a survey of its members in England and Wales entitled *Unacceptable Pupil Behaviour* (Neill, 2001). A total of 2,575 questionnaires, representing the composition of the teaching force in general, were returned. The most frequent of the serious problems witnessed by respondents were threats of pupil to pupil violence, with 83.2 per cent of respondents reporting it at least once a year and 43.4 per cent on a weekly basis. Regarding threats of physical violence to themselves, 34.5 per cent of respondents personally experienced this from a pupil at least once a year, and 4.6 per cent had experienced it from parents. Pushing, touching or other unwanted physical contact was personally experienced by 37 per cent of respondents at least once a year and by 8.9 per cent of respondents weekly; this was greater in secondary schools.

Bullying in schools

Research into bullying in schools has been quite extensive over the last decade. In a study by Smith and Shu (2000), 2,308 pupils aged 10 to 14 years from nineteen schools across England took part in a question-naire survey. While the schools were sampled from a cross-section of rural and urban areas, they do comprise schools previously concerned about bullying issues. It was found that 12.2 per cent of pupils experienced being bullied 'two or three times a month' or more. Younger pupils were more likely to report being bullied, but gender differences were not significant. And 2.9 per cent of pupils reported bullying others 'two or three times a month' or more. Boys reported being the bully more often than girls did, but age differences were not consistent. Being hit or physically bullied accounted for 21 per cent of bullying, with physical bullying being significantly more common in boys. These figures were lower than those obtained some seven years previously (Whitney and Smith, 1993), and the authors tentatively attribute this to the increase in anti-bullying activity in the participating schools and in the UK generally (Smith and Shu, 2000).

Action

Current national/regional policies regarding violence in school

Whilst nothing specific has been implemented to address violence in schools, several recent government initiatives have begun to tackle related issues. The Office for Standards in Education (OFSTED) was set up with a statutory responsibility to keep the Secretary of State for Education and Skills informed about 'spiritual, moral, social and cultural development of pupils [in] schools'. Its main aim is to improve educational quality and standards of achievement in schools, accomplished through regular independent school inspections which report on a range of educational issues including disruptive behaviour, and a review of each school's anti-bullying policy. Since September 1999, the Schools Standards and Framework Act (1998) has made it a legal requirement that all schools have a policy or framework for 'encouraging good behaviour and respect for others on the part of pupils and, in particular, preventing all forms of bullying among pupils'.

The National Healthy School Standard (NHSS) was launched by the government in October 1999, the aim being for all local education authorities to be involved in an accredited education and health partnership by March 2002. The national standard has a role in supporting the development of local healthy schools programmes, including activities that ensure schools become healthier places in which staff and pupils work and learn (National Healthy School Standard, 2000).

The most significant national initiative taken to reduce violence in schools is a special three-year government programme entitled Excellence in Cities. This initiative aims to address issues of underachievement, disaffection and social exclusion in targeted urban areas (Department for Education and Skills, 2002). Schools are awarded money if they can demonstrate that they have developed systems and practices for enhancing provision of, for example, projects for pupils who display aggressive or disruptive behaviour.

Each year schools receive money through the Social Inclusion Pupil Support Standards (Department for Education and Skills, 2002). For 2001/02, a total of £174 million has been allocated to local authorities as part of the government's continued drive to deal with bad behaviour and to tackle truancy. Of this total, £137 million is going directly into schools to tackle truancy, discipline and exclusions, of which £10 million will be used to support the establishment of Learning Support Units to ensure that disruptive pupils are taken out of the classroom.

In December 2000, the then Education and Employment Secretary launched an anti-bullying pack. This pack updated the 1994 publication *Don't Suffer in Silence* based on the findings of the Sheffield Anti-Bullying project, and contains a video for teachers to use as a curriculum resource (Department for Education and Employment, 2000; Department for Education and Skills, 2002). Themes covered in the pack include: whole-school policy, pupil perspectives, strategies to combat bullying, working through the curriculum, peer support and working with parents and the community. The pack is supported by a website (www.dfee.gov.uk/bullying), and a public information film to raise awareness. The department is also providing £180,000 in 2000/01 to help Parentline Plus to expand its helpline to deal with parents' calls about bullying.

Connexions (2001), a new guidance and advice service in England for all 13- to 19-year-olds, is an important initiative in the government's action plan for reaching out to young people at risk, which began full-scale operation in a number of areas from April 2001. Its key objective is to encourage more young people to stay in education or training, so that an increased number have the qualifications needed for further education and employment. It is available for all pupils, with a special emphasis on young adults engaged in offending behaviour or who experience chaotic lifestyles. Connexions will enhance school planning and provision in the area of personal development and work-related learning, including personal, social and health education, citizenship and Healthy Schools Standard work. It is delivered through a network of personal advisers working with schools and linking up with partner agencies in the statutory and voluntary sectors. Effective record keeping will be important to monitor the progress of young people, review interventions and contribute to the build-up of evidence-based practice.

Local initiatives or programmes

In March 1999, the Forum on Children and Violence launched a new campaign entitled *Towards a Non-violent Society: Checkpoints for Schools* (Varnava, 2000). The campaign offers a concise and practical guide enabling schools to review current activity and develop plans to promote non-violence as part of a whole-school policy, as well as assisting in monitoring and evaluating progress (National Children's Bureau, 2000). Two evaluations are under way: one by Vidal as part of the Connect UK-001 project (www.gold.ac.uk/connect), and one by Shaughnessy at the University of Surrey Roehampton (j.shaughnessy@roehampton.ac.uk). Based on Checkpoints in Schools and the many suggestions of young people, *Towards a Non-violent Society: Checkpoints for Young People* (Varnava, 2001) has recently been introduced for pupils moving from primary to secondary school, with the aim of raising awareness of and preventing violence involving pupils.

Leap Confronting Conflict was founded by the Leaveners (a Quaker community arts charity) in 1987, to explore the causes and consequences of conflict and violence in young people's lives. Leap aims to ensure that the active processes of conflict resolution and mediation lie at the heart of all personal and social education for young people. They have developed a range of projects including Confronting Conflict in Schools, which currently involves five secondary schools in the London borough of Tower Hamlets that experienced high levels of conflict and violence in the local community, spilling over into the schools. In 1999, a total of 480 pupils participated in this programme; a further twenty young peer trainers undertook rigorous residential training and then delivered workshops to younger pupils; and, in 1999, the local education authority decided to offer funding to all secondary schools in the borough, to enable them to participate in a rolling programme of conflict training over the next five years (Leap, 1999).

ChildLine in Partnership with Schools (CHIPS) was introduced into secondary schools in England, Scotland and Wales in October 1997, and to date in excess of 1,000 schools are involved (Turner, 2000). CHIPS is a partnership between ChildLine, young people and schools, the aim of which is to raise awareness about ChildLine, and to encourage schools to support their pupils in setting up projects run by and for pupils that tackle issues that affect their lives, such as bullying and violence. Feedback from 318 schools via a questionnaire survey suggests that CHIPS did raise awareness of ChildLine and issues such as bullying and violence in schools (Turner, 2000). Furthermore, many schools requested training in peer support. ChildLine have extended the success of CHIPS into primary schools with the launch of a new teacher's pack containing eight lesson plans based on some of the most common issues that primary school-age children phone ChildLine about, including bullying (ChildLine, 2000b).

Peer support systems

The Peer Support Forum was established in 1998 through collaboration between ChildLine/CHIPS and the Mental Health Foundation (see www.mhf.org.uk/peer/). It aims to promote peer support to enhance the emotional well-being of young people and challenge bullying and other forms of violence.

Peer support in schools concerns pupils helping pupils. It builds on the resources that friends spontaneously offer one another, and creates opportunities for young people to be active, responsible members of their community by, for example, supporting peers who are the victims of conflict. Peer support systems aim to facilitate the use of basic listening skills, empathy for the other's point of view, a problem-solving approach to interpersonal difficulties and a willingness to take a supportive role. The different types of peer support include Co-operative Group Work,

Circle Time, Circle of Friends, Befriending, Schoolwatch, Conflict Resolution/Mediation and Active Listening (Cowie and Wallace, 2000).

Circle Time

Circle Time is an example of the Co-operative Group Work approach; it is a time set aside each week in which teachers and pupils sit in a circle and take part in activities, games and discussion. The positive atmosphere that is generated in a well-managed circle can encourage group members to listen to one another, learn to take turns, give and receive affirmation, discuss difficult issues from a problem-solving stance, and keep to the rules – rules that *they* have played a part in formulating. Circle Time has been evaluated by Robinson and Maines (2000) using the case study method; they reported that Circle Time heightens young people's self-awareness, gives them a greater sense of personal mastery and improves group and social skills.

Circle of Friends

Sometimes known as 'circle of support', which originated in Canada, Circle of Friends is a method for building relationships around a pupil who is vulnerable to social exclusion because of disruptive behaviour, a behavioural difficulty, or peer relationship difficulties in their lives. It is currently used in the UK in more than 100 local authority primary and secondary schools (Neustatter, 2001). The method aims to: provide a support team to work with a vulnerable pupil; increase the active attempts of the peer group to intervene positively in that pupil's life; increase the level of acceptance and inclusion of the pupil; increase opportunities for the pupil to make friends in or outside the circle itself; and increase insight and understanding for the pupil into his/her own feelings and behaviour. It also aims to impact positively on relationship and organizational factors within schools. Case study evaluations confirm that Circle of Friends is a flexible and creative method of forming a peer network for individuals who experience difficulties in their relationships and behaviour (Newton and Wilson, 1999).

Befriending

Befriending systems involve the assignment of a pupil or pupils to 'be with' or 'befriend' a peer. Usually befrienders are volunteers, same-age peers or older pupils, who are selected by teachers (and sometimes existing befrienders) on the basis of their personal qualities. Usually there is some training in interpersonal skills, such as active listening, assertiveness and leadership. Studies of befriending indicate a number of advantages.

For vulnerable pupils, the experience of being befriended can be a critical part of the process of feeling more positive about themselves. Befrienders report that they benefit from the process, feeling more confident in themselves and learning to value other people more. Teachers frequently report that the school environment becomes safer and more caring following the introduction of a befriending scheme, and that peer relationships in general improve (Cowie and Sharp, 1996).

Schoolwatch

Schoolwatch is a pupil-organized initiative developed by South Wales Police to challenge antisocial behaviour as part of its Schools Liaison programme. It is now in operation in over 100 primary schools in South Wales. The Home Office Police Research Award Scheme has evaluated Schoolwatch. They found that, in comparison with control schools that had not participated in the scheme, the pupils in Schoolwatch schools reported that bullying had declined and felt happier and more valued than they had before the scheme was introduced. The main factor was the enthusiasm and ownership the pupils felt for their scheme (Warton and Barry, 1999).

Conflict resolution/mediation

This is a structured process in which a neutral third party assists voluntary participants to resolve their dispute. The aims are to: enable victim and perpetrator to identify offender liabilities and obligations and to find a means of restitution; empower young people themselves to defuse interpersonal disagreements among peers, including bullying, racist name-calling, fighting and quarrelling; ensure that each disputant comes away from the mediation with a positive 'win–win' experience and the sense that the outcome is fair to both sides. Where programmes have been evaluated, the responses are generally positive. These methods are reported to result in decreases in the incidence of aggressive behaviour, and improvements in school climate and the quality of pupils' relationships (Stacey, 2000).

Active listening

Active listening methods extend the befriending and mediation approaches into interventions that are based more overtly on a counselling model. Pupil helpers are trained and supervised to use active listening skills to support peers in distress. The aims are to: give helpers skills to deal with peers' interpersonal issues; help the victims of bullying;

challenge pupils who bully. In one secondary school, 60 per cent of peer supporters reported benefits arising directly from the interpersonal skills and teamwork acquired in the course of training, and 63 per cent believed that the service was having an impact on the school as a whole. The adults in charge of the schemes were unanimous in confirming that the work of the peer support service went beyond the help offered to individuals in need – valuable as that was – and that it affected the whole school (Naylor and Cowie, 1999).

In general, peer support methods are perceived positively by users and potential users, by teachers and by parents. Their greatest impact is in changing the ethos of the school to one that is more prosocial. The peer supporters – a proportion of whom are former victims – gain enormously in social skills, confidence and self-esteem. They also learn useful roles and responsibilities that serve them well in future careers. One disadvantage is that currently they are viewed as 'feminine' systems with only a small percentage of peer supporters (around 20 per cent) being boys (Cowie, 2000). The most effective systems appear to be those that adopt a befriending approach that is well integrated into the school community. Counselling based systems are more likely to be perceived with suspicion and simply not used (Cowie et al., 2002).

Relevant case studies

Case study I

This is a secondary school located in a London borough where in the early 1990s violence and conflict were heightened by racial tension. Pupils were prevented from achieving their potential and examination results were among the poorest in the borough. A near-riot in summer 1993 in a local shopping area prompted school management to search for ways in which they could move from a reactive stance to a more proactive role. This school implemented a Confronting Conflict Programme in collaboration with Leap (1998). The programme involved pupils being off-timetable for two days of intensive tutor group work; weekend training courses, both at the Leap centre and residentially, for pupil facilitators who then worked with younger pupils, including some sessions in local primary schools; and a weekend training course for staff volunteers to develop skills in facilitating workshop sessions for year ten tutor groups. Following the three-year programme, qualitative evidence suggested that high-level conflict experienced by both staff and pupils in the school had significantly decreased, and that bullying was less likely to escalate into physical violence (Leap, 1998).

Case study 2

The Conflict Resolution in Schools Programme (CRISP) (Leicestershire Mediation Service, 2000) currently operates in partnership with schools across Leicestershire to empower young people with the skills to manage human conflict effectively, and provide a safer, supportive learning environment. Within four schools across Leicestershire a needs assessment exercise revealed that 60 per cent of students said there was a fight every week, 81 per cent of students witnessed name-calling every day and 72 per cent of students said they witnessed rumour-spreading every week (Henry, 1999). In the second year of the programme, CRISP have delivered over 80 hours of staff INSET training to over 250 school staff and over fifty-five hours of personal, social and health education training to students; recruited and trained ninety-seven new mediators; delivered three local network days; and produced a newsletter and a compact disc. In one of the city schools, and one of the county schools, forty-five mediations involving 112 students were monitored; seventeen of those mediated were classified as being at risk of exclusion, and thirteen had special educational needs; forty-one of these mediations reached a successful resolution. Group interviews with eighty-eight peer mediators suggested that in schools where peer mediation is allowed to flourish, as well as providing an effective arena in which to resolve conflicts, it contributes to increased student responsibility, increased emotional literacy and ability to maintain stable relationships (Bitel, 2000).

Case study 3

In one secondary school, Hampstead School, befrienders known as 'peer partners' were trained to offer friendship and comfort to fellow students who had come as refugees to the UK, had seen violence and destruction, and were often far from family and friends. These young people were potentially vulnerable to loneliness, social exclusion and victimization. The peer partners set up an after-school homework/social club where pupils could come to study, relax or talk about issues of concern to them. At the club, they also gave advice and information, and offered emotional support to pupils who were upset. In addition, they raised funds for the project, and delivered speeches about the scheme within school and to outside audiences. Many of the pupils who were helped were so appreciative of the scheme that they volunteered later to become peer partners to 'repay' what they had gained (Demetriades, 1996).

Summary

- An extensive literature search reveals little in the way of definitions or descriptions of violence in schools.
- At the time of writing, there is no central register of violence in schools statistics available from government sources.
- With the exception of studies on pupil to pupil bullying, there is very little research into the nature and prevalence of violence in schools.
- There is an influential movement in the UK that takes account of risk factors in identifying sources of youth violence and pointers for intervention. This could suggest a way forward for schools.
- Several government initiatives and national/regional policies have been implemented in recent years to improve standards of behaviour in schools, including issues of underachievement, disaffection, social exclusion, bad behaviour, truancy, and bullying, but nothing *specifically* aimed at tackling violence in schools.
- A number of local initiatives tackling violence in schools are in place around the UK; these include a growing number of schemes involving peer support and conflict mediation. Some have been evaluated, in many cases with positive outcomes.

References

Bitel, M. (2000). *The Evaluation of Year 2 of Leicestershire Mediation Service's Conflict Resolution in Schools Programme.* Leicester: Charities Evaluation Services.

Budd, T. (1999). *Violence and Work: Findings from the British Crime Survey.* London: Home Office.

ChildLine (2000a). Annual Report. London: ChildLine, Studd Street, London N1 0QW.

ChildLine (2000b). *ChildLine Teacher's Pack.* London: ChildLine, Studd Street, London N1 0QW.

Connexions (2001). Online. Available HTTP: <http://www.connexions.gov.uk>.

Cowie, H. (2000). Bystanding or standing by: gender issues in coping with bullying in English schools. *Aggressive Behavior,* 26, 85–97.

Cowie, H., Naylor, P., Talamelli, L., Chauhan, P. and Smith, P.K. (2002). Knowledge, use of and attitudes towards peer support: a follow-up to the Prince's Trust survey. *Journal of Adolescence,* 25, 1–15.

Cowie, H. and Sharp, S. (1996). *Peer Counselling in Schools: A Time to Listen.* London: David Fulton.

Cowie, H. and Smith, P.K. (2001). Violence in Schools: A Perspective from the UK. In E. Debarbieux and C. Blaya (eds). *Violence in Schools: Ten Approaches in Europe.* Issy-les-Moulineaux: ESF. pp.181–195.

Cowie, H. and Wallace, P. (2000). *Peer Support in Action.* London: Sage. Online. Available HTTP: <http://www.peersupport.co.uk>.

Demetriades, A. (1996). Children of the Storm. In H. Cowie and S. Sharp (eds). *Peer Counselling in Schools: A Time to Listen.* London: David Fulton.

Department for Education and Employment (2000a). *Don't Suffer in Silence: An Anti-bullying Pack For Schools*. London: HMSO.

Department for Education and Employment (2000b). Private communication. Email from Denise Roberts, DfEE Enquiries, 18 December.

Department for Education and Skills (2002). Website: <http://www.dfes.gov.uk>.

Department of Education and Science (1989). *Discipline in Schools: Report of the Committee of Inquiry, chaired by Lord Elton*. London: HMSO.

Department of Education Northern Ireland (1999). *Northern Ireland Suspension and Expulsion Study (1996/97)*. DENI Research Briefing 1/99.

Farrington, D.P. (1998). Predictors, Causes and Correlates of Male Youth Violence. In M. Tonry and M.H. Moore (eds). *Youth Violence*. Chicago: University of Chicago Press.

Farrington, D.P. (2001). Risk factors for youth violence. Paper given at the International Conference on Violence in Schools and Public Policies, 5 March.

Farrington, D.P. and Welsh, B.C. (1999). Delinquency prevention using family-based interventions. *Children and Society*, 13, 287–303.

Gulbenkian Foundation (1995). *Children and Violence. Report of the Commission on Children and Violence*. London: Calouste Gulbenkian Foundation.

Hallam, S. and Castle, F. (1999). *Evaluation of the Behaviour and Discipline Pilot Projects (1996–1999) Supported Under the Standards Fund Programme*. DfEE Research Brief 163.

Henry, J. (1999). Talking peace in our schools. *Leicester Mercury*, 18 February.

Home Office (2000). Private communication. Email from Dr Vicki Harrington, Crime and Criminal Justice Unit, Research Development and Statistics Directorate, 12 December.

Leap Confronting Conflict (1998). Evaluation of the Confronting Conflict Programme in Morpeth School. September 1994–July 1997. Unpublished. Leap Confronting Conflict, The Leap Centre, 8 Lennox Road, London, N4 3NW.

Leap Confronting Conflict (1999). Annual Review 1999. Unpublished. Leap Confronting Conflict, The Leap Centre, 8 Lennox Road, London, N4 3NW.

Leicestershire Mediation Service (2000). Time To Talk. Annual Report 1999/2000. Unpublished. Leicestershire Mediation Service, 7th Floor, Epic House, Charles Street, Leicester, LE1 3SG.

Mellor, A. (1990). Bullying in Scottish secondary schools. *Spotlight 23*. Edinburgh, SCRE.

Mental Health Foundation (1999). *Bright Futures: Promoting Children and Young People's Mental Health*. London: MHF.

National Association of Head Teachers (2000). *Managing Security: Personal*. NAHT Professional Management Series PM018.

National Children's Bureau (2000). Website: <http://www.ncb.org.uk>.

National Curriculum (2000). Website: <http://www.nc.uk.net>.

National Healthy School Standard (2000). Website: <http://www.wiredforhealth.gov.uk>.

National Statistics (2000, 2001). Website: <http://www.statistics.gov.uk>

Naylor, P. and Cowie, H. (1999). The effectiveness of peer support systems in challenging school bullying: the perspectives and experiences of teachers and pupils. *Journal of Adolescence*, 22, 467–480.

Neill, S.R. St.J. (2001). *Unacceptable Pupil Behaviour: A Survey Analysed for the National Union of Teachers*. Warwick: University of Warwick, Institute of Education.

Neustatter, A. (2001). The power of love. *Guardian Education*, 17 April.

Newton, C. and Wilson, D. (1999). *Circle of Friends*. Dunstable: Folens.

Pitts, J. and Smith, P. (1995). *Preventing School Bullying*. London: Home Office Police Research Group, 50 Queen Anne's Gate, London SW1H 9AT.

Robinson, G. and Maines, B. (2000). *Safe to Tell*. London: The Book Factory.

Scottish Schools Ethos Network (2001). Website: <http://www.ethosnet.co.uk>.

Smith, P.K. and Sharp, S. (eds) (1994). *School Bullying: Insights and Perspectives*. London: Routledge.

Smith, P.K. and Shu, S. (2000). What good schools can do about bullying: findings from a survey in English schools after a decade of research and action. *Childhood*, 7, 193–212.

Stacey, H. (2000). Mediation and peer mediation. In H. Cowie and P. Wallace (eds). *Peer Support in Action*. London: Sage.

Turner, M. (2000). *Strategy Plan For CHIPS*. London: ChildLine, Studd Street, London N1 0QW.

Varnava, G. (2000). *Towards a Non-violent Society: Checkpoints for Schools*. London: National Children's Bureau/Forum on Children and Violence.

Varnava, G. (2001). *Towards a Non-violent Society: Checkpoints for Young People*. London: National Children's Bureau/Forum on Children and Violence.

Warton, K. and Barry, S. (1999). *Schoolwatch: An Evaluation*. London: Home Office, Research, Development and Statistics Directorate.

Whitney, I. and Smith, P.K. (1993). A survey of the nature and extent of bully/victim problems in junior/middle and secondary schools. *Educational Research*, 35, 3–25.

Wright, C., Weekes, D. and McGlaughlin, A. (2000). *'Race', Class and Gender in Exclusion from School*. London: Falmer Press.

Chapter 18

Tackling violence in schools

A report from Ireland

Mona O'Moore and Stephen Minton

Background

The country

Politically, the term 'Ireland' is used to refer to the Republic of Ireland (*Poblacht na hÉireann*) (an area of 70,280 km²), which came into being in 1948. It has a population of around 3.6 million; 58 per cent live in urban areas, 42 per cent in rural areas. The capital and chief administrative centre is Dublin (population 1.1 million). The Republic of Ireland is a constitutional republic, and is officially bilingual (English and Irish).

Most Irish people (93 per cent) are Roman Catholic by denomination; the Protestant minority numbers 3 per cent. The only distinct ethnic minority population, up until recent times, has been the Travelling community. In the last few years, Ireland has also become home to a small but growing population of economic migrants and refugees, the number of which looks set to continue (Department of Education and Science, 1998).

The school system

Education is compulsory for children between 6 and 16 years of age, under the Education (Welfare) Act (2000). Primary schools (of which there are 3,300 in Ireland, with 21,000 teachers and 490,000 pupils) will typically enrol children between 4 and 11 years of age. Second-level education establishments (of which there are 782 in Ireland, with 22,500 teachers and 370,000 pupils) cater for pupils between 12 and 18 years of age (Jordan, 1999). Progression is usually by one grade per year. The ratio of pupils to teachers is about 26:1 at the primary level, and 17:1 at the post-primary level (Department of Education and Science, 1993a). Primary schools usually have 40 to 300 pupils (a few up to 500); post-primary schools usually have 200 to 800 pupils.

Until 1960, no state provision had existed for the education of young people with mental, visual or hearing impairment in Ireland (Boldt and

Devine, 1998). Today, educational provision for pupils with special needs is made in both special schools and in special classes within ordinary schools. At the time of the most recent report of the Special Education Review Committee, 0.9 per cent of all pupils received their education in special schools (Department of Education and Science, 1993b).

Though not formally examined, social and personal health education (SPHE) is taught at both primary and post-primary levels during discrete SPHE time, and across the curriculum. Civil, social and political education, which is aimed at preparing pupils 'for active participatory citizenship', is a compulsory and examinable subject during the junior cycle of post-primary level education (Wylie, 1999).

Definitions and language

Olweus (1999a, p.12) defines physical aggression (violence and violent behaviour) as 'aggressive behaviour where the actor or perpetrator uses his or her own body or an object (including a weapon) to inflict (relatively serious) injury or discomfort upon another individual.' This definition, used for the purposes of this report, excludes purely verbal aggression, but includes fights between equals. However, most empirical studies of aggressive behaviour in schools in Ireland have focused on bullying rather than violence; and, as Olweus notes, 'there is a good deal of bullying without violence ... and, likewise, there is a good deal of violence that cannot be characterized as bullying' (Olweus, 1999a, p.12). Bullying is usually taken by Olweus and many other researchers to refer to repeated aggressive acts, in which there is an imbalance of power (Olweus, 1993; Roland, 1989; Roland and Idsøe, 2001; Smith and Sharp, 1994). When material from empirical studies into bullying in Irish schools is presented in this chapter, reference will be made to data pertaining to physical bullying exclusively as often as is possible.

Historical background

Discipline in Irish schools

Corporal punishment was abolished with effect from February 1982, by order of the Minister for Education (Irish National Teachers' Organization, 1993), and classroom discipline measures have changed accordingly (see Glendenning, 1999; Irish National Teachers' Organization, 1993; Jordan, 1999). Reports carried out by the Irish National Teachers' Organization (INTO) (1993, primary level) and the Department of Education and Science (primary and post-primary levels) indicated that although the general level of classroom indiscipline remained low, in many schools (particularly urban, economically disadvantaged and second level) a small core of persistently disruptive pupils existed.

Bullying

Despite the long-standing research tradition concerning bullying in Scandinavia (see Olweus, 1999a, 1999b; Roland, 1989), empirical studies of the nature and incidence of school bullying are very much a recent feature in Ireland. The first empirical studies, using relatively small samples, but yielding important, informative and indicative data, appeared in the late 1980s (Byrne, 1987; Mitchell and O'Moore, 1987; O'Moore and Hillery, 1989).

In 1993, the First National Conference on Bullying in Ireland was held (see O'Donnell, 1993), and the *Guidelines on Countering Bullying Behaviour in Primary and Post-primary Schools* were circulated to all schools (Department of Education and Science, 1993a) in September. The first nationwide study of bullying behaviour in Irish schools was carried out by O'Moore during 1993–1994. The results were presented to the International Conference on Research into Bullying Behaviour in Schools, which was held in October 1996 in Trinity College Dublin (O'Moore, Kirkham and Smith, 1997). Earlier that year (January 1996), the Anti-Bullying Research and Resource Centre had been established within the Teacher Education Department, Trinity College Dublin, with Dr O'Moore as its founder and co-ordinator.

Additionally, within the last three years, the three major teachers' unions in Ireland – the INTO, the ASTI (Association of Secondary Teachers, Ireland) and the TUI (Teachers' Union of Ireland) – have undertaken or commissioned surveys of the extent, nature and frequency of workplace bullying in schools. The results of these surveys are included in this report.

It should be noted that the National Crime Council of Ireland (2001) have included data regarding juvenile involvement in recorded crime in their recent report. However, the data, while broken down in four main offence categories – larceny, offences of violence, damage to property and sexual offences – does not provide information regarding where the offences occurred. Thus there is no information specific to school violence. However, the report does show a decline since 1992 in recorded crimes in all offence categories for juveniles except damage to property. The report emphasizes, however, that the figures may reflect recording practices and/or prosecution decisions rather than 'real' decreases in the number of offences being committed by juveniles.

Knowledge

Violence between pupils

A sample of 20,422 pupils – 9,599 primary (aged 8 to 12 years; 4,485 girls and 5,114 boys) and 10,843 second-level (aged 11 to 18 years; 6,633 girls and 4,210 boys) – took part in O'Moore, Kirkham and Smith's (1997) nationwide survey. These pupils were drawn from 531 schools (320 primary, 211 second-level). The initial aim of the study was to sample 10 per cent of primary and second-level schools in each of the twenty-six counties of the Republic of Ireland; this was achieved in the primary schools sample, and exceeded in the second-level sample, where 27 per cent of all second-level schools were represented. This survey will be regularly referred to during the course of this chapter.

Of the primary school children, 31.3 per cent (n=3,064) reported being bullied: 18.6 per cent 'once or twice'; 8.4 per cent 'sometimes'; 1.9 per cent once a week; and 2.4 per cent several times a week. Of the post-primary children, 15.6 per cent (n=1,695) reported being bullied: 10.8 per cent 'once or twice'; 2.9 per cent 'sometimes'; 0.7 per cent once a week; and 1.2 per cent several times a week. The bullying involved physical violence for 15 per cent of the primary school girl victims, 32 per cent of the primary school boy victims, 11 per cent of the post-primary girl victims, and 34.5 per cent of the post-primary boy victims (O'Moore, Kirkham and Smith, 1997).

Besides 'being hit or kicked', other types of physical bullying that appeared in the victims' comments were being spat or urinated upon, having fruit thrown at one, having one's head held in the toilet bowl, being kissed against one's will, and having one's clothes ripped off. Thirty post-primary pupils reported having been sexually harassed (O'Moore, Kirkham and Smith, 1997).

Violence from pupils towards teachers/school personnel

In ascertaining the prevalence, nature, severity and frequency of workplace bullying in schools, and with a view to generating recommendations for its reduction, INTO distributed 751 questionnaires to its members (the return rate was 54 per cent). Reports of physical abuse were comparatively rare in INTO's findings – just under 9 per cent of the sample, or thirty-five individuals, had been victim to this on at least one occasion (twenty-three on one occasion only; ten 'occasionally'; and two 'often'). Most often the perpetrator was a pupil (twenty-four cases), followed by parents (six cases) (Irish National Teachers' Organization, 1998).

In a similar survey amongst second-level teachers, the TUI commissioned Dr O'Moore to research 'the extent, nature and effects of workplace bullying in TUI schools and colleges throughout Ireland' (Teachers' Union of Ireland, 1999, p.15). One thousand teachers were randomly selected. Results, based on 407 respondents, indicated that 21.7 per cent of TUI staff (9.1 per cent men, 12.6 per cent women) had been bullied in the previous twelve months. This included physical abuse in 2.8 per cent of all cases (O'Moore, 1999). When the ASTI polled 1,000 of their members (with a 62 per cent return rate) some 32 per cent reported having suffered physical abuse during their teaching careers (Association of Secondary Teachers of Ireland, 1999). The perpetrators of this abusive behaviour were most often pupils and parents. It must be noted that the definition of physical abuse was sufficiently broad to include 'low level incidents such as pushing and door slamming' as well as 'slapping, kicking and assault' (Association of Secondary Teachers of Ireland, 1999, p.3).

Violence from teachers/school personnel towards pupils

Until recent years, members of the religious orders on behalf of the state made most of the educational provision, at both the primary and post-primary levels. Shamefully, instances of extreme physical violence under the guise of classroom 'discipline', and cases of sexual abuse, went unreported (or reports were disbelieved), quite literally for generations. *States of Fear*, a four-part series of television programmes on child abuse screened by RTE (Radio Telefís Éireann, the state's broadcasting service), featured harrowing accounts of abuse suffered by pupils at the hands of members of religious orders who ran the state's institutional schools. The programme, which began in April 1999, precipitated the disclosure of many other cases of abuse in institutional schools (O'Brien, 1999). By March 1999, legal proceedings had been initiated in 145 cases involving allegations of sexual or physical abuse of children while in institutions that were operated by or on behalf of the state.

Additionally, the *Guidelines on Countering Bullying Behaviour* (Department of Education and Science, 1993a) recognized that teaching and non-teaching school staff can 'unwittingly or otherwise, engage in, instigate or reinforce bullying behaviour in a number of ways.' However, no reliable statistics on this are available.

Violence between teachers/school personnel

ASTI's and INTO's surveys indicated that this is uncommon, or at least, very rarely reported. In INTO's results where members reported being a victim of physical abuse (which numbered thirty-five in total), the perpetrator was a member of the school personnel in just four of the cases – and in each of these four cases, the incident was a once-only occurrence. Likewise, ASTI (1999) found that the perpetrators of physical assault towards teachers were most often pupils (82 per cent of all cases).

There is, however, a perception that existing anti-bullying codes address the pupils' needs only, and not the needs of staff. This view was expressed by 77 per cent of the 73 per cent of teachers who reported that their school had an anti-bullying policy in INTO's survey, and 86 per cent of the 74 per cent of teachers who reported that their school had an anti-bullying policy in ASTI's survey (Association of Secondary Teachers of Ireland, 1999; Irish National Teachers' Organization, 1998). ASTI (1999, p.1) recommends that 'the school is to be organized in such a way as to reduce incidents of bullying amongst both staff and pupils'. On the basis of their results, both the TUI and the INTO have made similar recommendations.

Age

The Department of Education and Science's *Report on Discipline in Schools* indicated that a statistically significant higher rate of indiscipline exists in second-level schools than in primary schools (Department of Education and Science, 1997). However, and apparently by contrast, empirical studies into general bullying behaviour reveal that the incidence of bullying tends to reduce with age (Byrne, 1999; and see Smith et al., 1999). O'Moore, Kirkham and Smith's (1997) nationwide survey found approximate 'frequent' victimhood (bullied 'once a week or more often') incidence rates of 1 in 20 primary school pupils, and 1 in 50 post-primary school pupils, and also found the level of non-reporting of bullying behaviour to be positively correlated with age (O'Moore, Kirkham and Smith, 1997). Hence, ascertaining the relationship between age and involvement in violent behaviour is by no means simple.

Gender

Internationally, it has long been acknowledged that girls and boys tend to be involved to a different extent and in different types of bullying behaviour, with boys being relatively more represented in physical types of bullying (Olweus, 1978; Roland, 1989). These differences in typology were borne out in Ireland by O'Moore, Kirkham and Smith's (1997) nationwide study: whereas 15 per cent of the 1,306 bullied primary school girls, and 11 per cent of the 843 bullied post-primary girls reported having been 'hit' or 'kicked', 32 per cent of the 1,875 bullied primary school boys, and 34.5 per cent of the 986 bullied post-primary boys reported having been victim of such physical bullying.

Ethnicity

In 1997–1998, there were 6,300 Traveller children enrolled in Irish schools and educational centres (Department of Education and Science, 1998). Traveller children – boys in particular – have a reputation for fighting and classroom indiscipline; in understanding this, Carlson and Casavant (1995) refer to the cultural differences that exist between the settled and the Travelling communities in terms of their respective attitudes towards aggression. They cite Crawford and Gmelch (1974), who found that 'aggression is part of Traveller culture and is frequently rewarded in boys because it is felt that life is brutal and children must learn to fight to survive' (Carlson and Casavant, 1995, p.101). They also report that 'because of the extreme prejudice of settled people, Traveller children are often intimidated by settled classmates' (p.103); however, whether this intimidation includes physical violence is unclear from their literature, although 'name-calling' is mentioned.

As noted above, Ireland's resident foreign national population is, as yet, small in number. However, in O'Moore, Kirkham and Smith's nationwide study, 7 per cent of girls and 9 per cent of boys at the primary level, and 4.8 per cent of girls and 8.1 per cent of boys at the post-primary level indicated that 'I was called nasty names about my colour or race' (O'Moore, Kirkham and Smith, 1997).

Socioeconomic status and school type

Schools in Ireland are not designated 'disadvantaged' in themselves, but the area which they serve may be, according to socioeconomic and educational indicators such as high levels of unemployment, social housing, and low levels of literacy and numeracy. In the nationwide study, reports of bullying others were higher in schools of disadvantaged status; no significant relationship existed between advantaged/disadvantaged status and reports of being bullied. Additionally, bullying behaviour was significantly higher in second-level schools where there was a higher concentration of pupils from lower socioeconomic backgrounds (O'Moore, Kirkham and Smith, 1997).

Reports of being bullied and bullying others were more frequent in urban, rather than rural, primary schools; the reverse was found at the post-primary level. In neither case, however, did the findings reach statistical significance (O'Moore, Kirkham and Smith, 1997).

The same study examined possible effects of class size and school size. Class size was deemed 'small' if there were fourteen pupils or fewer; 'medium' for classes of fifteen to twenty-four pupils; and 'large' for classes of over twenty-five pupils. There was no relationship between class size and reports of either being bullied or bullying others in primary schools. In post-primary schools, reports of being bullied and bullying others were most frequent in small schools, although the analysis for reports of bullying others did not reach statistical significance.

School size was deemed 'small' if there were 199 pupils or fewer; 'medium' for schools of 200 to 499 pupils; and 'large' for schools of over 500 pupils. No relationship was found between school size and being bullied at the primary level, although reports of bullying others were at the highest levels in medium-sized primary schools, and at the lowest levels in large primary schools. At the post-primary level, reports of being bullied and bullying others alike were most frequent in small schools (O'Moore, Kirkham and Smith, 1997).

Action

National legislation

The Education (Welfare) Act (2000) was enacted on 5 July 2000; the objectives essentially focus upon school attendance and retention. Under this Act, schools are obliged to provide a code of behaviour clarifying the schools' duty of care and policy concerning violence, indiscipline and bullying. The code should contain elements that specify suspension and expulsion procedures (Glendenning, 1999). Failure on the part of the school to act in cases of violent behaviour resulting in causal injury to a member of staff or pupil now constitutes a legal breach of the school's duty of care.

The Safety, Health and Welfare at Work Act (1989) places employers under the obligation of a general duty of care to do whatever is necessary to ensure the safety of the workplace and the safety and health of the employee (Glendenning, 1999). School management authorities, as employers, are thereby required to ensure the health and safety of school pupils and personnel; the act recognizes indiscipline and violence as a health risk in schools (Jordan, 1999).

Child protection and service provision

The Department of Health and Children's National Children's Strategy (2000) is a ten-year plan that aims to improve the quality of children's lives in Ireland. The strategy underlines children's rights, and it is intended to give children a voice via the appointment of an Ombudsman for children, and the setting up of *Dáil na nOg* ('Parliament of the Young'). The strategy also aims to ensure children's lives are better understood (through increased support and resources for research), and to provide quality support and services for children (early intervention and preventive work will be stressed). The strategy has been implemented since October 2000, and will be evaluated by the biannual publication of a 'State of the nation' children's report (Department of Health and Children, 2000).

The Department of Health and Children's *Children First: National Guidelines for the Protection and Welfare of Children* (1999) are intended to 'support and guide health professionals, teachers, members of the Garda Síochána (police) and the many people in sporting, cultural, community and voluntary organizations who come into regular contact with children ... and are therefore in a position of responsibility in recognizing and responding to possible child abuse' (Department of Health and Children, 1999, p.9).

The Child Abuse Prevention Programme ('Stay Safe') was designed by representatives of the INTO in association with the Departments of Health and Education (Byrne, 1999). It was introduced into primary schools in 1991–1992 (see Lawlor and MacIntyre, 1991), and is now available to primary schools nationwide on request. The programme is aimed at 8- to 11-year-olds (Jordan, 1999); its aims are to prevent child abuse by equipping parents and teachers with the knowledge and skills necessary to protect the children under their care. Children are taught safety skills in the classroom, which are reinforced at home through discussion with parents. Additional goals of the programme include the raising of community awareness and encouraging the reporting of child abuse (Jordan, 1999; Lawlor and MacIntyre, 1991).

The Irish Society for the Prevention of Cruelty to Children (ISPCC) have operated Childline, a telephone helpline for children in trouble or danger, since 1988. In its first eleven years (1988–1999), the service handled more than 277,000 calls (Byrne, 1999). Other ISPCC initiatives include Steps, a '[nationwide] network of youth advice and counselling services' (Irish Society for the Prevention of Cruelty to Children, 1998b, p.2), and Crib (Children's Rights Information Bureaux), a nationwide network that provides information on children's rights and entitlements.

The Department of Education's Guidelines and Procedures

The *Guidelines on Violence in Schools* (Department of Education and Science, 1999) recommend that the school considers, and where appropriate implements, the raising of awareness amongst staff of policies concerning violence, bullying, discipline, health and safety and related issues through discussion at staff meetings and at other times (Glendenning, 1999). Also, visitor access to the school and to teachers should be restricted and security measures implemented; and a code of discipline, in which violent behaviour towards a teacher is deemed serious or gross misbehaviour that may warrant suspension, is to be drafted (Department of Education and Science, 1999; Glendenning, 1999).

Bullying had, before 1993, been seen entirely within the context of school discipline. The *Guidelines on Countering Bullying Behaviour* (Department of Education and Science, 1993a) aim 'to assist schools in devising school-based measures to prevent and deal with bullying behaviour' and 'to increase the awareness of bullying behaviour in the school as a whole, as well as those from the local community who interface with the school' (p.5). The importance of the active involvement of pupils (especially senior pupils), teaching and non-teaching staff, parents and guardians, local and community agencies, the school board and local inspectorate in the generation and implementation of anti-bullying policy was firmly underlined throughout. So too was clarity in the recording, reporting and investigation of bullying behaviour, and acting thereon; it was recommended that the prevention of bullying should be 'an integral part of a written Code of Behaviour and Discipline in all primary and post-primary schools' (p.11). The expansion of in-service and pre-service courses on aspects of bullying behaviour (to teachers and trainee teachers respectively) was seen as being of considerable benefit.

Unfortunately, one year after these guidelines were initiated, O'Moore, Kirkham and Smith's nationwide study on bullying found that 22 per cent of primary and 25 per cent of second-level schools had yet to develop a policy on bullying (O'Moore, 2000; O'Moore, Kirkham and Smith, 1997). Disappointingly, the passage of years has not led to a redressing of this inaction. In 1998, primary teachers' responses to their union's survey on workplace bullying indicated that 27 per cent of schools had no anti-bullying policy (Irish National Teachers' Organization, 1998); ASTI's survey of second-level teachers revealed that 26 per cent of second-level schools had no anti-bullying policy (Association of Secondary Teachers of Ireland, 1999). Perhaps the incidence of three bullying-related suicides (see Byrne, 1999; O'Moore, 2000; McSweeny, 2001) since the publication of the guidelines might mark out the urgency of countering this misattributed complacency and the 'ambivalence and lack of condemnation of bullying in society that is reflected in our schools' (O'Moore, 2000, p.99).

Two case studies

Case study I (Dublin): the Pathways Through Education project – raising the self-esteem of young people in school

In Scandinavia, Germany and England, victims of bullying have been found to test low in terms of global self-esteem scores (Björkqvist, Elman and Lagerspetz, 1982; Olweus, 1993; Lösel and Bliesener, 1999; Boulton and Smith, 1994). In Ireland, O'Moore and Kirkham (2001) note a self-esteem difference between victims who bully ('bully-victims') and 'pure' victims (victims who do not bully others). In an earlier Dublin study, both types of victims were found to have lower self-esteem than controls, but bully-victims had lower self-esteem scores than 'pure' victims (O'Moore, 1995). Bullies, too, were found to have lower self-esteem scores than control (non-involved) pupils (O'Moore, 1995). These early Dublin-based findings were later found to hold true at the nationwide level (O'Moore, 2000; O'Moore and Kirkham, 2001; O'Moore, Kirkham and Smith, 1997).

The Pathways Through Education programme aims at raising the self-esteem, motivation and confidence amongst students in inner city second-level schools that serve areas of disadvantage, in a series of innovative ways (Uhleman, 2000). Core issues of concern include the development of a whole-school approach to such initiatives, and the retention of students in second-level education. The range of interventions include:

- *Classroom interventions*: A double-class period (80 minutes) is delivered to first year students on a weekly basis, and to second year students on a monthly basis. A magazine composed by the young people involved in the project was produced, and peer leadership/mentoring programmes are offered in one of the schools.
- *Work with staff*: A project support group made up of teachers was established in each school; additionally, staff training, evening workshops and daytime consultancy with the classroom intervention team were made available.
- *Work with parents*: Parents' workshops are offered, and the classroom intervention team work closely with the home–school liaison teachers in the schools.

Evaluations of the first two years of the project indicated the classroom interventions to be very successful, and the work with teachers and parents to be mostly so. It was generally difficult to get parents involved, although some success was achieved through the workshops; as parental involvement is vital, it was recommended that the Pathways team develop still closer links with the designated home–school liaison teachers (Craig, 2000; Uhleman, 2000).

Quantitative indicators (obtained from school records) showed that participation in Pathways seemed to be associated with greater than average attendance levels for first year students, and a lower than average number of discipline offences (Craig, 2000). Qualitative measures (pupil evaluations) indicated an extremely favourable response from partaking students towards the project. This was also reflected in school principals' and parents' evaluations (Craig, 2000).

Case study 2 (Donegal): a pilot project to evaluate the effectiveness of a proposed national programme to prevent and counter bullying behaviour in Irish schools

Following the publication of the *Guidelines on Countering Bullying Behaviour in Primary and Post-primary Schools* (Department of Education and Science, 1993a) and in light of the high general incidence levels of bullying revealed by O'Moore, Kirkham and Smith's (1997) nationwide survey, it was felt that Irish schools could benefit from a model that incorporates the training of school management, teaching staff, parents and pupils. Dr O'Moore and her team submitted proposals to the Department of

Education and Science and the Calouste Gulbenkian Foundation stating an initial intention to conduct pilot work with a sample of the primary schools within the county of Donegal. After the successful completion of this pilot research, a national programme would be pursued. It is hoped that through this programme schools should see reductions in the levels of general indiscipline as well as those of bullying.

The proposed national programme is based on a Norwegian model, which was developed by the Ministry of Education in association with Stavanger College's Behavioural Research Centre, and successfully applied at a national level (Roland and Munthe, 1997). Four key elements are to be included in the national programme:

1 *Teachers' resource pack* Contains information about bullying behaviour (drawing on the Department of Education guidelines and the nationwide survey), with an emphasis on classroom management, the development of a positive atmosphere in class and school, staff leadership and parent–teacher co-operation.
2 *Parents' resource pack* Contains information on prevalence, types, causes, effects and indicators of bullying behaviour; also, how to deal with alleged or actual incidents of bullying.
3 *Work with pupils* Schools will be assisted in creating a climate that does not accept bullying. As part of a general awareness-raising campaign, pupils will have access to age-related handbooks, which include ideas for the prevention and countering of bullying in their class and school. Pupils will be encouraged, through peer leadership, to support children whom they witness being bullied.
4 *Training of a network of professionals* To provide boards of management, staff, pupils and parents with the necessary training and support to prevent and counter bullying in their school communities. Each county, depending on the number of its schools, should have ten to twenty professionals, who may be teachers, counsellors, educational psychologists or appropriate staff from local third-level establishments. A programme of workshops and seminars would be arranged for the 'professionals', centred upon preventive and intervention strategies, and the content of the information packs for parents, pupils and teachers.

In this pilot study, thirteen professional teachers in the county of Donegal participated in a training programme in order to develop the expertise required to co-ordinate anti-bullying programmes for teachers, pupils and parents in up to three schools each. Eleven of these teachers held an in-service day for teachers, and an after-school meeting for parents, as well as acting as an adviser/support to schools in relation to bullying problems thereafter.

In order to ascertain the overall effectiveness of the programme, pupils in the schools completed both pre- and post- programme modified versions of the Olweus bully/victim questionnaire. Similar studies that have preceded this, conducted elsewhere in Europe, have found disparate levels of programme success (see Olweus, 1993; and Roland and Munthe, 1997, in Norway). A study in Sheffield, England, in which staff of seventeen primary and seven post-primary schools were involved, recorded reductions of 17 per cent in reports of victimization, and 7 per cent in reports of bullying others at the primary level after the implementation of anti-bullying measures (Smith and Sharp, 1994).

In terms of lowering the incidence of pupils' involvement in bullying behaviour, as evidenced by their own responses to the pre- and post-programme Olweus questionnaires, the Donegal programme would appear to have been fairly successful. Within the last school term there were overall reductions of 21.5 per cent in reports of being victimized (from 39.0 per cent to 30.6 per cent of all pupils), and of 24 per cent in reports of having bullied others (from 28.7 per cent to 21.8 per cent of all pupils).

Sadly, the implementation of the anti-bullying programme had no positive effect on victims' willingness to report being bullied to teachers or parents, as was also the case in the primary schools in the Sheffield project. Eslea and Smith (1998, p.217) suggest that the issue of anti-bullying programmes failing to increase the reporting rate of bullying 'is not the indictment it at first seems'. They argue that anti-bullying programmes foster both increased teacher vigilance (the pupils have less need to report incidents) and increased pupil assertion (as bullying is taken seriously in a school running an anti-bullying programme, the mere threat of 'telling' works). Whether Eslea and Smith are over-optimistic in assuming the existence of these masking phenomena, though, remains to be seen. Perhaps the non-resolution of this particular point is a further demonstration of the fact that the need for careful evaluation studies of anti-bullying programmes is absolutely imperative.

Summary

It is only in the last fifteen years that the problems of violence and bullying in Irish schools have been addressed. Since then, however, we have seen a growing body of research and public awareness of this issue being at least partly translated into educational policy (*Guidelines on Violence in Schools*, 1999; *Guidelines on Countering Bullying Behaviour*, 1993), children's policy (*National Children's Strategy*, 2000; *Guidelines for the Protection and Welfare of Children*, 1999), curricular development (SPHE, CSPE) and legislature (Education (Welfare) Act 2000, Safety, Health and Welfare at Work Act 1989).

Notwithstanding this, violence in Irish schools has not been directly addressed. Empirical research has generally positioned physical violence as one of the many types of bullying. At the policy and legislative levels, interventions have focused upon somewhat broader issues within education such as bullying, discipline, welfare, citizenship, retention, equality of access, and educational disadvantage.

Studies from the late 1980s onwards revealed a higher incidence rate of bullying (including physical bullying) in Irish schools, compared with our contemporaries in Scandinavia. Early Dublin-based studies, and the nationwide survey conducted by O'Moore, Kirkham and Smith (1997) have provided a good indication of the incidence, frequency and typology of bullying and violent behaviour amongst pupils. More recent surveys, commissioned by the teachers' unions, have helped to provide a picture of the various forms of violence and bullying suffered by teachers in their workplace.

The second case study of this report, a pilot project to evaluate the effectiveness of a proposed national programme to prevent and counter bullying behaviour in Irish schools, has yielded very favourable results. In light of this, and all of the above, the next step must be the launching of a national programme to prevent and counter violence and bullying behaviour in Irish schools.

References

Association of Secondary Teachers of Ireland (1999). Press release. Dublin: ASTI.

Björkqvist, K., Elman, K. and Lagerspetz, K.M.J. (1982). Bullies and victims: their ego picture, ideal ego picture and normative ego picture. *Scandinavian Journal of Psychology*, 23, 307–313.

Boldt, S. and Devine, B. (1998). Educational Disadvantage in Ireland: Literature Review and Summary. In G. Doyle (ed.). *Demonstration Programme on Educational Disadvantage: Educational Disadvantage and Early School Leaving*. Dublin: Combat Poverty Agency.

Boulton, M.J. and Smith, P.K. (1994). Bully/victim problems among middle school children: stability, self-perceived competence and peer acceptance. *British Journal of Developmental Psychology*, 12, 315–329.

Byrne, B. (1987). A study of the incidence and nature of bullies and whipping boys (victims) in a Dublin city post-primary school. Unpublished Master's thesis, Trinity College, Dublin.

Byrne, B. (1999). Ireland. In P.K. Smith, Y. Morita, J. Junger-Tas, D. Olweus, R. Catalano and P. Slee (eds). *The Nature of School Bullying: A Cross-national Perspective*. London: Routledge.

Carlson, H.M. and Casavant, C.M. (1995). Education of Irish Traveller children: some social issues. *Irish Journal of Psychology*, 16, 100–116.

Craig, S. (2000). Final evaluation report to the 'Pathways Through Education' project. Dublin Institute of Technology/ 'Pathways Through Education' project document.

Department of Education and Science (1993a). *Guidelines on Countering Bully-ing Behaviour in Primary and Post-primary Schools*. Dublin: The Stationery Office.

Department of Education and Science (1993b). *Report of the Special Education Review Committee*. Dublin: The Stationery Office.

Department of Education and Science (1997). *Report on Discipline in Schools*. Dublin: The Stationery Office.

Department of Education and Science (1998). *A National Educational Psychological Service: Report of the Planning Group*. Dublin: The Stationery Office.

Department of Education and Science (1999). *Guidelines on Violence in Schools*. Dublin: The Stationery Office.

Department of Health and Children (1999). *Children First: National Guidelines for the Protection and Welfare of Children*. Dublin: The Stationery Office.

Department of Health and Children (2000). *The National Children's Strategy: Our Children – Their Lives*. Dublin: The Stationery Office.

Eslea, M. and Smith, P.K. (1998). The long-term effectiveness of anti-bullying work in primary schools. *Educational Research*, 40, 203–218.

Glendenning, D. (1999). *Education and the Law*. Dublin: Butterworths.

Irish National Teachers' Organization (1993). *Discipline in the Primary School: Report of a Survey Incorporating Aspects of Bullying in Schools*. Dublin: Irish National Teachers' Organization.

Irish National Teachers' Organization (1998). *INTO Consultative Conference on Education. Relationships and the School Community: Bullying and Other Issues. Interim Report*. Dublin: Irish National Teachers' Organization.

Irish Society for the Prevention of Cruelty to Children (1998a). *Childline*. Dublin: Irish Society for the Prevention of Cruelty to Children.

Irish Society for the Prevention of Cruelty to Children (1998b). *Crib: Children's Rights Information Bureau*. Dublin: Irish Society for the Prevention of Cruelty to Children.

Jordan, R. (1999). Ireland: National Activities, Programmes and Policies. In *Policies in the Member States on Safety at School and on Measures to Counter Violence in Schools*. Brussels: European Commission.

Lawlor, M. and MacIntyre, D. (1991). *Stay Safe Programme: Child Abuse Prevention Programme*. Dublin: Department of Health / Eastern Health Board.

Lösel, F. and Bliesener, T. (1999). Germany. In P.K. Smith, Y. Morita, J. Junger-Tas, D. Olweus, R. Catalano and P. Slee (eds). *The Nature of School Bullying: A Cross-national Perspective*. London: Routledge.

McSweeny, N. (2001). Lessons in brutality killed him. *Irish Examiner*, 11 October.

Mitchell, J. and O'Moore, A.M. (1987). In *Report of the European Teachers' Seminar on Bullying in Schools*. Strasbourg: Council for Cultural Co-operation.

National Crime Council (2001). Crime in Ireland: Trends and Patterns, 1950 to 1998. Online. Available HTTP: <http://www.ireland.com/newspaper/special/>.

O'Brien, T. (1999). Amendment could give victims of abuse time to sue. *Irish Times*, 29 April.

O'Donnell, V. (ed.) (1993). *Proceedings of the First National Conference on Bullying in Ireland*. Dublin: Campaign Against Bullying.

O'Moore, A.M. (1995). Bullying behaviour in children and adolescents in Ireland. *Children and Society*, 9, 54–72.

O'Moore, A.M. (1999). *Report on Workplace Bullying of Teachers' Union of Ireland Members*. Dublin: Teachers' Union of Ireland.

O'Moore, A.M. (2000). Critical issues for teacher training to counter bullying and victimization in Ireland. *Aggressive Behavior*, 26, 99–111.

O'Moore, A.M. and Hillery, B. (1989). Bullying in Dublin schools. *Irish Journal of Psychology*, 10, 426–441.

O'Moore, A.M. and Kirkham, C. (2001). Self-esteem and its relationship to bullying behavior. *Aggressive Behavior*, 27, 269–283.

O'Moore, A.M., Kirkham, C. and Smith, M. (1997). Bullying behaviour in Irish schools: a nationwide study. *Irish Journal of Psychology*, 18, 141–169.

Olweus, D. (1978). *Aggression in the Schools. Bullies and Whipping Boys*. Washington DC: Hemisphere Press (Wiley).

Olweus, D. (1993). *Bullying in Schools: What we Know and What we can Do*. Oxford: Blackwell.

Olweus, D. (1999a). Sweden. In P.K. Smith, Y. Morita, J. Junger-Tas, D. Olweus, R. Catalano and P. Slee (eds). *The Nature of School Bullying: A Cross-national Perspective*. London: Routledge.

Olweus, D. (1999b). Norway. In P.K. Smith, Y. Morita, J. Junger-Tas, D. Olweus, R. Catalano and P. Slee (eds). *The Nature of School Bullying: A Cross-national perspective*. London: Routledge.

Roland, E. (1989). Bullying: the Scandinavian Research Tradition. In D.P. Tattum and D. Lane (eds). *Bullying in Schools*. Stoke-on-Trent: Trentham Books.

Roland, E. and Idsøe, T. (2001). Aggression and bullying. *Aggressive Behavior*, 27, 446–462.

Roland, E. and Munthe, E. (1997). The 1996 Norwegian programme for preventing and managing bullying in schools. *Irish Journal of Psychology*, 18, 233–247.

Smith, P.K., Morita, Y., Junger-Tas, J., Olweus, D., Catalano, R. and Slee, P. (eds) (1999). *The Nature of School Bullying: A Cross-national Perspective*. London: Routledge.

Smith, P.K. and Sharp, S. (eds) (1994). *School Bullying: Insights and Perspectives*. London: Routledge.

Teachers' Union of Ireland (1999). TUI bullying survey: disturbing reading. *TUI News*, 21, 15.

Uhleman, J. (ed.) (2000). *Youthstart Prevent: The Report of the Transnational Project*. Helsinki: Helsinki University Press.

Wylie, K. (1999). Education for citizenship – a critical review of some current programmes in England and Ireland. *Irish Educational Studies*, 18, 91–102.

Part V

Commentaries

Chapter 19

Violence in schools

An Australian commentary

Phillip T. Slee

In recent years there has been an increasing global concern with the issue of school violence. A range of international conferences and publications have highlighted the growing concern in Europe, North America (e.g. Zimring, 1998) and the developing countries (e.g. Ohsako, 1997). Reactions to this concern appear to range from the notion that it represents a degree of 'moral panic', to the strong sense that there is something fundamentally going wrong in our schools. The seventeen European chapters in this book represent a considerable achievement in addressing the issue of school violence and provide a significant and substantial basis upon which to evaluate the educational, psychological, policy and programme development implications, in a cross-national context.

The generally similar format to the presentation of each chapter makes it relatively easy to overview the country presentations with respect to the topic, under a number of broad headings, including:

- issues of definition;
- knowledge regarding school violence;
- the nature of school bullying: an international perspective;
- a review of the effectiveness of school-based programmes.

In addition, in reading the various chapters it was apparent that a number of themes were interwoven throughout, including:

- the level of concern regarding school violence;
- violence as a community issue;
- the level at which interventions were directed, for example class, school, community;
- current trends/issues.

These themes will also be commented on in this chapter. There are many European country similarities to the emergence of school violence as an issue in Australia, and also some significant differences; in this commentary, where appropriate, comment will be made with reference to Australia. The issue of school violence is a global one, and so this chapter will begin with an evaluation of the general level of concern evident in each country, thereby providing a context for a consideration of other issues raised in the various chapters.

Level of concern regarding school violence

At an international level, media reports and an emerging body of research have drawn attention to the level of concern regarding school violence. In the USA, Mulvey and Cauffman (2001, p.797) note 'School violence, having been dubbed a crisis, permeates the national consciousness and media outlets'. The degree to which the level of concern is supported by factual evidence is a matter for debate. Stephens (1997) has interpreted school crime data released by the US Department of Education to indicate an increase in school violence, allied to a growing public perception. Alternatively, other researchers in the United States report a decline in school crime (e.g. Hyman et al., 1997).

Many of the seventeen European country reports in this book comment on the extent to which school violence has been a matter of concern. As noted in the French report in this volume, 'Since 1993 the problem of violence in school has been considered a public safety concern' (p.19). As noted in The Netherlands report in this volume, 'Possibly the focus on violence in the press and the media and the fact that many people no longer tolerate violence, can explain the feeling that everything is deteriorating nowadays' (p.70). For a small number of countries the issue of school violence has been a relatively recent concern. For example in the chapter on Greece it was observed that the issue of school violence was quite a new phenomenon. The author refers to a paper by Artinopoulou (1998) who had noted 'we do not recognize school violence as a social phenomenon'. In fact, the authors note that the issue was not broadly addressed at all, so as not to suggest that schools are a place of violence.

The whole issue regarding how best to raise the level of debate concerning school violence such that it can be subject to open discussion appears important. The Netherlands states 'in most Dutch schools matters of safety and security are being discussed more openly now' (this volume, p.76). It appears from reading the European chapters that various countries are at different points in their recognition of and willingness to debate the issue. In part these differences are related to political, cultural and historical factors. For example, the French report notes that the issue of school violence has lengthy historical and political overtones, with a strong sense that violence is seen as a social justice issue.

A similar concern regarding the level of debate has emerged in Australia in the last decade. As Reynolds (1991, p.1) noted, 'White Australia did not begin auspiciously. Violence accompanied the birth of the first settlement and was a constant presence during the formative years'. It could well be argued that violence as a way of life was entrenched and enshrined as part of the white colonization of Australia, where the island continent was viewed as a penal colony. Reynolds (1991) estimated that in the course of the white settlement of Australia over 2,000 European and 20,000 Aboriginal lives were sacrificed. The same author has rightly questioned whether this dark primal beginning has left a legacy of violence. Proponents of this view point to the extent to which violence appears embedded in the white Australian psyche, manifested in the extent to which many Australians eagerly embrace commitments to international conflicts (such as World War I and more recently the 'War Against Terror'). At a more general level the Australian Institute of Criminology Committee report (1990) identified a significant concern with the extent to which violence is perpetrated against those in authority such as police and teachers.

Social commentators such as Mackay (1999) point to the contradictory signs that violence is not as endemic in Australian society as some would suggest. There is an argument to be made that Australia is a relatively peaceful culture, as evidenced by the long tradition of parliamentary democracy and general lack of racial violence in a very multi-cultural setting. Australia shares in common with many of the European country reports evidence to the effect that schools are relatively safe places in terms of violence and the statistics available suggest that many forms of violence are in fact decreasing.

In 1994 an Australian Commonwealth Senate inquiry into school violence resulted in the publication of an influential report, *Sticks and Stones: A Report on Violence in Schools* (Commonwealth of Australia, 1994). This inquiry heralded a nationwide movement to address the issue of school violence, particularly bullying. While the report generally concluded that school violence was not an issue in Australian schools, bullying was. The inquiry raised significant questions regarding the frequency of violence in Australian culture and the impact of violence on the community, and identified the need for intervention programmes to reduce violence, particularly that associated with bullying.

Australia shares with many of the European countries the sense that the issue of school violence has been used by the media and sensationalized. Nonetheless, there is an emerging debate in Australia regarding the idea that violence is a social justice issue. The most marginalized in our society – the poor, the young, and the Indigenous – appear most at risk of victimization. In 1990 the Australian Institute of Criminology addressed the issue of violence in broader Australian society. The members of the committee noted a number of common factors associated with violence in Australia: it tends to be much greater for males, higher in urban areas (related to economically disadvantaged areas), associated with young adults, and linked in terms of victimization to Aboriginality.

Echoing the Australian findings, the Belgium report specifically identifies the patterns that have been noted regarding those most at risk for perpetration of violence and for victimization. The challenge highlighted by the European reports appears to be that of how best to raise the matter of school violence as an educational, social and political issue in a sustained manner in order to bring about some reasoned debate and encourage appropriate action. In a related manner, encouraging further debate around the issue hinges strongly on the availability of information and this was directly addressed in this volume.

Central register of violence data

In over half of the European countries, there is no central register for understanding, collecting and collating statistics on violence. However, in countries such as France it is noted that 'more accurate records of violent offences and infringements were started in 1993, mainly because of the apparently increasing number of assaults against students and teaching staff members' (this volume, p.19). Other countries such as Italy and Finland state that there is also some general record of the issue of violence. Thus, in Italy, juvenile crime statistics provide some information on violence. The Italian statistics are used to highlight that juvenile crime has, in fact, been decreasing with the exception of crime committed by 'baby gangs'.

The value of accurate statistical information is that it can help offset media efforts to sensationalize the issue of violence and public perceptions of a general increase in violence. The politically sensitive nature of the issue is well highlighted in the Portugese chapter, where it is noted that the Security Cabinet of the Ministry of Education had argued that 'a significant part of the growing feelings of insecurity, revealed by school communities, has its roots in increasing media attention and has no strong support in data about violence in schools' (this volume, page 122). As the authors recognize, the lack of a common understanding of the issue of violence, and inequalities in reporting incidents, highlight the need for countries to develop and maintain accurate records regarding school violence.

The debate concerning the nature and extent of violence in Australian culture is severely hampered by a general lack of any co-ordinated approach to data collection, collation and dissemination. This situation is not dissimilar to that reported by over two-thirds of the European countries in this publication. The Australian Bureau of Statistics does collect and disseminate statistics on the theme of crime and justice, for example juvenile crime (Australian Bureau of Statistics, 2000). Each state and territory similarly collects and collates information on crime and justice.

School violence

Less than a third of the European countries report that there exists any central data collation regarding the issue of school violence. In examining the location data for Australian crime reports relating to 'assaults' for the year 2000 (Australian Bureau of Statistics, 2000) it is apparent that the majority of assaults occur in private dwellings (34 per cent), in the community (23 per cent) in recreational areas (10 per cent), retail areas such as shops (7 per cent), in areas of justice, such as police stations and courts (4 per cent) and in education areas (3 per cent). The figures suggest that education areas are in the top ten places where violence occurs. In the 1990 Australian Institute of Criminology Report, it was noted that it is often in schools where aggressive or otherwise antisocial behaviour first becomes publicly apparent.

In the school context, Australia has the same lack of a national co-ordinated data collection base as many of the European countries; it shares many of the political features of the European countries, with a central government and regional or state authorities, and each of the major states and territories collects their own statistics regarding school violence generally as part of their school behaviour management policy. The political, geographic and administrative difficulties inherent in collating statistics on school violence mirror those reported by many of the European countries. Differences in definition, data collection and collation methods mean that it is difficult to compare figures across the states and territories in Australia.

Figures from the public school system in South Australia (Department of Education, Training and Employment – DETE) are illustrative as they relate to school violence. The figures pertain to incidents of school suspension which, as will become apparent, are generally related to violence. South Australia has a computerized method for recording school-based incidents that it has kept since 1999. In term three of school year 2000 the percentage of all students suspended was 1.6 per cent and this figure had been relatively stable for some years (Cox, 2002). The majority of suspensions in term three of school year 2002 were for: threatening the good order of the school (42 per cent); interfering with the rights of others (7 per cent); and threatening or perpetuating violence (29 per cent).

In a review of suspensions and expulsions in government schools in Australia, McMahon (2001) concluded that there was a great deal of inconsistency between the states and territories in how suspension and expulsion was applied. She called for a national overview of structures and practices to bring about greater procedural fairness in the application of suspension and expulsions. In reading many of the European country reports it appears that a similar recommendation would hold in relation to developing a statistical base in terms of school violence. It is apparent from reading the chapters that a much needed development concerns a co-ordinated national response to matters of definition, data collection and collation. There is much to learn from some countries that have managed significant gains in this regard. Such information then informs knowledge regarding school violence.

Knowledge regarding school violence

Many of the country reports call for greater knowledge about the issue of school violence, and this is of course directly linked to the issue of the extent to which data is available. Countries such as Austria, Belgium, Germany, Greece, and Luxembourg report that knowledge regarding school violence is limited. For example the Austrian report notes that 'Information on violence in schools is based on empirical studies, mostly in the form of diploma or doctoral theses' (this volume, p.85); the Luxembourg report states that 'There has been little systematic research on the specific topic of violence in schools' (this volume, p.52). This outlook mirrors a growing international call for greater understanding of the issue of school violence (Borum, 2000; Burns, Dean and Timm, 2001; Sullivan, 2000).

As already noted, in 1994 a Commonwealth Government inquiry into violence in Australian schools concluded that while violence was not a major problem in Australian schools, bullying was. A recommendation of the inquiry was for the development of intervention programmes to reduce school bullying. At a state level some governments (e.g. Western Australia, 1995; Australian Capital Tenitory, 1996; New South Wales, 1995) have funded investigations into school bullying and similarly reported that it is a major concern. To that end Australia shares similar concerns with countries such as Austria, Belgium, the United Kingdom, Finland, Germany and The Netherlands. The sentiment expressed by the Finnish report echoes that of many European reports: 'it appears to be incorrect to make a strict distinction between bullying and violence in schools in Finland. Rather, in most cases, severe violence appears to be the tip of the iceberg of bullying-related problems' (this volume, page 191).

Issues of definition

A number of the countries note that violence is distinguished from bullying. There appears to be general agreement that bullying is one part of violence, or that the terms 'bullying' and 'violence' are linked, as noted by Finland, Germany, Italy, Norway and Luxembourg.

Roy (1994) defines school violence as 'any situation where a member of the school community is intimidated, abused, threatened or assaulted by another member of that community'. Baker (1998, p.29) argues for the idea that 'School violence is probably best conceptualised as a range of antisocial behaviours on school campuses, ranging from oppositionality and bullying to assaults'. A comprehensive definition of violence is provided by Furlong et al.:

A public health and safety condition that often results from individual, social, economic, political, and institutional disregard for basic human needs. It includes physical and nonphysical harm which causes damage, pain, injury, or fear, and it disrupts the school environment and results in the debilitation of personal development which may lead to hopelessness and helplessness.

(Furlong et al., 1997, p.246)

In terms of the issue of school bullying, the general consensus of the European reports is that bullying is one part of violence, in accordance with the definition provided by Olweus (1993). The accepted understanding of bullying is that it is a particularly destructive form of aggression, defined as physical, verbal or psychological attack or intimidation that is intended to cause fear, distress or harm to the victim, and where the intimidation involves an imbalance of power in favour of the perpetrator. Typically there are repeated incidents over a period of time. Distinguishing features of this broadly accepted definition are the power imbalance and the repetition over time. Interestingly, over half of the countries cited a definition of bullying. Perhaps there needs to be some greater debate regarding the issue of definition with a view to reaching some consensus.

Violence as a community issue

The idea that violence is a wider community issue is gaining currency (Chappell, Grabonsky and Strang, 1991; Slee, 2001) and this is reflected in a number of European country reports. There are in fact significant advantages to nestling the issue of violence in a broad community context. For example, it is a less blameful orientation than considering it only as an organizational problem, which must be solved by education and school authorities. The fact that it is being seen as a community issue is reflected in the growing number of organizations expressing some concern about this aspect. In Australia, organizations such as 'Safety House', Child Help-Line, and the Department of Community Services through 'Parenting South Australia' are just a few examples of where the issue of violence has been addressed in the broader community context. To that end, Australia shares some programmes in common with the European countries (such as in providing telephone helplines as in the United Kingdom).

The movement towards the wider community initiative is underpinned by the writing of authors such as Etzioni (1995) and Tam (1996). In advocating a movement towards 'communitarianism', Etzioni describes the 'social webs of communities' as the 'webs that bind individuals, who would otherwise be on their own, into groups of people who care for one another and who help maintain a civic, social and moral order'. Drawing on similar concepts, there is an argument to be made that school violence detracts from the 'social capital' of a society (Coleman, 1988; Cox, 1995). Social capital was seen by the late James Coleman (1988) as an ingredient of the functioning of social relations among individuals. Significant elements of social capital include the extent to which individuals trust and have confidence in each other in the general community. As such, social capital is a resource residing in the social networks of the members of a community.

In an interesting parallel to the situation of Australia, the Austrian report states that 'Currently, the intention of Austrian educational policy is to strengthen school autonomy and reinforce co-operation between teachers, parents and pupils' (this volume, p.83). There is a similar move in the public education sector across Australia, underpinned by the general aim of strengthening school–community ties. A number of countries including Belgium, France, Iceland, Italy, Sweden and the United Kingdom describe innovative efforts and programmes to engage the broader community in addressing the issue of violence. For example the Icelandic report describes a parent management training programme to help parents who have children with behaviour problems, while the Ombudsman for Children in Iceland initiated a conference on school bullying. The very fact that Iceland has an Ombudsman for Children raises significant questions about the status of children in various countries and the political and social priorities attached to 'protecting' them from issues such as violence. Researchers are now examining the links between social capital and school outcomes, including students 'at risk' for being victims or perpetrators of violence (Runyan et al., 1997).

A number of European reports specifically mention the plight of children identified as 'at risk' for school violence. In the Belgium report a specific school programme is cited, identifying schools with 'special needs'. Similarly, in the Italian and United Kingdom reports particular mention is made regarding special needs children with emotional and behavioural problems. A number of European countries (Belgium, Iceland, Italy) identify certain groups of students with 'special needs' as particularly at risk for bullying. The French report broadens the discussion with the idea of 'social exclusion', adopting a socially critical line in suggesting the link between 'school violence and social unfairness' (this volume, p.22). The introduction of a social justice component to the issue of school violence is an important feature of the French chapter. It is interesting that with a number of significant exceptions, few of the European reports took up the issue of social justice and social inclusion as associated with school violence.

School bullying and violence

Outcomes of the international efforts to understand the nature of school bullying have resulted in significant publications; for example, the book edited by Smith, Morita, Junger-Tas, Olweus, Catalano and Slee (1999) drew together findings of research from over twenty-two countries. The evidence is now quite clear that bullying in schools is an international problem and the opinions expressed by the seventeen European countries certainly support this view. As noted in the Swedish report, 'There is no doubt that violence and bullying among schoolchildren is a widespread and serious problem' (this volume, p.223). Bullying is particularly a risk in groups such as school peer groups, from which the potential victim cannot readily escape.

The international research suggests that despite some cultural differences, many of the broad features of bullying are similar across different countries, and this is highlighted in many of the European country reports. For example Belgium, Germany, Greece, Italy, Iceland, Norway and the United Kingdom identify similarities in the nature of bullying. It is commonly found that many victims do not report bullying or seek help. There also appear to be characteristic sex differences, with boys using and experiencing more physical means of bullying and girls experiencing or using more indirect and relational means. An emerging body of research in Europe, the USA and Australia is addressing the issue of indirect and relational bullying (e.g. Owens, Slee and Shute, 2001, in Australia).

A number of European countries have also collected data at a national level. It does appear that the frequency with which students report they are bullied varies significantly from country to country; for example, Ireland reports a higher frequency of bullying than some other countries. Overall, the European research findings relating to frequency, type and effects of bullying generally hold true for Australian students subject to bullying (Rigby and Slee, 1999). Inter-country interpretations should be treated with caution as the matter of equivalence in data collection methods and definition of terms among other matters needs careful consideration.

Sexual harassment

In Australia, research within sociological and feminist frameworks and in the educational literature has highlighted the importance of broad cultural and social influences, such as male–female power differentials, on boys' victimization of girls, especially through sexual harassment (e.g. Gilbert and Gilbert, 1998; Mills, 2001).

Rigby (1998) has speculated that boys may bully to impress girls; it is also possible that they aim to impress other boys. In considering victimization of girls by boys, sexual harassment may seem an obvious issue, especially in the early high school years, when girls may be particularly sensitive to victimization based on their developing bodies and sexuality (indeed, even in preadolescence, a relationship has been found between girls' perceptions of sexual harassment and their body esteem; Murnen and Smolak, 2000). The Gender Equity Taskforce (1997) recognized the unacceptable impact of sexual harassment on girls (and some boys). However, the literature on aggression (and bullying more specifically) has had relatively little to say about sexual harassment. The sexual harassment literature is a separate one and, in stark contrast to the individualistic approach of the bullying literature, broad societal influences are seen as central.

As noted by Hudley et al. (2001), a particular behavioural episode involving harassment or bullying may be judged differently by perceivers differing in gender. Murnen and Smolak (2000) found that 10-year-old boys and girls have different perspectives on sexually toned behaviours from opposite-sex peers; girls are more likely to see the behaviours as frightening and boys as flattering. In Australia, boys generally are socialized to believe they have power over females, and even young boys sometimes use sexual aggression against girls and women. Martino (as reported in Mills, 2001) interviewed Australian adolescent boys about their views of masculinity, and concluded that status is conferred by peers on boys who display a particular type of heterosexual masculinity that involves denigrating 'anything that smacks of femininity' (p.39). Martino noted that such social and cultural practices limit the personal choices of both sexes. The importance of gaining an understanding of boys' perspectives is essential, since male attitudes towards violence contribute to resistance to preventive initiatives (Artz and Riecken, 2001).

A number of European reports directly address the issues of sexual harassment and ethnicity (e.g. France, Germany, Iceland, Ireland, The Netherlands). It appears particularly pertinent as a line of further research to consider these issues in the context of school violence generally. Of course, either implicitly or explicitly the issue of school safety is quite germane to the topic of school violence and bullying.

Safety from bullying

An important element of the definition of bullying relates to the question of a power imbalance between the bully and victim, and so safety at school is a pertinent question. A number of European countries specifically discuss the issue in their reports (e.g. Finland, France, The Netherlands). In referring to the Australian situation, Rigby and Slee (1999) have noted that the question of how safe schools are for students depends on how we define 'safety'. In contrast to some cultures, violent and life-threatening situations are relatively rare in Australian schools. The French report states that while official statistics indicate school is a relatively safe place for students, the '"black hole" of non-reported offences, the non-consideration of victims; and the inability to determine what the major delinquency problem is composed of (namely minor delinquencies)' lead to some serious questioning of the 'official statistics' (this volume, p.20). Interestingly, Stewart and Cope (1997) make the point that there is a growing concern amongst Australian teachers that some students feel so unsafe at school that they have resorted to weapon carrying in order to defend themselves.

In a large-scale sample, Australian students were asked if school is a safe place for young people who find it hard to defend themselves from attack from other students. Among both males and females, less than 20 per cent see school as a 'safe' place for vulnerable students (Rigby and Slee, 1999). Of the students who report being bullied at school, over 9 per cent report that they have truanted and over 15 per cent report 'thinking about' staying away from school (Rigby and Slee, 1999). School bullying then raises the question of equity and access for some students in relation to education. Stewart and Cope (1997, p.36) note that the issue of school safety 'indicates the need for school administrators and classroom practitioners to initiate programs in their schools that will provide students with an awareness of – among others – their legal rights and responsibilities'. Only a small number of European reports raise the legal issue relating to school bullying, which is similar to the situation in Australia (Slee and Ford, 1999). It appears that in only a very few European countries has legislation been enacted relating specifically to school bullying. Some serious further consideration is needed of the legal rights of school students apropos school violence and bullying.

School-based programmes to reduce bullying

As Eslea and Smith (1998, p.203) noted, 'Most, if not all, children experience bullying at some time in their lives: they may be the victim, they may be the bully, or they may witness the suffering of others'. Australian schools are now being strongly encouraged to develop anti-bullying policies, grievance procedures and intervention programmes. The promotion of mental health through schools, by encouraging positive peer relationships and reducing bullying and sexism, is central to the Australian National Action Plan for Promotion, Prevention and Early Intervention for Mental Health (Commonwealth Department of Health and Aged Care, 2000a, 2000b).

The European country reports document a varied range of local and national intervention studies to reduce bullying. In some countries very little has been done (e.g. Denmark, Greece). The Danish report notes that 'No specific and systematic efforts (long-term action or plans, research studies, etc.) are currently being made about violence or bullying in schools at a national level – either related to statistics or to prevention' (this volume, p.241). Other country reports indicate that there have been many initiatives but little evaluation (e.g. Austria, Germany). Finally, a number of countries report extensive evaluations (e.g. Norway, United Kingdom). Many reports call for more extensive, longitudinal research to provide the basis for evidence-based practice to guide school bullying interventions. The underlying theme, shared with Australia, is the lack of an extensive, well-documented body of empirical research relating to the effectiveness of interventions; and only a limited number of such evaluations have been conducted in Australia (e.g. Slee, 2001; Clearihan et al., 2000).

It was difficult to ascertain from the country reports what legislative protection from school violence was in place either at a national or regional level. Countries such as Germany, Ireland, Sweden and the United Kingdom specifically highlighted policy directives; for example the Swedish report states that 'The policy of creating a safe environment in Swedish schools has a long tradition' (this volume, p.224). Overall, it appears that considerably more needs to be done at a policy level to take account of and address the needs of young people. Certainly, a number of countries provided significant exemplars of innovative ways that young people had been consulted regarding their needs and views. The Danish report cited a 'youth parliament' initiative and the German report described setting up a 'violence commission' modelled on that of France and the USA. A number of country reports called for specific teacher training regarding the issue of violence (e.g. Spain and the United Kingdom). It does appear obvious that a critical element in any violence prevention programme should involve the education of those directly working with students, including teachers, police and social workers.

School violence and bullying – more than a duty of care

The issue of school violence and bullying has broadened to embrace the idea that it is a community issue and not simply a school problem whose responsibility it is to address. It is now understood far more clearly that the issue is really about relationships. Simplistically, a great deal of research, especially on bullying, has focused on the relationship between perpetrator and victim. Now it is understood that the relationship also incorporates the bystanders who witness the bullying and that these bystanders have a very active role to play in encouraging or discouraging the bullying. More broadly still, the relationships extend well beyond the school bounds to embrace the family and the broader community. One way to understand why bullying has attracted so much attention in the last few years is to consider the issue from a relationship perspective. Bullying has always been with us, but it is only now that the national and international community is beginning to voice its collective concern that it is an unacceptable aspect of human relationships.

Conclusion

In this chapter it is argued that violence in school is an issue that crosses individual, school, community, state and international boundaries, as the European reports in this book attest to. Its impact and effects are indeed far-reaching and now well-documented and substantiated in the psychological research. Most significantly, it has now crossed the boundary of what was once regarded by some, if not many, as 'acceptable' behaviour. In reviewing the informative chapters from the various European countries presented in this book a number of themes emerged, including:

- a call for co-ordinated international research into school violence free of short-term politically expedient needs;
- the co-ordinated development and evaluation of comprehensive intervention programmes addressing school violence;
- the development of greater international awareness raising concerning school violence;
- the education of those who act 'in loco parentis' in relation to children, regarding the damaging impact of school violence on all concerned;
- a link between violence in schools and the level of community health and well-being in terms of factors such as poverty and crime rate.

Each country report challenges us to take up the issue of school violence with some urgency. A few key avenues for further inquiry are identified, including the social justice and social exclusion issues associated with school violence. It is also apparent from the reports that historical and cultural factors impact significantly on the understanding and awareness of the issue. To that end, significant implications emerge in relation to the development of intervention programmes that should be contextualized and not simply copied from another country. Significantly, more research into the topic is needed to better inform 'best practice' intervention programmes and avoid embracing ill-founded programmes designed to meet some short-term political or social agenda. In sum, the underlying message of many, if not most of the chapters in relation to school violence, is that in acting in the best interests of those deemed to be most vulnerable, the community would be seen to be fulfilling broader civic, social and moral imperatives.

References

Artinopoulu, V. (1998). Promoting prosocial behaviour as a school violence prevention policy: the Case of Greece. Paper presented at the workshop: Prosocial Pupil Development. Nijmegen, ITS, The Netherlands, June 26–27.

Artz, S. and Riecken, T. (2001). What, so what, then what? The gender gap in school-based violence and its implications for child and youth care practice. *Child and Youth Care Forum*, 26, 291–303.

Australian Bureau of Statistics (2000). *Recorded Crime in Australia: Companion Data*. Canberra: ACT. Catalogue No. 4510.0.

Australian Institute of Criminology (1990). *Violence: Directions for Australia*. Canberra. Australian Institute of Criminology.

Baker, J.A. (1998). Are we missing the forest for the trees? Considering the social context of school violence. *Journal of School Psychology*, 36, 29–44.

Borum, R. (2000). Assessing violence among youth. *Journal of Clinical Psychology*, 56, 1,263–1,288.

Burns, M.K., Dean, V. and Timm, S. (2001). Assessment of violence potential among school children: beyond profiling. *Psychology in the Schools*, 38, 239–247.

Chappell, D., Grabonsky, P. and Strang, H. (1991). *Australian Violence: Contemporary Perspectives*. Canberra: Australian Institute of Criminology.

Clearihan, S., Slee, P.T., Souter, M., Gascoigne, P., Nicholls, A., Burgan, M. and Gee, J. (2000). Anti Violence Bullying Prevention Project. Paper presented at the Victims of Crime Conference. South Australia. Adelaide 25–26 May.

Coleman, J. (1988). Social capital in the creation of human capital. *American Journal of Sociology*, 94, 95–120.

Commonwealth of Australia (1994). *Sticks and Stones: A Report on Violence in Schools*. Canberra: Australia Publishing Service.

Commonwealth Department of Health and Aged Care (2000a). *National Action Plan for Promotion, Prevention and Early Intervention for Mental Health 2000*. Canberra: Mental Health and Special Programs Branch, Commonwealth Department of Health and Aged Care.

Commonwealth Department of Health and Aged Care (2000b). *Promotion, Prevention and Early Intervention for Mental Health: A Monograph*. Canberra: Mental Health and Special Programs Branch, Commonwealth Department of Health and Aged Care.

Cox, E. (1995). The Boyer Lectures. Australian Broadcasting Commission.

Cox, G. (2002). Personal communication. Department of Education, Training and Employment.

Eslea, M. and Smith, P.K. (1998). The long-term effectiveness of anti-bullying work in primary schools. *Educational Research*, 40, 203–218.

Etzioni, E. (1995). *New Communitarian Thinking, Persons, Virtues, Institutions, and Communities*. Virginia: University Press.

Furlong, M.J., Morrison, G.M., Chung, A., Bates, M. and Morrison, R.I. (1997). *School Violence: Children's Needs*. Bethesda, MD: National Association of School Psychologists.

Gender Equity Taskforce for the Ministerial Council on Education, Employment, Training and Youth Affairs (1997). *Gender Equity: A Framework for Australian Schools*. Canberra: ACT on behalf of MCEETYA.

Gilbert, R. and Gilbert, P. (1998). *Masculinity Goes to School*. St. Leonards, NSW: Allen and Unwin.

Hudley, C., Wakefield, W.D., Britsch, B., Cho, S.-J., Smith, T. and DeMorat, M. (2001). Multiple perceptions of children's aggression: Differences across neighborhood, age, gender, and perceiver. *Psychology in the Schools*, 38, 43–56.

Hyman, I., Dabbany, A., Blum, M., Weiler, E., Brooks-Klein, V. and Polako, M. (1997). *School Discipline and School Violence: The Teacher Variable Approach*. Needham Heights, MA: Allyn & Bacon.

Mackay, H. (1999). *Turning Point. Australians Choosing their Future*. Sydney: Macmillan.

McMahon, R. (2001). Suspensions and expulsions in government schools. *Rights Now*. June, 7–8.

Mills, M. (2001). *Challenging Violence in Schools: An Issue of Masculinities*. Milton Keynes: Open University Press.

Mulvey, E.P. and Cauffman, E. (2001). The inherent limits of predicting school violence. *American Psychologist*, 56, 797–802.

Murnen, S.K. and Smolak, L. (2000). The experience of sexual harassment among grade-school students: early socialization of female subordination? *Sex Roles*, 43, 1–17.

Ohsako, T. (ed.) (1997). *Violence at School: Global Issues and Interventions*. Paris: International Bureau of Education.

Olweus, D. (1993). *Bullying in Schools: What we Know and What we can Do*. Oxford: Blackwell.

Owens, L., Slee, P. and Shute, R. (2001). Victimization among Teenage Girls: What can be Done about Indirect Harassment? In J. Juvonen and S. Graham (eds). *Peer Harassment in School: The Plight of the Vulnerable and Victimized*. New York: Guilford. pp.215–241.

Reynolds, H. (1991). Violence in Australian History. In D. Chappell, P. Grabonsky and H. Strang (eds). *Australian Violence: Contemporary Perspectives*. Canberra: Australian Institute of Criminology. pp.13–23.

Rigby, K. (1998). Gender and Bullying in Schools. In P. Slee and K. Rigby (eds). *Children's Peer Relations*. London: Routledge. pp.47–60.

Rigby, K. and Slee, P. (1999). The Nature of School Bullying: Australia. In P.K. Smith, Y. Morita, J. Junger-Tas, D. Olweus and P. Slee (eds). *The Nature of School Bullying: A Cross-national Perspective*. London: Routledge.

Roy, M. (1994). Violence in Australian schools. *Criminology Australia*, 6, 16–19.

Runyan, D.K., Hunter, W.M., Socolar, R.R.S., Amaya-Jackson, L., English, D., Landsverk, J., Dubowitz, H., Browne, D.H., Bangdiwala, S.I. and Mathew, R.M.

(1997). Children who prosper in unfavorable environments: the relationship to social capital. *Pediatrics*, 101, 12–19.

Slee, P.T. (2001). *The PEACE Pack: A Program for Reducing Bullying in our Schools.* Adelaide: Flinders University. 3rd edition.

Slee, P.T. and Ford, D. (1999). Bullying is a serious issue – it is a crime! *Australian and New Zealand Journal of Law and Education*, 4, 23–39.

Smith, P.K., Morita, Y., Junger-Tas, J., Olweus, D., Catalano, R. and Slee, P. (eds) (1999). *The Nature of School Bullying: A Cross-national Perspective.* London: Routledge.

Stephens, R.D. (1997). National Trends in School Violence: Statistics with Prevention Strategies. In A.P. Goldstein and J.C. Conoley (eds). *School Violence Intervention: A Practical Application Handbook.* New York: Guilford. pp.72–90.

Stewart, D. and Cope, B. (1997). Judicious behaviour management. *Australia New Zealand Education Law Association*, 4, 35–43.

Stewart, D.J. and Knott, A.E. (1998). Peer student bullying, harassment and violence in Australian schools: a discussion of issues and legal remedies. A paper presented to the ANZELA conference, October. Canberra.

Sullivan, K. (2000). *The Anti-Bullying Handbook.* Auckland, Melbourne, Oxford and New York: Oxford University Press.

Tam, H. (1996). Education and the communitarian movement. *Pastoral Care in Education*, 14, 3.

Zimring, F.E. (1998). *American Youth Violence.* New York: Oxford University Press.

Chapter 20

Violence in schools

The view from Israel

Rami Benbenishty and Ron Avi Astor

A Talmudic expression says *'Sadna d'araha chad hoo'* – the heart of the world is the same, across many different places. Indeed, the efforts described by the countries represented in this book demonstrate how universal concerns surrounding issues of bullies and victims are present across diverse cultural contexts in Europe. Nevertheless, in addition to the common cross-national components of the bully/victim phenomena, the detailed explanations provided about bullying and victimization in each country also suggest a rich and diverse tapestry of approaches, definitions, and methods that could contribute to a better empirical understanding of the bully/victim phenomena.

This book presents detailed empirical descriptive evidence of the bullying/victim phenomena across many cultural contexts. Knowing how different countries approach and understand bullying is an important step in furthering theory development. These kinds of descriptions highlight the role of culture and social context as it interacts with bully/victim issues. From a more pragmatic view, this kind of cross-national comparison also allows for the exchange of ideas surrounding intervention and educational policy.

We believe this book has advanced the two overarching goals of theory development and intervention information exchange between cultures and countries. The fact that these chapters are organized similarly facilitates comparisons between countries. The fact that all the chapters are in English is a great contribution to the global community concerned with bullying and victimization. Ironically, this book highlights how limited we are in our ability to access knowledge accumulated in other countries. The chapters cite a wide range of studies conducted in each country. Unfortunately, because of language barriers, readers may have limited access to the original work cited. Given the recent technological advances in automatic translation, it may be feasible to create an international clearinghouse that contains empirical studies conducted in a wide range of countries, accessible to users in several languages.

Our primary aim in this chapter is to comment on the chapters from the point of view of researchers who are studying bullying/victimization under the wider umbrella of 'school violence' in Israel. Given our space limitations, we decided to focus on a rather limited set of issues that we found particularly interesting. We will address cross-country comparisons, anti-bullying interventions and implications for research on bullying and school violence.

Cross-country comparisons

One of the important functions of this compendium of chapters is to allow cross-country comparisons. Such comparative data could be used to gain a perspective on how extreme the situation is in one's country. Such comparisons may also have a strong positive or negative public impact. For instance, Menesini and Modiano (chapter 10) report that comparative research showed that school violence was reported in Italy at a higher level than that which had been found in other European and Western countries (being about twice as high as in England and almost three times higher than in Norway). The major response of Italian newspapers and television programmes to these data brought about awareness in schools. School heads and staff in general began to be interested and to study the issue.

Alternatively though, distorted or partially reported cross-national comparisons could have negative social outcomes. For example, in Israel, the findings of international comparative studies have been used to 'demonize' Israeli youth. For instance, a few months ago, in the wake of a series of reports on youth violence, the front page of the largest daily newspaper published a chart derived from an international study (TIMMS) presenting the Israeli students as the 'most violent' in the world. This chart became 'the talk of the day' among the Israeli public. While this comparison contributed to the public awareness of the problem, the reports also served to incite negative public feelings towards youth and schools.

Given the potential positive and negative contributions of comparisons derived from this book in the future, it is important that we examine comparisons critically and use them cautiously. We would like to point out two major aspects that should be considered when cross-country comparisons are being made – definitional issues and variations in context.

Definitional issues

The chapters from different countries show clearly that definitions of the term 'bully' vary. This could have a dramatic impact on the collection and interpretation of cross-national data/studies. For instance, in Harel, Kenny and Rahav's study of youth health risk behaviour (1997), Israeli students were asked whether they were bullied and the question stated that they were being asked about *Hatrada* (harassment), *Hatzaka* (teasing), and *Biryonoot* (bullying). Each of these words has quite a different meaning in Hebrew. The word for bullying strongly implies physical force exerted by a strong/well-built student (a 'thug' or 'goon'). The other two words are often used to describe a weaker student nagging, teasing, and 'getting on the nerves' of another student, possibly stronger than the perpetrator. We wonder how students in different cultures synthesize and integrate their own culturally specific terms when responding to questions about bullying.

This issue becomes even more complicated when findings are reported in the media. Invariably, the term bullying is used, as if it captures all three different behaviours. We believe that the Israeli public's immediate perception is that the figures reported in surveys reflect physical violence by strong students attacking others. The public is not aware that these figures also include other behaviours that have negative implications, but do not involve physical violence.

When comparisons are made across countries, one should be very careful in interpretation. For instance, Harel, Kenny and Rahav (1997) report on bullying frequency in Israel and compare it to bullying frequency in twenty-four other European countries that participated in a World Health Organization study. The chapters in the present book suggest strongly that the meanings and connotations of the word bully vary widely across countries, and such cross-country comparisons should be made very cautiously.

One way to overcome this difficulty is to include an array of specific behaviours in conjunction with using more abstract terms that have different meanings and connotations in various countries. We are attempting this approach in Israel. The authors have conducted a national study of school violence in Israel (Benbenishty, Zeira and Astor, 2000). We focused on victimization to *specific and concrete* violent acts. We presented the students with a list of violent acts and asked whether they were victims of each of these acts in the last month. The items related to school victimization in several areas – verbal-emotional (e.g. a student cursed you, a student insulted you), threats (e.g. a student threatened to hurt you, students threatened you on the way to and from school, a student threatened you with a knife), mild physical infraction (e.g. a student pushed and shoved you) and serious physical violence (e.g. you were cut by a knife, you were involved in a fight and required medical attention). We think that the meaning and connotation of these behavioural events is quite common across countries. It may be a better strategy to compare how many students report that they were threatened with a knife in various countries, rather than only compare how many of them said that they were bullied. Findings from Iceland seem to support our point

– those who reported having been punched (36 per cent) were about twice as many as those who reported having been subjected to 'violence' during the same twelve months. Hence, the more general term seems to have a different meaning than the concrete and specific violent acts.

Perhaps a better way to examine the interrelationships between reports on bullying, and those on victimization to specific and concrete violent acts, is to assess them within the same study. This approach could help determine whether the differences between reports on bullying, and those on victimization to specific violent acts, are minor, or perhaps reflect the deeper conceptual distinctions between the concepts of bullying and school violence (Olweus, 1999). In our new national study of school violence in Israel we presented secondary school students with questions related to bullying, as well as questions about victimization to specific violent acts. We are also in the midst of conducting case studies in schools that serve different cultural groups (Orthodox Jew, Hassidic Jew, Beduin, Druze, Christian Arab, etc.). We hope that our survey and qualitative findings will contribute to the discussion about the meaning of bullying and the degree to which the term has different cultural connotations. From a theoretical perspective these kinds of studies could help us better understand the relationships between school violence behaviours and bullying.

Contextual differences

Another important issue to consider when making cross-country comparisons is the *context* of school violence. Comparing bullying rates without understanding the different contexts may be quite misleading. Researchers who study their own country may be unaware of how unique their environment is, and how it influences rates of bullying and school violence. There are several context characteristics that may be responsible for a significant amount of the variation among the countries reporting in this book.

Varying school contexts

A basic assumption when we compare bullying and school violence across countries is that a school is a school is a school. Obviously, the school systems described in this book have much in common. Nevertheless, the chapters also reveal major systemic variations along organizational, social, and political dimensions that may have direct implications on rates of school violence, and on intervention effectiveness. Some variations are in the organizational structure and mission of the schools, some are in the age populations they serve. For instance, in Italy there are three sectors – primary elementary school (ages 6 to 11), secondary middle school (11 to 14), and secondary education (15 to 19). In Ireland, primary schools cater to children aged 4 to 11, and second-level education to children 12 to 18. In Finland, children enter primary schools at the age of 7. In Belgium nearly all students attend nursery schools from the ages of 2.5 to 6, and primary education is for children aged 6 to 12, whereas in Portugal pre-school education is for children aged 3 to 6 and is not compulsory, and the basic compulsory education is divided into three grades lasting four, three and two years, respectively.

These different age groups and the different organizational school structures may have substantial implications for school violence. For instance, having children that range widely in age within the same school building may expose younger students to much more bullying by older students than school systems in which age groups are separated physically. Other educational practices may be vitally important in the effectiveness or non-effectiveness of programmes. It was interesting to learn that in Portugal, students who make poor progress tend to be retained in the same grade more than one year; this is not very common in Israel (and we suspect in other countries). The presence of older students in a class, especially students who are failing academically, could have a major impact on levels of threat and fear experienced by younger classmates. Similarly, the exclusion or inclusion of students with special needs may have a significant impact on rates of violence in schools. Variations in mainstreaming of special needs students among countries in Europe may be responsible for different rates of bullying experienced in these systems. Other structural issues such as average school and class sizes, the availability of support staff, and student to teacher ratio may also have an important impact on schools in different educational systems.

In terms of the social context that may affect school violence, we found the issue of minorities especially interesting. Ethnic minorities were mentioned as more vulnerable groups in several countries (e.g. Greece, Italy, Germany, Spain and Ireland). It would be important to try to identify what explains this vulnerability in terms of being victims/perpetrators of school violence. It is possible that some of the risk factors are associated with students' lower socioeconomic status and lack of parental resources. It is also possible that at least in some countries, students and staff target minorities because of fear/hate of foreigners. Houndoumadi, Pateraki and Doanidou (chapter 11) report that in Greece only 38 per cent of the teachers surveyed believed that children of immigrants should be able to enrol in any school, while the remainder believed that they should attend special schools set up for these children. Similarly, O'Moore and Minton (chapter 18) cite a study in Ireland that indicates that because of prejudice, Traveller children are being intimidated by settled classmates.

It seems reasonable to hypothesize that different social, cultural, and school circumstances create diverse patterns of victimization and perpetration among minority youth. It is possible that these variations could be addressed by different types of interventions. A comparative study focusing on the relationship between bullying and the characteristics of minorities could make an important contribution to our understanding of the dynamics of school violence, as well as to efforts to address this problem among minority children. Such a study should not be limited to reporting the minority status of children. We suggest a more descriptive approach that addresses a wide range of issues, such as economic characteristics of minority students within each country, to what extent minority students see themselves as part of the majority society (or prefer to maintain a minority identity), whether minority students tend to cluster in certain schools and create their own school within a school, what the attitudes are of other students towards minority students, and similar issues. This rich description will help scholars and policy makers across Europe understand better the relationship between school violence and minorities (for an interesting discussion of the roots of minority violence in French schools, see Debarbieux, Blaya and Vidal, chapter 2 of this volume).

Some of the social-contextual factors that impact on school violence and bullying can be identified, examined, and compared across countries in a straightforward manner. Other contextual aspects are much subtler. For instance, from our reading of the chapters it seems that the ideologies regarding the function of the school in society, the relative roles, the professional authority and power position of parents, students, teachers, and principals *vis-à-vis* each other may be quite different across Europe. In the same spirit, Debarbieux and his associates highlight comparative studies that contrast the school model in France, other European countries, England and the United States, and show major differences. These differences could have a major impact on the acceptability of interventions in certain countries, and their relevance for some groups compared with others. In Israel, for instance, we think that certain groups of parents feel more empowered to influence school policies and are more involved than other groups (e.g. veteran Israelis compared with new immigrants). Similarly, it seems that the ability to involve parents in school violence programmes would differ for economically deprived and excluded families compared with parents with more social resources.

Finally, when we examined the descriptions of various social contexts in which schools operate, we were surprised not to find reviews of the role of religion and religious schools. We think that value systems and ideology related to religion and parochial schools may have influenced violence-related issues strongly. For instance, in Israel we found that students in Jewish religious primary schools reported more physical maltreatment by staff than children in Jewish non-religious schools (Benbenishty, Zeira and Astor, in press). Further, whereas in primary schools violence was slightly more prevalent in Jewish religious schools, the situation was dramatically different in high schools – school violence levels in Jewish religious high schools are very low. We also found that the more orthodox religious schools tended to address the issue of school violence differently from other schools. For instance, principals in these schools refused to discuss this issue with their students, believing that these discussions would have negative effects by 'bringing bad ideas to students' heads'. It will be important to examine whether the prevalence of school violence and the school responses towards these phenomena in Europe are influenced by religious and ideological practices.

One way to learn more about the ways in which contextual differences among countries impact on school violence is to examine their impact within each of the countries. Hence, studies that ascertain the relative impact of contextual issues on school violence can inform us about the potential contribution of various contextual aspects to school violence. The students' minority status, the socioeconomic status of the school neighbourhood and of the students' parents, and the availability of resources in and out of the school are among the issues that can be studied. The effects of these environmental context characteristics can be compared with those of the within-school context and climate. A recent study conducted in Israel (Khuri-Kassabri, 2002) shows that school climate may contribute to levels of school violence more than the characteristics of the schools' outside environment (such as socioeconomic status and crime rates in the neighbourhood). If these findings are replicated in other countries, it will help build our ability to identify what aspects of the school context contribute to school violence.

Interventions

The chapters describe a wide array of different types of interventions. The presentation of these interventions is one of the book's most valuable contributions, as readers are exposed to various approaches to and ideas about a wide range of anti-bullying programmes. We think that educators and policy makers around the world will find many of the ideas very relevant to their needs. In fact, in a recent exchange we had with students in the Israeli school of educational leadership, we shared what we learned about the 'time-out' schools described in the chapter from Belgium (and in France). They were unaware of this type of intervention, and several of them thought that it might be a solution to some of the challenges we face in Israel.

Levels of exposure to anti-bullying interventions

None of the chapters gave an estimate of how many students and schools are exposed to interventions aimed at reducing school violence. From our reading of the chapters we suspect that only a fraction of children and schools are involved in anti-bullying interventions. In many cases the interventions are part of time-limited projects that are implemented in select areas or schools. We think that assessments of prevalence and depth of exposure to programmes should accompany all future national reviews of the efforts to prevent school violence.

Focused versus holistic programmes

Compared with the literature from the United States, European countries seem to have a clear preference for more holistic, whole-school interventions, which is evident in the broad range of issues targeted by these interventions, as well as the wide array of organizations and government departments involved in these projects. Thus, the focus in many European programmes is not limited to bullying and violence but covers more comprehensive issues such as democracy, participation, and citizenship (e.g. United Kingdom, Belgium, Norway). This is true for some Israeli projects as well. In the Israeli city of Herzelya, for instance, the city-wide mobilization is around democracy and tolerance. Anti-violence is seen within the framework of disseminating the principles of democracy and non-prejudice in everyday life. Such a general approach, in contrast to programmes that focus mainly on school violence and bullying, has advantages, but limitations as well.

On the one hand, when anti-violence programmes are integrated into everyday curricula and do not constitute specialized programmes, they utilize regular funds and structures and therefore their sustainability over time is more secure. Furthermore, in terms of the ideology and the philosophy of education, non-violent and prosocial behaviours should be addressed as an integral part of everyday practice and not as a special and separate effort. On the other hand, when anti-violence themes are part of everyday curricula, the danger is of diluting anti-violence programmes by not addressing content matters and skills that are particularly relevant, as proven empirically, to the prevention and treatment of violence.

In Israel we are beginning to see some evidence that the more general and holistic life skills programmes that include violence or bullying components have little or no effect on violence-related issues. Such findings suggest the need for much more focused interventions. One important source of such programmes is the pool of interventions developed in the United States, which typically are based on a theory of the causes of violence and consist of structured curricula accompanied by detailed manuals and materials. For instance, Fraser et al. (2000) developed a programme called *Making Choices: Social Problem-solving Skills for Children*, based on Crick and Dodge's (1994) social information processing model. This is a structured programme that is based on a manual and training materials. In our meetings with educators we heard many of them asking for such well-structured and focused interventions.

Flexibility in selection and implementation

The various reports raise the question – how flexible should schools be in selecting and implementing their anti-bullying programmes? To what extent should schools be allowed and motivated to select which programmes they would like to implement and to tailor these programmes to their needs? There are advantages and disadvantages to having a nationwide programme that is clear and set, versus having a programme that is very flexible and adaptable to each school.

The implementation of a formal programme, required of all schools in the country or a region, has many advantages. It ensures that all schools participate (and not only the more proactive and effective schools), enough resources can be allocated, training can be provided to all teachers and schools involved, etc. The investment in creating materials such as video-cassettes and training materials (as described, for instance, in the United Kingdom and Norway) is huge. A large base of users and participants in a programme facilitates the support and ongoing improvements in the programme, while sporadic small-scale programmes may be quite limited in the support they could muster. Many educators in Israel complain that anti-violence programmes are small-scale, short-lived, and poorly supported. Therefore, these programmes do not get a fair chance to evolve and make a significant difference. An alternative model suggested by many educators is a focus on a limited number of programmes that are implemented in a standardized manner. This way, they believe, it would be possible to get the resources required to make a significant change.

A standard formalized intervention may not suit the needs of all schools. When the principal and staff in a school do not feel that a programme suits its needs, they do not co-operate with implementation of the programme, and can sabotage it in many ways. Hence, there are advantages to programmes that are based on grass-roots efforts, involve the school community in creative ways, and ensure the relevance of the programme to the unique strengths and needs of the school and the community. The chapter on Germany provides an example of a country in which there are huge variations among regions in the ways these programmes are being implemented. It may be unwise to ask all these diverse regions to utilize the same programmes without tailoring them to their unique contexts.

In Israel, we have similar dilemmas surrounding the national programme implementation. The balance today is tipped towards providing flexibility to each school and allowing schools to adapt programmes to their specific needs. Schools, however, are left with little guidance and do not receive much support from a central unit specializing in this issue. For instance, schools in Israel recently received a list of all anti-violence programmes offered by various organizations. This list was not accompanied by information (such as cost and evidence for effectiveness) that could help principals make informed choices.

We think that general guidelines to schools should be disseminated about the basic principles proven effective in the development of local efforts to deal with bullying and violence. Hence, schools and regions will have the flexibility of selecting among supported modules, as well as the freedom to create their own projects that reflect their local needs, strengths and resources.

Teacher training

One of the most important (and neglected) aspects of intervention is teacher training. Findings in Iceland indicate that teachers felt that they did not know how to deal with violence. This report parallels findings from our national study in which homeroom (class) teachers and principals said that they did not get training during their teacher education and that they felt they need more training. Based on our findings we recommended that the Israeli Ministry of Education increase their support of teacher training in schools of education. Training teachers already in the field is another area that should be explored further. Based on the present book, it seems that some European countries have already identified this shortcoming and provide resources to support teacher education (e.g. United Kingdom, Finland, France). One of the more promising ideas is to create a teacher group that specializes in bullying and is a resource for programmes in their region.

Interventions: evaluation and monitoring

Most countries report that little has been done to evaluate the range of interventions employed (e.g. Austria, Germany, Greece). Clearly, it would be important to have empirical evaluations that examine the effectiveness of intervention programmes. Anti-violence and anti-bullying programmes are complex, composed of various interventions, target many outcomes and populations, and are implemented in diverse contexts. Whereas in some cases it is possible and meaningful to evaluate such programmes using strong experimental designs, in many other circumstances it would prove impossible. Consequently, many intervention programmes are carried out for years without any evaluation (e.g. Menesini and Modiano from Italy describe a programme that is in its eleventh year and is being evaluated only now).

For the situations in which experimental designs are not feasible or desirable, we advocate an alternative approach – ongoing monitoring of school violence and bullying. The idea of monitoring is to collect data systematically and continuously so that schools can assess what their current levels and patterns of violence are, and how they are changing over time. Ongoing monitoring and immediate feedback to users can help identify changes in levels of violence, prompt modifications in current practices, and indicate to what extent these changes are associated with better outcomes. The feedback loop should be quick so that schools can get information on their levels of success throughout the implementation process (Benbenishty, Astor and Zeira, in press).

The authors of this chapter implemented such a monitoring system in Israel. In this project, all schools in the Herzelya district (more than twenty-five schools and about 10,000 students) conducted annual student surveys and asked about their victimization, and perpetration of violence in school. All schools used the same instrument and design. The questionnaire was similar to the one used in the national study, so district findings could be compared with relevant findings in the national survey, findings of each school in the district could be compared with the district-level findings, and findings of each grade level in the school could be compared with the overall findings in the school. The survey is being repeated every year (this year is the third in a row).

Thus, each of the schools and the district as a whole can identify changes in levels and patterns of victimization. Schools used their reports to assess their situation and plan interventions that focus on the areas students identified as problematic. Ongoing monitoring helps schools assess whether the measures they take are influencing levels of violence. Schools that implement a specific anti-violence programme that targets certain outcomes can use the feedback to ascertain whether their goals are being achieved. A formative evaluation of this project identified many benefits, as well as difficulties that should be overcome in future implementations (Benbenishty and Astor, 2002).

Research

The chapters in this book report on a large number of research studies on school violence and bullying. Unfortunately, the great majority of these studies were not reported in widely available research journals, which is regrettable because researchers from around the world could have learned from these European studies. Nevertheless, the book raises many interesting research-related issues. In this chapter we already commented on some methodological points and proposed future studies. In the following sections we would like to focus our comments on several additional areas of research that require special attention in the future.

Research on teachers, principals and parents

As could be expected, most of the research in this area focuses on students' perspectives. There is little research on teachers' views, and there is almost no research on the perspectives of principals and parents. We think that each member of the school community has an important contribution to make to the understanding and the treatment of school violence. Therefore, it is essential that these diverse perspectives be studied. Furthermore, it is important to compare these different points of view. Data on major discrepancies between the views of school staff and students in the same schools can be informative, and provide fruitful insights as to the sources of school violence and the ways to address it.

Consider, for instance, recent findings in our national study. We found that there are many significant and consistent differences between students, homeroom teachers, and principals. These discrepancies had a clear direction: students reported victimization and assessed their schools as having a violence problem much more than their homeroom teachers did. Principals saw and heard of even less violence than their teachers. Clearly, in order to mobilize the staff to address school violence it is essential to see their point of view and help them realize how different it is from what students actually feel and experience.

We could not find any study of parents' perspectives on school violence. We think this point of view is important because parents are a critical component of the school community and may contribute significantly to violence reduction and prevention of the perpetration and victimization of their children. Recently we initiated a study of parents' perspectives on violence in their children's schools. Among the issues we are investigating is the interface between the parents and the teachers – the degree to which parents feel that teachers share information with them, listen to their concerns, and are willing to engage them in efforts to prevent violence.

Victimization of students by staff

Atria and Spiel (chapter 6) comment that there is a lack of studies in Austria investigating violence by teachers against students. Indeed, few chapters even mention this issue. We find this gap in the literature quite disturbing. Although corporal punishment is explicitly prohibited in most if not all European countries, the issue of maltreatment perpetrated by school staff should not be neglected. There is a sharp contrast between the significant negative ramifications of physical and emotional maltreatment by adults who are expected to protect the pupil and the little attention to this area (see also a comment in Olweus, 1999).

Our studies in Israel (e.g. Benbenishty, Zeira and Astor, in press) strongly suggest that victimization (especially emotional) by staff is not negligible in prevalence and is directed more at younger male students, coming from families from lower socioeconomic status. Further, there are cultural differences in staff maltreatment. We found, for instance, that physical maltreatment of primary students was more prevalent in Arab schools. Among Jewish schools, physical maltreatment was higher in religious compared with non-religious schools. O'Moore and Minton's comments (chapter 18) on the situation in Ireland seem to echo this relationship by reporting on physical maltreatment in state institutional schools run by religious orders. Further research is required in order to understand the dynamics that lead to victimization by staff, the more vulnerable groups, and the relative effectiveness of various interventions in this area.

Multi-level design and analysis

It is interesting to note that although the school violence literature and interventions emphasize the role of the school context, there is little research that examines school context variables systematically. Notable exceptions are O'Moore's study in Ireland (O'Moore, Kirkham and Smith, 1997) and studies conducted in Norway by the Centre of Behavioural Research. The authors of these studies were able to make comparisons among schools based on their socioeconomic status. Further, they examined the possible effects of class size and school size on levels of school violence. Most other studies, however, focus only on student characteristics associated with bullying.

We recommend that future studies employ multi-level designs and statistical analyses that address variables on several levels simultaneously: individual students, classes, schools, and school neighbourhood characteristics. Such studies could examine school violence and bullying, ask what factors explain these phenomena and estimate the relative contributions of (a) characteristics of individual students who are bullies or victims, (b) school-level variables (such as climate, class size), and (c) neighbourhood characteristics (such as poverty and crime). Such studies can also identify the relative contribution of the socioeconomic–political context of the school environment (such as the economic status of students' families, proportion of minorities in the school, etc.).

In our national study we employed a two-level design (students within schools). We gathered information on individual students, as well as on the characteristics of the school (e.g. number of students, average class size, climate), the students' families (e.g. education, poverty, family size), and the school neighbourhood (e.g. unemployment, education, poverty and crime). A recent study (Khury-Kassabri, 2002) utilized Hierarchical Linear Modelling (Raudenbush et al., 2000) to identify the relative contribution of these variables to levels of school violence. The study provides strong evidence that this type of analysis could contribute significantly to the understanding of the impact of school context on violence. Furthermore, the study indicates strongly that the factors that explain school violence in one group of schools may not be relevant in another group of schools. To illustrate, the study shows that whereas the socioeconomic status of the school neighbourhood is strongly related to students' reports of victimization in Arab schools, this factor has almost no relationship with victimization in Jewish schools.

Periodic national and regional representative studies

One of the major surprises we had in reviewing the chapters is the lack of reports on national studies based on representative samples. One exception is the study carried out in 1997 by O'Moore and her associates in Ireland. We were especially surprised given the fact that the World Health Organization is conducting periodic studies of Health Behaviors in School Aged Children (HBSC) in European countries. In fact, the Israeli team published a report (Harel, Kenny and Rahav, 1997) that compares bullying statistics (year 1994) from twenty-four European countries (among them Germany, France, Finland, Norway, Sweden, and French and Flemish Belgium). The same study has been repeated in 1998 (official reports are not yet available). It is puzzling that the WHO study did not get much attention in this book.

We think that it is essential to carry out national studies based on representative samples. Studies collecting data on students, teachers and principals as well as on school and neighbourhood characteristics can provide a solid base for policy making nationally. Furthermore, it is important to repeat these studies at regular intervals of two to three years in order to assess changes. If national studies are not feasible in certain countries, we strongly recommend conducting such studies on a regional basis.

Finally, the Connect network that produced this report has proven to be a very strong and viable co-operative research effort across Europe. As such, it can become the cornerstone of ongoing school violence assessment throughout Europe. On the basis of the lessons learned from this co-operation and the comparisons conducted so far, it will be possible to agree on an instrument and design that can be applied across Europe. A cross-country comparative research that combines the students' perspective, the views of teachers and principals, and information on characteristics of the school and its environment can provide a rich source of information for policy making and planning in each country, in addition to valuable comparisons. The fruits of the current effort can become the seeds of the next project that targets school violence and aims to bring peace to our youth.

References

Benbenishty, R. and Astor, R.A. (2002). *Monitoring School Violence: Linking National, District and School Site Data. Evaluation of the First Two Years of a Pilot Project. A Research Report.* Jerusalem: Hebrew University and Ann Arbor, Mich.: University of Michigan.

Benbenishty, R., Astor, R.A. and Zeira, A. (in press). Monitoring school violence on the site level: linking national-, district-, and school-level data over time. *School Violence.*

Benbenishty, R., Zeira, A. and Astor, R.A. (2000). *A National Study of School Violence in Israel.* Jerusalem: Hebrew University.

Benbenishty, R., Zeira, A. and Astor, R.A. (in press). Children's reports of emotional, physical, and sexual maltreatment by educational staff in Israel. *Child Abuse and Neglect.*

Crick, N.R. and Dodge, K. (1994). A review and reformulation of social information processing mechanisms in children's social adjustment. *Psychological Bulletin,* 115, 74–101.

Fraser, M.W., Nash, J.K., Galinsky, M.E. and Darwin, K.M. (2000). *Making Choices: Social Problem-solving Skills for Children.* Washington, DC: NASW Press.

Harel, Y., Kenny, D. and Rahav, G. (1997). *Health Behaviors in School-Aged Children (HBSC): A World Health Organization Cross-national Study.* Jerusalem: Brookdale Institute.

Khuri-Kassabri, M. (2002). An ecological model of factors associated with school violence. Doctoral dissertation submitted to the Hebrew University, Jerusalem.

Olweus, D. (1999). Norway. In P.K. Smith, Y. Morita, J. Junger-Tas, D. Olweus, R. Catalano and P. Slee (eds). *The Nature of School Bullying: A Cross-national Perspective.* London: Routledge. pp.28–48.

O'Moore, A.M., Kirkham, C. and Smith, M. (1997). Bullying behaviour in Irish schools: a nationwide study. *Irish Journal of Psychology,* 18, 141–169.

Raudenbush, S., Bryk, A., Cheong, Y.F. and Congdon, R. (2000). HLM5: *Hierarchical Linear and Nonlinear Modeling.* Lincolnwood, IL: Scientific Software International.

Chapter 21

The complexity of school violence

Commentary from the US

John Devine and Hal A. Lawson

Violence in Schools: The Response in Europe is an important contribution to research and evaluation, policy and practice. Our review of the seventeen country reports is couched in our appreciation for colleagues' contributions. Like our European colleagues, our approach to school violence mixes humility, a sense of urgency and impatience. Our impatience stems from our perceptions of institutional inertia, especially inertia that derives from problem avoidance and denial. When the problem is ignored and neglected, school violence is reinforced, or at least, condoned. This state of affairs is cause for moral outrage, and it is dangerous, not merely to schools, but to every democratic society.

Like our colleagues, we are committed to the development of cross-national learning and innovation networks. This timely book facilitates network development. The most effective networks are animated by collaborative, action-oriented conversations. This review is designed to promote these conversations. In accordance with our charge from the editor, our analysis has a primary purpose and a secondary purpose. Our primary purpose is to respond critically to the European report chapters. Our secondary purpose is to report developments in our host nation, the United States (US).

We try to avoid re-examining the ground already explored in *The Nature of Bullying: A Cross-national Perspective* (Smith et. al., 1999), but build on its foundation and investigate how its findings are being applied in school and community contexts throughout Europe. We also explore what the two sides of the Atlantic can learn from one another.

Our analysis includes a descriptive component and a critical, normative component. The descriptive component addresses current research, policy and practice. The critical, normative component signals future needs and directions. Both components are influenced by our biographies, and they are interwoven in our analysis. In brief, our analysis is selective. It is not necessarily representative of all of the current thinking in the US. In fact, the diversity we cull from the European chapters mirrors the diversity in research, policy and practice in the US.

Cross-national differences

We begin by offering an important qualification aimed at preventing any suspicion of arrogance. Evaluative comparisons indicating the superiority of one nation's approach are inappropriate, unwarranted and dangerous. To our knowledge, no one has all of the answers to the school violence problem. In fact, the search for the 'right' questions is a commonality on both sides of the Atlantic. Cross-national diversity cannot be wished away. For example, national policy environments vary (Esping-Anderson, 1999). In turn, school systems vary, and so do the relations among school systems and other child and family-serving systems.

Corporal punishment, including punishment in schools, is another important difference. For example, the authors from Finland note that in their nation, as in other Scandinavian countries, corporal punishment is prohibited by law and not only at school, but within homes. By contrast, only one state in the US, Minnesota (where many are of Scandinavian descent) forbids corporal punishment even by parents. Far worse, the US is one of only six nations today that still employs capital punishment on youth and executes children (as young as sixteen) (Gilligan, 2001).

Furthermore, school governance systems vary. In contrast to the US, European nations exhibit more centralized, national authority for public schools. In the US the authority for maintaining and administering the public schools has always resided in the fifty states. The scale of public schooling is instrumental in the decentralization of authority. Public schooling involves some 16,411 public school districts; 91,000 schools employ 2.8 million teachers who serve 46.9 million students.

However, this conventional contrast also is changing. As the country reports make clear, many of the European countries are delegating more responsibility to their provinces, counties and municipalities in order to strengthen local school autonomy. In the same vein, the US scene is also changing. Prior to 1965, the US federal government's role was limited principally to guidance, via selective policies; federal financial assistance to the states was quite peripheral. In contrast, today Washington sends $120 billion per year to the states for various educational initiatives and diverse programmes. A notable example is the Safe and Drug-Free Schools Program of the US Department of Education. This programme dispenses grants of over $600 million per year for school security programmes, including safety technology, crisis management consultants and software. A lesson learned from this initiative is that enormous amounts of money, while indispensable, are not enough. Practice, policy and research in the US are constrained by competing definitions of school violence, including its manifestations, causes and remedies.

Defining school violence

What is school violence? How prevalent is it? Is it a universal concern, or is it specific to some kind(s) of school(s)? Is it place-bound (e.g. limited to certain cities)? What causes it? Who are the victims? Who are the perpetrators? Who determines the boundaries and parameters for these questions? Who decides who decides? These questions are associated with *the theory of the school violence problem* (Lawson, 2001). The theory of the problem pinpoints two practical questions. What's wrong that needs fixing? And, what's good and proper that needs to be restored, maintained and fortified? Arguably, understanding of the theory of the school violence problem is the key to intervention effectiveness and appropriateness. If understanding of school violence's manifestations and causes is limited and flawed, it is not likely to be remedied or prevented.

National, regional and local differences

Differences in the theory of the school violence problem are noteworthy. Intra-national and international differences in the theory of the problem recommend (somewhat) unique interventions and, in turn, research, evaluation and record keeping strategies. These differences also suggest the dangers of wholesale, uncritical borrowing of interventions employed in other national and local contexts, i.e. contexts in which a different theory of the problem often operates. For example, Amsterdam, Paris, London and New York share the status of being big cities, but uncritically lumping them together for school violence interventions may be a mistake.

Bullying versus violence

This caution also applies to the dominant definition of the school violence problem in this book. The dominant definition is bullying. Despite this basic consensus, questions remain about whether bullying is operationalized consistently across every nation. The earliest research on bullying was conducted by Dan Olweus in Sweden and Norway in the early 1970s (Olweus, 1993; Rigby, 1996). National awareness campaigns and intervention projects date from that period, and no doubt they have been instrumental in popularizing the school violence-as-bullying approach. With notable exceptions (e.g. France, Spain), the majority of the European reports in this volume employ Olweus' (1999) definitions of bullying. This approach offers many benefits. It also includes a limitation.

Olweus (1999) offered an important distinction between *bullying* and *violence*. Notably: 'there is a good deal of bullying without violence and likewise, there is a good deal of violence that cannot be characterized as bullying'. Our reading of these chapters yields the following conclusion:

this key distinction between bullying and violence is not made evident in many of the chapters. Apparently, bullying trumps violence. The Ireland chapter expressed the definitional issue succinctly: 'most empirical studies of aggressive behaviour in schools in Ireland have focused on bullying rather than on violence.'

What is bullying? Hazler et al. make explicit the essential components of bullying:

> The starting-point for recognition of bullying situations in the context of schools is a definition (Hazler, 1996; Olweus, 1996a; Schuster, 1996; Smith et al., 1999) that is highly consistent internationally across programmes and in its placement of emphasis on several key factors: Bullying is the repeated (not just once) harming of another through words or physical attack on the school grounds or on the way to or from school. The act of bullying is unfair, because the bully is either stronger or more verbally or socially skilled than the victim(s). An individual or group may carry these actions out.
>
> (Hazler et al., 2001, p.134)

Hazler et al. emphasize that it is the combination of these factors that creates a bullying situation. This combination differentiates bullying from other forms of play, teasing or fighting.

The US context: violence trumps bullying

This European emphasis on bullying is not evident in the US. Owing in part to the US media, 'school violence' or 'dangerous schools' or 'youth gangs' are more popular than bullying. Only recently have US researchers, largely under the influence of European pioneers such as Olweus and Smith, set their sights on bullying as a specific research topic in schools. A simple database search tells the whole story: in a typical US university library catalogue one finds only eighteen entries under 'bullying', but 108 books on school violence. In the same vein, when one checks the US Department of Justice website (http://ojjdp.ncjrs.org/) one finds 500 documents under 'school violence' and only 188 on 'bullying'.

Gendered violence: 'boys will be boys'

The political and societal context in which American educators and administrators, social and health service professionals, parents and students find themselves is important. This context includes the pervasive gun culture, the tendency to rely on technological 'quick fixes' to deal with security issues, dominant ideas of what it means to be a man and how boyhood leads to healthy manhood, and the domination of the TV, cinema and advertising industries. In this context, 'bullying' still appears to many Americans to be just a part of young people's experience. Even one Supreme Court Justice, in commenting on a school sexual harassment case, opined that such behaviour was just a 'normal part of growing up'.

It is in this cultural climate that William Pollack (1999) identified an unwritten 'boy's code' at the heart of the American socialization process, that dictates that 'boys will be boys'; that boys should be tough, that they should demand respect, that they should not show deep emotion, and that they should never cry. Pollack's work on boys parallels Mary Pipher's *Reviving Ophelia* (1994) and Carol Gilligan's *In a Different Voice* (1982) on the topic of girls' socialization.

Regarding the gender role socialization issue, perhaps the most unusual report emanated from Denmark. This frankly stated that 'the Danish approach to bullying' is that it is conceived somehow 'as a natural thing that everybody experiences at some time'. It noted some common views on bullying, such as 'Being bullied will strengthen you.' At the same time, the report admitted that 'bullying is bad', that the problem of bullying and violence is evident, and that ways must be found to deal with it.

If gender matters in both bullying and violence – and we suggest that it does – then there are some omissions in the European reports. Sexual harassment, a form of gendered violence, receives scant attention. It is a growing issue in the US. Similarly, domestic violence is not mentioned in the European reports. Domestic violence typically involves male-induced crimes against women.

Exceptions to the exclusive emphasis on bullying

The Belgian report explains the dominant emphasis on bullying in relation to the pervasive influence of Scandinavian, Anglo-Saxon and Dutch publications. The authors add that the broader notion of 'violence in schools' has become very common in recent years, especially in Wallonia.

Other exceptions to the school violence-as-bullying approach merit attention. The report from France, for example, draws on the work of Debarbieux (1996). Following the work of Roche (1994), he employs the concept of 'incivility' at school. Victims of these small offences (incivilities) experience a 'global feeling of disorder'. The large majority of these small offences go undetected and are in fact on the increase, at the very time when the more serious offences are decreasing. These 'incivilities' occur at the border of conventional behaviour and are one of the main factors in the deterioration of school climate.

Above all, the French report promotes an approach to the theory of the problem that differs from the top-down, externally defined approach. Violence, this report's authors recommend, must include the 'subject-ive', lived experiences of children and youth. By extension, the lived experiences of teachers and other adults also merit inclusion in theories of the problem and data regarding its incidence, prevalence, manifestations and causes.

The French report emphasizes school climate, including pervasive insecurity. Insecurity is commonplace in the US. Many US inner-city educators and guards confide to researchers that they feel thankful if they can just finish the academic year without incident. In the American context, fear is a close companion of insecurity.

Bullying relates to student orientations and actions. The report from Germany provides an important reminder: violence often includes relations among adults at the school. Incivility may encompass these interactions, and it may relate to staff morale, recruitment and retention.

On both sides of the Atlantic, staff turnover is related to school characteristics, location, insecurity, fear and violence. As in the inner ring suburbs of Paris (home to immigrants), in comparable areas of US cities, teacher and principal turnover is high. Vicious cycles appear to be involved here. Staff turnover erodes the school's prosocial normative climate. Staff turnover and student turnover ('Travelling students' in the report from Ireland) destabilize entire schools.

These emergent commonalities suggest an innovative approach to the theory of the school violence problem. Where the interactions among individuals and groups of all ages are concerned, incivility may be a better sensitizing construct than bullying. In other words, incivility may be a better way to think about the entire range of attitudes and behaviours that need to be addressed. (Antisocial behaviour, the idea used in the Belgium report, appears to be a synonym.)

For example, this same 'incivility effect' was noted for New York City inner-city schools (Devine, 1996) and by Bourgois (1995) for inner-city drug gangs on the streets of Harlem among whom 'regular displays of violence' are necessary and essential within a 'culture of violence' whose roots are to be found ultimately in the dominant society itself. Anderson's (1999) 'streetwise youth' demonstrate unsettling incivility in community contexts with norms that support it, or at least do not address it.

Incivilities are not restricted to the school in the same way that 'bullying' approaches are. The mere fact that they are not so restricted indicates the limitations of walled-in theories of the problem (e.g. bullying) and the selection of interventions. Walling in approaches also wall out alternatives (Lawson, 2001). In other words, the ecologies for incivilities must be taken into account: school, family, peer group and community ecologies. Bourdieu's theorizing is relevant here (Bourdieu and Wacquant, 1992). It involves the relationship between 'habitus' and 'field'. Simply stated, these aggressive behaviours have an internal logic within the context of the code of the streets (Anderson, 1999) and within the context of a 'culture of terror'.

The social geography of school violence and social-structural causes

Place and local context matter in every analysis. In other words, there is a social-geographic dimension to the school violence problem, and it is inseparable from the racial, ethnic and socio-economic composition of the children, youth and families served by the school (Lawson, 2001). The reports from Belgium, France and Ireland emphasize the place-specific challenges associated with ethnic and racial diversity and low socio-economic status. These reports are indicative of social-structural causes of the school violence problem, causes that are not amenable to interventions designed for individual children and youth and groups of students. Psychological theories and interventions continue to dominate thinking and practice.

Psychological theories

These social-structural mechanisms do not rule out social-psychological theorizing and interventions. For example, an important conceptual breakthrough was achieved in the work of Twemlow, Fonagy and Sacco (2001) by expanding the traditional bully/victim dyad to the triad of bully/victim/bystander. This psychoanalytically based model accounts for bystanders of the victim type, the bully type and the avoidant bystander. Their analysis of confused or ambivalent 'bystanding' in the context of high schools opens new possibilities for prevention, for intervention and for altruism (for a related analysis, see Salmivalli, Huttenen and Lagerspetz, 1997).

Violence involving property and goods

Violence is not merely an interpersonal relationship. It also includes symbolic violence and the destruction of goods, and it is also manifested in graffiti. The Portugal report alludes to this same phenomenon when it describes many of the violent situations as coming from 'students' frustrations and resulting in the destruction of property'. The report alludes to those who consider that school violence can be solved within the pedagogical field and not so much through policing tactics.

School climate and pedagogy

School climate is a key factor in violence's causes and remedies in some of the European reports and in some schools in the United States. The study of school violence converges at this point with the whole field of critical pedagogy (Apple, 1993; Willis, 1981; Bowles and Gintis, 1977). To what extent are school violence policies and practices integral to school improvement? Or, are these policies and practices merely tacked on to real school priorities and operations? The European chapters offer mixed insights into these questions.

The American wake-up call

A key question is this: are we looking at a conflation of the terms 'bullying' and 'school violence', or are we looking at two quite distinct phenomena? Readers who have not followed developments in the US may benefit from the following reminder about the speed with which violence develops. Many so-called 'spree shootings' erupted in rural and suburban American schools in the late 1990s. If there is such a thing as a key threshold point, the Columbine tragedy was it. Two high school students entered Columbine High School armed with two sawn-off shot-guns, a semi-automatic pistol, a 9-millimetre semi-automatic rifle, and over 30 pipe bombs, grenades and other explosives. They quickly killed twelve students and a teacher. They also wounded twenty-three others before taking their own lives. After Columbine, the conclusion was clear: *kids killing other kids and their teachers was not merely an 'inner-city schools issue'.* This brutal violence could happen anywhere.

Bullying was implicated at Columbine. As the media began to expose all of the details, the bully/victim aspects of these incidents became quite clear. In a sense, Columbine mobilized and sensitized middle-class America to school violence in the same way in which the events of 11 September 2001 later sensitized Americans to global terrorism. Main-stream America suddenly realized that it was not immune either from the violence of our 'ghetto' neighbourhoods or from global violence.

But this awareness has not meant that we have learned to question our most cherished assumptions about the mosaic of root causes for school viol-ence. The National Rifle Association with its advocacy of gun ownership became, in 2001, the top lobbyist group in Washington and is deemed by many to have even been one of the key players in deciding the last presidential elections. It is important to identify political and ideological patterns underlying these school violence incidents rather than just seeing them as mere expressions of spectacular violence perpetrated by disturbed youth.

Three years after Columbine, the citizens of Colorado are still debating in the state legislature the wisdom of allowing citizens to carry concealed handguns. In some rural US schools, where high school youth routinely hunt animals for their family's food supply, kids still bring their guns to school in their pick-up trucks, and their parents support them. No wonder metal detectors and surveillance technologies are imperative in the US. In contrast, we looked for, but did not find, in the European chapters, reference to metal detectors and other surveillance equipment in schools.

The effects of gun-related violence and the threats of homicide are pervasive in many US schools. For example, ten years after three school murders in New York City schools the Board of Education is still relying on metal detectors, security guards and the police. They use military language; for example, they talk about the need to 'secure the perimeter' of crowded urban high schools. Fear, insecurity and a sense of crisis are commonplace in some of these schools.

Even prior to Columbine, many school districts had begun to require each school to formulate an 'emergency crisis plan', anticipating the eventual school yard shooter. Even after it became clear that both Eric Harris and Dylan Klebod, the perpetrators of the Columbine massacre, had been both bullies and bully-victims, the issue of bullying took a back seat to the proper deployment of SWAT teams (i.e., rapid deployment teams consisting of paramilitary police), the lawsuits against the county, and basic issue of survival. In this heated environment, it was deemed far more urgent to place the emphasis on school security, crisis preparedness training, security assessments, gang intervention, insurance liability issues, the management of bomb threats, threat assessment, the legality of concealed weapons, and 'media relations' in a time of crisis. Using federal funds, high-priced 'security' consultants have been hired by many school districts and state legislatures have enacted 'tough-love' laws and zero-tolerance legislation.

Planning interventions

The theory of the school violence problem is instrumental in intervention planning, and it also structures research and evaluation undertaken in each nation. How this problem is operationalized weighs heavily in how it will be addressed; who addresses it; who is accountable for it; and whether it will be solved (Lawson, 2001). Debarbieux, Blaya and Vidal (chapter 2 of this volume) depart from the exclusive reliance on the bullying-as-violence approach. They put it this way:

> This scientific debate is also a fundamental strategic one: should we protect the school from its environment and external aggression, or should a genuine partnership with the inhabitants of the area be the solution? Should the school be deeply involved in the outside community life or just be a school in a neighbourhood (Debarbieux, 1994)? Are the causes of violence in school totally external, or is school responsible too?

Answers to these questions about the theory of the problem determine the choice of interventions. Many of the interventions in the European reports are walled in; they are limited to the school. Apparently, violence that occurs outside the school is 'someone else's problem'. When this approach reigns, extra-school violence is not addressed in the school, even though this violence affects school attendance, academic performance and behaviour.

Child abuse and neglect (CAN) provides an important case in point. There is no mention of CAN in the European reports. This oversight poses significant problems. In the US, longitudinal studies of CAN victims indicate both short- and long-term consequences. School problems and other personal social problems (e.g. substance abuse, delinquency) are among the short-term effects. CAN's long-term effects include health problems, mental health problems, employment problems, domestic violence, substance abuse, and more child abuse and neglect. Left undetected and unaddressed, CAN is part of a disturbing intergenerational pattern that harms children and families and imposes serious constraints on schools. What anti-violence crusade can hope to achieve its aims when CAN persists?

In the US, teachers are charged with reporting suspected cases of child abuse and neglect. The main idea is that teachers identify CAN and then they refer the problem to social and health service providers. In this sense, schools and community agencies are supposed to work in partnership, connecting walled-in and community-based approaches for addressing CAN and other forms of violence. In truth, this important plan has loopholes. Teachers receive scant training for this awesome responsibility. They may not view CAN reporting as part of their responsibility. Variability is commonplace. Under reporting is suspected. Staff turnover often erodes partnerships.

Fledgling partnerships described in the reports from Belgium, Iceland, Ireland, Norway and Sweden take into account the relations among school, family and community violence. These partnerships are matched by a growing community schools movement in the United States (www.communityschools.org). Community- and neighbourhood-based partnerships are developing on both sides of the Atlantic. For example, neighbourhood-based child protection and family support initiatives (some designed to prevent CAN) are under way in the US and in England. Community-based substance abuse cessation and prevention initiatives have also been mounted. Unfortunately, many of these approaches are categorical; they are not integrated effectively with school improvement.

Commonalities from Europe

Reading across the spectrum of the reports from all seventeen European countries, one is struck by several commonalities. In almost all countries, violence and aggression in schools emerged as a serious issue, with severe incidents occurring almost everywhere. More and more children of immigrants have been enrolled in schools throughout the continent, and everywhere schools are struggling with xenophobia and with the problems associated with bilingualism. Many of the countries now tend to strengthen school autonomy or at least promote financial autonomy.

All reports valorized empirical research studies and most regretted the lack of a more systematic empirical research approach to school violence. They all recognized that their respective countries had developed a wealth of materials, projects and initiatives. But almost all felt that the programmes had not had careful evaluations. Many are participating in the international project 'Health Behaviour in School-aged Children'. Almost all countries employ the Olweus definition of bullying or some modification of it. In the past decade many of these countries have been rocked by a series of spectacular violent school-associated incidents.

Crisis preparation in the US

The most notable trend in the US is the intense focus on 'crisis preparedness'. After the events of September 11, the Bush administration has asked all schools to review their plans for dealing with a crisis, including school shootings, suicides and large-scale disasters such as the terrorism of September 11. Schools are exhorted to have a professional security assessment and to work with police, fire and emergency services to develop joint plans. Grants are going to business firms specializing in 'school security assessments' that may include reviewing a school's 'crisis preparedness plan', security guard and school police staffing patterns and training, physical security measures and the like. Funds are available for acquiring metal detectors, electronic locks, surveillance cameras, and other related equipment and technology. One fruitful area for future transnational research would be to contrast the phenomenal growth of the security guard and police-in-the-school industry in the US, with the quite different approach described in the chapter on France in placing a *conseiller principal d'éducation* in each secondary school for school discipline and, since 1997, *aide-éducateurs* for mediation, and assistance with violence prevention.

Knowledge gaps and international differences

Several of the reports expressed regret over the lack of a central register of statistics for violent incidents in the schools. Bullying apparently is declining. Several of the European countries have shown a significant decline in bullying activity due, no doubt, to the anti-bullying campaigns and other activities in each of the reports.

Bullying data are not as important in the US. Given the lack of any widespread national anti-bullying campaign, even in any of the states, measurement of decline would be meaningless. The National School Safety Center (www.nssc1.org) is one of the most reliable sources of information on school safety and school climate. They collect abstracts of studies from a variety of agencies and organizations. The data they present are relevant for the purpose of our cross-national comparisons. For example, a *Journal of the American Medical Association* study of 15,686 public and private school students at all grade levels, found that 30 per cent of all the children had ever been bullied, 16 per cent said that they had been bullied occasionally during the current term and 8 per cent had been bullied at least weekly; 13 per cent reported that they had bullied other children (Nansel et al., 2001).

These data are consistent with another poll in which more than two-thirds of 14- to 17-year-olds surveyed reported that there is a group at their school that sometimes or frequently intimidates them, often with no or few consequences (www.empowered.org). While many of the victims responded by isolating themselves, almost a third of respondents said victims usually plan ways to get back at intimidators. Only a third of students believe that the school penalizes students who engage in intimidation. Other recent studies that bear on our topic may be found at www.emkf.org, www.alfred.edu/news, www.peds.umn.edu/peds-adol, and at http://www2.cdc.gov/mmwr/mmwr_ss.html. The latter study indicates that between 2 and 16 per cent of high school students felt too unsafe to go to school and 17 per cent carried a weapon during the thirty days preceding the survey.

Most American school staff members would agree with a statement in the Ireland report. This suggests that most surveys and anti-bullying codes address the pupils' needs only, and not the needs of the staff. And, although statistics differ dramatically (depending on each researcher's methodology), some US surveys agree with many of the European reports; for example, the surveys in Spain that indicated that 60 to 72 per cent of teachers considered the lack of school discipline a problem. Like the Spanish SAVE model, the best evaluated American models stress the need to involve all of the members of the educational community in the design and development of the school's organization (the 'whole-school' model). Similarly, the Italian chapter describes a whole-school policy against bullying model that was carried out successfully in Lucca, with a progressive decrease in bullying.

US Government officials are constantly reassuring citizens that, despite the sensational incidents recounted in the news media, schools are the 'safest place children could be'. The Bureau of Justice Statistics' report *Indicators of School Crime and Safety 2000* seems to support this contention. In effect, between 1992 and 1998 violent victimization rates at schools dropped from 48 crimes per 1,000 students to 43 per 1,000. At the same time, there were 60 violent deaths at school between 1 July 1997 and

30 June 1998 including 47 homicides, 12 suicides and one teenager killed by the police in the line of duty. The federal government's *Annual Report on School Safety* for the year 2000 (Departments of Education and Justice, 2000) states reassuringly that 'overall school crime continues to drop'. They can also somehow conclude optimistically that 'violent deaths at school are extremely rare' since only 'thirty-four deaths were reported in 1998–99 compared to the high of 49 deaths in the academic year 1995–96.' But perhaps the most startling statistic is that the number of multiple-victim homicides at schools increased from one in 1994–1995 to five in 1997–1998. In all, there were 251 school-associated violent deaths between 1992 and 1999, of which the overwhelming majority were deaths by firearms (195). The ubiquity of guns, legal and illegal, inside and outside of schools in the US is the single largest contrast between European and American schools.

Where crimes and violence occur: key data

Three important points raised in the German chapter about statistics would seem to apply across the board to most of the countries surveyed, namely, that serious crimes occur very rarely in schools, that the typical form of violence is verbal violence, and that there are differing research opinions regarding whether there is a rise in violence or not. In Germany, as in many countries, the media commonly proclaim a rise in violence whereas most of the scholarly studies see a lessening of school violence along with the decrease in youth violence generally.

Activities and programmes to address the problem

Some US approaches to understanding why youths become violent and programmes to counteract school violence appear to converge with those described for Europe. The United Kingdom report, for instance, discusses the work of the Commission convened by the Gulbenkian Foundation, one of whose key principles was that all discipline should be positive and that children should be taught prosocial values and behaviour, including non-violent conflict resolution. Similarly, the Austria report described the project Social Learning that began in 1984 and soon became one of the most frequently applied programmes in the country. Its activities consist in teachers' self-reflection and self-presentation, attention and acceptance of others, feedback and rule definition, coping with conflicts, establishing teams, and evaluation.

The Center for Social and Emotional Education in New York City, started in the mid-1990s, has become the national leader in fostering effective social and emotional learning (SEL) for children and adolescents. Their operating assumption is that social and emotional learning is as important a component of schools as reading, writing and arithmetic. To this end, they provide professional development opportunities for teachers, training to parent associations and consultation to schools in their effort to translate research and best practices to educational materials and resources for use in schools, homes, communities and universities (Cohen, 1999, 2001). Many of the teacher-training programmes mentioned in the chapter on Spain in which teachers themselves are active in designing the course content would seem to resonate with this SEL theme. The Life Skills programme in Iceland, in a similar way, addresses issues such as human rights, gender equality and the protection of the environment, as well as violence in the schools.

The American over-emphasis on crisis preparedness training – to the detriment of social and emotional learning – has already been mentioned. But one of the happier outcomes in reaction to the recent convulsive events in the US – the spate of spree shootings, the September 11 terrorist attacks – has been for schools and school systems to combine a high-quality school crisis intervention model (e.g. Lichtenstein et al., 1995) with the social and emotional learning models such as the one described above. Unfortunately, there are still many states that are simply content with drawing up 'checklists' for maintaining safe school environments that stress security staffing, criminal activities and response to incidents rather than taking a more proactive stance.

The comprehensive case study presented on the Gran School in the Norwegian chapter also picks up many of the components of the SEL approach mentioned above. At Gran, the head teacher and staff are described as having 'lost control' and the social power had passed into the hands of a large group of unruly adolescents. The Centre for Behavioural Research was able to mobilize an impressive and energetic intervention that included support for the school staff, changing school routines and teaching methods, opening the school outside regular hours, breaking up hard-core gang activities using sports and other activities and improving the school's relationships with the parents of immigrant students. Gradually, the school changed.

Several of the projects mentioned appear to be practical in import, and they may be replicable, or at least, applicable in the US. For example, there is no US national equivalent to ChildLine in Partnership with Schools in England, Scotland and Wales, a free British telephone helpline for children and young people in trouble or danger, although various cities and communities have their own helplines and their suicide prevention lines. Another British programme that American schools could almost certainly profit from would be the Forum on Children and Violence campaign that promotes non-violence as a whole-school policy. Circle Time, a British type of teacher–pupil support group, has its counterparts in several American inner-city schools where small groups of students meet with a teacher either every morning or three days a week. It appears to work better in the smaller school settings rather than in the overcrowded bigger schools. More generally, any one of the states could profit from the application of the kind of pilot programme designed to evaluate the effectiveness of the anti-bullying programme launched in Donegal (Irish report).

The report from Sweden makes clear that schools that are most in danger are those where the focus is completely limited to measures taken in acute situations and where preventive measures are not well articulated. The report then outlines a series of methods for reducing bullying, notable among which is the Olweus method that attempts to carry out preventive work at three levels – the level of the schools, the classroom, and the individual pupil and the pupil's parents.

The German report added another element to this whole-school approach: the finding that consent between teachers on intervention or prevention arrangements can reduce violence at school. They suggest an intervention that works primarily through regular discussions about behavioural rules in classes (for example about supporting attacked schoolmates to stop aggressive behaviour and to encourage positive behaviour).

Another contrast often neglected in comparative educational studies is school size. In Iceland the largest upper secondary schools have around 1,500 students. In Brooklyn (one of the most impoverished of the five boroughs of New York City), the twenty largest high schools have an average enrolment of 2,776 students, with three schools going as high as 4,000 to 4,200 students. Relative school sizes of this magnitude, many of which are known to be among the most troubled in the city, forces one to question the validity of Olweus' (1996b) assertion that 'the size of the class or school appears to be of negligible importance for the relative frequency or level of bully/victim problems'. One of the most promising developments on the US scene is the fact that educators are turning increasingly to small schools as a way of preventing violence (Klonsky, 2002). Here is one area that is ripe for an international research programme.

The report from The Netherlands makes the important point that in that country:

> A growing number of schools make use of participatory schemes regarding safety and youngsters, such as peer education and peer counselling. This is one way of dealing with problems of social cohesion and social bonding within schools: making students more responsible tends to provoke more responsible behaviour. Schools are steadily learning that students are not only part of 'the problem', but can also be a constructive part of the solution.

Concluding observations

These European reports indicate that school violence can be simplified considerably and categorized neatly. In fact, it may be desirable and appropriate to do so in some nations. Operationalized as bullying, and separated from other acts of violence (physical, symbolic and moral), it is amenable to walled-in, school-specific approaches. More specifically, bullying can be matched with targeted record-keeping and tailored interventions. Conventional schooling's emphasis on students, academic achievement, and the key roles of their teachers (tutors) are not disturbed by this walled-in approach. To be sure, teachers may be asked to do more, but the boundaries of the school and the professional power and authority of educators, are not disturbed when violence is simplified.

Some of the reports from Europe mirror findings from school communities in the US. In these cases, school violence is a complex phenomenon. It is multi-determined, and it requires multiple levels of intervention. Walled-in approaches must be accompanied by comprehensive interventions that include the media, families, community agencies, and the justice system. These expanded approaches often require place-specific tailoring, and they require policy change.

Intra-national and international diversity weigh in on this matter. The question is not one or the other; combinations of school-based and community-based approaches are warranted. Given the emergent understanding of school violence, all such approaches require built-in evaluation and research mechanisms.

Many of the reports conclude with regret that more systematic research based on empirical evidence on the topic of violence has not been carried out. Authors express hope that more scientific evaluations of intervention programmes will be carried out. The data presented in the 'knowledge' sections demonstrate the high importance the respective authors place on juvenile crime statistics, and on quantitative information and measurable objectives in tracking the increase or decrease of the various phenomena associated with school violence (percentages of students bullied, gender differences, etc.) through self-report studies, police reports and the like.

At least two main dangers derive from this concentration on so-called 'rigorously scientific' approaches. The first is methodological: in valorizing quantitative research and correlational analysis (based on the model of the natural sciences), non-positivist qualitative research and discourse analysis may be relegated to the margins (Morrow, 2000). Qualitative approaches, including empowerment-oriented, ethnographic evaluation (Fetterman, 2001) may be one of the strongest tools for probing the intricacies and subtle complexities in the area of school violence, in part because they represent the voices and stories of victims, perpetrators and bystanders (as suggested in the report from France).

The second problem is substantive, and it derives from the methodological problem. By concentrating on exact measurement and the counting of incidents, the individual student (or teacher, or parent) becomes the unit of analysis in research work. This 'bean counting approach' rules out larger social entities: the institution of the school, the ministry of education, pedagogical philosophies and other overarching structures. Our point is this: the concentration on individual violent acts and the 'psychologizing' of the theory of the problem often masks the underlying social inequities, including the social-structural causes identified earlier in this analysis. In short, root causes are not identified and addressed. The knowledge base for practice and policy is therefore flawed.

This positivist tendency in Europe is evident in the dominant American paradigms for youth violence research as well (see US Department of Health and Human Services, 2001). Perhaps one reason that these scientific reports with their 'hard data' methods do not seem to be able to convince the public or spur to action is that their conclusions are so obvious: more boys than girls indicated that they had been bullied or victimized, there are higher rates of bullying in vocational schools, younger students have been found to be victims more frequently than older pupils, and so forth.

Fortunately, all of the countries surveyed presented case studies and snippets of descriptive material of a qualitative nature that revealed structural factors at work in the construction of school violence. The Greek report states that 'overcrowding and sharing of premises in shifts was related to a climate of lesser involvement in the school [thereby] facilitating . . . the expression of physical violence'; it also disclosed that vandalism has been extensive and of great concern and offered the interpretation by some researchers that this form of violence may be an expression of 'just retaliation' by the students, who report experiencing the school as the perpetrator of violence against them.

The report from Luxembourg offers a future objective for all European countries. It states that one of the most important priorities will be to formulate and realize a nationwide policy against violence; and, to carry out more systematic research on the specific topic of violence in schools. This mandate appears to have universal import. It certainly is relevant to the US context.

This commonality provides a reminder about others we must identify and explore. It also serves as a reminder about the importance of cross-national learning, development and improvement networks. This book is an important instrument for these networks. We anticipate future international exchanges and networking that benefit everyone. After all, school violence affects people from all walks of life in diverse places around the world. We are pleased to join these networks because we in the US have much to learn from our European colleagues. Our analysis of the European chapters thus concludes with a note of gratitude for our colleagues' contributions to research, policy and practice.

References

Anderson, E. (1999). *Code of the Street: Decency, Violence, and the Moral Life of the Inner City.* New York: W.W. Norton and Company.

Apple, M.W. (1993). *Official Knowledge.* New York: Routledge.

Bourdieu, P. and Wacquant, L. (1992). *An Invitation to Reflexive Sociology.* Chicago: University of Chicago Press.

Bourgois, P. (1995). *In Search of Respect: Selling Crack in El Barrio.* Cambridge: Cambridge University Press.

Bowles, S. and Gintis, H. (1977). *Schooling in Capitalist America.* New York: Basic Books.

Bureau of Justice Statistics. *Indicators of School Crime and Safety 2000.* Online. Available HTTP: <http://nces.ed.gov/pubsearch/pubsinfo.asp?pubid=2001017>.

Cohen, J. (ed.) (1999). *Educating Minds and Hearts: Social and Emotional Learning and the Passage into Adolescence.* New York: Teachers College Press.

Cohen, J. (ed.) (2001). *Caring Classrooms/Intelligent Schools: The Social Emotional Education of Young Children.* New York: Teachers College Press.

Debarbieux, E. (1994). Ecole du quartier ou école dans le quartiere. Violence et limites de l'école. *Migrants-formation,* 97.

Debarbieux, E. (1996). *La Violence en Milieu Scolaire. 1: Etats des Lieux.* Paris: ESF.

Departments of Education and Justice (2000). *Annual Report on School Safety.* Online. Available HTTP: <http://www.ed.gov/offices/OESO/SDFS/publications.html>.

Devine, John (1996). *Maximum Security: The Culture of Violence in Inner-City Schools.* Chicago: University of Chicago Press.

Esping-Anderson, G. (1999). *Social Foundations of Postindustrial Economies.* Oxford and New York: Oxford University Press.

Fetterman, David M. (2001). *The Foundations of Empowerment Evaluation.* Thousand Oaks, CA: Sage Publications.

Gilligan, C. (1982). *In a Different Voice.* Cambridge: Harvard University Press.

Gilligan, J. (2001). *Preventing Violence.* New York: Thames & Hudson.

Hazler, R.J. (1996). *Breaking the Cycle of Violence: Interventions for Bullying and Victimization.* Bristol, Pa.: Accelerated Development.

Hazler, R.J., Miller, D., Carney, J. and Green, S. (2001). Adult recognition of school bullying situations. *Educational Research,* 43, 133–146.

Klonsky, M. (2002). How smaller schools prevent school violence. *Educational Leadership,* February.

Lawson, H. (2001). Reformulating the school violence problem: implications for research, policy, and practice. Paper presented at the International Conference on School Violence and Public Policies, UNESCO, Paris, France.

Lichtenstein, R., Schonfeld, D., Kline, M. and Speese-Lineham, D. (1995). *How to Prepare for and Respond to a Crisis.* Association for Supervision and Curriculum and Development, 250 N. Pitt Street, Alexandria, VA. 22314, USA.

Morrow, R.A. (2000). Social Theory and Educational Research: Reframing the Quantitative-qualitative Distinction through a Critical Theory of Methodology. In K. McClafferty, C. Torres and T. Mitchell (eds). *Challenges of Urban Education: Sociological Perspectives for the Next Century.* Albany: SUNY Press.

Nansel, T.R., Overpeck, M., Pilla, R.S., Ruan, W.J., Simons-Morton, B. and Scheidt, P. (2001). Bullying behaviours in US youth: prevalence and association with psychosocial adjustment. *Journal of the American Medical Association,* 285 (16), 2094–2100.

Olweus, D. (1993). *Bullying at School: What we Know and What we can Do.* Oxford: Blackwell.

Olweus, D. (1996a). Bully/victim problems at school: facts and effective intervention. *Journal of Emotional and Behavioral Problems,* 5, 15–22.

Olweus, D. (1996b). Bullying at School: Knowledge Base and an Effective Intervention Program. In C. Ferris and T. Grisso (eds). *Understanding Aggressive Behavior in Children.* New York: New York Academy of Sciences.

Olweus, D. (1999). Sweden. In P.K. Smith, Y. Morita, J. Junger-Tas, D. Olweus, R. Catalano and P. Slee (eds). *The Nature of Bullying: A Cross-national Perspective.* London: Routledge.

Pipher, M. (1994). *Reviving Ophelia.* New York: Grosset Putnam.

Pollack, W. (1999). *Real Boys: Rescuing our Sons from the Myths of Boyhood.* New York: Henry Holt & Company.

Rigby, K. (1996). *Bullying in Schools: And What to Do About It.* Melbourne: Australian Council for Educational Research.

Roche, S. (1994). *Insécurités et libertés.* Paris: Le Seuil.

Salmivalli, C., Huttenen, A. and Lagerspetz, K.M.J. (1997). Peer networks and bullying in schools. *Scandinavian Journal of Psychology,* 38, 305–312.

Schuster, B. (1996). Rejection, exclusion, and harassment at work and at schools. *European Psychologist,* 1, 293–309.

Smith, P.K., Morita, Y., Junger-Tas, J., Olweus, D., Catalano, R. and Slee, P. (eds) (1999). *The Nature of Bullying: A Cross-national Perspective.* London: Routledge.

Twemlow, S., Fonagy, P. and Sacco, F. (2001). An innovative psychodynamically influenced intervention to reduce school violence. *Journal of American Academy of Child and Adolescent Psychiatry,* 40, 377–379.

US Department of Health and Human Services (2001). *Youth Violence: A Report of the Surgeon General.* Rockville, MD: Department of Health and Human Services.

Willis, P. (1981). *Learning to Labor.* New York: Columbia University Press.

Name index

Subject index